Liberty's Prisoners

EARLY AMERICAN STUDIES

Series editors:
Daniel K. Richter, Kathleen M. Brown,
Max Cavitch, and David Waldstreicher

Exploring neglected aspects of our colonial,
revolutionary, and early national history and culture,
Early American Studies reinterprets familiar themes
and events in fresh ways. Interdisciplinary in character,
and with a special emphasis on the period from about
1600 to 1850, the series is published in partnership with
the McNeil Center for Early American Studies.

A complete list of books in the series
is available from the publisher.

Liberty's Prisoners

Carceral Culture in Early America

Jen Manion

PENN

UNIVERSITY OF PENNSYLVANIA PRESS

PHILADELPHIA

Published by
University of Pennsylvania Press
Philadelphia, Pennsylvania 19104-4112
www.upenn.edu/pennpress

Printed in the United States of America
on acid-free paper

1 3 5 7 9 10 8 6 4 2

Library of Congress Cataloging-in-Publication Data
ISBN 978-0-8122-4757-2

For my teachers

CONTENTS

〜

Illustrations follow page 134

ABBREVIATIONS

⌐

BOI	Inspectors of the Jail and Penitentiary House, Philadelphia Prisons System, PCA
HSP	Historical Society of Pennsylvania, Philadelphia
MAG	Magdalen Society of Philadelphia, HSP
MCD	Mayor's Court Docket, PCA
PCA	Philadelphia City Archives
PFT	Prisoners for Trial Docket, Philadelphia Prisons System, PCA
PG	*Pennsylvania Gazette*
PMHB	*Pennsylvania Magazine of History and Biography*
PPS	Pennsylvania Prison Society, HSP
PSA	Pennsylvania State Archives, Harrisburg
PSAMPP	Philadelphia Society for Alleviating the Miseries of Public Prisons, HSP
PSD	Prison Sentence Docket, Philadelphia Prisons System, PCA
Statutes	*The Statutes at Large of Pennsylvania from 1681 to 1801*, ed. James T. Mitchell, Henry Flanders, et al. (Harrisburg: Clarence M. Busch, State Printer of Pennsylvania, 1896)
VAG	Vagrancy Docket, Philadelphia Prisons System, PCA

Introduction

WHEN THE WAR with Great Britain finally came to an end, Pennsylvania's legislature moved quickly to enact what it had first approved in the state constitution of 1776: major revisions to the penal code to reduce the number of capital crimes and put an end to harsh punishment.[1] Under the newly democratic government, more men than ever before gained importance in the body politic.[2] But the Revolutionary promises—life, liberty, happiness—were quickly foreclosed by a revised penal system that disguised its violence under the rubric of humanitarianism, replaced slavery as the disciplinary authority in African American lives, and prized the property rights of the few over the human rights of the many. A diverse class of white men, from ruling elites to middling artisans, cast their lot with the penitentiary system, hoping it would make them better men, bring back the gender roles of old, cultivate industrious habits, contain the threat of free blacks and immigrants, and regulate illicit sex. It was a tall order, made more challenging by the resistance of lower-class men working as watchmen, keepers, and guards who refused their orders, African Americans who fought back against unjust laws and people who claimed possession of them, Irish immigrants who stole items of small value to survive after serving out or abandoning their indentures, and working women who refused to give up their jobs and retreat from public life into the domestic fantasy of republicanism. When economic depression struck and crime rates spiked, the underclasses seemed more threatening than ever before.[3] Elites did not stand idly by but rather invoked the authority of enlightened justice to reassert hierarchy and order. They used punishment to classify and segregate people along lines of difference—crime, class, gender, race, and age—in order to identify those who might one day stand as citizens if properly reformed.

Women were both marginal and yet immensely important figures in this process. In 1784, President of the Pennsylvania Supreme Executive Council John Dickinson argued that punishments in general should be "less severe" for everyone than previously enforced under British rule, but especially those "inflicted upon women."[4] In 1785, public debate over the role of punishment in society focused on the plight of one particular woman— Eleanor Glass. She caught the eye of a member of the Pennsylvania grand jury who visited the county jail. He was outraged that people convicted of minor offenses and unable to pay their fees might face indefinite confinement.[5] The juror felt that Glass—a white woman—was being cruelly incarcerated beyond reason and endured great suffering that was more than any person should bear. Glass's case was part of a larger debate about punishment in the young nation. Women—and ideas about them—played a crucial role in the social and political life of the early republic.[6]

Eleanor Glass was no republican mother; nor were the thousands of women whose lives serve as the basis for this book.[7] Glass and women like her stand at the center of the evolving story of the impact of the post-Revolutionary expansion of punishment on the lives of the poor. Her situation was not terribly unusual for the anonymous and forgotten masses that lived beyond the borders marked for citizens in the new republic. She was convicted of assault and battery on another woman, Mrs. Evitt, and fined six pence. Glass was confined to the prison because she could pay neither the fine nor the court fees. The juror noted that Glass's case was "unparalleled" and that through the denial of her liberty, the "rights of human nature [were] villainously violated."[8] Accusations that punishment violated human rights would quickly fade away in the coming years as the orderly, controlled penitentiary became the premier emblem of American democracy.[9] Glass and others like her became liberty's prisoners.

The cultivation of sensibility was at the heart of the refinement of punishment, much as it was to the entire nation-building project.[10] The language of feeling helped early Americans distance themselves from British barbarity. The juror who wrote on behalf of Glass described her situation as something that should "Excite our commiseration, abhorrence, and contempt."[11] In doing so, he focused not on questions of legality but on the emotions her situation compelled him to feel. Feelings were fragile—and could be manipulated. In the outcry over Glass, others took a less sympathetic approach, blaming Glass for her own troubles and warning the public not to worry about her. Under the pen name Veritas, one man wrote,

"There was no danger that a stroller, without home and without character, (and such she appeared to be) would be injured in her morals by remaining in goal."[12] Writing for those aspiring to cultivate their humanitarian sensibilities, Veritas explained his aim was to prevent unnecessary worry or concern on the part of the "generous public, whose feelings are always roused by a tale of inhumanity and distress." He rejected the idea that Glass was mistreated in any way, and felt the other juror's letter would elicit inappropriate compassion, concern, and sympathy on the part of the public. The struggle to determine the line between reasonable and excessive feeling as well as appropriate and misdirected compassion defined both penal reform and masculinity. The expansion of punishment was not a cold, calculated gesture of distant hands but rather a messy, intimate, and contested process that unfolded over time. Reformers, judges, Inspectors, and lawyers enjoyed the highly charged and emotional meetings they had with society's most vulnerable women, as it enabled them to recalibrate the tension and reach of patriarchal authority into something more elastic and broadly shared—appropriate for democracy.[13]

This diverse group of elite white men had a great deal at stake in re-establishing social order and hierarchy in the aftermath of the American Revolution. By defining themselves against an increasingly vocal and growing group of others—free blacks, laborers, immigrants, and women—they aspired to define an American national identity with themselves at the center.[14] But men from diverse social ranks would also publicly jockey with each other for power and authority. From the attorney general to one of the nameless prison guards, accusations of incompetence, wrongdoing, or inhumanity were never more than a turn of the newspaper page away. In the public discussion of the Glass case, two other members of the 1785 grand jury, Francis Wade and Francis Gurney, felt the need to defend the attorney general, William Bradford. They asserted that the problems discovered by the grand jury in prison were "not owing to a want of attention or humanity" on his part. They also defended the keeper in his decision not to put Glass forward for a pardon.[15] Guards, keepers, reformers, Inspectors, judges, and jurors would all be subjects of praise and contempt, sometimes unexpectedly, as the rules and expectations for punishment changed.

The burgeoning press played a vital role in publicizing these controversies. The official report of this grand jury was overseen by chief justice of the Supreme Court of Pennsylvania, Thomas McKean, and published alongside the letters. It called for the introduction of public punishment for prisoners as a way for them to earn money to pay off fines and fees.[16] The first great wave of penal reform began in publications like the *Freeman's Journal*, the *Pennsylvania Packet*, and the *Pennsylvania Gazette*, which brought the question of incarceration and human rights to early national audiences. The press thrust questions of punishment and democracy onto the table: What was the purpose of punishment? To which class of prisoners should it be tailored? Could labor be used to generate revenue in punishment? Should those unable to pay fees be pardoned? Would women be disciplined and punished in the same ways as men, or be judged with consideration of their sex? How could one system produce diverse and at times competing aims, such as reform, deterrence, punishment, justice, and profit? Women occupied a central place in these debates, yet have been overlooked by generations of historians. The question of women's role in punishment is a significant one, tied to nothing less than the question of women's place in the nation.

*   *   *

The refinement and expansion of punishment has been the focus of many important historical studies.[17] Once celebrated as the pinnacle of Enlightenment thought, the penitentiary has been exposed as a powerful tool of social and individual manipulation.[18] Historian David Rothman's classic study *The Discovery of the Asylum* placed the penitentiary alongside the poorhouse, hospital, and asylum on a continuum of institutions that advanced the state's effort to establish order and assert greater social control in the unstable decades of the early nineteenth century. His critical approach to institutions designed by well-intended reformers—and long heralded as safety nets for the sick and poor—laid the foundation for numerous studies to follow. Foucault's sweeping treatise *Discipline and Punish* identified the ever more subtle mechanisms of control and punishment that came into fashion, culminating in the development of a hardened "criminal identity" for those imprisoned.[19] The prison became a brilliant companion to industrialization, training the ordered, disciplined workforce that the economy required.[20] Democracy and its promise of freedom and justice required the right kind of punishment—a context in which the denial of liberty made perfect sense.[21] The rise of a liberal political ideology and the growth of institutional disciplinary regimes fueled each other. Isolating the guilty from society became the only way to ensure that neither innocent citizens nor the broader aims of justice would be corrupted.[22] Together, these studies show how in the span of just two generations, from the 1790s to the 1830s, social, political, and economic forces together transformed punishment from a public spectacle into a private one; from a corporal experience into a spiritual one; from a one-time event into a period of time in one's life.

Ideas about race, gender, and sexuality—long neglected from serious examination in studies of the penitentiary's nascent years—were central, driving forces in the transformation of punishment. As an intersectional study of crime, this book helps us to better understand who was in prison, why, and what impact this had on the development of the penitentiary. Punishment was defined in relation to and on the backs of a diverse and motley crew of both male and female European immigrants, laboring poor Irish and Anglo-Americans, and African Americans enslaved, bound, and free. But prison offered something different to everyone who entered its doors. As elite and middling Americans embraced ideals of femininity defined by whiteness, domesticity, and submission, the prison was used to cultivate submission and domesticity among chiefly Irish and African American working poor. White women were least likely to be imprisoned and most likely to be pardoned. Together, men of all racial and ethnic groups might find a path to citizenship by embracing religious instruction, laboring in the workshop, and striking a proper balance between being sufficiently repentant and ambitiously independent, a pursuit shared by elite men as well. Social norms that were raced, classed, and gendered would determine who was punished and what happened once the person was imprisoned.[23] Only by looking at the role of race and gender in creating order can we understand how the penitentiary was constituted and recognize the important role punishment played in manipulating social norms in the early republic.

The court and prison records documenting these experiences are both rich and sparse, full of details about one aspect of a case and missing vital others.[24] The records are nearly as chaotic as the lives of the men and women captured by them, as unpredictable as the period that produced them.[25] By combining quantitative social history methods with discourse analysis, this study finds meaning where previously there was thought to be none. Close attention to the language used and its possible meanings allows for what critic Barbara Johnson describes as a "teasing out of warring forces of signification within the text itself."[26] These forces of signification—

phrases both often repeated and unique—allow us to see the ways language produced meaning.[27] By examining women as subjects of punishment alongside "the idea of women" as criminals, the central role of gender in the creation of the penitentiary is illuminated.[28] Not only were women always there—before the courts, in the jails, and on the stock and pillory— but ideas about women and their relationship to crime, punishment, and reform were central topics of consideration.

This project has expanded greatly since it began. I was once content with showing that women were imprisoned in significant numbers for a range of crimes throughout these formative years.[29] Without diaries or let- ters written by the women themselves, I accepted that I would never really know what they thought, felt, or strived for. But other scholars have pushed me to find more meaning in these records. I have come to see the records of women's criminality and the actions that led to their arrest as a window into their intentions, aspirations, and constraints. The records provide an important vantage point for an analysis of race, sex, power, and difference, building on generations of important work in social history that has high- lighted agency in the lives of those marginalized by political history.[30] This work provides an important counter to decades—even centuries—of invisi- bility and powerlessness. Social history has increasingly been critiqued as out of fashion—and even naïve—as part of a larger trend in the profession away from politically engaged scholarship. But scholars in the growing field of critical prison studies have pushed back, showing how incomplete our understanding of state authority has been without attention to the actions, thoughts, and experiences of those subjected to its reach.[31] Showing that domestic servants and enslaved people ran away, disobeyed, and stole from their captors makes visible the fear and vulnerability of some of the city's most powerful men and women. This triangulation of authority, resistance, and imprisonment was enabled by the shifting political economy, in which long-standing dependency on slavery and servitude gave way to wage labor and new social hierarchies. While the severing of relationships of depen- dency may have saved elites, artisans, and businessmen money in the short run, it created a whole new set of problems. Many Philadelphians suffered from widespread poverty and turned to petty theft as a means of survival. The rampant threat of petty theft exposed the weaknesses of this new politi- cal economy, while the prison was used to cover up this failing. Severe punishments for minor larceny would get people off the streets, provide a false sense of social and economic stability, and shift the blame onto the poor, fueling racist and anti-immigrant sentiment.

Reading prison records for evidence of agency adds a much-needed dimension to how we understand institutional authority and policy-making. In prison, inmates refused to work, plotted their escape, formed close bonds, shared stories, skills, and secrets, had sex, and nursed those who were sick. Obedience to rules, acceptance of work assignments, and general good behavior could be as manipulative as obvious resistance. Inmates would strategically attempt to shape their own destiny by winning the praise of the keeper, Inspectors, or reformers, and in turn the privileges those people could offer: food, alcohol, clothing, bedding, visitation, loans, and even pardons. Inmates might turn to each other to learn skills that might make them more skilled workers—or more effective thieves. Out from under the watchful eye of a parent or master, an inmate might find it easier to enjoy friendship, community, sex, or other forms of intimacy. While confinement itself was a denial of freedom, it may have been welcomed by the servant or enslaved person who escaped an abusive master— and tasted freedom for a few days or even weeks before being captured. This view provides a long-needed counter to the pervasive view of punishment as a totalizing vehicle of social control.

Sexual activity was also a crucial site of liberal thinking and policy-making.[32] Foucault used the term "bio-power" to describe the extension of power over individual and collective bodies in advancing larger social or political goals.[33] Sex was at the heart of punishment—and punishment was a vital component of the early American national identity.[34] Attorney General William Bradford disavowed the legacy of British barbarism by rejecting the old logic used to govern punishment for sex crimes such as rape and sodomy. Enlightened punishment was widely lauded by American elites as emblematic of social progress from the staid and tyrannical authority of the British. The restriction of certain kinds of sex always had larger aims. Sex was the central subject of debate during the two most important moments in the history of the penitentiary: its creation in 1790 and the construction of the first building designed for solitary confinement in 1829. Nothing alarmed judges, elites, and reformers like the threat of uncontrolled sex between prisoners. Historians of sexuality have revealed the dynamic, layered, and changing meaning of sexuality in early America.[35] We have learned a lot about the expressions of desire, love, and lust deemed criminal through our extensive reliance on court records. This study adds to the literature by turning the area of focus from the docket books to the prison itself; it is less concerned with how sex landed people in prison than with what kinds of sex people had and what it meant, once they were imprisoned.[36]

Examination of the role of women and gender in punishment requires simultaneous analysis of the role of race, with particular consideration of African American women and the legacy of slavery.[37] Slavery came to an end in a multitude of ways over nearly a century of American history, from state level abolition, beginning with Pennsylvania in 1780, to the Emancipation Proclamation in 1863. When we examine this crucial period—the transition from slavery to freedom and its relationship to punishment—we must do so carefully, considering the specificities of time and place.[38] The much-studied transition from slavery to freedom in Southern states during Reconstruction had little in common with the passing of abolition acts in all Northern states by 1804.[39] Punishment was influenced by the transition from slavery to freedom in substantial if sometimes unpredictable ways. For example, the Pennsylvania Gradual Abolition Act of 1780 privileged an abstract notion of liberty but actually preserved the institution of slavery for a whole generation of African Americans. At the same time, enslaved people throughout Pennsylvania secured their own freedom by running away or buying it. The availability of casual laborers and increasing prominence of abolition rhetoric together made slavery less economically and politically desirable.[40] States of unfreedom—enslavement, indentured servitude, and imprisonment—were defined and transformed in tandem. These histories of slavery and racism intersect with gendered norms of criminality and reform in important ways.

Consider the case of Alice Clifton. In 1787, Alice Clifton gave birth on the second floor of the Barthalomew residence in Philadelphia, where she lived as a slave.[41] Alice claimed the child was born dead, but came under suspicion for killing the child because the newborn's throat was slit. Alice came to trial during a time when court attitudes toward infanticide were beginning to shift from a presumption of a mother's guilt to her innocence.[42] New laws required more positive evidence of actual violence against the infant for a charge of infanticide to stick. The criterion for determining likely guilt was no longer the perceived sexual licentiousness of the woman but rather the quality of maternal love she exhibited.[43] Two doctors testified that the child was born dead—a result of either miscarriage or death during childbirth. Their testimony was further substantiated by Alice's owners, the Barthalomews, who did not hear a child cry or make any noise while they were gathered in the dining room, right below the room where Alice gave birth. The central question on which Alice's case hinged was why she would slit the child's neck if it was born dead. Alice claimed she was afraid it would cry. This response, along with a razor mark on the child's neck, stood as evidence that the child was born alive—and that Alice killed it. After only three hours of deliberation, the jury found Alice guilty of murder and sentenced her to death. Just as quickly, the Supreme Executive Council of the state pardoned her.

Clifton's case serves as a window into both black women's powerlessness in the legal system and the idea that justice was also possible for them.[44] The basis for her pardon is unknown, but like many other pardons, it served a crucial role in both the cultivation of sensibility and the expansion of punishment. By granting selective pardons and extending individual acts of forgiveness to sympathetic defendants, the state deflected critiques of the expansion of penal authority. Progressive reformers who recommended pardons could position themselves against the state and remain detached from the violence of punishment. With each reconfiguration of punishment, mostly in the name of creating a system that was less vicious and more humane, its reach expanded, establishing cultural norms and social roles that extended far outside the prison gates.

There are many parallels between enslavement and imprisonment. This connection has been demonstrated in compelling work by scholars and activists calling for recognition that mass incarceration has become a structural substitute for slavery in oppressing African Americans.[45] The post-Revolutionary promise of liberty made the threat of imprisonment possible, even necessary. For African Americans, imprisonment reinscribed the dialectic between slavery and freedom.[46] Punishment—like slavery—cut people off from their families and communities. Only by destroying the family could a person's social relations be entirely remade, as reformer Dr. Benjamin Rush indeed hoped would happen.[47] Two schools of thought have emerged in the quest to understand the impact of slavery on African American communities. The concept of "social death" coined by sociologist Orlando Patterson has been widely used to describe the devastation and isolation of slavery. Scholars of slave resistance have set their work in opposition to this concept, showing the many ways that enslaved people claimed their humanity and shaped their destiny despite their circumstances.[48] As historian Vincent Brown has argued, "social death" as a concept was never intended by Patterson to describe daily life but rather was a "distillation" of the larger study meant "to reduce them to a least common denominator that could reveal the essence of slavery."[49] Turning to this somewhat more elastic concept of "social death" as a way to understand punishment in early America serves three vital purposes. First, it points to the important connection between systems of social regulation that restricted the life chances for African Americans across time and space, from North to South, in slavery and in freedom.[50] Second, it highlights the powerful role of ideology in punishment. No better phrase captures the effect the penitentiary was meant to have on those who passed through its doors. Third, it compels us to assess the gap between ideology and experience, as it quickly becomes apparent that those in prison lived highly social, communal, and interactive lives. Somewhere between the articulated goals of punishment and tidy notes in the prison record books we must look for the people—with complicated pasts and uncertain futures—who filled the nation's first penitentiary.

*   *   *

Philadelphia's old Walnut Street Jail was opened in 1776, designated a penitentiary in 1790, and closed for good in 1835. Walnut Street Prison, as it was called after 1790, served multiple functions at both state and local levels. As the only state penitentiary from 1790 to 1818, it housed those sentenced to imprisonment of one year or more from anywhere in the state.[51] It also served as the county jail for Philadelphia, housing anyone convicted before the Mayor's Court, regardless of charge or sentence, from its opening in 1776 to its closing in 1835.[52] A number of other prisons were built during this time. Arch Street Prison opened in Philadelphia in 1817 to house debtors and witnesses; it was repurposed in 1823 to house prisoners for trial and vagrants.[53] In 1818, Western State Penitentiary was opened in the western part of the state so that convicts would not have to be transported hundreds of miles to Philadelphia. Only with the opening of Eastern State Penitentiary in Philadelphia in 1829 were convicts finally entirely separated from other all classes of prisoners. Moyamensing County Prison was opened in 1835 to vagrants and untried prisoners, eventually replacing Arch Street.[54]

Philadelphia is the ideal site for an examination of early American punishment. Not only was it the most important city in the young nation, but it was also the birthplace of the penitentiary. No other community invested as much time, energy, or money in redesigning the penal system, from top to bottom. Pennsylvania jurists, reformers, and intellectuals were deeply engaged with Enlightenment philosophies regarding punishment, citing earlier writings such as Montesquieu's 1748 essay *The Spirit of Laws* and Cesare Beccaria's 1764 *Essay on Crimes and Punishments* repeatedly.[55] Often described as the father of criminal justice, Beccaria argued that punishments should be proportional to crimes, established on a scale, and consistently applied. None of those things could be said about Pennsylvania's colonial penal system, but many sought to make them happen.[56] Leading jurist and founding father James Wilson was well versed in European political and legal theory and embraced Becarria's idea that the prevention of crimes should be the main objective of criminal law and that such punishments should be moderate, speedy, and certain.[57]

With the opening of Eastern State Penitentiary, Pennsylvania elites put themselves on the map as pioneers who promised to revolutionize punishment and cure society of its social ailments in the process. The introduction of solitary confinement, the thoughtfully designed building, and regimented guidelines drew elites, politicians, and reporters from all across the United States and Europe. The modern penitentiary was celebrated as representative of moderate, rational punishment. Everyone agreed that Eastern State Penitentiary changed the nature of punishment forever—for better and for worse. But the slate of history was not wiped clean when the heavy gates of the first modern penitentiary finally opened. The construction of Eastern State on the site of an old apple orchard was authorized in 1821 amid fierce debates over inmate sex, the lack of reform, and failed manufactures.[58] Decades of disputes over the true aim of punishment, political fights over control of the courts and the Board of Inspectors, high rates of recidivism, and financial mismanagement all came to a head in the tumultuous decade of the 1820s. A prison revolt in March 1820 resulted in hundreds of men getting through layers of security, and brought the entire system to its knees. Only one outer gate stood between them and freedom on Sixth Street before the military started firing, killing one and injuring a few others.[59] The great chronicler of Pennsylvania penal history, Negley Teeters, reflected on the significance of the cornerstone dedication for Eastern State on May 22, 1823, "At last the dream of a quarter century was on the threshold of realization."[60] After nearly four decades of disappointment, frustration, and conflict, many looked to the new building as a final chance to turn the system around. Even the penitentiary's most ardent supporters would struggle to maintain a fraction of the hope and idealism that defined reformers of earlier decades.

*   *   *

Liberty's Prisoners focuses on the chaos and messiness that marked the first two generations of penal reform, from 1785 to 1835. The first two chapters focus on the central principles of reformative incarceration: work and sentiment. Intense debate over eighteenth-century penal theory resulted in a plan for the penitentiary that privileged labor over corporal or capital punishment, cherished sentiment and the cultivation of feelings, and identified the family as a source of both negative influence and positive leverage. Each of these components of punishment advanced white supremacist and highly gendered ideals that positioned national belonging far outside the reach of poor, immigrant women and nearly all African Americans.

Chapter 1 examines the central role of labor in punishment. The rigid sexual division of labor was exposed in 1786 by the introduction of public punishment, as men were sent to clean the streets and women were left behind in the workhouse. Though women were excluded as formal subjects of reform, they proved exemplary workers and model inmates, providing reformers with inspiration and hope as men—true subjects of reform— failed their charge at every turn. Women in prison might begin to carve out the expectation that women, too, could be model citizens by submitting to expectations. The prison served as a disciplinary tool for masters who chose to imprison runaway or disobedient servants or slaves for as long as they wished. When indentured servants or the enslaved ran away, stole household goods, or both, their masters went crazy. Threatened by their own inability to control the behavior of those bound to them by law, elites turned to the state for help. But servants and the enslaved used this punishment to their own aims as well; some refused to leave the prison, preferring their communal containment in jail to whatever abuse or mistreatment awaited them back at home. Chapter 2 shows the powerful and manipulative force of feeling in driving reform efforts. Reformers placed themselves between inmates and the callous arm of the state, claiming an incredible amount of authority and hoping to improve themselves as much as anything. Family was an important part of sentimental reform. Isolating the guilty from their families was a key component of punishment. Prisoners

austin reed

revealed the value of family in their lives in requesting pardons. They knew the language of feeling and the value of gender norms as well, presenting themselves in particular ways that were most likely to elicit compassion and recommendations of pardons. For those devastated by being estranged from their families, imprisonment would serve as leverage to provide incentive to reform.

Women and men of the lower sorts understood social and economic hierarchy better than anyone. They were subject to the orders and whims of those who provided them with food, shelter, or money in exchange for work. Already living on the edge, they were incredibly vulnerable in times of greater economic instability, as was the case in the early decades of the nineteenth century. Chapter 3 charts the efforts of women who were inspired by social chaos, political rhetoric, need, or want to claim something for themselves: a voice, a valued object, a night on the town, community, and yes, even freedom. Women in public refused to be invisible and contained within the domestic sphere. Women were punished for things that men did without a second thought: walking the streets at night, drinking in public, and exchanging sex and money. Poor women were arrested just for being in the streets at the wrong time or in the wrong place—especially if they were African American. The prison was filled with people held under the highly subjective and loosely applied vagrancy law. As law enforcement efforts increased, there were always women who refused to relent. Colonial vagrancy statutes were modified to criminalize the early national poor just as African Americans rushed to the city in search of freedom.

The penitentiary was designed to facilitate a strict ordering and classification of people along lines of difference. Sloppy at first, the process of using sex, race, age, and criminal classification to categorize and separate people was nearly perfected by the 1820s. In place of real opportunities for personal transformation, skill development, and even religious conversion, authorities relied on segregation and isolation as a way to establish order, setting a dangerous precedent. Chapters 4 and 5 explore the role of sex and race in prison, two ideas that dramatically shaped punishment and ultimately served as justification for its failures. Chapter 4 charts the impact of the abolition of slavery on the expansion of the penal system and the role of punishment in making race. Debates over the constitutionality of slavery, the place of free blacks in society, and the root causes of racial difference all shaped punishment. As early as 1780, the state modified its oppressive regulation of African Americans in form, but not substance. Chapter 5 interrogates the significance of sex and sexuality in the expansion and refinement of punishment. If concerns about heterosexual sex defined the 1780s, by the 1820s they gave way to fears of same sex—or at least sodomy. Generating public alarm about sex was the single most effective political strategy in getting new laws passed and budgets approved for the expansion of punishment. Prisons were spaces for inmates to learn from each other, experiment consensually, or even assault each other—away from the watchful eyes of masters, parents, and keepers.

The expansion of punishment had major and lasting implications for African Americans, immigrants, and the poor.[61] Leading jurists and progressive elites used the penal system to discipline and punish diverse citizens in ways that advanced social hierarchies rooted in race, gender, class, and sexual differences. This process helped to justify and stabilize liberalism's exclusionary framework.[62] None of this was beyond the understanding of regular people, who knew better than most the forces that limited their own upward mobility. Women and men who eventually ended up in prison might embrace or flout the conventions expected of their race, class, or gender as it served their needs or desires at any given moment. *Liberty's Prisoners* shows that those who were subject to surveillance and regulation were not blank canvases for social experimentation but rather played an active part in instigating, manipulating, resisting, and shaping these forces.

༽

CHAPTER 1

Rebellious Workers

EARLY AMERICAN CULTURE was rife with contradictions. The War for Independence upset long-standing social hierarchies among white men while leaving white women, African Americans, and laboring people with little to show for their efforts. Victory ensured that the economic interests of Anglo-American merchants would no longer be thwarted by the political or economic whims of the British, making the war little more than a lateral move. When British aristocrats and elites went packing, wealthy and learned Anglo-American men took their places as heads of state, industry, and society. The working poor, indentured, enslaved, and even middling men and women whose efforts proved vital to the war's success expected something more: a leveling of old social and political hierarchies, greater economic opportunities, and freedom from bondage. But only a few conditions changed. The passage of the 1780 Gradual Abolition Act made Pennsylvania the first state to legislate against slavery while preserving the institution for another generation, as the Act famously did not free a single enslaved person. Non-land owning white men were granted voting rights, Northern states increasingly abolished slavery, and middling and elite women had more opportunities for formal education. As doors opened for the middling sorts, others belonging to the "lower sorts," including vagrants, the poor, unskilled workers, the enslaved, bound servants, immigrants, free blacks, and servants, remained shut out. Poverty and its attendant life circumstances (homelessness, unemployment, living on streets, illness, begging, relying on religious or public charity) would threaten the American experiment more than the British military ever could. Those suffering greatly under the volatile economy of the early republic were targeted as the source of a social problem rather than result of an economic one.

Elites believed that a faulty, outdated penal law contributed to chaos and lawlessness, inspiring a dedicated effort to transform official responses to the rebellions, crime, and poverty of the masses.

In Philadelphia, as in many other seaport cities, the compact design of neighborhoods put rich and poor in close proximity to each other. The density of Philadelphia and New York in 1800 was unparalleled in North America, with a population of 40,000 people per square mile compared to the national average of six.[1] The two cities were becoming more like London—a city with 129,000 residents in just over one square mile in 1801—and less like anywhere else in the United States.[2] Cities also had distinctly different demographic trends from their rural counterparts, including more free blacks, female heads of household, and young white men.[3] The widespread reliance on enslaved, bound, or hired domestic help brought the laboring poor into the homes of middling and elite Philadelphians alike. Domestic workers who were enslaved or bound were treated as dependents and received housing and food as part of their arrangement—no small security in a city teeming with formerly enslaved and immigrant newcomers desperate for work and housing. But even this came at a price. Working women were generally denied the freedoms enjoyed by their male counterparts. If male laborers were viewed as "a footloose and potentially rebellious element in society," the women who worked predominantly as hired or bound house servants were greatly restricted by the watchful eye of their employers, with whom they probably lived.[4] Watchful or needy masters and mistresses scrutinized their comings and goings, demanded their constant availability, and subjected them to untold abuses.

The revolutionary promises of liberty and the opportunity to pursue happiness were not materializing for this group of servants and free laborers, leading many to seize them for themselves.[5] Enslaved African Americans along with indentured servants and domestic workers of African, Irish, and English descent clamored for a taste of freedom from tyranny and suffering in their daily lives. They challenged the abuse and authority of masters, mistresses, and employers. They came together to share frustrations, aspirations, and plots. They ran away, disobeyed orders, threatened masters, and stole from the homes of their employers.[6] Most significantly, they denied their labor to those who felt entitled to it, by custom and by law. Seeking their own piece of the revolution's promise, this group upset the economic and social hierarchy. A majority of elite and middling Philadelphian households were dependent on the labor of this group and indulged in theatrical hyperbole when articulating their fears of and frustrations with such bold demonstrations of resistance. As a last resort, they turned to the state for help and had their servants or slaves imprisoned to punish them and regain control. The jail was freely used throughout the colonial era by slaveholders and masters of servants to punish them for not working hard enough, disobeying, or running away.[7] The penitentiary would serve this same function in the post-Revolutionary period—but in a vastly expanded way.

The refusal of those enslaved or bound to work combined with the inability of others to find adequate employment put labor at the heart of social disorder in the decades following the war. Hard labor became the hallmark of a new system enacted through a series of laws passed between 1786 and 1794 that reduced the number of capital crimes, outlawed corporal punishment, and introduced imprisonment as the premier punishment. By reinstituting bound labor through punishment, elites aimed to discipline this recalcitrant workforce, exhort money for the state from their labor, and instill republican family values on the working poor. A strict sexual division of labor was imposed, requiring male convicts to clean the public streets while women worked behind closed doors. This was the first of many efforts to organize and segregate prisoners along lines of difference. Certain kinds of work were already more commonly associated with either men or women, but institutional labor regimes would exacerbate—even naturalize—these distinctions. Though the work of women in the eighteenth-century city was very diverse and often public, institutional labor regimes were narrow in scope and increasingly hidden. Prison labor not only foreshadowed but also accelerated the diminishing scope and value of women's work more broadly by the mid-nineteenth century at the same time that more white women and free blacks were becoming household heads in Philadelphia, from 1790 to 1830.[8]

If labor served as a dead end for women, it offered the realization of the full potential of punishment exacted against men. The opportunity for structured, institutionalized labor might literally help transform convicts into workers.[9] For men of all racial and ethnic groups, the prison initially offered the chance for reform. The opportunity to work in a manufactory was a path to redemption and even citizenship for men who embraced it. But for men who knew slavery, indentured servitude, impressment, and other systems of exploited labor, being forced to work without pay was not the olive branch it was touted to be.[10] The penitentiary promised humane treatment, opportunity for quiet reflection, and religious counsel, in part to avoid comparisons to slavery.[11] While moral reformation served as the ideological basis for the penitentiary, labor provided its economic justification. But the nature of work also produced its own ideologies, including the fortification of a heterosexual political economy that ensured women's political and economic dependence on men, even though so many men proved unable or unwilling to be depended upon.

Public Punishment

A new era in punishment began when men dressed in blue and brown striped uniforms of coarse fabric and woolen caps took to the city streets with shovels, brooms, and wheelbarrows to make up for their crimes. Men who previously may have been pushed around the city from public square to public square in a cage, subject to whips, stones, and a good old public shaming were now expected to contribute to the greater good. When elite Philadelphian Ann Warder went out for a walk one spring day in 1787, she confronted a group of men cleaning the streets, harassing strangers, and begging for money. Warder wrote, "They have an iron collar around their neck and waist to which a long chain is fastened and at the end a heavy ball. As they proceed with their work this is taken up and thrown before them."[12] Warder complained about the situation and suggested that the guards needed to be more effective in preventing people from speaking to the prisoners—and giving them money.[13] This scenario captures one of the many paradoxes of penal reform: public labor was instituted as punishment for lawlessness—and further contributed to public disorder and the discomfort of the city's elite denizens in the process.

American reforms followed British policies in many ways, including public punishment. Even before debates over public punishment in Pennsylvania flooded the papers, evidence from the British experiment with the practice was printed in the *Pennsylvania Gazette*. The late Dr. Fothergill had argued that if the purpose of public punishment was to deter as much as to punish, the condemned should be paraded in front of those most likely to offend.[14] He added, "I do not mean, however, that they should go at large, though in chains and with keepers. They should be kept as much as possible from all converse with the public, and yet be seen by them." Fothergill identified the challenge of encouraging visibility while denying communication. Public punishment in Pennsylvania differed from its British counterpart in that it paraded convicts through the middle of crowded city streets rather than restricting them to labor on the wharves, away from public view.

Public labor was authorized by the 1786 Act to Amend the Penal Laws of the State, the first major penal reform bill passed after independence. The popular bill was devised under the rule of Pennsylvania's radical constitution of 1776 and passed into law a decade later by the liberal Constitutionalists then in power, signaling widespread support for the bill's contents. This issue proved more unifying and less controversial than many other topics of the day.[15] The new law required public punishment of all convicts at "continued hard labor . . . in streets of cities and towns, and upon the highways of the open country and other public works."[16] The act officially served three major functions: to offset the expense of caring for convicts in prison; to discourage criminals through shame and embarrassment from resuming a life of crime; and to deter others from resorting to crime. While much was made of the power of shame and deterrence, it was the financial piece that made the bill popular. The idea that the prisoners would earn money to provide restitution, cover court fees, and pay for their own upkeep was popular among judges who relied on fees for payment, elites wary of footing the tax bill for public institutions, and a general public suspicious of an expansive and strong government.

While elite men agreed on the bill's contents, workers and city officials were another matter as men jostled for power and authority under the new government. The city's street commissioners refused to follow the law and use prisoners as workers, claiming that to do so would interfere with those men already employed at cleaning the streets. Such conflicts between elites and workers were increasingly common as white men—except for the working poor—embraced their newfound political power and elites struggled to assert their authority in less autocratic ways.[17] Chief Justice of the Supreme Court of Pennsylvania Thomas McKean eventually forced the commissioners to hire convicts. Funds were transferred from the city to the county budget at a rate of one shilling nine pence per day as wages.[18] This rate was considerably lower than the going rate for workingmen engaging in other jobs throughout the city, such as cooking or cleaning.[19] The financial arrangement seemed ideal for all parties except the prisoners themselves, who would scarcely see much of their earnings. The city benefited from cheap labor while the county was earning income to offset the costs of imprisonment. Officials hoped that by sparing the public the financial burden of supporting prisoners, they would be free to experiment with new forms of punishment. McKean supported penal reform generally and public labor in particular because it had a revenue-generating scheme that would finance the expansion of the prison.[20]

Visibly humiliating labor provided a new twist on the old practice of public shaming. The practice of public shaming was used by many colonies with impunity, subjecting women and men to the stock, pillory, branding, and public carting.[21] Pennsylvania Quakers, however, were less violent than New England Puritans or those in the culture of violence that characterized the slaveholding southern colonies. The fact that they shied away from forms of corporal punishment widely used by other colonies and championed in the mother country has been attributed to their aversion to "unusual cruelty, suffering and the shedding of blood."[22] Quakers generally resorted to fines over corporal punishment, making this reinvigorated call for shame in punishment curious. But rather than reflect the public shaming of old, punishment by public labor was a forward-looking response to the breakdown in social hierarchy and deference that propelled the revolution. The combination of hard work and public shame was the perfect tool—timely and necessary—for reasserting not just law and order, but hierarchy.[23]

The reform aspect of public punishment hinged on prisoners having certain emotional reactions to their experience. It was essential that those subjected to it embrace a feeling of disgrace. The law itself stated that labor was to be "publicly and disgracefully imposed" while the dress of prisoners was to be "formed with every mark of disgrace."[24] Outfits marked with bold, unattractive stripes made from the coarsest of fabrics were one component. The iron collar around one's neck, attached by a chain to a heavy metal ball, was certainly a mark of degradation. On top of all that, convicts were to be "disgracefully treated" in every imaginable way. Reformers believed that deep personal shame was a key ingredient in motivating people to try to change their ways.[25] But creating conditions to incite a feeling of disgrace was easier said than done. Two seemingly competing forces made public punishment short-lived and untenable: the sentimental project of elites and the rejection of both authority and reform by those condemned.

First, consider the actions of the men. The men sentenced to public punishment became known as "wheelbarrow men" because they pushed wheelbarrows through the streets. They embraced this collective identity imposed on them and redirected it for their own aims.[26] Wheelbarrow men themselves refused to embody and express the feelings reformers desired or predicted. Convicts did not defer to authority, bury their heads in shame, or succumb under the weight of guilt and remorse. Rather, they maintained their own agendas. They embraced the opportunity to get out of the prison, talk to each other freely, and interact with the public. They taunted people walking by as they cleaned the streets. They begged for money. They were not diminished or disgraced by public punishment.

Rather, they were emboldened. A group of wheelbarrow men plotted a great escape from the prison. The plot was "previously laid," since they had a coordinated strategy of "calling attention of the keepers to the main gate" while others climbed the walls of the yard. Mostly armed with knives and stones, a group of "about eighty" nearly succeeded in breaking through an iron gate before an assistant keeper "fired several shot at them." When all was said and done, one was killed and seven were wounded.[27] They threatened people with violence, including the city's squire. Some claimed that if they got their hands on the squire, Mr. Pollard, "They would cut his hair off and disfigure him so that he should not be known."[28] In September 1787, several escaped by "getting into the common sewer" and were only captured "after a long and vigilant subterraneous pursuit."[29] The largest escape occurred in 1788, when a group of thirty-three prisoners fled the grounds, few of whom were eventually recaptured. Some attribute an "unusual number of highway robberies and burglaries" later that year to this bunch, and this was widely thought a result of the wheelbarrow law.[30] Wheelbarrow men from Philadelphia routinely escaped. In the summer of 1788, four men were picked up in Baltimore as vagrants who were described as "wheelbarrow men from Pennsylvania."[31] They were again put out to work "on the public roads" of Baltimore County. In January 1789 several wheelbarrow men tried to escape from the jail in Philadelphia "by digging under the foundation of the building." The jailor fired at and killed two or three of them.[32] Noted for his hair, "cut remarkably short," James Smith, also known as William Johnson, escaped the wheelbarrow in Philadelphia before being jailed in New Jersey for horse stealing. Weeks before, two other men were caught and charged with a housebreaking in New York. These men were reportedly described as "A part of the wheelbarrow gentry from Philadelphia, and which lately struck so much terror in the inhabitants of that city."[33] Most significantly, one group of four men escaped together and quickly robbed a man they allegedly identified while working in the street at the wheelbarrow. The incident escalated, and the man was murdered. The wheelbarrow men were caught, convicted, and executed for this crime.[34]

The actions of the escapees created a climate of fear in the city, threatening not only the viability of penal reform but also the very validity of government. People felt unsafe, and the young state appeared weak, unable to control even convicts. Philadelphia was well established as the home of state government and an important place for national political meetings. The chaos threatened not just the city but also the still weak and vulnerable national government. The ongoing violence created an obstacle for those promoting the city of Philadelphia as the ideal capital for the new nation. In 1788, the legislators claimed that Philadelphia was, "A place where lawless and wandering banditti of wheelbarrow men and the unwholesome effluvia of dirty streets, with many other nuisances, might endanger their health or lives, every hour of the day and night."[35] Members of the General Assembly remarked that Philadelphia had better clean up its act if it hoped to have the Congress relocate there from New York, as it later would in 1790. Others warned that no one was safe walking on the streets of Philadelphia in the evening unless within reach of the night watch, an early form of neighborhood policing.[36]

Dr. Benjamin Rush was the first to publicly outline the ways that public punishment undermined the sentimental project. Rush was a prominent physician who would become a leading voice in efforts to transform punishment. The basis for Rush's critique was the idea that public punishment had the potential to elicit sympathy for criminals from an unsuspecting public.[37] Rush believed that sympathy and compassion misdirected at prisoners laboring in public would be socially disastrous – inspiring rage at the state for inflicting punishment and possibly deadening sympathy for those truly worthy.[38] When Rush delivered these ideas before a meeting of the Society for Promoting Political Inquiries at Benjamin Franklin's house on March 9, 1787, those in attendance enthusiastically embraced his critique.[39] Rush's lecture and its dissemination in printed form would inspire and shape public debate on the subject for years, until the law was repealed in 1790. His arguments incited fear in lawyers, judges, and reformers that convicts working in chains in the city streets would elicit excessive or improper emotions in its citizens. Further, he feared that harsh punishments led to a hardened people—exactly the opposite of what he aspired to for himself and his community.[40]

Public punishment was by all counts a disaster. It made the city seem less safe rather than more safe. It was not crime itself, however, that created social chaos but rather ineffective punishment. It inspired an expansion of policing efforts that ultimately targeted the poor. It is easy to cite Rush's essay as the basis for abandoning public punishment, but to do so obscures the impact of actual rebellion, violence, and disorder. Rush's ideas about the confused emotions and moral corruption of innocent bystanders changed the conversation from one of the real resistance and violence of the wheelbarrow men to a more distant intellectual exercise in hypothetical interactions. Looking back on the end of public punishment, reformer Caleb Lownes centered his critique on the prisoners themselves, noting how punishment failed to reform them. Lownes plainly states, *"Disgraceful labour or treatment* of any kind, it has not had, nor can have, any valuable tendency towards restoring an offender to usefulness in society, and it is therefore discontinued."[41] This most public, visible, and physical of punishments failed because those targeted refused to internalize its lessons. Public punishment did not instigate an appropriate response in the hearts and minds of the prisoners, regardless of its emotional impact on citizens.

The actions of the wheelbarrow men and the public debates over the significance of this policy obscured the existence of women in prison. While the rhetoric up to this point suggests that men alone were the targets of penal reform measures, this was simply not the case. Ample evidence shows women laboring away in a workhouse during this period. In 1787, the Acting Committee of the Philadelphia Society for Alleviating the Miseries of Public Prisons (PSAMPP) reported that women in the workhouse were busy "spinning &c. and making shifts for the men."[42] A workhouse calendar from 1789 confirms that female convicts, vagrants, and runaways worked side by side, including three women who were convicted of stealing.[43] Anyone who read the *Pennsylvania Gazette* would be reminded of the women in prison by the advertisements that asked for "Any old blankets, shoes, stockings, mens and womens apparel" to be delivered to the prison.[44] From 1787 through 1790, women constituted anywhere from 10.4 to 21.9 percent of the convict population and nearly half of all inmates when vagrants and runaways were included.[45] There are a number of reasons women were not ordered to labor in the street alongside men.

Women and men were distinct entities under English common law. The legal and social distinctions between men and women were deemed to be a substantive basis for different treatment by the courts. This distinction was adopted by the American legal system and remained in place well into the late nineteenth century, designated by the phrase "from the consideration of her sex."[46] Married men were responsible for the actions of their wives. Women who broke the law were at times given the benefit of the doubt before the courts, assuming that they were under the influence of a man. Women who broke the law were simply less significant than men who did the same. They were already held in the lowest regard by male judges, reformers, and elites. There was no need to make a spectacle of them through public shaming because women in prison were believed to be already disgraced. Furthermore, the public shaming of dissolute women might further taint the public viewing the spectacle. And so most reformers were content to assess the effectiveness of the penal law as it pertained to men. In his characterization of the failure of public punishment, Rush focused solely on the wheelbarrow men. In a 1787 letter to New York reformer John Coakley Lettsom, Rush wrote, "From the experience of our citizens of the bad effects of our wheelbarrow law (as 'tis called), it will probably be repealed. This I hope will pave the way for the adoption of solitude and labor as the means of not only punishing but reforming criminals."[47] Rush, like most others, ignored the impact of the law on women in prison, quite possibly presuming that it did not have any.

But the fact that public punishment was not applied to women had lasting consequences. Chiefly, it ensured that the dominant public perception of criminality was male. Convict men were hypervisible in both the streets and the press as wheelbarrow men raised havoc, resisted authority, and made great escapes. While the behavior of prisoners was cited as a significant reason for the abolition of public labor in 1790, it was actually the behavior of male prisoners that necessitated the change. The failure of public punishments inspired reforms that dramatically affected prisoners' of both sexes for decades—even centuries—to come. The four years of public punishment (1786–1790) were critical for marking the male body as the physical embodiment of criminality and transforming the meaning and function of punishment.[48] They inspired the adoption of punishment by hard labor in a far more controllable, predictable environment—behind the walls of the penitentiary.

Runaways

Wheelbarrow men were not the only group to resist order, discipline, or punishment in the streets, institutions, and homes of the city. Five women escaped from prison in 1796. Three white women, Pricilla Roberts, Catherine Lynch, and Joan Holland, made it all the way to Baltimore before being recaptured.[49] Two others, African American Phebe Mines and Irish Margaret McGill, also escaped through the dungeon and into Sixth Street with the group as well.[50] Women also regularly contested the terms of their employment, indenture, enslavement, and imprisonment. They negotiated with employers, resisted masters, and sometimes escaped altogether. The 1780s and 1790s were record decades for enslaved and bound workers rising up against authorities in seeking freedom. From 1780 to 1789, in the city of Philadelphia alone, over four hundred enslaved people either were manumitted or ran away.[51] In the 1790s, more bound servants and enslaved people were imprisoned for running away or standing up to abusive masters than ever before.[52] Women who were caught running away or resisting the terms of their employment constituted the largest single category of those charged with vagrancy—as one-third of all vagrants in 1795.[53] As news spread of the Haitian Revolution in which enslaved blacks took up arms against their oppressors, African Americans were inspired to believe that they too could free themselves from the bonds of slavery.

Advertisements for runaway servants, enslaved people, and escaped convicts used nearly identical language and formats, signaling the groups were held in similarly low regard. People placed ads to announce and describe those who ran away, often calling for someone to deliver the runaway person to the nearest jail if captured.[54] When an enslaved woman named Dina ran away in search of freedom, she had not committed any crime. For innocent enslaved and convicted people in search of freedom, the ads usually ended with a line similar to the one concerning Dina: "Whoever takes up said Negroe Woman and secures her in any gaol, so that her master may have her again, shall have THREE POUNDS reward, and reasonable charges, if brought home, paid by David Carson."[55] Readers were thus encouraged to identify, capture, and transport runaway servants and slaves to the prison for holding—treating them as criminals. While an increasing number of Pennsylvanians supported the abolition of slavery by 1780, many people still felt differently when it came to their own servants or slaves. Even leading prison reformers who were antislavery advocates were content to accept this function of the prison as a place to contain those seeking freedom.

Vagrancy laws provided the legal justification for the imprisonment of runaways. They were loosely defined yet powerful tools used to reassert social and economic hierarchies. The vagrancy records themselves did not distinguish clearly between servant and slave when recording instances of runaways. Rather, they designate only the category of "master" or "mistress" in referring to the aggrieved party. The ambiguity of status in the records challenges us to think more carefully not only about the blurred boundaries between the two but also about the limits of freedom more broadly for both groups. While servant and slave remained distinct legal categories, they were increasingly treated similarly under the law after the Gradual Abolition Act created a new class of African American servants.[56] Significant numbers of African Americans would have been servants rather than slaves, as gradual abolition required children of slaves to serve terms of extended servitude to age twenty-eight.[57] African American women working as domestics in the 1790s could have been enslaved, servants, or hired. Of the nearly two thousand free blacks in Philadelphia in 1790, half were women who worked in white households.[58] Regardless of status, they were all vulnerable to the same treatment. Poor whites, especially bound servants, also faced harrowing treatment at the hands of masters and jailers. In Philadelphia during this period, the sad truth was that the working lives of servants of both European and African descent were remarkably limited and with many parallels to enslavement.[59] Neither the spirit of the American Revolution nor post-Revolutionary penal reforms changed any of this.

Though Anglo-Americans controlled the political, legal, and economic systems that shaped the lives of African Americans as well as servants of European descent, they seemed genuinely upset and threatened by expressions of resistance and disobedience. But it is precisely this structural imbalance that requires us to skeptically assess the fairness of any law that criminalized acts of freedom seeking in a time and place that celebrated freedom seeking from British rule, arbitrary authority, and the like. It is difficult to take seriously concerns about the disobedient servants, free blacks, and rebellious workers when the state was aligned with those who claimed ownership over their lives, bodies, and time, and laws were easily bent to this aim. From the earliest years of the Pennsylvania colony, laws punished runaway servants with five extra days in service for each day absent.[60] Imprisonment of runaways was one step in a disciplinary process aimed at returning them to their proper place.[61]

The increase in the number of African Americans running away, fighting with, or otherwise disobeying their masters fueled the growing animosity of elite whites toward free blacks. When a black woman named Patience refused to work, her master had her charged "with being a refractory and disorderly negroe woman who refuses to perform any kind of labour for her subsistence."[62] When an African American servant named Jantie left the service of Joseph Elton, she successfully evaded authorities for over a week. Upon her capture, she spent four days in the vagrancy ward before her enraged master had her "delivered to Mrs. Weed" at the prison for an undeclared charge—and a punishment we can scarcely imagine.[63] Patience and Jantie were two of dozens of black women who challenged those who claimed possession of them, and got a brief taste of freedom, however elusive. The prison also served as a holding tank for those suspected of being slaves. One woman named Sall from Little Creek in Delaware was held for eleven months on the unconfirmed assumption that she was a slave.[64] Masters had complete discretion over how long to leave slaves or servants locked up and how many lashes to have administered by the jailer.

The prison was not necessarily a totalizing institution of social control but could also serve as an intermediate space that constantly changed in response to challenges from within and without. Freedom was mediated through the prison in two directions. While the prison served as a tool of elites to manage a resistant labor force, workers also used the prison as a way to resist the abuses of servitude and conspire about ways to escape or to survive once released.[65] Victorie ran away from John Imbert on July 29, 1795. She was captured and imprisoned under charge of being his slave. Authorities doubted this claim, and Mayor Hilary Baker called for an investigation and imprisonment of Victorie until a judge decided to release her. John Imbert reclaimed her on August 2nd, but she quickly ran away again, only to be re-imprisoned on August 3rd. Such determination to escape despite near certain capture suggests Victorie had a profound claim to freedom. These records of runaways, however, scarcely document the trauma and horrors experienced by those enslaved.[66] The official reporting of runaways in the newspapers and court records are one-sided. They do not tell us why Victorie ran away or how she was feeling. But we can discern that for the enslaved Victorie, risking life in prison was better than life with John Imbert. She remained in prison for two months, possibly until he could find someone else to buy her time. While short of freedom, Victorie may have felt relief at the chance to get away from a much-hated abusive master.[67] The prison could also serve as a safe haven from slaveholders. When four children ranging in age from four to twelve were discovered in the Washington City Jail, one jailer reported that the children's aunt placed them there "to keep them out of the hands of a man, who wished to sell them as slaves." Even though the conditions of the jail were horrid, and one of the children suffered with scant clothing and illness, their beloved relative felt this terrible circumstance gave them a better chance at life and freedom.[68]

The extent to which servants and slaves tried to shape their own fate in the face of great opposition was remarkable. Some servants ran away repeatedly or refused to leave prison to return to the home of their captor. When twelve-year-old Clarissa Morris ran away from Margaret Tucker of South Fourth Street, Tucker offered a one-dollar reward and reasonable charges for the return of Morris, a woman described as mulatto and objectified in an advertisement as having "frizzled hair, a good set of teeth, and is narrow visaged."[69] Once Tucker recovered Morris, Tucker decided to sell the remainder of her term of indenture to someone else. Tucker may have obscured Morris's rebellious spirit when negotiating the sale, but it could not be suppressed for long.[70] Morris ran away from her new master, George Springer. She again was picked up on vagrancy charges in February 1807 and sentenced to one month for running away.[71] This group of women frustrated their owners so much that the latter relented in selling or trading them. Samuel Clarkson offered a five-dollar reward in the *Philadelphia Gazette* for the delivery of his servant Susanna Ware, whom he described as "an indented Irish servant, aged about 26 years, of a fair complection, her features rather coarse, she took with her several changes of clothes."[72] Ware enjoyed three weeks of freedom before being picked up and held on vagrancy charges in November 1795.[73] Clarkson left her in prison for sixty days, signaling that he had lost control of her and resorted to extreme measures to discipline her. The fact that she stole from him extended her punishment and increased the likelihood that he would search for someone to buy or trade the remaining time of her indenture. Elizabeth Folmer ran away from her master Thomas Palmer and "remained absent six or seven weeks."[74] Similar to Morris and Ware were Anna Guster and George Roth, who ran away from a term of bound servitude on the farm of Charles Greguire.[75] When captured, they refused to go back to his farm. He left them in prison, waiting for them to change their minds or for someone else to buy out their indentures. Roth eventually gave in and was discharged back to Greguire's farm in December, but Anna held out for two more months.[76] Even though the cards were stacked against them, each of these women got a taste of freedom. This process offered servants and slaves the hope of a different kind of life: a less abusive master, or one step closer to freedom.

Masters and mistresses were more likely to seek the assistance of the state in disciplining servants and slaves of African descent than the vast population of English and Irish servants, signaling their discomfort with controlling the African American members of their households and an expectation that the state would help them regulate its black residents.[77] When African American Phebe Bowers allegedly "threaten[ed] the life of her mistress Rebecca Conway" she was punished by imprisonment without trial and denied bread for fourteen days.[78] In 1790, over half of the masters and mistresses exercised their discretion to release their prisoners in less than the standard term of thirty days. For example, Mila was discharged after only four days. She was described as "the property of William Lewis, esq" and he ordered her discharge and delivery to a Mr Todd.[79] Elizabeth Nen was held for only fifteen days, having run away from "her master" Henry Clanse.[80] The conditions in prison were deplorable; inmates were often stripped of their clothing, minimally fed, and left to defecate in their own cells. Only the most refractory and uncontrollable of white servants were punished in this manner. When Elizabeth McCoy was charged with "obstinately refusing to obey the lawfull commands of her Mistress Mary Robinson," she was imprisoned for only three days but denied bread.[81] The harsher punishment of African Americans has several explanations. Whites consistently felt more entitled to black labor than they did to that of native born whites or even immigrants who might share their own European ancestry. For whites, slavery still reflected a financial investment, making the rebellion of a slave both a social and a financial threat, whereas servants could more easily be replaced. African Americans may have been more likely to attempt freedom than others—and were probably more often mistreated in the first place.

Women of both European and African ancestry were imprisoned together. Sarah Evans and Elizabeth Folmer both arrived on September 17, 1795. Evans received a very strict punishment upon escaping her apprenticeship to Joshua Peeling. She was kept in prison for four months before being discharged to the almshouse.[82] One can only imagine her ordeal—and the stories she and other women would share during those four months. Elizabeth Folmer had it comparatively easy. Though she left her master Thomas Palmer, she was released from prison after two weeks. Even more importantly, she experienced "six or seven weeks" of freedom before being caught in the first place.[83] When Evans and Folmer arrived, an enslaved woman named Jane was already there, serving thirty days on charges of "being a very refractory disobedient girl and of absenting herself from her mistress service."[84] When Margaret Mullen entered the prison on September 18th, she would have met a number of other runaways and possibly shared a room with Sarah, Elizabeth, or Jane. Mullen was bound to John Cardner and punished for five days for her attempt at escape.[85] Despite the harsh conditions of the prison, the companionship of other young women who shared their plight may have been a welcome relief from the strict orders, overbearing meddling, or abuse of a master or mistress.

Men of wealth and political power were especially frustrated by the resistance and rebellion of their domestic help during this contentious period and were twice as likely as women to file charges for the punishment and capture of runaways.[86] In 1791, Nance, was charged with thirty days of hard labor for "being disorderly and disobedient to her master William Pollard Esq."[87] Eliza Johnson was described as a "mullato" and charged with "very bad behavior to her master Hugh McCollough."[88] Matilda Pringle was a bound servant who ran away from Doctor James Tate.[89] Eleanor Moor was charged with "disorderly behaviour by her master Hugh Moon," while Rebecca "negress" was charged for "misbehavior to her master."[90] A gutsy young woman described as "Marinet blk girl" was charged "on the solemn affirmation of John McLeed with being his indentured sevt. And greatly misbehaving herself towards her said master and his family."[91] In 1791, Catharine Frame was said to be "misbehaving herself toward her master and mistress Hugh Saveing and wife and being with child and refusing to tell the father of it," and sent to prison "to be kept at labour thirty days" as punishment.[92] The fact that men with social capital and political authority struggled to maintain order in their own homes is dramatically revealing. If women in their service refused their authority, how could they expect deference of their wives or command the respect of colleagues? Such challenges to their authority could have a ripple effect that would be uncomfortable at best, disastrous at worst. Rather than respect the increasing attempts of servants and those enslaved to grasp freedom and autonomy, elites chose to denigrate the character of the lower sorts and embrace the expansion of penal authority.

This list of powerful, learned men who imprisoned their female domestic help for challenging their authority goes on. Emanuel Eyre was appointed to the Philadelphia County Assembly with four others in an announcement that also named sheriffs, coroners, and the commissioner John Baker. On July 1, 1790, an enslaved woman named Phillis was "charged with deserting her masters service Emanuel Eyres to be kept at hard labour for one month." She was held for 26 days.[93] When Francis Hopkinson died, Williams Lewis was appointed judge of the District Court for the District of Pennsylvania by the president of the United States in July 1791. Not long before, Lewis had ordered an enslaved woman Mila first to prison for disobedience and then to a Mr. Todd, likely as a sale.[94] Edward was the mathematical and writing master at the English School of the Philadelphia Academy. He and his wife charged Justina, their "negress" servant, with "behaving herself exceedingly indolent and disobedient." She was released September 11, 1795, by Hilary Baker.[95] Alice Cassady was punished for running away from Captain John Foster in July of 1795 and then by John Kean, a successful merchant, in September of that same year.[96] Peter Blight was named a director of the Insurance Company of North America in January 1795. Months later, he ordered his servant Catharine Louise Figg to prison for stealing from him and running away. She was discharged after two months.[97] Men sought the help of the state in managing the laboring women in their lives.

Conflict between female laborers and the women who controlled their labor were also common.[98] Mistresses were rarely sympathetic allies of their bound laborers but instead turned to the state for assistance with disciplining and punishing those who refused their orders. Widows especially struggled. Mary Meredith was widowed when her husband Daniel, a brass founder, died in 1777.[99] In 1790, Mary struggled to maintain her authority over the eslaved Dinah. Dinah was charged with "being idle disorderly and disobedient towards her mistress Mary Meredith to be kept at labour thirty days."[100] Dinah was released after just two weeks, signaling that Mary needed Dinah back helping in the house. The widow Souder charged her servant Sarah Morton with assault and threatening.[101] Souder was probably married to Casper Souder, who had owned a tavern in Northern Liberties. He must have died sometime between 1784 and 1795.[102] In 1790, Nancy was charged with "disobeying the lawful commands of her mistress to be kept at hard labour," though she stayed in prison for only four days.[103] Servant and enslaved women could terrorize their mistresses just as some mistresses surely terrorized their workers. In 1795, Calypso was held for "being a very ill tempered and of behaving very indolent toward her mistress madam [?] and others."[104] The conflict between enslaved and bound workers and privileged women who owned their labor was not mollified by any sense of shared suffering or the marginalization of their sex. Mistresses reported more difficulty with insubordination than masters did. While men would mostly be away from home conducting business, meeting with friends, or visiting coffeehouses, women worked closely with servants and slaves in accomplishing domestic tasks, day in and day out. Mistresses constantly ordered, monitored, and disciplined their servants and slaves, making the possibility for direct conflict even greater. The ideological basis for elites to treat domestic help with mistrust, contempt, and violence was already established by the institution of slavery. For example, in Berks County, just outside Philadelphia, a white woman named Elizabeth Bishop murdered her black female servant without consequence in 1772, even though the evidence established her guilt.[105]

The slave labor economy defined social roles and expectations in ways that justified systemic violence against African Americans. As Thavolia Glymph has shown, enslaved women in a later period in the U.S. South were expected to undertake an extensive, often impossible list of tasks and "to do these things in silence and reverence, barefooted and ill-clothed."[106] When enslaved women questioned, challenged, or failed to meet these impossible expectations, they could be beaten, abused, or sold away from loved ones.[107] The anecdotes cited from the vagrancy dockets capture what Glymph describes as "a kind of warring intimacy" between mistresses and those enslaved.[108] Even the most minor challenge or imperfection could be viewed by a mistress as justification for extreme violence. Just as slaveholding mistresses were not held accountable for their role in household violence, the same can be said of Philadelphia's elite men and women. Spared the association with violent overseers who might enforce discipline in the plantation South, elite whites in the city turned to the state to enact violence and impose order for them.

Prison Labor

The early years of manufacturing coincided with the quest for new ways to discipline rebellious workers. While some states still relied on corporal punishment, capital punishment, and general ill treatment of the condemned, Pennsylvanians were eager to expand on the almshouse-style institutional labor regimes and transform prisoners into a disciplined workforce. British reformers provided Pennsylvanians with the idea of building self-sustaining, lucrative manufacturing systems inside of prisons. Just months after Benjamin Rush delivered his lecture against public punishment at Benjamin Franklin's house, many in attendance became charter members of the Philadelphia Society for Alleviating the Miseries of Public Prisons. PSAMPP members exchanged frequent letters with their British counterparts about prison labor and published a pamphlet full of anecdotes from British prisons.[109] PSAMPP sought to assure the public of the value and effectiveness of prison-based manufactories by citing the general order achieved in British prisons by this system. A manufactory of a Norfolk, England, prison specialized in cutting logwood and working with hemp to turn it into a usable material. The beating, heckling, and spinning of hemp was very dirty and smelly—and quickly adopted in Walnut Street Prison shortly thereafter. Who better to do the most distasteful tasks than prisoners?

While the impetus and support for introducing labor in prison came from British reformers, it was also rooted in the distinctly American impulse to develop a manufactory system that could free it from dependence on British imports. Advocates for manufacturing claimed the long-term financial viability of a sovereign state hinged on an increase in production.[110] One commentator asserted that manufacturing was key to the wealth and future of the nation, claiming, "A nation composed of farmers, without a due intermixture of manufacturers and mechanics, must, sooner or later, degenerate to the condition of mere labourers."[111] Manufacturing innovations were featured in local magazines and newspapers. In rural Pennsylvania, the spinning wheel was touted as a "fashionable piece of family furniture."[112] Some believed the popularity of spinning, along with the establishment of looms, cultivation of flax, and efforts to increase the quantity of wool would enable the United States to become independent. Artisans and manufacturers regularly complained about the waste of the nation's wealth on the purchase of imported goods that were either unnecessary or could just as easily be produced in the colonies.[113] As textile manufacturing grew, it played an increasingly important role in expanding Pennsylvania's involvement in the Atlantic trade.[114] Groups of manufacturers, merchants, and capitalists came together to promote their views in organizations such as the Pennsylvania Society for the Encouragement of Manufactures and the Useful Arts, formed in 1787—the same year as PSAMPP.[115] The two groups had much in common, including expanding the productive capacity of the nation and putting convicts, vagrants, runaways, and immigrants to work. Arguments for putting the idle, poor, and criminal classes to work were circular. For those living outside the law, hard work would provide the discipline and structure they needed to allow for the reordering of their minds. For poor people, labor would keep them from a state of idleness, which was thought to lead to lawlessness. Idleness, then, was the greatest source of chaos and evil; it moved a poor person to a life of crime and stood in the way of a convict's reformation.

The development of a penal system with labor at its core was intimately linked to this larger economic and political culture. Pennsylvania was the first state to embrace this connection when it passed An Act to Reform the Penal Laws of this State in 1790. The act required that the offender "undergo a servitude of any term or time" up to ten years while being "kept at such labor and fed and clothed."[116] With this directive, the modern penitentiary was made. This new system of punishment was put to the test at Walnut Street Jail, officially renamed Walnut Street Prison in 1790 with the passage of this law. The key distinctions would be forced labor behind closed doors and a newly authorized Board of Inspectors to oversee operations and management. Walnut Street Prison served as the nation's first penitentiary and the destination for all those convicted and sentenced to one year or more in prison from across the state of Pennsylvania.

The Board of Inspectors quickly declared three goals for the new system: public security, reformation, and humane treatment of prisoners.[117] An explicit concern with the treatment and well being of prisoners reflected an entirely new attitude toward those condemned. The belief that those convicted of serious offenses against society should be attended to rather than cast away seemed a radical departure from early modern corporal punishment.[118] But this proposed humane treatment quickly became rigidly inhumane, defined by the strict ordering, regulation, and manipulation of bodies. The Board aspired to instill order in ways large and small; first, they restricted interaction with outsiders, prohibited drinking, and separated men and women. That part was easy and served to support the chief aim of punishment: the promotion of "habits of industry" through "solitude, low diet, and hard labor."[119] Labor was still at the heart of punishment, but to what end? The widely documented aims of penal labor—to punish, to generate revenue, and to reform—could easily be at odds with each other.[120]

Judges, prison guards, and reformers debated the real aim of prison labor. Was work intended to make the penitentiary self-sufficient, contribute to industry, or reform the inmates? Benjamin Rush and other visionaries believed that successful manufactories would signal successful punishment, defined by the transformation of convicts into productive liberal subjects. Rush insisted punishment should combine hard labor with bodily pain, solitude, watchfulness, silence, cleanliness, and a simple diet, and that these conditions would encourage individual transformation.[121] Inspectors quickly departed from a literal interpretation of the law that called for labor "of the hardest and most servile kind" when they recognized that the most profitable labor was often not the most servile.[122] When profit motives and reform motives contradicted each other, there was no clear consensus as to which was more highly prized. Hard labor in prison seemed like an ideal remedy for a range of social and economic ills. It would serve as punishment for those who refused or were unable to live and work in the ways that elites had hoped. Elites had very specific expectations for how the poor and working classes should live their lives: work hard, avoid the streets at night, attend church, and be honest, respectful, modest, and submissive.[123] Those who failed or refused any one of these things were more likely to end up in prison, a place that was now thought to be capable of providing proper discipline to transform them into productive workers.

The work of inmates was grouped and managed first according to sexual difference.[124] Authorities were generally ambivalent about women inside early American prisons. They did not make special rules for them but informally modified the policies as they saw fit.[125] Women were grouped all together by sex. Men were also grouped together by sex but then further divided by the type of work they performed. When the Board put Francis Higgins in charge of overseeing the labor in prison, they asked him to keep a record of the work of each group, listing "women convicts" as a group and then detailing the work of men as "shoemakers, woolcarders, weavers, carpenters, logwood chippers."[126] While women were put to work doing tasks that were considered unskilled but which they presumably already knew how to do, men were offered the opportunity to learn a trade in the prison workhouse that they could then use to "maintain themselves and become useful members of society."[127] Inspectors boasted, for instance, of the large number of apprentices who worked in the shoemaking division. Male prisoners were offered the opportunity to earn wages from their labor to cover their costs, and then give the surplus to their families. The Inspectors reported paying the wife of an inmate from his wages "to assist her in her present embarrassments."[128] While men's manufactories were unpredictable in their productivity, they did generate revenue, produce goods, and offer skill development to some inmates, some of the time.

Men's work was divided into two major categories—one for able-bodied men and another for those men who were too old, weak, or infirm to do "men's" work. Such a distinction created a class of prisoners who did not fit neatly into the prison labor system based on sexual difference. Too old or weak or infirm to work in the men's manufactories, these men were assigned some of the same tasks as the women.[129] This was an accepted fact of life: the declining physical abilities of men who lived very hard lives marked by poverty, movement, and manual labor. The creation of a second category of work for men who were unable to do men's work revealed the temporality and fragility of the division along lines of sexual difference. It did not, however, open up opportunities for young, strong, robust, or skilled women who might take their place. The disruption of the gendered order of labor was a one-way street. Men could safely take up women's work, but women, however capable or strong, were not permitted to do the work of men.

Valuation of women's work was generally half that given to men's, a signal of their inferior position in the labor market more generally.[130] An early group of Inspectors valued the work of women cooks and washers at one shilling six pence. The male cook, designated "the first cook," was allotted three shillings three pence.[131] In 1809, the value of women's work was set at twenty-five cents per day for those "Spinners, washers, and other able bodied whose employment is irregular."[132] The same report assesses thirty cents a day to "able bodied men whose employment is irregular." The value of women's work actually declined over time. In 1812, it was set at "no more than 20 cents per day."[133] By 1816, one week of work in prison earned women one-third to one-half of what men earned.[134] Women's work was also used as a justification for serving female prisoners smaller quantities of food than men. Because their tasks were "less laborious" than men's, they received the "same quality" of mush, potatoes, and bread but in smaller portions than the men received.[135] This distinction between the valuation of men and women's work was made passively. The Board presented their resolution that the payment for women's labor be lowered using passive voice. The report claimed that because "no particular price is fixed" to women's work, it was worth less than work that had a fixed price; yet the Inspectors themselves made the decision not to assign it a specific value. Just as men's wages were determined by the number of pairs of shoes produced or number of nails headed, women's work could have been valued by the number of shifts made or yards of flax spun. But it was not so valued.

While the Inspectors refused to recognize the value of women's labor, others following the debates over penal reform noticed that women in prison labored productively and diligently—even as men were causing chaos in the streets with wheelbarrows. An essay in the *American Museum*, possibly written by the publisher Mathew Carey, highlighted women's institutional labor: "Hitherto the female criminals, condemned to labour, have been prudently placed in the work-house, where, it is said, their earnings have been equal to the cost of their food and clothes."[136] Women served as model prisoners and showed how the system of forced labor could be economically advantageous, while wheelbarrow men demonstrated chaos, violence, and resistance. Even those women who were considered dissolute and incorrigible could be transformed by imprisonment and "gradually reconciled to labour and industry." The key to this process was a careful balance between discipline and encouragement, delivered through a "strict but not cruel superintendence."[137] The *American Museum* was a popular publication that enjoyed a diverse readership, including some of the most powerful men in the country.[138] Failure to address the gendered dimensions of penal reform, then, was intentional—and not because people did not realize that women were imprisoned.

Women's productive labor was in fact vital to the maintenance of the institution.[139] By the 1790s, women made the clothing for both themselves and male prisoners. Inspector Lownes reported, "Most of the clothing, at present, is spun, wove, and made up in the house, and is designed to be so altogether in future."[140] This was modeled after the system used in the House of Employment, where women were reportedly employed at "carding, spinning, knitting, sewing, & c." for decades.[141] Spinning was a common task for women and a staple of institutional work regimes.[142] Women produced coarse linen for other convicts to wear and fine linen for sale to the public.[143] Women worked at "washing and cleaning their apartments."[144] Vagrant women were left with the more repulsive task of "picking Hair."[145] Inmates picked a variety of materials for various uses: hair for bedding, okum for building, and wool for clothing. Picking hair was a "disgusting" assignment that reportedly could "create distemper." A former inmate complained that the smell was so awful as "to cause many of them to vomit, and set all hands to coughing."[146]

The number of references to naked prisoners or those "said to have no cloathing" highlights the urgency of the task at hand for women charged with making clothes. The Visiting Committee of PSAMPP reported in 1804 one "young woman of the name of Sarah Keys who is said to have no cloathing but a shift, Sarah Hopple in near the same situation."[147] The material used to make the clothing was "tow-linen," the grade of material often used for "wagon-covers and house-cloths, not even bleached."[148] This was the same grade of cloth specially imported to clothe slaves in Caribbean and southern colonies. Men assisted women with clothing production, as they wove the fabric while women "made up" the article itself.[149] This was consistent with artisan work practices also going out of fashion during the period. Women and children spun, men wove, and women sewed the clothing. Women's labor in prison was both indispensable and hidden, much as the work of enslaved and indentured servants was for centuries. The system of sex-segregated labor in which women produced much of the clothing and bedding used by prisoners cultivated a culture of men's domestic dependence on women and women's economic dependence on men in return. The prison-based economic system exploited women's labor for the gain of the institution. As a prisoner, a woman sustained male prisoners for nothing in return.[150]

African American and first generation immigrant women faced greater limitations and were disproportionately restricted to domestic work as servants, seamstresses, and laundresses. It was generally impossible for women to earn enough money to cover their expenses, pay off fines or fees, and have anything to keep for themselves. The only existing record of a financial account for a woman in the penitentiary's early years reveals that the low pay rate scarcely came close. The account of Elizabeth Clinton from York County covers the period from December 31, 1803, to April 15, 1804. In that time, she received provisions worth $13.60 along with shoes $.93, blankets $2.50, and clothes $5.98, costing a total of $23.01. Her total earnings paled in comparison. She was "compensated" $5.00 for her washing and $7.60 for her sewing, a total of $12.60, leaving her indebted to the institution for $10.41.[151] Records such as these were more commonly kept for prisoners from counties outside Philadelphia because city commissioners sought reimbursement from surrounding counties.

The fulfillment of the domestic tasks of the penitentiary necessitated a steady flow of women into the prison. This remarkable dimension of the relationship between gender and punishment has scarcely been acknowledged by either reformers or historians. This correlation is only noted in a reprinted account from a British prison that PSAMPP circulated in 1790. The passage argued that a larger prison could hold more women who could do more work—and even be offered more diverse duties.[152] The system required the imprisonment of enough women to get the work of the prison done. Inspectors may have welcomed the imprisonment of skilled spinster Mary Davis and others like her who could train women and oversee the production of clothing.[153] A consistent population of women in prison enabled the management to ensure sufficient coverage of certain tasks, such as cleaning, spinning, making clothing, and caretaking. This is verified by the fact that women's prison activity was always productive and never punitive. While a treadmill was authorized to be built in the city's prisons, it was directed at men "to be used as a species of hard labour for such male prisoners as are liable to be placed to such punishment."[154] Popular opinion was against having women on the treadmill because there were other forms of employment more "congenial to the habits of their sex."[155] This remark refers not only to labor that was not physical but more importantly for work that was domestically productive.

Institutional work regimes narrowly defined and undervalued the productive labor of women, but beyond the walls of the prison, women's work took many different forms and played a crucial role in early American economies.[156] Women worked in public markets, both formal and illicit, selling and bartering goods. They kept shops, taverns, and inns. Servants and slaves would handle whatever tasks they were assigned in homes, shops, and markets before picking up side jobs to earn extra money in their free time. For poor women, work always expanded far beyond the four walls of home. Economic pressures as early as the 1760s forced even middling women to take on some paid work.[157] In the 1790s, one-third of female heads of household worked as retail dealers or hucksters while another one-quarter worked as innkeepers and boardinghouse managers.[158] Others worked as schoolmistresses, midwives, nurses, cooks, seamstresses, mantua makers, and milliners.[159] Working women filled the streets of Philadelphia every day, selling their wares, shopping at markets, and running errands for themselves, their families, and their employers.[160] But even these efforts were challenged by crackdowns on tippling houses, hucksters, disorderly houses, prostitutes, and fences—all important sites of work for women.

Accurate accounting of women's wealth can be difficult to find because of highly gendered assessment practices by constables.[161] But there is no mistaking how quickly a woman could go from being productively self-sufficient to unemployed and destitute. Almshouse records show the economic vulnerability of women despite the range of jobs they held. Ann Robeson kept a store with her husband on Second Street near the corner of Black House Alley, but he had deserted her many years ago.[162] Mary Conkline was a chambermaid at the city tavern, with a "bad sore leg" that eventually made it impossible for her to do her job.[163] Both women turned to the almshouse for support. Mr. Martin's indentured servant Ann Dames was subject to fits that made her "incapable of being serviceable to him" and leading him to take her to the almshouse himself.[164] Women who long worked in the service of others at the city hospital were especially vulnerable to illness themselves. Jenny Byrnes worked as a nurse in one of the hospital wards but became too sick to continue.[165] Mary Hall served as the long-time cook at the city hospital before succumbing to illness and old age, making her a "very old helpless woman."[166] Both women were admitted to the almshouse. Women who worked hard to piece together a living in health and youth could easily become sidelined by illness, injury, abandonment, or age. The line between dutiful worker and dependent was both thin and blurry.

While penal reformers had grand visions for turning male criminals into skilled and productive shoemakers, carpenters, nailers, and weavers, they did not train women in midwifery, mantua making, nursing, bartending, or bookkeeping.[167] Women's work in prison was restricted to laundry, cleaning, spinning, and sewing—jobs leftover for the unskilled and poor and yet necessary for the maintenance of all prisons. The relegation of women's work to distinctly domestic, unskilled, undervalued labor had several consequences. It aligned the disproportionately African American and immigrant inmates with forced domestic work, reasserting their proper place as servants in the homes of others despite the abolition of slavery and abandonment of indentured servitude. This particular sexual division of labor advanced a racialized notion of work that was not formalized within the institution until decades later. Second, it foreclosed on the wide array of work skills that women might have developed to succeed independently in the new republic, promoting instead their financial dependence on men and, as a result, reinscribing a heterosexual political economy.

But even women's work outside prisons became less visible and less valued as a market-based economy developed in the early republic. As Jeanne Boydston has shown, women, like men, adjusted to the changing market forces that defined this precapitalist moment. While some women's work might take place in the home, it still involved taking in out-work or increasing domestic production of items for sale or trade at the market. For women, even the visibly productive elements of household labor were becoming increasingly devalued.[168] The fact that so many women engaged in so many different forms of public labor became obscured by men's struggles to secure wage work for themselves. Working poor families long relied on the contribution of women's wages to meet the basic necessities of food, fuel, shelter, and clothing; those slightly better off may have used the income women earned to cover "the extra expenses of taxes, medical bills, candles, soap."[169] The economy of early America was like a roller coaster. It caused nothing less than a crisis in the heterosexual political economy, breaking up families, forcing men to migrate for work and women into the marketplace. Most jobs were tied to the maritime economy, and both natural and international forces shaped the success of merchants, retailers, shipbuilders, and mariners.[170] Even skilled, able-bodied workingmen became less secure in their wage-earning ability—and less able to provide for their dependents. In spite of this—or possibly because of it—men's work became more valued and visible. Long-standing recognition of the family as an economic unit was gradually replaced by the idea of the male breadwinner. And so women in prison were trained not to take on one of the diverse and profitable jobs that gave women an important place in the colonial economy but rather to assume the position of economic dependent. Women's labor in prison at the end of the eighteenth century not only forecast but also helped to reassert a heterosexual political economy that erased the value of their work.

Submission

Reports of women's submission to penal authorities and their embrace of institutional work assignments stood as powerful testimonies for liberal reform, even as women themselves were largely excluded from liberalism's promises. Women's work in prison was less monitored than men's, leaving ample opportunity for women to refuse to work, joke around, or even fight with each other. But misbehavior was rarely documented. Instead, in institutional records from 1794 to 1835, women were *nearly always* reported to be working hard. In 1801, the Visiting Committee of the Acting Committee of

PSAMPP noted great productivity among the women despite the fact that
"idleness remains among men."[171] The women vagrants were "generally if
not all employed." As the years went by, the Committee noted that women
were either working in similar numbers as before or at an even higher rate.
In 1804 it described the women's wing as "in a better situation generally than
sometimes heretofore there being more of them employed."[172] In 1805 the
Committee found many prisoners needed clothing and upon purchasing
linen reported that one piece of it was "made into 11 shifts and 13 shirts"
by female inmates.[173] The keeper reported that it took the women "their
whole time nearly" to get their work done, a sign they worked steadily and
dutifully.[174]

Though reformers refused to speak of women's work in anything but
the passive voice, they did repeatedly recognize their productivity. The Visiting Committee pointed out "Flannell was made into shirts and shifts by
the vagrant female prisoners."[175] Two of the women who received the shifts,
Kitty Spencer and Mary Ford, were being held in the dungeon. Kitty,
described as "almost naked," really needed much more than a shift.[176] Kitty
was a nineteen-year-old African American woman sentenced to nine
months at hard labor for stealing, of all things, clothing.[177] And so reformers noted that women helped to clothe other women in prison but did so
passively.

Reports of female productivity were juxtaposed with those of male idleness. Men were reported positively only in the earliest years.[178] But even
then, reports of male idleness outnumbered positive accounts. In 1795, the
Inspectors noted, "The stone cutters do not cut the quantity of stone they
are capable of."[179] The following year, a detailed scheme of punishment
through food deprivation was established for those in the nail factory who
did not work to their potential. The Inspectors reported that prisoners who
failed to complete a "reasonable days work" would be denied breakfast for
the first day and both breakfast and dinner should they underproduce for
two consecutive days. Continued failure to meet the requirements resulted
in solitary confinement.[180] In October 1820, the Visiting Committee noted,
"About 20 females were spinning and knitting for the convicts, the males
have not employment."[181] Constant reporting of male idleness fueled ongoing debates about the role of labor in punishment and the effectiveness of
punishment more broadly.

Men's manufactories were a disaster not just from a labor standpoint
but also from a management one. Inspectors struggled to effectively

manage the prison manufactories. Unable to sell nails made in the prison, they offered them at a discount to the public; unable to sell linen, they turned to a local warehouse, and then years later to auctions. They expanded store space in the front of the prison to better exhibit the available goods in hopes of increasing sales.[182] Sometimes they overestimated the demand or realized that goods produced by prisoners did not have as high a value on the open market as anticipated.[183] Some charged that prison manufactories undermined the free market.[184] As early as 1798, Inspectors realized the institution was deeply in debt from the "extensive credit" that was extended toward the prison manufactories.[185] After years of struggling to make the manufactories profitable, Inspectors decided the prison would stop purchasing raw materials for the prisoners to craft into goods for sale. They closed down the store where goods produced in the prison had been sold for years. Inspectors reported that it was better to have convicts work "for individuals who furnish the materials," saving them the trouble of purchasing supplies and assuming debt.[186] The prison thus resorted to contracting out the prisoners' labor to the highest bidder.[187] As a result, the convicts worked for "customers" who paid a set price to the keeper for labor while providing the convicts with the necessary materials.[188]

These failing manufactories quickly inspired vocal criticism from those who felt that the primary purpose of the penitentiary—moral reform—was being subjugated to profit. In 1812, Judge Jacob Rush, brother of Dr. Benjamin Rush, claimed that the practice of making "money out of the bodies of convicts" could actually "destroy their souls."[189] Judge Rush condemned the way that labor came to dominate the institution at the expense of other concerns, calling the law a "public fraud" that claimed to reform criminals while instead nurturing them in a "school for vice." Roberts Vaux later echoed the argument that attention to profit over punishment led to doom. Vaux scoffed, "The grand object was not so much the punishment and reform of the criminals, as a pecuniary balance, at the year's end" as if financial concerns were beneath moral ones.[190] In 1821, even the Inspectors themselves admitted the failure of their prison manufactory because it both lost money and failed to reform inmates.[191] The failure of manufacturing was one thing, but the failure of punishment was not an option. During these hard times, reformers and Inspectors looked to the women's side of the prison for inspiration.

Women served as a crucial site of optimism and hope for Inspectors, reformers, and jailers during a challenging, unstable period for two reasons:

they seemed to work more dutifully than the men, and they more easily adopted a submissive disposition. Even when women rebelled against orders, men in charge did not take these challenges to their authority seriously. Rather, when women did not work to their full potential or challenged their authority, keepers responded to them very differently than they did to the men. Reform was nothing if not gendered, and it demanded different things of men and women in prison. For instance, on occasions that women were not working to their potential, reformers generally made excuses for them. In their January 1799 report, Inspectors noted "many idle" women convicts and described women vagrants and prisoners for trial as "many idle some dirty and some ragged."[192] They did not blame the women for their behavior, however, noting instead that they were "unable to procure a sufficient number of spinning wheels to employ all the women," particularly since many of the wheels were destroyed in a fire started by the men. When women did not work efficiently or dutifully, the Inspectors generally had an excuse for it.

Women who resisted the orders were easily handled by skilled guards who knew how to manipulate and cultivate submission from them. One woman, "an old offender" who tried to burn the prison down in the early 1790s, was described as "ungovernable" and "of an extreme bad character." But she was no match for a keeper who knew how to handle her emotions and cultivate her submission. Inspector Caleb Lownes recalled that once she realized the keeper "was easy" and did not provoke her "to keep up her passions" she was left with no reason to resent him and thereby "at length submitted."[193] Submission was the necessary state for this particular woman—or any woman—to achieve. This woman not only obeyed all the rules of the house after this incident, but promised that she would "perform two days work, each day" for the duration of her stay. Hard work and appropriate submissiveness were expected from women in prison.

There are several explanations for such dramatically different responses to men and women's idleness. Women were viewed as easily reformable because they worked hard and demonstrated the expected deference to male authority figures most of the time.[194] By demanding deference and submission of the female convicts—two traits central to women's proper role in society—reformers ensured women would have a greater likelihood of reformation than the men. Inspectors had less to prove in overseeing the women. Female prisoners were trained to assume their proper roles in the heterosexual political economy: as domestic caretakers, economic dependents, and subordinate followers of men. Inspectors did not aspire to make independent, self-sustaining productive citizens of women in prison. There was no path to citizenship for women inside the prison—and few options for them once outside it.

Enslaved and bound women of African descent who challenged the authority of white men and women who claimed possession of them were also no match for the disciplinary regime of the prison. While many references to women in prison avoid mention of race or ethnicity, one visitor made special note of how easily black women received and submitted to the authority of the white keepers. Robert Turnbull, a young lawyer visiting from South Carolina, toured the prison and wrote extensively of his experience. His essay was widely read both domestically and in Europe and powerfully demonstrates the insidious correlation between enslavement and imprisonment in dictating the power relationship between white men and black women.[195] Representations of black women having positive experiences in prison advanced liberal ideals of individual advancement in the face of massive structural obstacles. When visiting the women's ward, Turnbull was most fascinated by "a young negress" who requested a discharge, though having served less than half her two-year sentence. He reported that her conduct "had been regularly pleasing" and her work ethic admirable. Although her request was rejected, Turnbull was impressed with how she received the bad news, writing, "She declared herself satisfied with his reasoning, and resumed her employment at the spinning-wheel with cheerfulness and activity."[196] Thus black women prisoners served a critical political and discursive function as emblems of model inmates. Turnbull characterized imprisonment as a positive force in the lives of black women that strengthened the ideological legitimacy of institutional punishment.[197] Black women in particular were used to advance the idea that punishment promised to be a positive force in their lives, just as racist justifications of slavery portrayed the enslaved as happy and taking pleasure in their work in service to their master. Each time a reformer highlighted the successful reform of a black woman in prison, he or she justified the expansion of incarceration.

Accounts of female prisoners—African American, European immigrants, and a few Anglo- and Irish Americans—embracing their captors were vital in reassuring reformers and Inspectors of their own benevolence.

Turnbull described a vivid scene of heartfelt reunion between women prisoners and a keeper who had been away. He wrote, "With the most heartfelt expressions of joy, they hastened from their seats to welcome him on his return, and on his part, he received them with a mixed sense of tenderness and satisfaction."[198] This was celebrated as evidence that characteristics of sentimentality were adopted in the prison itself, enabling the keeper to serve as "a protector—an instructor—not an ironhearted overseer!" This language of benevolent paternalism aimed to obscure the violence of punishment and distinguish it from slavery. These expansive feelings shared by inmates and keepers characterized a soft, warm, and comfortable paternalism expected of the family, not the state. Women prisoners were to be reformed through their relationships within the prison family, which further bolstered the heterosexual political economy.

*   *   *

Women's labor was deemed a great success because women dutifully complied with their work orders, thereby demonstrating both the viability and the effectiveness of institutional punishment. This seemed to be the right remedy for those rebellious runaways and others who refused to work and resisted the authority of those who claimed a right to their labor. Forced labor under the watchful eye of a jailer was hardly a change from the conditions under which many women regularly labored, in either slavery or freedom. Men who proved resistant to authority under the wheelbarrow law continued to undermine efforts of the state to discipline them into a productive labor force.

The privilege of presiding over the domestic sphere was increasingly held up as the proper place for women, even as some middling and elite Anglo-American women agitated for women's education, equality, and political power. While some men might tolerate or even embrace changes demanded by their own wives and daughters, they did not extend this view to the masses, the poor, or the organization of the prison. Rather, penal authority pushed back against all sorts of challenges to the social order. Enslaved, bound, or hired working women would have squeezed domestic work in between other wage-earning duties, but this was not an option in prison. The predominantly Irish and African American women who filled the prison were marked as capable of only the most undervalued forms of work.

The prison was at the forefront of a movement that narrowed the possibilities for women's work and lives in the American city. Much of the ideological work of labor was unspoken. The sexual division of labor was hardly explained or celebrated, but it was more highly prized than profit. The strict adherence to this principle reveals how invested the state was in naturalizing differences and establishing the social category of gender. The great accomplishment of this period was the largely invisible way in which the sexual division of labor became formalized. Only where women were concerned was the totalizing effect of penal labor realized. Women's labor was not profitable per se, but it was indispensable. This process served to naturalize a feminine gender that was both incapable of skilled work and fundamentally submissive. There was no way out for women. Those who refused to work, spoke out against visitors, or generally misbehaved were deemed incorrigible, fallen, and worse than male criminals. Those who worked quietly, submitting to penal authority and serving as model inmates to observers, were credited with nothing more than being women—if more properly so than when they first arrived.

⮑

CHAPTER 2

Sentimental Families

WHILE THE WAR for Independence from Britain looms large in its impact on late eighteenth-century American politics and culture, older forces, including the Enlightenment and the Great Awakening, inspired a great deal of social transformation as well. The Enlightenment was characterized as "the age of reason," in which human progress would be measured through advances in science, medicine, technology, culture, and politics. Enlightenment writers from Cesare Beccaria to Montesquieu produced progressive theories of criminal justice that rejected the legacy of European brutality and aimed to put logic, predictability, and fairness at the heart of punishment. In part because of the tremendous importance of these writings, the revolutionary generation relished the opportunity to craft laws fit for democracy. While these ideas inspired many people to question long-standing practices of violent, corporal, and excessive punishment, the Great Awakening compelled large numbers of Protestants to take action to alleviate the suffering of the masses and pursue salvation for themselves. Together, these forces shaped a culture of humanitarian sensibility among elite and middling men and women.

When botanist and future Massachusetts senator Manasseh Cutler visited Philadelphia in 1787, he met with many local luminaries, including Benjamin Rush, Benjamin Franklin, and Charles Willson Peale. Cutler stayed at the well-appointed Indian Queen on Third Street between Market and Chestnut, along with several men attending the Constitutional Convention. Cutler's hosts wined and dined him, canceling other appointments to spend time with him and show off the best of what their city had to offer. Cutler was part of a new generation of men who asserted themselves as leaders in the revolution's wake.[1] Humanitarian sensibility required that

Cutler cultivate an awareness of everything around him. On his walk around the area of the State House and over past Walnut Street Jail, Cutler's senses were awakened in ways both positive and negative. He described the walk around the State House as being full of "beauty and elegance," only to have his own experience of "pleasure and amusement" diminished by "one circumstance that must forever be disgusting." Cutler contrasted the elegance of the prison building with "its unsavory contents." He seemed appalled that it was impossible for him to escape the sights and sounds of the inmates, complaining, "In short, whatever part of the mall you are in, this cage of unclean birds is constantly in your view and their doleful cries attack your ears." Cutler was made very uncomfortable by the prisoners' disruption. He claimed, "Your ears are constantly insulted with their Billingsgate language, or your feelings wounded with their pitiful complaints." His remarks expose the limits of the sentimental project. Though sensibility required that he intervene in social matters and mitigate the suffering of others, Cutler seemed more rattled by his own discomfort than that of those imprisoned.[2]

The cultivation of sensibility was a central value for this generation of elite and learned men. They embraced sensibility—"human sensitivity of perception"—as a way to improve themselves and transform society.[3] Late eighteenth-century sensibility combined both reason and feeling in what could be an uneasy balancing act.[4] Men aspired to balance between the embrace of feeling and a fear of the effects of too much feeling in themselves and others. The expansion of penal authority was rooted in this tenuous quest. Early American culture privileged sentiment as a valued individual pursuit. Sensibility had its roots in eighteenth-century England and later "broadened the arena within which humanitarian feeling was encouraged to operate."[5] Reformers targeted many different groups with their efforts, including the poor, the enslaved, alcoholics, immigrants, and prisoners.

The legacy of European punishment and popular perceptions of inmates together made prison an implicitly degraded, vile, and hardened place. When public punishment brought the degradation of the prison into the city streets, Pennsylvania's leading statesmen were moved to action. The sentimental project would face its ultimate test in working with liberty's prisoners. Far from politically neutral, however, it became a vehicle for the naturalization of sexual differences while imposing white upper- and middle-class family values on predominantly African American and Irish working and poor people. By reaching out to men and women in prison, offering assessments of their progress and assistance in securing pardons from the governor, male reformers could cultivate a refined, controlled, and benevolent masculinity. They stood in contrast to the brash, aggressive, unfeeling keepers and guards who maintained ultimate authority over inmates. They sought to differentiate themselves from men of lower classes who were "hardened" while encouraging gendered notions of work and dependency among those imprisoned.

The sentimental family became an important idea in punishment, as it was in larger social discourses.[6] Punishment called for imprisonment and total isolation from one's family. This manipulation of family ties and dependencies was dynamic, contradictory, and violent, though done in the name of enlightenment and progress. Visitation with loved ones was restricted while reformers inserted themselves forcibly into the lives of the imprisoned, asserting their own ideas of proper visitation. When given the chance to articulate their needs and dreams in petitions for pardons, inmates crafted stories of love, loss, and family that were highly gendered and sentimental. Ideals such as virtue that had long been cast outside the reach of immigrants, African Americans, and poor native-born whites were embraced by these very groups as they sought to establish themselves as worthy of respect, pardon, and even citizenship. Women in prison claimed a feminine subjectivity for themselves that was anchored not only in family and motherhood but also in work.

Pardons

Several of Pennsylvania's delegates to the Constitutional Convention—Benjamin Franklin, James Wilson, Jared Ingersoll, and Thomas Mifflin—would play key roles in redefining and enforcing the penal laws of Pennsylvania. PSAMPP was incorporated in 1787 and became the nation's leading prison reform organization. Reformers of relatively modest means, including artisans, ministers, and shopkeepers, joined with political leaders, merchants, and local elites in devising a revised system of punishment. White men collaborated across class in doing this work, to some extent. Quaker Caleb Lownes, an ironworker by trade, and shopkeeper John Connelly devised the organizational structure of the Board of Inspectors while

elite men including Benjamin Franklin and Benjamin Rush held the spot-
light.[7] One justification of the need for visits by PSAMPP was that keepers
were insufficiently feeling and not tending to the basic needs of prisoners.
The powerful group of men who came together through PSAMPP had no
problem blaming the workingmen employed as jailers and turnkeys for the
problems that marked the jail. When Quaker merchant Samuel Rowland
Fisher was imprisoned by the British during the war, he had harsh words
for the keeper of Philadelphia's Old Stone Prison. Fisher described Stokeley
Hossman as "the most unfeeling Man that I remember to have met with
. . . a rough, hard-hearted Man."[8] Fisher criticized the actions of lesser,
working-class men using the language of feeling—something Philadelphia's
elite began to do more and more after the war. The jailor who oversaw
Walnut Street Jail in the 1780s, Mr. Reynolds, also resisted imposition of
politicians and reformers. He ignored the demands of the Supreme Executive Council on a number of issues by refusing to admit ministers to preach
and by not releasing pardoned prisoners who still owed fees. Reynolds
claimed he took orders only from the sheriff—not from the state's governing body and certainly not from a group of self-righteous humanitarians.[9]
For many years, Reynolds did a job no one wanted, for very little pay. He
resented the half-hearted meddling and micromanagement offered by his
betters. But right or wrong, they would ultimately prevail. Reynolds was
accused of exploiting the broken system to the detriment of inmates for his
own wealth, extorting extra fees for luxuries such as alcohol. By most official counts, he was corrupt and eventually removed from his position.

Inspectors wanted a keeper who embraced their ideas and gave up the
penal ways of old. Reynold's replacement, Elijah Weed, was popular among
Inspectors because he supported their efforts. The keeper, long an officer
charged with being tough and hard in superintendence of criminals, was
now expected to embrace an authority anchored in sensibility and feeling.
This partly explains why upon his death, Mary Weed, Elijah's wife, was
appointed to his position for a brief period despite the widespread disap-
proval of women's involvement in prison work at that time.[10] One visitor
claimed, "The office of gaoler cannot be repugnant to the feelings of a well-
inclined individual."[11] And so Inspectors felt it was a vital part of their job
to instate a man of feeling at the top. One thing was clear to them: while a
feeling man might become more feeling, and a hardened man might
become more hardened, the two did not switch places. Even with a new
keeper in place, they visited regularly.

Male reformers who served on the Visiting Committee of PSAMPP visited the prison weekly. While their official mission was to "alleviate the miseries" of the prison, the visits fulfilled other needs as well. Miseries were defined in terms of lack and excess: lack of clothing, bedding, food, and medical care along with too much freedom of movement, interaction with outsiders, and access to alcohol. Most obviously, the visits provided crucial emotional experiences for the men that enhanced their ability to feel sympathy and compassion for others. Progressive elite men believed that reform work gave them the opportunity to demonstrate sensitivity, generosity, and humanitarianism—in addition to cultivating their own sensibility.[12] Benjamin Rush shared this sentiment in a letter to fellow reformer John Coakley Lettsom, "I have the pleasure of informing you that, from the influence of our Prison Society, a reformation has lately taken place in the jail of this city in favor not only of humanity but of virtue in general." Proud of the impact of their work on others and themselves, Rush declared, "One thing is certain, that if no alleviation is given by them to human misery, men grow good by attempting it."[13] This emergence of feeling in the nineteenth century was vital. As Jan Lewis has argued, "To show feeling was to prove oneself fully alive." But excessive compassion could be destructive. Reformers embraced opportunities to learn about the hardship of others but resisted getting drawn in too closely to others' pain.[14]

The pardon became an important site of humanitarian intervention for this generation of reformers beginning in 1787. From this moment onward, men representing benevolent organizations would visit the prison and report their assessment of physically suffering individuals. They received petitions from prisoners begging for release and would determine whether or not they were worthy of recommendation to the governor for pardon. The system actually provided countless opportunities for strange men with authority granted by the governor to meddle in the lives of inmates—both men and women, predominantly poor. They would identify those individuals whom they deemed worthy of better care, support, or release. They would make formal recommendations to the governor or Supreme Executive Council and informal offerings of blankets, clothing, food, and prayers.[15] The creation and expansion of institutionalized authority were accompanied by an increase in individual attention for specific prisoners from interested reformers who might mediate between them and the increasingly anonymous state. The organization's impact was extraordinary. Shortly after its creation, PSAMPP was flooded with petitions from prisoners. Most petitions represented individual prisoners, although occasionally groups authored them as well. Prisoners pleaded with courts, reformers, and even the Supreme Executive Council of the state concerning a wide range of issues, from their inability to pay fines to their treatment at the hands of jailers. Individuals begged for forgiveness of court-imposed fines or prison fees that all too often were the only thing standing between them and freedom.

Men and women in prison articulated their needs in slightly different ways. By its very nature, the petition required recognition of one's dependency and helplessness. For women, the genre was fitting—at least in theory. Just as gender norms requiring female dependency may have made it easy for reformers to assist female inmates, those same roles may have made it harder for women in prison—disproportionately impoverished—to pass the "character" tests rooted in social norms that were also raced and classed. PSAMPP concluded, for example, that Catherine Haas did not deserve their intervention because she was "of a bad character and since last visit was convicted and sentenced to hard labour in the work house."[16] For women, "bad character" was a catchall phrase for a wide range of behaviors, including cursing, prostitution, simple vagrancy, drunkenness, petty theft, or not showing proper deference to authorities. For men, an expression of submission might garner praise from reformers while undermining the men's claim to citizenship in the new republic. The core qualities of the liberal subject—individual agency, accountability, and responsibility—were beyond the reach of men in prison, who were forced to beg their betters for help.[17] The petitions served as highly gendered narratives of dependency.[18] This vulnerable class of people negotiated dominant expectations regarding family life and gender roles while seeking the assistance of the reformers.

Progressive reformers did not have to look far for evidence of the harsh cruelty of the state, or of their own benevolence. Prisoner Elizabeth Donovan begged the reformers to rescue her from the "hard-hearted" keeper by "throwing" herself on their "bounty and goodness."[19] Elizabeth appealed to them through the lens of their growing philosophical commitment to a humanitarian sensibility that had been until recently a feminine pursuit. Donovan's insistence that the reformers were the kind of virtuous gentlemen who could override the authority of the state (embodied by the wicked keeper) fueled their understanding of reform's mission and affirmed their own sense of benevolence. Petitions further served to defend and justify penal authority in the first place. Prisoners did not call on revolutionary principles of justice or liberty or democracy in requesting assistance. Rather, they appealed to the reformer's individual humanity, mercy, kindness, or charity.

Female inmates had to navigate dominant views of motherhood in their appeals. Susey Mines' petition was filled with references to her family, although not the kind reformers would want to hear; a republican mother she was not. Mines blamed her daughter for her imprisonment and claimed she had no idea her daughter was stealing and then storing the items at her home. Mines wrote that she "would not permit her daughter or her goods inside of her doors" if she knew her daughter was a thief. Mines's situation was not unusual, as many women were charged with possessing, receiving, or selling stolen goods rather than with actual theft. Once in prison, Mines wrote of her suffering in an exceptionally descriptive way, a practice more common among female than male petitioners. Mines emphasized the survival of her family and based her request for assistance on their needs. She stated that she had "a family [of] small distress[ed] children [to] provide for which are now in a most suffering condition and starved and cold winter just approaching," and appealed to the "merciful kindness and humanity" of the reformers to help her and prevent her and her family "from perishing this winter." Like other women who raised the needs of their family in petitions, this mother named children but never mentioned a husband.[20]

The number of references to women who appeared to be sole providers for themselves and their families is striking. Sarah Collier cited the distress of her children as the primary basis for her appeal and explicitly referenced their dependence on her. Speaking of herself in the third person, Collier wrote, "She humbly hopes that your honour will grant her liberation as her confinement will only serve to increase her distress as her children are almost helpless and chiefly depending on their parent['s] industry."[21] Women believed that motherhood was the right chord to strike with male reformers who held the key to their freedom. The concept of republican motherhood was already circulating, carving out an important role for women's domestic leadership in shaping the polity. Women like Collier risked judgment of failure about their parenting skills and life choices, but they still believed drawing attention to their role as mothers was their best hope in convincing their visitors to recommend them for a pardon.

Elizabeth Elliot wrote to the Supreme Executive Council of the state requesting remission of fines for her conviction for selling liquor without a license. Elliot did not claim innocence but begged remission from the ten-pound fine. She probably supported herself and her family through her tippling house. Though she did not present the suffering of her children as the basis for her request, she did end her appeal by stating, "Your unfortunate petitioner is a poor widow who hath a family of five small children."[22] In cases such as Elizabeth's, it was clear that she did not have a husband. The absence of references to male providers signals several things. One, women without the economic support or political authority of men were more likely to be imprisoned. Two, female petitioners were more successful in appealing to the sympathies of reformers if they presented themselves as single women with children. In the absence of a named husband, progressive men would assert their own patriarchal benevolence, offering financial or legal relief to women who were failed by other men.

Petitioners exhibited varying degrees of deference, with women's petitions generally more excessive in their demonstrations of both suffering and submission. In November 1787, prisoner Catharine Usoons sent a letter to John Morrison, a coppersmith and charter member of PSAMPP. Her petition deployed themes that would resonate with her male audience by deferring to Morrison, emphasizing her own vulnerability and dependency, and highlighting her role as a mother. She pleaded, "To your honour the dismal and deplorable situation I now labour under with my young infant at my breast, have not any cloaths to put on and am almost starved . . . I hope your honour will take it into your charitable consideration as it will never lay in my power to pay the restitution lay'd on me wile I lay in Jail and I have been here 18 months and suffer'd inconsiderable, and I am afraid myself and child will starve this winter without your honour."[23] Catharine's appeal offered PSAMPP members a range of ways to help her. Short of actually paying the fees for her release, PSAMPP could see to it that she received some clothing—at least the standard shift—and adequate food. Written expressions of submission by women reinforced their appropriate position vis-à-vis men and served as evidence of their successful reformation. By demanding deference and submission from female convicts—two traits central to women's proper role in society—reformers ensured women would have a greater likelihood of reformation than the men. The rhetorical submission of the petition only further enforced this.

Male petitioners had a host of different issues to navigate. Manliness was measured by independence for men in the early republic. The working poor, servants, slaves, and imprisoned men strove for *expressions* of

independence in place of actual financial independence.[24] Male prisoners
were eager to reassert themselves as providers for their families, and this
idea often shaped the basis and tone of their petitions. They were not
looking for handouts but merely the opportunity—both noble and
appropriate–to support their wives and children. James Parkins wrote,
"Your well known sensibility and the goodness of your heart I flatter myself
will be an advocate for a whole family and by your benevolence and kind
influence I anxiously wish that a drooping family may once more smile and
thank their generous benefactors."[25] Parkins made his case based on the
collective needs of his family rather than his individual desires. Other men
wrote explicitly about the particular family members who depended on
them. Alexander Drian's petition to the Supreme Executive Council cited
the needs of his two-year-old child and wife in critical condition as grounds
for leniency and a remission of his fine.[26] John McCrum begged to be
released so that he could "go work honestly for my bread and my wife as I
always did before," adding that he would rather be dead than to see his
"wife suffer as she does."[27] Prisoners worried about their families and
believed that the well-being of innocent women and children would inspire
the benevolent reformers to help them. This turned out to be true in many
cases. For example, the Visiting Committee of PSAMPP advocated the payment of the dollar fine that kept prisoner William Ketsel from being with
and supporting his "wife and three children."[28] The idea that men deserved
the opportunity for success because their families were dependent on them
only became stronger in Philadelphia during this period, as wage labor
replaced long-standing terms of servitude or slavery for society's most
vulnerable.

Gendered notions of economic self-sufficiency and independence were
less forgiving of men who needed assistance.[29] This is precisely why male
prisoners framed their requests in more expansive terms. Jacob James could
not make the complete bail he was offered and ended up in jail awaiting
trial—a common cause of people's imprisonment. James basically
requested a loan from PSAMPP for his bail money and promised to pay
the debt back weekly until it was discharged. This was an unusual and
creative request. He rooted his appeal, however, in the needs of his family
and his desire to take care of them. James wrote, "Hon[ore]d Sir I have a
wife and one child in grate distress on the account of my being in this place
and can not be any help to them."[30] James entered a dependent relationship
with his benefactors based on his desire for freedom. He (and others like

him) staked a claim to independence (and therefore manliness) by asserting his relationship to his dependents.[31]

Patrick Kain claimed to have unknowingly harbored two escaped convicts and ended up in prison as a result. Kain offered several reasons why PSAMPP should assist him, none as powerfully or dramatically stated as his need to provide for his family. Obviously distraught, he proclaimed, "I have a wife and three small children and have myself lost a leg in the service of the country and have sailed since 7 voyages with Capt. Cunningham and if I am detained here and loose the chance of a berth god knows what will become of my wife and children."[32] Men never cited their children alone as those in need of their aid, suggesting they were never expected to be the primary or sole caretakers of children. Men could be providers for families, not caretakers of children. Thus, they referred to their wives and families, in marked contrast to women, who often described themselves as the sole custodians of children.

Despite hints of things to come, including a decrease in use of the language of deference and an increase in the use of petitions for collective political action, the petitions written by prisoners in Walnut Street Jail from 1787 to 1789 are more reflective of the petition's past than of its future. Even the more assertive and entitled petitions penned by debtors would not have raised the ire of reformers. They were still petitions, after all, a genre of communication that "acknowledged the power of the rulers and the dependence of the aggrieved."[33] Prisoners were nothing if not dependent—and reformers were happy to oblige requests that did not threaten this hierarchy. Still, imprisoned men were placed in an impossible position: they had to practice deference and obedience while demonstrating the markers of citizenship—independence, agency, and strength. The petition only further highlighted this tension, which can be seen in attempts by some men to assert themselves more boldly. Men used the petition in multiple ways, attempting to navigate the paradoxical relationship between submission and self-determination. They did this most persuasively not by rooting their arguments in claims of independence, liberty, democracy, or citizenship, but rather through their own relations of dependency—by framing themselves as providers and caretakers for wives and children.

Prisoners of both sexes wrote desperately, longingly, and mournfully about the plight of their families during their imprisonment. Their only hope was to appeal to the whims, sensibilities, or conscience of those men who positioned themselves as arbiters of justice and suffering. PSAMPP

members received significant public recognition for their work. One commentator downplayed the fact that most were economically successfully and
politically powerful, stating, "Nothing further need be said, respecting the
members who come to their relief, but that they are men, engaged in the
noblest office that can employ human nature, that of mitigating the miseries of their fellow creatures."[34] But it was precisely their status that empow-
ered them to advocate the creation of the penitentiary and then to mediate
the intimate family relationships of those trapped inside.[35] Gendered representations of desire and dependency helped stabilize the heterosexual
political economy by assuring reformers that men and women in prison
understood and aspired to social and economic roles rooted in sexual
difference.[36]

*   *   *

Reformers embraced their role in recommending pardons partly because
this process deflected attention from the expansion of punishment and its
brutal consequences for immigrants and African Americans. Individual
pardons provided a counter to concerns that the penal system was a substitute for slavery, an extension of the slave labor economy, or a tool to contain the poor masses. The opportunity to pardon strengthened the belief of
benevolent reformers and abolitionists alike that human consideration—
and even justice—might be possible for African Americans, immigrants,
women, and all of those with no formal say in legal matters. Widespread
use of the pardon in the first decade of the penitentiary reflects both optimism and pragmatism. PSAMPP's first recommendation for pardon was
for a black man convicted of arson. In 1787, Barrack Martin along with his
wife, Tamar, were charged with arson. It was decided that there was no case
against her (ignoramus), but he was convicted of arson and sentenced to
death in 1787.[37] Martin was said to "voluntarily and maliciously, on the 28th
Feb. 1787, set[ting] fire to and burn[ing], in the township of Lower Dublin,
one barn, one stable, and one out house, the property of a certain Susannah
Morris, containing 10,000 lbs weight of hay."[38] The Supreme Executive
Council ordered a pardon for Martin shortly after his conviction. PSAMPP
members discovered that despite this order, he was still being held in prison
in irons. They recommended him "to the care of the Acting Committee"
on May 31, 1787. Two weeks later, the Acting Committee reported that his
irons were removed, and they soon received verification of his pardon and

noted the council was "ready for his liberation."[39] Martin's pardon was inspired by the early zeal of humanitarian reformers.

And so the pardons flowed. Reformers and Inspectors would visit prisoners and make recommendations to the governor. Reform proponents argued that pardons were essential to the penitentiary system because they gave jailers and reformers a way to entice convicts to good behavior. Pardons were also "freely granted to make room for new-comers."[40] In 1795 and 1799, roughly half of the women sentenced received early releases. Pardons were more frequent and of greater length (about four months) during 1795 than in 1799, when the average dropped to one month. But politicians and reformers continued to clash over the use of pardons. Many Pennsylvania judges and politicians were convinced that certainty and proportionality of punishment were key to the system's success. This idea was central to Cesare Beccaria's theory of punishment, which had inspired an earlier generation of reformers. Judge Jacob Rush argued that pardons should never be granted in response to convict pleas of sorrow, guilt, or regret. Granting pardon to those who repented would "give license to men to break laws as they pleased," while rendering the penal system and government weak, vulnerable, and ineffective.[41] This view was widely adopted, as the percentage of pardons dropped dramatically in the early years of the nineteenth century. By 1807, only 11 percent of prisoners received pardons.

Debates over pardons never subsided. Occasionally they were granted on humanitarian grounds, such as the pregnancy of a woman, but otherwise were typically linked to evidence of reformation. The criteria for pardons were as follows: "The convicts who demean themselves best, and are most submissive to the rules and orders of the jail, are rewarded by a recommendation to the governor."[42] In 1820, Governor William Findlay refused to accept the Board's recommendations and demanded more information in response to critics who claimed he pardoned too freely and was responsible for freeing a violent man.[43] President of the Board of Inspectors Thomas Bradford, Jr., begged for the reinstatement of the pardon and continued to advocate the use of pardons as a tool of reform. As he explained in a letter to the governor, pardons were a key to making prisoners more orderly and hardworking: "The stimulus to industry and obedience was hope and hence pardons were frequent. . . . Hope of reward and fear of punishment in the cells were the powerful and efficient agents in maintaining the admirable discipline which then existed in the prisons."[44] Successive governors rejected the plea. Fewer than 6 percent of the women convicted in 1823 received such pardons.[45] By 1830, the Board of Inspectors was begging the governor—then George Wolf—to reinstate the use of pardons on their recommendation. They devised a three-part classification system for determining an individual's worthiness of pardon. The governor believed that too liberal a policy would disturb the peace of society and that the public deserved to know why a prisoner was pardoned.

Others felt racial and gender norms still figured largely into pardons and that the governor used his own subjective means to grant them. Both were true. Women could also earn a pardon by promising to resume dependency on their parents. Evidence of family ties could prove crucial in justifying a pardon and early release from prison. Artimissa Gardner was sentenced to three months in prison for running a disorderly house. She swore to visiting reformers not only that she was anxious "to pursue a virtuous course of life" but also that she wanted to return to her mother who lived near New York. PSAMPP inquired about the legitimacy of her claim, her own word not being enough, but the prospect of this outcome was always thought preferable to releasing a woman back to the streets.[46] After Ann Setzimmous was imprisoned on charges of stealing fifty dollars from one person and something else from another, Inspectors had her released on the condition that she go home and live with her parents in the country.[47] Young women resuming dependency on family were pardoned while older black men languished in prison. A group visiting Walnut Street Prison in 1827 commented on several older men of color who were unjustly held. The visitors hinted at a racist jury system that was only compounded by a pardoning system corrupted by money and connections.[48]

Isolation from Family

In its founding constitution, PSAMPP invoked the unification of the family of mankind as a central goal of their efforts, stating "By the aids of humanity, their undue and illegal sufferings may be prevented; the links, which should bind the whole family of mankind together under all circumstances, be preserved unbroken."[49] It was widely agreed by men of state and reform that a breakdown in domestic authority led to crime and mischief in the first place. Patriarchal authority had many faces and forms.[50] Male heads of household, benevolent social reformers, and agents of the state would all exert control over the lives of poor women and men in different ways.[51]

When intimate patriarchy failed, they were happy to step in. Denied the opportunity to live with and labor on behalf of their own families, prisoners were forced to work as servants in a different house—the penitentiary.[52] This grave violation of the family occurred simultaneously with the production of the nuclear family as "the family" in broader circles.[53] Rather than being taught how to cultivate social relationships and familial relationships with their own kin, prisoners were forced to live in a distorted prison family organized around an overly simplified heterosexual political economy. Punishment stood against marriage and family, suggesting that the path of reformative incarceration was never really meant to lead to citizenship at all.

Penal authority was a double-edged sword when it came to women and marriage. On the one hand, unmarried women were disproportionately punished. On the other hand, penal authority also worked against the marriages of prisoners. The introduction of the penitentiary as the premier punishment actually *undermined* marriage. Women were cut off from the familial sphere and subject to an ever-expansive institutional patriarchy disguised by the rubric of humanitarian sensibility.[54] This violation of the family by progressive elites in the name of humanitarian reform shows what little regard they had for the family ties of the immigrant and African American poor who filled the jails. The denial of family life for prisoners further distinguished them from the middling and elite whites who embraced marriage as a foundational relationship for the nation. Divorced from the central social relationship rooted in sexual difference—marriage— prisoners were both literally and ideologically blocked from participating in citizenship.

When Rush laid out his critique of public punishment, he also outlined his vision for what should take its place: imprisonment and complete separation from one's family and community. His logic was that because liberty was so valued, imprisonment would be greatly feared. Rush wrote, "Personal liberty is so dear to all men, that the loss of it, for an indefinite time, is a punishment so severe, that death has often been preferred to it." He envisioned *complete* removal from society to a remote location engineered to be difficult to reach and ominous to behold. Rush stated, "Let the avenue to the house be rendered difficult and gloomy by mountains or morasses."[55] For such a forward thinking man of the Scottish Enlightenment, this description sounds oddly medieval, reminiscent of the kind of dungeons and castles that were scattered across Europe. It was also the opposite of new ideas in circulation about the sublime effects of nature and natural beauty on the mind and soul.[56]

Popular depictions of the pain inflicted on families by punishment feature heterosexual couples shattered by the imprisonment of the husband. A 1796 poem portrayed the experience of imprisonment through the eyes of the woman left behind: "Say, does a wife, to want consign'd, / While weeping babes surround her bed, / Peep through, and see the fetters bind / Those hands, that earn'd their daily bread?"[57] The poem centers on a nuclear family thrown into a state of sadness and want at the loss of their provider. Other portrayals focused less on finances and more on love. One poem captures the intense severity of isolation for a man denied his love. This prisoner exclaims, "My days were dull, my nights were long! My evening dreams, My morning schemes Were how to break that cruel chain, And, Jenny, be with you again."[58] The message in these stories was loud and clear: prison destroyed families. Prison inspired sadness, longing, worry, frustration, loneliness, anger, boredom, guilt, and poverty. These depictions celebrated families that were destroyed by the imprisonment of a man. But rather than lying around crying, as popular anecdotes portrayed, women had to take care of business. When her husband was imprisoned, Abigail McAlpines reported "[I] work in att my [ne]dedel which I hope will maintain me and my little girl decently," not only during his imprisonment but even after his release when he went off to sea to earn some money for the family.[59] The reality of family economies, particularly for those of the lower sort who disproportionately filled Philadelphia's prison, was always more complex than the situation idealized by the reform agenda.

Punishment defined by Rush centered on the manipulation of the emotions of prisoners while protecting the emotions of innocent citizens. Imprisonment would impose a range of overwhelming feelings of loss, loneliness, sadness, and remorse on the guilty. Inmates would be forced to submit to the authority of the state, which had total control over their release. The imagined future reunion with loved ones—anticipation, relief, and joy—was just as important to Rush as the temporary exile from family and society. Rush explained, "By preserving this passion alive, we furnish a principle, which, in time, may become an overmatch for those vicious habits, which separated criminals from their friends, and from society."[60] This desire for reunion gets stronger with age, burning inside the prisoner, and driving him or her to want to change. Rush wrote, "I already hear the inhabitants of our villages and townships counting the years that shall complete the reformation of one of their citizens."[61] He argued against banishment on the grounds that permanent exile destroyed the motivation of reunion with one's family.

Rush sought to make the case that prison was a more severe punishment than either public labor or death. He argued that imprisonment was the most severe punishment precisely because it forced separation from family. Rush wrote, "An attachment to kindred and society is one of the strongest feelings in the human heart. A separation from them, therefore, has ever been considered as one of the severest punishments that can be inflicted upon man."[62] Rush's proposal for this approach to punishment echoed sentiments expressed in an abolitionist essay about the problem of slavery: "When we consider the cruel invasion of every right of humanity, in forcing the unhappy Africans from their native land, and all those tender connections which rational beings hold dear."[63] Though Rush and his contemporaries would deny that their prized institution reproduced that one increasingly reviled, the parallels between enslavement and imprisonment are obvious.

Cutting people off from family and friends may have seemed an ingenious punishment to Rush and his contemporaries, but for African Americans both free and enslaved, it had a deep, dark, historic resonance. Ripping people from home, family networks, and loved ones was a routine practice of enslavement.[64] The violence of such destruction and isolation was justified under an economic system that privileged slaveholder profits and whims over the kinship networks, family, and emotional needs of African Americans.[65] As the institution of slavery was gradually eroding in the North, the institution of the penitentiary was being devised and rapidly expanded. Just ten years after passage of the Gradual Abolition Act paved the way for the end of slavery, the state of Pennsylvania enacted a revised penal law that allowed for containment not only of African Americans, but also of immigrants and the poor. Along with freedom came a new legal and social apparatus to deny freedom.[66] Such seeming contradictions were ubiquitous. For example, Rush himself joined the antislavery society while remaining in possession of his own slave for many years.[67] Rush, like so many other elites, justified this with the belief that blacks did not value freedom as much as whites. Only then could the connection between slavery and punishment be an afterthought. Prison was an ideal punishment if one presumed that liberty was "a good that belongs to all in the same way."[68] Ideologies of racism and liberalism became intertwined, enabling the expansion of an institution rooted in slavery during the era of slavery's abolition.[69]

Forced labor was also a familiar economic and social relationship for the many presently and formerly indentured servants who populated the prison in large numbers. By sentencing convicts to "servitude," the state reappropriated a classification long used to describe desperately poor people who were isolated from their own families while working in the homes of others, often under contract.[70] While servants labored under an economic debt determined by the terms of their indenture, prisoners labored under a social one that placed an individual's obligation to the state ahead of his or her obligation to their family.[71] Rush did not comment on how closely his proposed scheme for punishment resembled slavery or indentured servitude. No one did. But while indentured servitude was becoming irrelevant due to changing economic realities, debates over slavery raged nationally.

At least one person thought separating people from their families was too harsh a punishment. On his visit to Philadelphia, abolitionist Jacques Pierre Brissot de Warville detailed the pain of this separation: "By imprisonment, you snatch a man from his wife, his children, his friends; you deprive him of their succor and consolation; you plunge him into grief and mortification; you cut him off from all those connections which render his existence of any importance."[72] But for Rush, this pain was necessary to compel the personal transformation he hoped punishment would effect. Only then would the power of the family reunion be realized. Rush wrote of the hypothetical inmate's family, "I behold them running to meet him on the day of his deliverance.—His friends and family bathe his cheeks with tears of joy; and the universal shout of the neighborhood is, 'This our brother was lost and is found—was dead, and is alive.'"[73] Themes of sin, atonement, and redemption reminiscent of the parable of the prodigal son resonate in Rush's plan. For Rush, each inmate had the potential to be a prodigal son, able to see the error of his ways, repent, and be reborn under the right conditions. Rush's brother, Judge Jacob Rush, concurred. For both Rush brothers, suffering was a crucial component of punishment. Judge Jacob Rush argued, "The voice of nature has uniformly demanded *sufferings* as the proper atonement of guilt, and that sorrow *alone* is not a sufficient expiation."[74] Only through suffering and repentance could one find salvation—and be worthy of readmittance to the polity.[75]

Because family was both so prized and so perilous, family would be denied those who violated the law. Family ties were already stretched for everyone by years of extended separations caused by war, politics, and economic necessity.[76] The actual consequence of imprisonment for most families was financial peril. Laboring families required income from all their members, including adult men and women as well as older children. The imprisonment of either a man or a woman would result in a lost source of income for the family. If a prisoner was the single or primary earner in his or her family, this would be devastating. The famous bigamist, kidnapper, and counterfeiter Ann Carson described herself as the primary earner in her family, and the chaos her imprisonment triggered. She reported, "My family were, by my confinement, thrown into a state bordering on distraction; ever accustomed to have me at the head of both business and household, they knew not how to proceed without my presence."[77] Carson was one of many who served as the anchor of *both* home and work for a family. No one disputes the fact that Carson was a successful businesswoman who ran a small shop dealing in fine china and other imports. She was one of a sizable number of women in Philadelphia who managed their own businesses and asserted their economic independence in the process. Women like Carson exhibited a great degree of innovation, autonomy, and success while navigating the economic and social constraints of the city. Her family's hardship was a real and tangible consequence of her imprisonment.

Carson was not exactly a typical prisoner—her crimes were more serious, diverse, and publicized than those of most women. She probably earned more money as well. But she was part of a large group of women whose personal and family economies were thrown into chaos by imprisonment. Women imprisoned without trial for minor social transgressions under the vagrancy act faced incredible challenges.[78] Who would run Elizabeth Ferguson's beerhouse while she sat in prison for thirty-six hours on charges of intoxication? How much income did Mary Williams lose when she was held with five other women on charges of running a disorderly house? Did Mary Brown, a free black widow who labored as a washerwoman, lose clients when she was locked up for socializing with friends and deemed a "riotous" disturber of the peace?[79] Constables, night watchmen, clerks, and judges did not trouble themselves with these questions—though they freely complained of the consequences when women were unable to support themselves.

Imprisonment could destroy a woman's ability to earn money, keep a job, and raise her children. Institutional policies regarding children ranged from indifference to strict superintendence. Either could be devastating to mother, child, and their relationship. Some women moved between the almshouse and the prison, reflecting a cycle of poverty and imprisonment with no clear way out. Other women were devastated to learn that their children were bound out when they were in prison. In colonial times, infants and very young children could accompany their mothers to jail. This practice persisted in the first few decades of the nineteenth century.[80] Women with very young infants or who actually gave birth in prison were allowed to keep them by their side. In 1787, Catherine Usoons pleaded for some relief from prison or labor or both, in part because she was working "with my young infant at my breast."[81] The Visiting Committee reported that "some females" furnished "a gift" of clothing for a child recently born in the prison in 1800.[82] Inspectors John Harrison and John Bacon noted on April 28, 1817, that a prisoner Dobly Miller gave birth to a boy.[83] Other women had children of indeterminate ages with them. For example, in 1800, a woman named Ruth Moore, who appealed to the mayor for a discharge, was described by the Visiting Committee as "an Indian Woman with her child."[84] In 1804, reformers mentioned prisoner "Ann Keating and her child," as well as reporting the purchase of two yards of flannel for Mary Gale's child.[85] These children were probably infants or very, very young. The fact that women would keep their young children with them in prison was utterly shocking and astounding to reformers who complained about the practice. Writing to the Supreme Executive Council, PSAMPP members noted, "Children both in the goal and workhouse are frequently suffered to remain with their parents whereby they are initiated in early life to scenes of debauchery dishonesty and wickedness of every kind."[86] Reformers sought to rid the prison of children for their own protection, despite the fact that many had nowhere to go. A single, divorced, or widowed woman's children would have been removed to the almshouse or bound to a local family if other relatives were not available to take care of them during their mother's imprisonment.[87]

Poor African American and Irish families were already deemed to be places of depravity and corruption by many middling and elite men and women of the period. Reformers specifically believed the working class was failing at its primary function of producing disciplined workers.[88] Chief Justice McKean of the Supreme Court of Pennsylvania argued that the children of slaves, though legally entitled to freedom by virtue of their birth after March 1, 1780, would be better off remaining in service to a white master than raised by "poor and ignorant parents."[89] Many others simply believed that the children of the poor were prone to mischief and corruption.[90] Both signaled a breakdown in proper domestic authority in the home, with consequences for social order in the present and economic order in the future. Those seeking to reform prostitutes also blamed a lack of family discipline, giving children the opportunity to associate with dangerous people and make bad decisions that quickly led to immorality and even crime.[91] Judge Jacob Rush tried to make the connection between domestic authority and the stability of the nation whenever possible. Judge Rush claimed there was an abundance of evidence to show "that a republican government can be supported on no *other* foundation than the virtue of the people. And it is equally clear, *this* virtue must originate in *domestic* education, in obedience to *parental* authority, and in a love of order."[92] Judge Rush proposed a rather strict schedule for children so as "to impress them with habits of *early* subordination to private authority, in order to lay a proper foundation of obedience to *public* government and the laws of the land."[93] This was not all that different from the routinization of prison life that his brother Benjamin promoted: a distorted, punitive family household.

White reformers and state authorities thought nothing of removing children from poor Irish or African American families. Increasingly, institutionalization meant forced separation for a mother and her child, since these women were deemed inadequate parents. Devastatingly, imprisoned women could have their children taken away from them. The high rate of single mothers and female-headed households made prison a real structural disadvantage for these families. When Mary Barry was charged with multiple larcenies in the summer of 1792, her three children were admitted to the almshouse. It is likely that the financial burden of raising three children on her own motivated her thefts in the first place. Barry worked in partnership with two men, Henry McKeans and Richard McGuire, in breaking into both the home and the store of Samuel and Myers Fisher on the west side of Front Street.[94] They also broke into the stores of tobacconist William Miller on the north side of Front Street and shopkeeper Henry Manley on South Market, stealing some tea, one gammon, and a cotton stripe.[95] When Barry herself was imprisoned and awaiting trial, her three children—James Barry, age three, Eleanor Barry, age six, and Elizabeth Welch, age thirteen—were admitted to the Almshouse.[96] The almshouse might provide a decent temporary home for those with nowhere to go, but there was always a danger the children would be bound out as servants.

It was one thing for the almshouse to provide temporary support and care for children with parents in prison. Women could envision a future, a freedom, in which they would be reunited with their children. The state, however, had other priorities. The law authorized the Guardians of the Poor to apprentice any poor children who became orphaned, abandoned, or recipients of public support, including in the almshouse.[97] This law was expansive and subjectively applied.[98] The process of indenturing children out to labor in other families served to keep the cost of poor relief to a minimum and to provide young boys with skills.[99] When they were old enough, the girls were sent to work as house servants while the boys might apprentice with a farmer or tradesman.[100] For poor parents unable to provide for their children or simply deemed unfit, this practice was devastating. Some women fought this practice with all their might. One woman, whose daughter Isabella was forcibly taken from her, found out where her child was bound and went there to retrieve her. After taking "her away by force" from the master John C. Schneeds, the mother was arrested and imprisoned. The child was admitted to the almshouse.[101] This was an absolute tragedy for everyone involved.

For Martha Jefferies, the forced indenture of her granddaughter was the final tragic step in a long, hard life. Martha Jefferies arrived in Virginia from England in 1737 at age twelve as an indentured servant.[102] She probably served out her indenture and continued working in the area for years. In 1767, she gave birth to her daughter Margaret in Augusta Staunton Town, Virginia. Martha made her way north to Philadelphia with her daughter. Unable to find any work—or enough work—or simply tired of working so hard for so little, they participated in the city's vast informal economy. In 1794, they were charged with diverse larcenies. Martha, already sixty-nine, received a six-month sentence, while Margaret served a full year for this charge. In September 1795, they were charged with keeping a disorderly house. With the mother and daughter in and out of prison and reputed to run a disorderly house, the state decided enough was enough. Margaret's daughter Martha, named after her grandmother, was indentured to William Donaldson of Philadelphia for eleven years as a seven-year-old in 1799. We do not know how Margaret or Martha felt about this. Were they relieved their daughter/granddaughter might be provided for in a good home, fearful for her well-being, despondent the child was taken from them, or all the above?

Many women found themselves in the almshouse after being freed from prison, instead of having the imagined reunion with family that Rush envisioned. For those without family, work, or resources, it was no easy task making it in freedom. After Catherine McCoy spent over a week in jail for "being frequently intoxicated, abusive and troublesome" to her neighbors she was taken to the almshouse by the Constable. McCoy was kept apart from her husband and son.[103] Twenty-four-year-old Rebecca Williams served six months in jail before being transferred to the almshouse.[104] Illness commonly required women simply to go to the almshouse for basic care. Rose Thornton, described as "a frequent customer to the workhouse and goal," sadly found herself sick and was admitted to the almshouse in September 1792. Mary Ann Kelley was in and out of both the almshouse and the prison over the years. In 1797, she was treated for venereal disease and sent from the almshouse to the prison for "clamorous and disorderly conduct." This back-and-forth continued. By July 1800, she was married and known as Ann Wallace, still only twenty years old and suffering from cancer and in need of support.[105] After a life in and out of the jail and almshouse, Margaret Doyle (aka Margaret Dyer and Margaret Skinner) became very ill and died in the almshouse on October 14, 1790. The record described her as "a noted woman who hath been often here, at the jail workhouse." For most female prisoners, the scenario envisioned by Rush of happy reunions between reformed prisoners and their families would simply never be.

Visitation Restrictions

Women convicts occupied a semipublic sphere, enclosed within prison walls yet on display for those men—ministers, politicians, reformers, judges, and Inspectors—who wanted to view them. This semipublic position created space for them to manipulate public perceptions of female criminality.[106] On display for self-appointed humanitarians, these women might inspire modest offerings to alleviate their suffering, such as clothing, firewood for heat, meals on special occasions, or even afternoon tea. Such viewings, however, did far more for the male visitors than for the women themselves. When face-to-face with women in a great state of vulnerability and need, reformers could affirm their own status as benevolent men of refined sensibility with even the smallest gestures of assistance.

Institutional patriarchy had many faces. PSAMPP appealed to the legislature to create a Board of Inspectors for the prison that would oversee daily operations and report to jurists, reformers, and the public. While regular overlap existed between PSAMPP members and the Board of Inspectors, they functioned in distinct realms of society. PSAMPP was a private, volunteer benevolent association; the Board was an arm of the state. PSAMPP members pushed for the creation of the Board in the first place in 1790, but the records of their Visiting Committee show they were never entirely satisfied with the Board's ability to maintain the prison properly.[107] The Inspectors set prison policy and determined who would be permitted to visit and under what circumstances. Both groups of men had ongoing relationships with the women in prison in the early republic. Members of the Acting Committee of PSAMPP conducted detailed character assessments of female prisoners and determined their worthiness for pardons, remissions, or discharge. They assessed living conditions and determined if they needed clothing, blankets, or medical care. Male reformers who visited women in prison engaged in basic caretaking activities. Men sought to embrace feminine qualities and do the reform work themselves.[108] They walked a tightrope between embracing feeling—a marker of masculinity— and becoming feminine themselves.[109] Most frequently, they acquired and delivered blankets and clothing for the destitute women, though occasionally these offerings included food or medicine as well.[110] They ordered blankets to protect women from "the cold weather," and in the warmer months, they provided linen for shifts to be made by prisoners—or occasionally actual "shirts, shifts, and trowsers" that were already made.[111] Reformers were indiscriminate regarding which class of prisoners they assisted, and put out calls for used clothing from the people of the city in order to more properly clothe both vagrants and prisoners for trial.[112] It was not uncommon for the men to order thirty blankets at a time to be distributed among men and women of all classes.[113]

Upheaval in Pennsylvania politics resulted in the removal of Quakers from important offices all across the city, including the Board of Inspectors, which would now be chosen by the city council.[114] Longtime Quaker activists condemned new political leaders who were less inclined to embrace feeling and reason in punishment. New York reformer Thomas Eddy saw this change as having a negative effect on penal reform. In speaking of the penitentiary, he wrote, "those who most contributed to its establishment and support, are displaced to make way for new men, wholly unfit to manage its concerns."[115] PSAMPP became "an organization of protest and of opposition" that criticized the shortcomings of the Board for doing an inadequate job.[116] The tension between PSAMPP and the Inspectors can be

seen in this visit, as a complaint by the reformers about the state of prisoners prompted an official of the prison to report that the Inspectors "intend
furnishing blankets to the two vagrant departments." This was not good
enough, and the visitors still ordered the purchase of flannel for clothing
and cloth for sheets.[117] Two years later, similar conditions persisted
throughout the prison, though this time it was remarked that the Inspectors
provided the vagrants with "an adequate number of blankets," meaning
that PSAMPP would save considerable funds because it would not have to
purchase these supplies themselves.[118]

In the early 1800s, the Visiting Committee began naming those to whom
they provided clothing. This served both practical and emotional purposes.
On the one hand, by keeping track of who received clothing allowances,
reformers could curb the practice of prisoners selling their clothes to others
in exchange for contraband or cash. Emotionally, it showed that Visiting Committee members were paying close attention to the women—
humanizing them, even creating subjectivities for the objects of their attention.[119] The descriptions of individual recipients were vivid and personal.
On March 8, 1804, the committee reported its distribution of five shifts,
noting, "They found a young woman of the name of Sarah Keys who is
said to have no clothing but a shift; Sarah Hopple in near the same situation."[120] This same group took it upon itself to make extra visits to the
prison without the Committee and boasted of its efforts in securing the
freedom of three women, one child, and two men. These included debtor
Mary Cox, prisoner Ann Keating and her child, debtor and prisoner Elizabeth Coxe, and two men who had served their terms but remained for want
of a small fee, Isaac Jones and James Gregory.[121] Consistently, however,
basic supplies and furnishings were wanting. Twenty years into the penal
reform movement, conditions were nearly identical to those reported for
Walnut Street's predecessor—Old Stone Prison at Third and Market streets,
where "Many of [the prisoners] were almost naked and without shirts, and
no bedding of any kind."[122] When Inspectors Roberts Vaux and Thomas
Wistar visited the prison in 1809, they reported that many vagrant men and
women were without basic shirts and shifts, the sick ward lacked sheets,
and as usual, blankets were in short supply. This cycle of hardship and
relief, marked by nakedness and then the receipt of clothing, was the process that helped men who visited the prison "grow" according to Rush.

Inspectors had authorized a veritable parade of public officials including
clergy, politicians, reformers, foreign dignitaries, lawyers, and local officials

to visit the prison.[123] This list is detailed in the first official set of printed rules, which ordered the turnkey to admit the following people: "Inspectors, Keeper, his Deputies, Servants or Assistants, Officers and Ministers of Justice, Counsellors or Attornies at Law, *employed by a Prisoner*, Ministers of the Gospel, or persons producing a written license signed by two of the said Inspectors; and the latter only, in his presence or some one of the Officers of the Prison."[124] This list of appropriate official visitors advanced a patriarchal system of power and supervision, as a white man filled every single one of these occupations. Only the lawyer might explicitly have had the best interest of the inmate at heart—but who could afford one of those? In 1811, the Board passed a resolution that permitted the unregulated visitation of any man who had previously been an Inspector "to visit the interior of the prison, whenever such citizen may think proper."[125] These men no longer needed to serve officially on the Visiting Committee to stop by the prison.

Even *seeing* these degraded and suffering women (something many men of their station hoped to avoid by sweeping the streets of vagrants) would enhance their sense of their own humanity. This visitation ritual might best be described as pornographic. The reformers experienced their very own peep show, guaranteed to stimulate the heart and the mind, week in and week out. As Karen Halttunen has argued, those who sought to be marked by exquisite sensibility found pain to be both unacceptable and alluring, and at times eroticized it.[126] Women were forced to perform vulnerability, some of them grabbed from the streets for the most minor offenses, and many of them stripped of some or all of their clothes by more seasoned inmates upon arrival. Put in cages with small groups of other women, on display for the select group of visitors, they simply waited. It was known that the institution provided vagrants only with food, not clothing.[127] No one questioned the motives or morality of humanitarian men coming into weekly contact with the half-naked women. These elites were described as "some of the most respectable citizens of Philadelphia" and seemed beyond reproach.[128] What was the alternative, when Inspectors and jailers seemed content to let women go without even clothing or blankets? By portraying women in prison as naked and vulnerable, reformers offered up a particular truth that helped generate sympathy for women in prison. It also obscured the existence of women's rage, violence, and rebellion.

But the question of propriety and women's right to privacy from the male gaze was a real one. Architect Jeremy Bentham was concerned about the possibilities of male authority figures watching female inmates when he designed the panopticon plan in 1791. Bentham wrote about the different scenarios that might occur: "A male Inspector will have some view of a female Cell; and *vice versa*, though it be less material, a female Inspector will have a similar view of a male Cell." Bentham suggested the viewing of a naked male prisoner by a female Inspector would be "less material," however absurd and unlikely that scenario might be. Bentham's design was intended to deny privacy for everyone. And yet there was something about the idea that women might unknowingly be watched that unsettled him. He saw that the perfection of his design would create scenarios that ran counter to popular social convention, and tried to modify it. He claimed that it would be possible to designate a portion of the cell that would always be outside the view of an Inspector walking on a different floor, ensuring a female inmate the opportunity to undress without fear of being watched.

Bentham argued that decency required this, but there is no evidence that this idea was carried forward.[129] In fact, Bentham provided the logic to prove any special measures unnecessary. He argued that female prisoners would never be entirely alone, outside the watchful gaze of other women. This would serve to protect them—not from male Inspectors—but from their own cunning, which might incite them to engage in indecency to intentionally catch the eye of a male Inspector. Bentham determined that women—fundamentally corrupting seductresses—were not in need of protection. The watchful eyes of other female inmates, he wrote, "affords sufficient security against any voluntary trespasses against decency that might be committed by a female prisoner, through impudence, or in the design of making an improper impression upon the sensibility of an Inspector of the other sex."[130] Women in prison were fundamentally degraded to begin with, leaving the visitors and guards vulnerable to their seduction and alleviating the need for concern about the women.

*   *   *

The issue of who could visit prisoners, when, and under what circumstances was an ongoing subject of debate. While rules were regularly updated to accommodate strangers, there was no provision in the 1792 rules for visitation by family members, including parents, spouses, siblings, or children. This was no accident. Officials thought the casual comings and goings of people in colonial jails undermined punishment. PSAMPP members identified "intemperance and thoughtless folly" as the "parents" of crime. Further, socialization was at the heart of crime. The Inspectors agreed, reporting, "The character of the convict is generally social to a fault; the vices of social life have heralded the ruin of his fortunes and his hopes, and, when deprived of the society of his companions in vicious indulgences and guilt, he reads and listens with eagerness, because he is relieved by the variety from the weariness of his solitude."[131] Total isolation from loved ones was in order.[132] There is no doubt that Rush believed this. He even experimented with mild forms of solitary punishment on his own children, writing, "I have in one instance confined my two eldest sons in separate rooms for two days. The impression which this punishment has left upon them I believe will never wear away, nor do I think it will ever require to be repeated."[133] All along, Rush envisioned that punishment would isolate the condemned as much as possible from everyone. The fact that Rush experimented with these methods on his own children shows just how strongly reformers associated domestic authority with penal authority.

Visitation rules for debtors were always considerably looser than those for other groups of inmates. Debtors always had great freedom to receive visitors. A group of male debtors complained about the treatment of their visitors, "That our friends, wives, & c have been & daly are search'd in the most insulting & indecent manner for spirituous liquor, which whenever discovered is taken from them."[134] This letter illustrates the distinctive position of debtors whose previous class position supported their expectation of receiving respect and authority they did not receive in prison. Similarly, they expected their female visitors to be treated with a sensitivity and delicacy known to no other women in prison. When elite revolutionary leader Robert Morris was imprisoned for debt, his family practically moved in with him. His wife and daughter spent a considerable amount of time in his cell, freely moving in and out of the prison and joining him for meals regularly.[135] While publicly shamed by his debt, the financier of the revolution still benefited from social norms that required delicate treatment of his wife and daughter.

Debtors were permitted frequent visitors because they had to rely on their own resources and the generosity of friends and family for food, clothing, and fuel. After the Act for the Relief and Support of Poor Confined Debtors was passed in 1792, they were officially to be provided with fuel, blankets, and food by the institution, making reformers more willing to assist debtors in need.[136] This change also increased the ability of the prison to regulate their visitation. Initially, the marital relationship was privileged in the visitation policies of the debtors prison. Social standing (if no longer class position) linked debtors more strongly to the dominant cultural norms of reformers than the convicts and vagrants across the yard. The new rules of 1804 stated that "no male" could visit a woman prisoner and no woman could go to a man's room "except the wife of some one of them at a time unless in cases of sickness of a prisoner and the physician directs a nurse."[137] While men were permitted to have a primary caretaker in the form of a wife or nurse visit them in prison, women were granted no such exception. Policies seemed to unfold in response to specific circumstances rather than formal logic. On more than one occasion, the mother of a debtor sought admission despite the lack of official permission to visit. Deciding mothers did not belong to the cast of characters who brought vice and chaos to the debtors apartment, Inspectors added mothers to the list of permissible visitors in 1808. The policy was again updated seven years later, this time to address several problems stemming from an inability to keep track of visitors coming and going. Visitors were restricted to once-daily visits, with the exception of lawyers, physicians, runners, or designated family members, including "the wife husband father or mother."[138] This subtle change in policy expanded in several gendered ways—namely, by welcoming fathers and husbands to the realm of caretaking and concern for their debtor children and wives. Not only could wives now be debtors, but men could worry about, care for, and visit their imprisoned kin.

As time passed, Inspectors realized they needed to establish clearer and updated visitation guidelines for all areas of the prison. Most dramatically, the updated visitation policy denied inmates physical contact with their visitors. Rather, the meeting was restricted to fifteen minutes within earshot of a keeper so he could "hear all that passes" in the meeting. Furthermore, a door would now separate the two, "the wooden grated door shall be shut and all conversation with the prisoners shall be through both the grates."[139] This restriction would be devastating for visitors and inmates alike, denied the opportunity to touch, feel, or hold loved ones during the brief encounters permitted. Just as the visitation policy denied physical contact with inmates, it expanded the range of people who could visit and clarified the role of sexual difference and marital status. Rule One stated, "No men shall be permitted to visit the women's apartments unless in the company of one or more of the Inspectors of the Prison; and no woman shall be permitted to visit any other part of the prison than the women's apartments, unless it be such as desire to meet with the prisoners in the meeting house on the first day of the week for the purpose of communicating religious instruction."[140] These general rules governed the prison itself and were meant to apply to all visitors, including ministers, lawyers, and reformers. Furthermore, the policy stated that convicts who were "diligent in their work" and properly behaved would be permitted visitation, but only by "their husbands or wives, parents or children once in three months." This expansive consideration of families succeeded where previous policies failed, acknowledging the important role of parents and children rather than solely privileging marriage.

Eight years later, on April 15, 1816, it was clarified that children needed to be in the custody of a parent or have the permission of an Inspector to enter the prison.[141] This change in policy affected men and women differently. Male prisoners were more likely to have some woman—be it the mother of the children, a lover, wife, mother, sister, or friend—take care of their children while they were imprisoned and bring the children to visit them when possible. Women in prison, however, were disproportionately single parents. Who would bring their children to meet them? In some cases, a woman would have a relative care for her children, but just as often they would become wards of the state. The policy was again updated in 1816, with an additional restriction added that put more conditions on the visitation of children. Children were permitted to visit only in the company of an Inspector or a parent who received permission from an Inspector. No one other than religious people could visit on Sundays. Suddenly the opportunities for children to remain connected to their parents were further diminished.[142]

Rules determining which people were legitimate visitors gradually loosened over the years. *Who* could visit became less important than *how* the visit was managed. The new 1828 policy read, "The relatives and friends of such prisoners as behave well are permitted to see and converse with them through both the grates; the wooden grated door being shut, and a keeper in the entry to hear all that passes—the interview not to last more than fifteen minutes; this is allowed once in three months by an order of the visiting Inspector."[143] The reference to visitors makes no distinction of sex, nor does it privilege family members specifically. It no longer officially mattered if the visitor was the spouse, sibling, parent, or child of an inmate. What mattered was how the prisoner interacted with a visitor—not who that person was. While official policy moved away from the privileging of particular family members, there remained great latitude for Inspectors and guards to interpret the rules as they saw fit. Nonetheless, marriage was an officially privileged status for only twenty years, from 1808 to 1828.[144]

Intimate Patriarchy

Following the revolution, the state formally increased the power and authority given to men in the domestic sphere. Women turned less often to the courts for protection from their husbands—and courts were less likely to grant it.[145] Courts were reluctant to intervene when men abused their dependents, instead respecting family privacy. Marriage was, after all, a social contract intended to protect the male head of household from the state.[146] Elites everywhere exerted themselves over said dependents as well as local governments in an attempt "to bring order to the wider society."[147] Dependents, including wives, children, servants, and slaves, had little contact with the state, since the head of household served as the ruling authority.[148] And yet none of this prevented wives, children, servants, and slaves from clamoring for greater freedoms in the post-Revolutionary period.[149] Challenges to domestic authority contributed to an expansion of the penal state. As Carole Shammas has shown, "Patriarchs were supposed to control the movement of their dependents; when they no longer could do so, the system fell apart."[150]

Revolutionary writers had little patience for the patriarchal domination of old, calling instead for a more equal partnership between husband and wife.[151] Marriage played an increasingly important role in cultivating virtue and stability in the lives of middling and elite white men and women.[152] Republican ideology valued marriage between a man and a woman, not only because they were now to be "conjugal equals" but even more importantly because their relationship was to be a model for "all the relationships in the society and the polity."[153] Virtuous women were the key to a virtuous family, while men reserved for themselves the task of cultivating moral sensibility throughout society. Even though marriage was portrayed as a model partnership for republicanism, its practical reach was shrinking. The state no longer stood in defense of the marriage bond as it had in colonial times. The Pennsylvania divorce law of 1786 made it much easier for wives to divorce their husbands.[154] Greater numbers of women chose to remain single or asked for divorce.[155] Policing of marriage and its violations were also on the decline. None of the handful of women who were charged with adultery in this period were convicted.[156] Women were released when charges were dropped or small fines and securities were paid.[157] The most common complaints in adultery cases were made by their husbands or by the wives of men with whom they were allegedly behaving adulterously. Charges against women were taken seriously only when questions of paternity and child support were involved—issues that inspired men to charge women with adultery disproportionately in New England. But no such pattern emerged in Pennsylvania, where twice as many men as women were charged and pardoned in equal numbers.[158]

The diminished remnant of intimate patriarchy was quickly and quietly replaced by the state. This relationship between intimate and institutional patriarchy proved to be fluid and dynamic. As a state-financed arm of patriarchal authority, the prison would discipline those who had already challenged the more intimate figures of authority in their lives—husbands, fathers, masters, mistresses, and neighbors.[159] Countless court and prison records reveal the failings of domestic authority over women, children, servants, and slaves.[160] These women would be punished twice, first for challenging the rules of domestic authority in the first place, second for the alleged crime committed. The loosening of marriage laws and seemingly widespread use of self-divorce were exciting developments for some women, with mixed implications.[161] The divergence between the ideology and the reality of republican marriage was a constant source of tension. Single women were tremendously economically vulnerable, especially if they had children and especially if they were African American or first generation immigrants. The freedom to be single came with social stigma and economic peril to boot—with penal authorities not far behind. Those women who tried to survive outside the institution of marriage, whether by desire or necessity, were targets of constables and watchmen on the look out for "masterless" people in the public streets, especially at night.

Women who left their husbands faced serious economic challenges. Many participated in informal economies such as selling used or stolen goods and became more vulnerable to arrest.[162] When George Miller alerted the public that his wife Margaret "has absconded from her bed and board" he declared that people should not "trust her on his account."[163] Margaret struggled to make her own living through conventional work and was arrested for being "a common and abandoned prostitute" in 1790. In 1791 she was charged with stealing clothing along with Mary Nance and Catherine Ralston and released a month later on September 8, 1791.[164] When Martha Jones left her husband David in June 1803, he ran an ad in *Poulson's American Daily Advertiser* warning people not to trust her on his account, because she "sometime past left my Bed and Board without any just cause."[165] Martha Jones was arrested in 1807 for drunken, disorderly conduct and swearing.[166] Mary Bray faced arrest after leaving her husband Joseph in October 1806.[167] On April 1, 1807, she was accused of stealing a purse with $23 from a man named Peter.[168] When Ann Morris left her husband Thomas in 1813, he placed an ad in the *Democratic Press* saying that she had absented herself from his bed and board and that he would not pay her debts.[169] Just over a year later, Ann, a young black woman, was arrested with an older white man named Edward Collins, charged with larceny, and sentenced to two years and a one-dollar fine.[170] Morris was in and out of prison on later charges of robbery and assault.[171] Freed by social custom and legal reforms to leave husbands who were abusive, controlling, or undesirable, some women found themselves facing impossible economic obstacles in single life.[172]

*   *   *

Paternalism still figured strongly in criminal law. Women engaged in high-stakes crimes such as burglary and counterfeiting generally did so in partnership with men.[173] When they were caught, women were convicted of lesser charges than the men or none at all. This practice was rooted in both the English common law of coverture that made wives legal nonentities and strong cultural associations of men with criminality.[174] Women were at great advantage during trials because both legal and social precedent assumed their innocence and/or victimhood. Some women rightly benefited from these presumptions, while others were able to use the weight of history and ideology to get away with breaking the law. Women involved in burglary cases, for example, were often convicted of receiving stolen goods but not actually stealing them. When the Pennsylvania Supreme Court charged Mary Barry and Henry McKeever with burglarizing the home of James Twain and William Brown, McKeever was convicted, while Barry was found not guilty of burglary and guilty of receiving stolen goods, a misdemeanor.[175] Such outcomes were not uncommon. Consider Ann Price, a thirty-seven-year-old white woman from Maryland who was charged by seven different plaintiffs for burglary or stealing with a group of both male and female accomplices.[176] In a trial before the Pennsylvania Supreme Court of Oyer and Terminer against Price, William Vallue, and Paul Vandam, the trio were convicted of diverse larcenies. The men were sentenced to ten years hard labor while Price received only a two-year sentence for the charge of receiving stolen goods.[177] While serving her time, Price managed to escape by hiding in the yard while the keeper William Pidgeon believed she was sick in bed. She was captured and brought back to prison with two extra years added to her sentence.[178]

When the men and women charged together were legally married, the women might not receive any punishment at all. When country yeomen Charles Boyles and his wife Mary were charged with stealing six silver tea aprons, one silver tablespoon, and two pairs of leather shoes belonging to lawyer John Shock (in addition to Peter Shock's black velvet cape), Mary was found not guilty, while Charles was sentenced to eighteen months in prison.[179] Samuel Davis and his wife, Christina, stole sixty pounds of coffee belonging to John Forester. Christina was acquitted while Samuel was found guilty.[180] When Reuben and Hannah Freshwater were tried before the Chester County Court of Oyer and Terminer for burglary in 1816, he was found guilty and sent to prison in Philadelphia, while she was released. Freshwater broke into the home of Joseph McMinn and stole eight promissory notes worth fifty dollars, among other items.[181] This pattern of wives' acquittals can be seen across a range of property crimes but is especially the case for those carrying punishments of one year or longer.

Counterfeiting required an upfront investment in materials that few women could finance on their own, but they were often a part of counterfeit rings with men. In 1795, a group of three men and one woman used a rural location as their base while producing and passing five- and ten-dollar bills. They were charged and tried by the Lancaster County Court of Oyer and Terminer. While the three men were convicted on three counts, the lone woman, Margaret Price of Derby, England, was found guilty on only one. Margaret's husband, M. Joseph Price, was sentenced to the most severe term—sixteen years—while the other two men received fifteen years. "From the consideration of her sex" Margaret was sentenced to the shortest term allowed—four years and a fifty-dollar fine. Then she was pardoned and discharged on April 26, 1796 after just one year and two months into her sentence. Joseph Price also received a pardon, serving only one year and four months of the sixteen-year term.[182]

When women and men engaged in high-stakes burglaries together, men bore the weight of social and legal responsibility. Though John McCrum claimed that "a bad woman that [he] got acquainted with and bad company" led him to burglarize the home of Charles Willson Peale, the "bad woman" herself, Elizabeth Emery, got off easy.[183] McCrum was sentenced to seven years for his lead role in the incident, while Emery received a much lighter sentence of one year for knowingly receiving the stolen goods.[184] It is hard to know what inspired Emery to visit McCrum in prison after she herself was released. Did she hope to find out where the remaining stolen goods were stashed so she could cash in? Or did she feel a guilty obligation that McCrum received such a long sentence? Once visiting McCrum, she became the subject of an interrogation by PSAMPP members John Connelly, Benjamin Shaw, and John Olden to expose the corrupt practices of keeper Reynolds. The newly formed PSAMPP was desperate to clean up the prison and get rid of Reynolds. When they interviewed Emery at the workhouse, she confirmed their greatest fears of Reynolds's corruption and abuse of power. Emery reported a long tale of being asked by McCrum to retrieve stolen goods to return to Charles Wilson Peale because McCrum had come to know him as a "friend and brother" during his frequent visits to the jail.[185] She also reported that she retrieved a bundle of goods containing spoons, tea and coffee pots, salt containers, and candlesticks that he had previously stolen from George Clymer and hidden in a buckwheat stack near a tavern on Race Street. She gave candlesticks and tablespoons to keeper Reynolds in exchange for "one guenia and one quart of spirits" that he gave to McCrum.[186] After McCrumm himself was released on a pardon, he sent Emery back to the prison to meet with Reynolds and retrieve some of the goods Reynolds was holding for him. The items turned out to be "two pistols and four keys." McCrumm used the pistols to assist his robbery of two silver watches that he in turn delivered to the prison turnkey through Emery in exchange for a quart of spirits and some cash.[187] Emery was McCrumm's accomplice and possibly lover while his wife suffered alone, a "stranger in the city."[188] They likely shared profits from the plunder but there was little loyalty between the two. Instead, she betrayed both McCrum and keeper Reynolds in exposing the role of Reynolds in trading stolen goods for cash and spirits with prisoners.[189]

Even if individual women did lure men into criminal acts as McCrumm alleged, legal precedent, economic realities, and social custom all pointed the finger at men when it came to orchestrating a serious crime.[190] In fact, few women achieved public notoriety for any crimes other than infanticide. The fact that women were seldom responsible for the most violent offenses or most egregious cons fueled public investment in the belief that men— not women—were more likely to be innately dangerous. All this changed in the 1820s when news of Ann Carson's life and crimes hit the papers. Her circumstances were both remarkable and rather ordinary. Like so many women, she moved on when her seafaring husband failed to return after a number of years, assuming he had died at sea or abandoned her. Upon his return, a confrontation ensued in which he was killed and her new lover held responsible. Some might say her first crime was adultery, but her real troubles began when she tried to secure a pardon for her lover, Richard Smith, by plotting to kidnap Pennsylvania Governor Snyder. Acquitted of this crime, she was later convicted as an accessory to burglary and counterfeiting. When issuing the conviction, City Recorder Joseph Reed, Esq., pointed out the infamous and spectacular nature of Carson's adventures: "It has never before happened within my experience or information, that any individual of either sex has been involved in such a variety and number of crimes as have been imputed, and no doubt justly, to you." Furthermore, Reed emphasized the severity of Carson's charges in both gender specific and gender neutral language. "They are crimes which degrade your sex and dishonor human nature."[191] Whatever dispensations Carson had received along the way as a white middle-class woman of some education and relative standing, she had long exhausted them. While she was said to have degraded her sex, there was no reference to her being "manly" or "masculine" or claiming some sort of criminal territory that belonged to men. No, it was clear that a woman—this woman, any woman—could create a significant criminal network to achieve devious aims.

Carson showed that women, too, could be guilty of the most egregious crimes. Her actions and the publicity she generated exposed the failure of intimate patriarchy once and for all. She was named "too dangerous a woman to be lightly sentenced, or soon liberated" not only for the magnitude of her crimes but for her skill in "collecting convicts about her immediately on their discharge from prison" and keeping up relations with those who remained in prison after her own release.[192] Carson was bashed in the press upon the publication of her memoir, *The History of the Celebrated Mrs. Ann Carson*, in 1822.[193] One essay claimed, "It is a reproach to our police that such a book is publicly advertised and sold in our city. Its details of crime, however glossed over, are calculated injuriously to affect the morals of young people."[194] The *New-Yorker* printed a scathing review in 1839 of the expanded and revised story of Carson's life published by Mrs. Mary Clarke. It referred to the *Memoirs* as "the abortion of a Mrs. M. Clarke—one of those female, literary Cyprians, who prostitutes their small abilities for lucre."[195] This tone is carried throughout the essay, which argues, "such filthy fuel should be burned only by the common hangman" that they dare not even bother to task their "faithful black" with its destruction. The least inflammatory statement might reflect the true cause of the hyperbole—fear of the effects of its dissemination: "Tell a story of the effects of vice to the young and it is more likely to operate as an incentive than an admonition."[196] The *New-Yorker* review was scathing because it forced the public to remember what it sought to forget. If middle-class women from good families could turn out like Carson, what was to prevent any woman from following in her footsteps?

* * *

The embrace of humanitarian sensibility inspired elites to want to feel good about the methods they used to control others. They distanced themselves from corporal punishment, excessive reliance on capital punishment, and violence more generally. To differentiate themselves from the British, reformers used bold, inspired declarations of change and reform. Yet they never put that much distance between themselves and the more mundane forces of history: continuity, assimilation, and capitulation. Much of English common law went unchallenged and remained the basis of the legal code in the United States.[197] The benevolent interventions by reformers on behalf of individual prisoners served to mask the systemic negative force that penal authority exerted on the lives of the poor.[198] Such acts of individual forgiveness and generosity helped to offset worries that the expansion of the infrastructure to control the criminal, disorderly, or poor might be unjust—or worse, undemocratic.

For prisoners, an imagined reunion with family never happened. The continuum between the almshouse and the prison was especially evident in the lives of women, as so many passed through the doors of both institutions in the course of their lives. It is easy to conclude that the aim of punishment was to control the poor. But the misleading promises of penal reform were far more insidious and destructive than that. Prison became a place for those whose lives failed to embrace or reflect the economic and emotional contours of the domestic nuclear family that was increasingly cherished as a prized social relation. Women who were single or on their own from a young age were more often imprisoned and blamed for their plight. Elaborate rules about visitation showed which relationships were most valued, but scarcely came close to capturing the networks of relationships that people created for themselves. Everyone who lived outside intimate patriarchy by refusing the authority of a father, husband, or master could become a subject of state regulation. The limitations of economic opportunities for African American and Irish immigrant women combined with the demands of motherhood generally left them more vulnerable than men.

Reformers may have wanted to help prisoners when they inserted themselves into the system as buffers between inmates and the callous arm of the state.[199] These minor interventions, however, proved devastating for the long-term prospects of justice. First, imposition of sentimental masculinity on punishment in place of the allegedly vengeful approach of working-class men did nothing but inspire resentment in prison staff. Second, it reinscribed a forced relationship of dependency by immigrant, African American, and native-born poor women on elite white men, an arrangement not very different from slavery or indentured servitude. Yes, the donations of clothing, blankets, and on special occasions, food, also improved daily life inside the prison. These individual gestures ultimately served to distract and disarm critics from the real injustices. The fact remains that these disproportionately African American, Irish, and poor working women were subject to objectifying and manipulative visitation rituals. Liberal reform made the men involved feel better about themselves while playing a key role in expanding the reach and structure of the prison system. Eventually, the culture of the prison proved to be beyond the reach of the sentimental project.

⌐

CHAPTER 3

Dangerous Publics

WOMEN MAINTAINED A visible presence in the public life of the early American city. African American, Anglo-American, and European immigrants occupied city streets, outdoor markets, public squares, taverns, and public houses. There were many forces drawing people out into public spaces, including food, fun, and friendship. People lived in crowded houses, disorderly houses, boarding houses, homes belonging to masters, and even the almshouse, compelling them to seek time in a spacious park, a break from supervision, or a chance for some fresh air. Some met lovers, or hoped to find one; others went to work selling used, stolen, or slightly damaged goods or preying on unsuspecting people to steal from them. Women who enjoyed some degree of financial stability and autonomy also worked in public, managing boarding houses, shops, schools, taverns, and disorderly houses. Most women lived visibly public lives, either by desire or necessity, though the public activities of the working poor were the most visible and contested.

Public women challenged patriarchal authority and ideals in many ways. Women without the economic support of a family, husband, or man struggled to survive on the pitiful wages paid to servants, washerwomen, and seamstresses. Those who had served out indentures, escaped slavery, or left abusive husbands, along with those who had been abandoned by parents, husbands, or lovers, could find themselves choosing between a number of terrible options: the risk of imprisonment for stealing, the risk of disease from sex work, or the almshouse. Many turned to the informal economy, which included stealing, threatening the security of elites and middling sorts in their own homes. Other women traded their time, affection, and sex for money. Both modes of exchange—involving goods and affections—figured prominently in urban street culture, but only those engaged in the latter were stigmatized as a socially degraded class.

Philadelphia was home to a diverse and exciting nighttime culture defined by the traditions, food, and music of people from all over the world. Newly arrived immigrants, mariners passing through, runaway slaves, and a diverse cast of "locals" gave life to the city streets and establishments, especially at night, when the day's work was done.[1] City life was also accompanied by a fair amount of violence. Women running businesses such as taverns, bawdy houses, market stalls, and fences might get into disputes with customers or have to help settle a conflict between them. Alcohol fueled tensions between friends, lovers, and strangers and was blamed for a high number of assaults. The prison had a revolving door for women facing charges of minor assault who were discharged after paying a small fine. Reformers sought to remove the excessive violence in punishment and thereby obscure the role of violence in American nation building.[2] But everywhere one looked, from war to slavery to taverns to the streets, the legacy of violence persisted, making public life truly—not just rhetorically—dangerous.

Women's claim to public life became contested in the early years of the nineteenth century. The ideology of "separate spheres" took root, calling for women to retreat to the domestic sphere while men reigned over public matters such as politics, economics, and ideas.[3] While this ideology was once thought of as a call to keep women from entering political life, we now see it also as a reaction against women's participation in political cultures following the revolution.[4] If ideologies condemned the public lives of working women, vagrancy laws enforced that goal through attacks on hucksters and the criminalization of prostitutes. Vagrancy statutes were aggressively used to get women off the streets and deny them access to economic opportunities. The criminalization of street culture was formalized in Philadelphia in 1789 when those charged with vagrancy were taken to prison rather than the almshouse. Elites including Tench Coxe and Jacob Rush saw vagrants as a threat to democracy. They viewed idleness and vice as a result of democracy's freedoms. This logic positioned the most vulnerable workers as a threat to democracy rather than its backbone. Aggressive enforcement of antivagrancy statutes enabled city officials to crack down on everyone. By saving the harshest condemnation for those involved in sex work, officials and reformers together denigrated all women who worked in public.

Poverty

Philadelphia's strategies for addressing the rising number of poor, unemployed, and rootless people in the city was nearly identical to that adopted throughout England earlier in the century.[5] In 1749, the colony invited the laboring poor to join vagrants and disorderly people in the workhouse so that they might contribute to the cost of their care. The shift from outrelief to workhouses reflected changing attitudes toward the causes of poverty. Even then, however, no more than 100 of the city's 11,000 residents relied on public alms. The British no longer sympathized with unskilled or semiskilled workers, who were most vulnerable during economic recessions, but rather attributed poverty to individual moral failings and laziness. When faced with a crisis in the 1760s, colonials looked to the motherland and followed suit, embracing ideology and practice in one fell swoop.[6] The Seven Years' War had a dramatic impact on Philadelphia, disrupting production, trade relations, supplies, and markets while dumping boatloads of refugees and new immigrants on its wharves. Urban poverty became a reality after 1762, and attitudes toward the poor and strategies for poor relief changed forever.[7]

The antivagrancy legislation of 1766 formed the legal basis for widespread imprisonment without trial that would come to define women's relationship to prison. The Act for the Better Employment, Relief and Support of the Poor called for "rogues, vagabonds and other idle dissolute and disorderly persons" to be committed to the house of employment in the almshouse.[8] The Guardians of the Poor interpreted this law as empowering them to reserve the almshouse for the "better sort" of poor and send the "vicious" poor to labor in the prison workhouse.[9] Those who caught the eye of constables or watchmen were required to provide proof of their employment. Failure to do so resulted in a term of forced "hard labor" for up to three months. The act was amended in 1767 to reduce the term of containment to thirty days.[10] As poor relief became institutionalized, people were denied their freedom for being poor. Not everyone agreed with the embrace of this British tradition. Benjamin Franklin believed the English had created a permanent class of impoverished idlers by their poor relief schemes and opposed these changes, but to no avail.[11]

City officials believed that men and women brought poverty on themselves, in part by failing to embrace a heterosexual nuclear family with a clear gendered division of labor. For decades, poor relief officials remained more forgiving of women than men who needed help. The number of women and children combined slightly outnumbered the men admitted to almhouses and houses of employment. For example, in 1785 poor relief officials admitted 182 women, 64 children, and 231 men to the almshouse."[12] Those admitted were largely described as "naked, helpless and emaciated with poverty and disease." Gendered notions of dependency and submission made it much easier for women to seem worthy. Women were expected to be economically and socially dependent on men, providing only supplemental income for the family as needed. Those who were appropriately dependent would be taken care of—if not by their husbands, then by poor relief officials who recognized their need. But the trade-off for this support was to be considered fundamentally dependent—and not really capable of assuming the responsibilities of citizenship. Women who were not sufficiently dependent and men who were insufficiently independent were punished by denial of aid.[13]

Guardians of the Poor pleaded with the legislature to relieve them of the burden of reforming the idle poor, believing it took away from their central mission to aid the honest and industrious poor. The legislature approved these desired revisions in 1789 by allowing for the actual imprisonment of vagrants. Constables examined "all vagrant and disorderly persons" by day, and watchmen delivered "vagrants, rioters or thieves" to the courthouse by night.[14] This expansive application of vagrancy laws allowed for instant imprisonment for thirty days without trial, solidifying the criminalization of poverty.[15] Women who refused to work or planned to leave the almshouse to socialize with friends, earn some money, or simply get out from under the guard's watchful eye for a few hours risked being deemed unfit and sent to prison instead. This new policy had the unintended consequence of reducing the almshouse population to those most feeble or infirm, leaving the manufactories with fewer able-bodied workers and inspiring further critique of the institution's managers.[16] By the early years of the nineteenth century, poor relief and almshouse admissions were tightly restricted, leaving more and more of the poor to fend for themselves. With a heightened focus on productive labor within the house of employment, managers helped create the template for the institutional labor system later adopted in prison.[17]

Women who remained at home and were by all counts moral and worthy (usually widows) still received out-work from the managers.[18] This bridge between out-relief (which was no longer available) and institutionalization was made selectively available to those who were identified as "industrious women and heads of families," and involved supplies of "flax, hemp, cotton, [or] wool" to be manufactured in their own homes.[19] This concession in allowing certain people to receive aid in their homes further stigmatized public life while rewarding women who remained at home. This arrangement also helped stave off critics of other forms of poor relief by showing the poor could contribute to their own aid. Even the committee charged with helping the poor felt the need to hammer home this sense of duty and exchange, describing the poor as people who "have nothing but their labour to bestow, [and] on this labour the public has a right to insist."[20] While life in the almshouse was never easy, it was less dangerous and unhealthy than many imagined.[21]

The 1790s were marked by increasing stigmatization of poverty and a growing conviction that the poor needed close supervision and regulation, in the almshouse and on the street.[22] Once privileged over men in the eyes of poor relief officials, women who failed or refused to conform to gendered standards of dependency and worthiness were marked as the "vicious" poor and would be sent to prison.[23] The managers of the almshouse were fed up with inmates who refused to work, were ungrateful for their treatment, or stole from the institution. They referred to inmate Margaret Hunsh as a "worthless hussy," Mary Gordon as a "drunken nuisance," and Mary McCalla as "of very bad character."[24] Directors kept a "black book" of women who challenged their authority and drank alcohol when they left the house, sometimes with permission, sometimes by escaping. Ann Craig was cited for coming home "intoxicated" after receiving permission to go out. Some women were punished severely and repeatedly for this behavior.[25] Margaret Cooper, Abigail Burket, Elizabeth Brown, and many others were "sent to the cells" for returning to the almshouse intoxicated.[26] Life in the almshouse was very much like life in prison.

The appointment of a high constable for the city in 1798 further confirmed the official attempt to rid the streets of poor and working people. His charge was clear:

to walk through the streets, lanes and alleys of the city of Philadelphia, daily, with his mace in his hand, taking such rounds that in a reasonable time he shall visit all parts of the city, and examine all vagrants, beggars, and such others, as shall fall under the description of idle and disorderly persons, by any act of assembly of this state, as to the place of their residence, and the mode they pursue of

acquiring a livelihood, and upon refusal to give him an account
thereof, or not giving a satisfactory account, to apprehend, and carry
such persons before the mayor or records, or some one of the aldermen, to be dealt with according to law.[27]

Local authorities challenged those staking a claim to autonomy in public
by trying to reestablish the authority of a "master, merchant, or importer"
over the individual and avoid a situation where they would "become
chargeable to the city, town, or county where they are found."[28] This
financial explanation served to justify the practice and obscure the highly
racialized and gendered enforcement of applicable laws.

The broadly worded and loosely interpreted vagrancy law served policing authorities in Pennsylvania rather well, granting them considerable
latitude in its application.[29] Two major categories of vagrancy charges pre-
dominate from 1790 to 1830: disorderly behavior and drunkenness.[30]
Throughout the 1790s, a significant percentage of vagrants included those
charged with being disorderly for running away from or disobeying masters. In the 1790s one was likely held for something that one did—such as
Bridge Cummings for "behaving in a disorderly manner and disturbing the
neighbors."[31] A much smaller number of Irish women were also charged
for cohabitating with or harboring African Americans. For example, George
Feganders accused Dianna Smith, Elizabeth Boyd, Sarah McNullitz, and
Catharine Carr with being idle vagrants who harbored African Americans.
Just a week earlier, Mary Connor was held on the same charge. In these
cases, Irish women caught the eyes of authorities for sharing housing with
African Americans but punished them as vagrants.[32] Social norms and
policing priorities shifted gradually over the years, from disobedience to
authority to unemployment to consequences of drinking. By 1807, one was
more likely to be held for something one did not have, such as a job or a
home, than for how one behaved. Sarah Snider was taken in for "having
no legal residence." Fewer and fewer vagrants were described as "disorderly," while increasing numbers were classified as "idle."[33] The fact that
idleness became a dominant charge against women reveals several important aspects of the contradictions in gendered ideology of the period.
Women on the streets who did not have proof of their work were punished
not because they failed to secure a job in a factory spinning thread in the
nearby mills of Manayunk, but because they refused to labor in the domestic realm as someone's wife or dutiful daughter. Women on the streets who

could be "spoken for" by respectable men were not imprisoned, while single women who lived by the informal economy were frequently charged and sent to prison.

The city cracked down on poor women who worked in low-end retailing known as "huckstering": reselling used or damaged goods on the street.[34] The city went to great lengths to restrict the informal economy and prevent hucksters from doing business in the marketplace. A city ordinance assigned a five-dollar penalty to any "Person who follows the business of a huckster, or of selling provisions, vegetables, nuts or fruits at second hand, shall at any time sell, or offer for sale, within the limits of the market, any provisions."[35] Formally, this law ensured that people would not have an opportunity to sell goods to the public without paying the required fee to the city for vending in the market. Vendors were charged rent for the market stalls—a fixed portion of which went to pay the clerks of the market, giving each of them a personal incentive for cracking down on hucksters. And so every person who could sell without paying rent for a stall disrupted the earnings of the clerk.[36] But legislation disparaging hucksters went far beyond the issue of fees, claiming them to be a social nuisance and "insignificant" to the market economy.[37] The attack on hucksters was a direct outgrowth of new ideals that sought to domesticate women, declaring their proper place was in the home, not the market.[38] While all working women were subject to censure as more people embraced this new gendered order, hucksters were targets of particular scorn. As Candice Harrison has shown, hucksters were perceived as "dangerous, aggressive, and unfeminine," far from the image of the wholesome rural women who sold goods in the country.[39] Rather, hucksters, like prostitutes, made the streets a threatening place. The city further restricted the selling of popular street foods, including boiled Indian corn, pickled oysters, and pepper pots, by local vendors after official market hours or on nearby streets, further curbing working-class street culture.[40]

Watchmen charged with enforcing the laws were known to abuse their power and violate those very same laws themselves. They were commonly the subject of complaints to the mayor for their bad public behavior, though such scandals rarely reached the papers. Correspondence with Mayor Joseph Watson reveals a revolving door of night watchmen due to their inappropriate behavior. William Hines begged for work again after having had his character impugned by a woman and another watchman. The details of this indiscretion are absent but he asserted his own behavior was tame compared to the transgressions of other officers. He wrote, "I did [to] inform you of all that has taken place which has come to my knowledge since my first acquaintance with publick officers respecting the conduct you would no doubt be convinced that my crime bad as it is it is but trifling to compare to the crimes committed by some officers who are very familiar with your honor."[41] Two men, George Nagel and John Crox, begged him for work after having been suspended from their jobs as watchmen for a serious (though unspecified) charge alleged against them after five years of public service. They pleaded on the basis of their need to support their families.[42] William Cammron wrote on behalf of a group of his neighbors on Fifth Street to then Mayor Watson to report violence and abuse of a night watchman. He reported the watchmen violently dragged a man across the street and said, "Dam you I'll knock your brains," while hitting him so hard that he made "blood spill out onto the pavement"[43] Regardless of such accusations and admissions of misconduct, the reach and authority of the watchmen were never questioned.

It is widely known that Philadelphians turned against the poor in the 1820s, but evidence of their criminalization began much earlier. The idea that democratic freedom would necessarily create an underclass of rebels who would resist work and embrace a life of "idleness" became a common refrain. This logic—promoted by Tench Coxe, Assistant Secretary of the Treasury of the United States—turned a structural economic problem into an individual moral one. Coxe argued that a free government would inevitably "produce vicious habits and disobedience to the laws" among citizens who were impoverished or idle. Coxe promoted manufacturing as a way to solve the problem of unemployment for the virtuous poor who were willing to work.[44] Members of the Pennsylvania Society for Promotion of Public Economy did a study of the causes of poverty and concluded that "idleness, intemperance, and sickness" were the chief causes.[45] Such beliefs were crucial to advancing the idea that crime and poverty were rooted in individual weakness rather than systemic failures. Americanus, a contributor to the *Columbian Magazine*, agreed. He described the young people who spent their days "begging" and "huckstering" as well as women receiving public assistance as a public nuisance.[46] Coxe was not alone in stoking the flames of fear of the underclasses. The crusade against the vices of the poor— including sex and drinking—were also taken up by Bishop William White, head of both PSAMPP and the Magdalen Society for reforming prostitutes, and Judge Jacob Rush, brother of the famed reformer Dr. Benjamin Rush.

Sex

The extensive toleration of sex outside marriage after the revolution spared many city residents charges for things like bastardy, adultery, fornication, and bigamy that had been considered serious crimes not long before. But most of the benefits of passing over prosecution of these cases extended disproportionately to men and crossed class, leaving the everyday street harassment of the working classes intact. The policing of women in public was a highly subjective endeavor. Constables and night watchmen exercised tremendous discretion in deciding that certain women—those too poor, too loud, too sexual, too drunk, or too independent—did not deserve to be free. In 1795, Mary Carlisle was charged with "being a very disorderly woman" and sentenced under the vagrancy law to thirty days at hard labor in Walnut Street Prison without trial.[47] Her record was typical on many counts and she was held for thirty days. Mary was charged for "being" a certain way—not because she actually did anything. The charge against Mary also declared her "unfit to be at liberty," revealing a belief that was widely held but rarely spoken.

Women were charged with vagrancy in numbers equal to men, though for different reasons.[48] Women were less likely than men to be charged with assault, arson, running away from their masters, disobeying their masters, or general vagrancy. Women were more likely, however, to be charged with being drunken or disorderly. Women suspected of engaging in prostitution were imprisoned for thirty days without trial. Men who paid women for sex were not charged or imprisoned for anything. Women hanging out in bars, the streets, and other public spaces with other women—or perhaps more significantly, without men—would be picked up and imprisoned under vagrancy laws. Men doing the same thing were simply being men. What constituted a transgression on the part of a woman was more subjective, especially concerning behaviors normalized for men and stigmatized for women: sex and drinking.

A number of phrases were used to describe alleged or suspected prostitutes. Martha Patterson was charged with "being an idle dissolute person and common street walker," while Margaret Miller was considered "a common and abandoned prostitute."[49] Nancy Sumers was "a disorderly vagrant having no visible means of making a living but by prostitution."[50] The suggestive record of Ann Galagher and Rebecca Williams describes "two very disorderly girls who were apprehended strolling about the streets at a very late hour last night."[51] Sarah Gault (alias Snow) was characterized as being "an idle disorderly, and lewd woman."[52] Elizabeth Duffy, Hester Clark, Rachel Lane, Elizabeth Watson, and Mary Porter were together charged with "being idle strolling vagrants following no legal means for support" and spent thirty days in prison in 1823.[53] In the case of some, such as Margaret Miller, their reputation preceded them, leaving them vulnerable to random lock-up. Ann Galagher and Rebecca Williams were out late at night, together in the streets—sufficient reason for the night watchmen to pick them up. Without husbands and unable to provide proof of employment, independent women of the lower classes who were out partying or walking around without men would all have been suspected of prostitution. Black women were especially vulnerable to accusation and prosecution.[54]

Foreign visitors remarked on the wide availability of prostitutes throughout the period, both in disorderly houses and in the streets.[55] Even if women were not charged criminally for prostitution, they were regularly picked up off the streets and condemned by authorities, jailors, and reformers alike.[56] Prostitutes faced a double standard with law enforcement officials and risked violence at the hands of their clients. Helen Jewett was a sex worker in a fashionable New York house until a regular client killed her, only to be found innocent.[57] Charges against prostitutes emphasized morality and social order, even though it was obvious that women from diverse circumstances turned to prostitution as a way to supplement their income. Adding insult to injury was the fact that watchmen described suspected prostitutes as "idle" when their illegal employment is what compelled their arrest in the first place. Those suspected of prostitution were never the majority of vagrants, however.[58] Even if we presumed that "disorderly" always signaled sex work (which it did not) this still only defined 41 percent of those charged in the 1790s and 31 percent in the early decades of the 1800s.[59]

Those engaged in sex work were not necessarily deemed entirely lost during this period. The Magdalen Society was founded to help those women who wanted to change their lives, repent, and find their way back to a more "honest" way of life.[60] Members of the Magdalen Society held as their mission "To aid in restoring to the paths of virtue to be instrumental in recovering to honest rank in life, those unhappy females, who, in an unguarded hour, have been robbed of that innocence, and sunk into wretchedness and guilt, and being affected with remorse at the misery of their situation, are desirous of returning to a life of rectitude, if they clearly saw an opening thereto."[61] Members would comb the almshouse and prison for possible recruits, though often found the women not ready to commit themselves to the program. Those visiting the almshouse reported, "There were several young females in the public alms house of this city who have been led astray from the paths of virtue and in order to enquire more particularly into their situation and the propriety of extending assistance to them or either of them, several managers of the committee visited them but on conversation and strict investigation it is the option of the cmt that they cannot at present be taken under its immediate care."[62] Later, after numerous visits, they decided the young woman in the almshouse, who would become Magdalen number three (Jane Orbeson), was truly "desirous to live a reformed life, and to obtain her living hereafter by honest industry," so they placed her at service with "a respectable family"[63] Prison Inspectors recommended a number of women "who appeared to merit the attention of this committee" but upon "examination and diligent inquiry" the Society decided they were not "suitable" for their charity.[64] Magdalens were trained and supervised in the domestic arts along with extensive prayer and Bible study. Those deemed success stories would be placed at service in a religious home, married off, or reconciled to their parents. Most Magdalens were from the local tristate area, especially after 1814.[65]

Society members were most likely to take on the case of a woman who claimed she was promised marriage and then abandoned or who came from "reputable" parents in the first place. Women who were failed by intimate patriarchy were worthy recipients of their aid. Young and wronged in love was a common attribution. Nineteen-year-old Magdalen number seven was seduced by a man who left her, though she did not give up easily, following him to Philadelphia before taking up residence in a disorderly house.[66] Number fifteen was a seventeen-year-old from New York State who had been "despoiled" by a young man who frequently visited her family and "gained her affections." Her parents disapproved of him when he proposed marriage. She ran off with him "under promise of marriage to Philadelphia," but he left her "pregnant and diseased."[67] Number sixteen also fell for a promise of marriage, but instead "lived in habits of prostitution" with a man for four years, from age fifteen.[68] Twenty-two-year-old number seventeen from Holland was seduced by an American shipmaster who brought her here under promise of marriage, only to find out when they arrived that he was already married.[69]

Those who were abandoned by parents through indenture or death were also subjects of the committee's compassion. Number eighteen came to Philadelphia from Ireland with her parents and was "seduced by a Spaniard" before she was even twelve. She lived with him for many years and birthed several children, all of whom died.[70] Number thirteen was left abandoned at age five when her parents died. She was twenty-seven now. Born in Philadelphia, she married a man in Maryland and had four children by him. Her husband "communicated disease to her and then deserted her."[71] Number nineteen was born in Delaware and bound to a widow when her parents died. She lived out her time in Philadelphia and "was sometimes after enticed to houses of ill fame and lived a wretched life about seven years until she was compelled by sickness to seek relief in the almshouse where she was visited by several managers."[72] The following was reported about number twenty:

> 30 years of age born in Ireland her parents being both dead she came to phila in the year 1793 and was bound to a person who kept a public house with whom she served out her time, after which she was seduced by a person of considerable note in this city and by him placed out to boarding for some years by whom she had one child, since which she has continued to live an unchaste life in all near ten years and being cast off by the person who had placed her to board and being left in a destitute situation she applied to a member of the society.[73]

Those in the Magdalen Society eventually changed their view of the women they were allegedly rescuing. They were less invested in the details of a woman's life or the circumstances that brought her to their door. They referred to the young women as "evil." It is not surprising they were defensive about their work or resentful of the young women. Of the twenty-five women under their care in the year 1828, only five of them could be considered success stories: two reconciled with their parents and three were placed at service. Another twelve women clearly exposed the failings of the organization: five left the house without permission, six were discharged for improper conduct, and one was discharged at her request.[74] Directors of the Magdalen Society complained of similar issues that plagued the prison: those more experienced in crime or vice targeted younger, more innocent girls, making classification, segregation, and separate confinement the only way to remedy "this evil."[75] Increasingly, in the streets and in institutions, being able to distinguish the lapsed from the truly fallen became the only way to ensure that vice would not spread to the masses.

Drinking

American elites believed that freedom made the existence of vice both more likely and more threatening. Judge Jacob Rush led the judicial charge against vice and immorality. Judge Rush was appointed to the Pennsylvania Supreme Court by fellow Federalist Governor Mifflin, serving for seven years before becoming President Judge of the Third Circuit in Reading in 1791.[76] Judge Rush was well educated, elitist, and puritanical. He publicly condemned other judges for being "unread" and promoted strict enforcement of the Blue Law of 1794 that made gambling, drinking, adultery, swearing, and breaking the Sabbath all punishable by imprisonment.[77] The law banned "unlawful game, hunting, shooting, sport or diversion" along with any work other than "of necessity and charity" on Sundays.[78] Anyone sixteen years of age or older who spoke a "profane curse or oath" would be fined or imprisoned if unable to pay the fine. Similar punishment for "excessive drinking of spirits, vinous, or other strong liquors."[79] A ban on gambling specifically targeted those who "play at cards, dice, billiards, bowls, shuffleboard, or any game of hazard or address, for money, or other valuable thing," (113). Licensed tavern keepers, housekeepers, and liquor store owners risked losing their licenses if they were convicted of encouraging or serving alcohol to people betting on "address, harzard or cock-fighting, bullet-playing, or horse-raising."[80] Additionally, the number of taverns and public houses would soon be restricted and regulated by licensing because they were known to "promote habits of idleness and debauchery."[81] Rather than view drinking and gambling as convenient distractions for the poor and working masses, elites felt both activities hindered the productivity of workers and threatened the order of society.

Judge Rush did his best to spread his views to grand juries throughout the state. In his speech at the Luzerne County Court in August 1800, he asserted that vice, if undeterred, would ultimately destroy the young nation. He claimed that vice and immorality "proved the bane and ruin of thousands of individuals; the scourge of nations, and bottomless gulph in which all the vast empires that ever existed, have been finally swallowed up."[82] For

Judge Rush, *the people* were a source of danger, and the only way to save the country was to reform their morals.[83]

Judge Rush's moralizing was too much even for some of his judicial colleagues. In one of his more extreme gestures, he ordered constables to arrest and imprison young boys for playing ball on Sundays. He invoked Pennsylvania founder William Penn in defense of his unpopular beliefs. Just because Penn advocated freedom of religion did not mean he tolerated immoral behavior, Rush claimed. He asserted that Penn would have sought legal action against "the drunkard, the swearer, the adulterer, the Sabbath-breaker, the gambler." While two young ball-playing boys might not seem like an obvious threat to the casual observer, then or now, Rush, an eternal pessimist, saw a slippery slope in every indiscretion, however minor. Judge Rush claimed that "If government may inflict punishments on acts of immorality which endanger its existence, such as murder and felony, it may lawfully forbid everything that incites or leads to the commission of such offences."[84] His logic of criminal progression granted wide latitude to all attempting to restrict it.

The result of Judge Rush's fanaticism can be seen in the imprisonment of a number of women for swearing, yelling, and lying. A woman charged with "Swearing profusely by God, twice, and by Jesus once," reported to the jail clerk that her name was "Honest Woman." Frustrating his attempt to record her identity, he wrote "(Calls Herself)" under the record where her name is listed as Honest Woman.[85] Sarah Engles received a sentence of 4,800 hours to atone for the charge of "swearing two hundred profane oaths by the name of God, Jesus Christ, and The Holy Ghost."[86] Hannah Johnson, Lydia Armstrong, Sarah Davis, Charlotte Palmer, and Sarah Williams were each charged with "hollaring murder" on separate occasions.[87] Accused fortune teller Mary Hawse was held for ten days in 1795 for "being a drunken idle vagrant who goes about obtaining money from ignorant and young people under pretence of telling fortunes."[88] Mary Thompson was picked up on suspicion of a different kind of fraud, "with being a vagrant who pretends that she has lost her husband and of having two children in the small pox both of which is false."[89] These minor irreverent expressions, shouts of panic, and trivial deceptions were each the foundation on which the great nation could falter. Under Judge Rush's watch, every person would be held accountable.

Judge Rush truly feared that the future of the nation would be determined not by the hard work, integrity, and grand accomplishments of the

elites but rather by its lowest common denominator: the lazy and morally
weak lower sort. Rush explained, "It cannot then be denied, that the public
prosperity of our land, depends upon the virtue of the people, and that the
practice of vice, like a cancer in the natural body, will at last extend itself
to the vitals of the country, and cut off our national existence."[90] The threat
outlined by Rush was taken seriously by the state, though not always at the
highest levels in exactly the ways he wished. Criminal courts were still
reserved for more threatening defendants: those accused of property crimes
and deadly violence.[91] The regulation of drinking, sex, swearing, and loitering fell to constables, night watchmen, and jailors, with a great deal of
flexibility. Most people were thrown in prison under vagrancy laws and
ignored until their release. Rush, however, took particular interest in prosecuting drinking.

Laborers, servants, and those formerly enslaved developed a strong public culture of their own in post-Revolutionary Philadelphia, frequenting the
streets, parks, neighborhood bars, and bawdy houses after work and socializing together late into the evening.[92] Such practices raised the ire of urban
elites who used the expanded network of constables and watchmen to
police and punish public disturbances. In a typical case, watchman George
Sheed, Jr., charged Sarah Brown, a twenty-eight-year-old black woman,
with being drunken and disorderly and disturbing the peace.[93] Drinking
was an important part of sociality and bonding for men of all classes in
eighteenth-century Pennsylvania.[94] Women's drinking was largely hidden
from view, reserved for the private sphere. But for poor women, the lines
between public and private were not so clear. Women working as slaves or
servants in other people's homes needed to leave home to create personal
time and space for themselves. Others lived in tight quarters, sharing homes
with family, relatives, and boarders, while still others were homeless or in
the almshouse. Whatever the specifics, plenty of women found reason to
venture into taverns, public houses, and the streets in search of a drink.

Women's alcohol use was well documented in the vagrancy records, as
nearly one-third of all charges from 1790 to 1823 had to do with alcohol.[95]
Margaret Fosset was held for "drunkenness to be kept at hard labour thirty
six hours," while Mary Evans was "charged with being found in the market
intoxicated, with strong liquor, to suffer thirty six hours imprisonment."[96]
The leniency exhibited by these two sentences was fleeting, partly as a result
of Judge Rush's beloved 1794 Act Concerning Vice and Immorality. After
its passage, those charged with being drunk were routinely imprisoned for

thirty days. In 1795, Mary Hawes was "found on the 9th inst drunk in Chestnut Street to be kept till she be sober and from thence 30 days at hard labor." Punishment for public drunkenness ebbed and flowed over the years. Heightened enforcement in the 1790s mellowed out in the early years of the nineteenth century.

When Irishwoman Mary Lane checked into the almshouse in November 1790, she was a single woman with two young children under age three. She was also described as "a very noted drunken disorderly woman."[97] Lane reportedly left the residence and was eventually brought back "in a cart and very drunk" around nine o'clock in the evening. Lane spent much of her life navigating between the prison and the almshouse as need and circumstance required.[98] The population of the prison and the almshouse swelled during the winter months when seaport and farm work dried up and fuel costs rose. Institutions cleared out during the warm months when life on the streets was more tolerable and seasonal employment more readily available.

A woman's enjoyment of drinking might destroy her marriage. When Ann Floyd was admitted to the almshouse, it was as much to "relieve her distressed husband" as anything. She had not committed any public crime, but was accused of "stealing his clothes and pawning them away for liquor, and destroying everything he brings into the house." She was held at the almshouse at the request of her husband, who refused to admit her into their home.[99] Other women were reputedly drunk along with their husbands. On March 15, 1812, John Christy entered the almshouse "infamously drunk." His wife Catherine was later brought in by two men who said "they found her in the mud corner of 9th and Pine Street." She was described as "ten times worse" than her husband. Both were put in the cells of the almshouse, which was rather like a prison anyway.[100]

Public concern about the connection between poverty and intemperance escalated in the 1820s.[101] A two-tiered approach to public drunkenness was devised, distinguishing between charges for simple drunkenness and charges for being drunk and idle. For example, a simple charge of drunkenness was met with a twenty-four-hour sentence and generally applied to women like Mary Cobb who were "intoxicated with strong liquor." By 1823, at least 20 percent of women charged with drunkenness served less than thirty days, unlike in the 1790s. The new law clarified the difference between casual intoxication and a life on the margins defined by unemployment or homelessness. Elizabeth Shaw, named for multiple offenses, including idleness, drunkenness, and vagrancy, was sentenced to and served the thirty-day maximum.[102]

The crackdown on drinking included heightened regulation of those who sold alcohol without licenses. Selling alcohol provided a vital source of income for poor white women. Women turned to this to supplement other forms of work such as keeping a boarding house or working as a seamstress. These women were still poor—often unable to pay the fine, ranging from five to fifty dollars, that came along with a conviction, but still better off than the poorest of women. This is also indicated by the fact that only white women were convicted of this offense. Of the sixteen women who served time in prison between 1820 and 1835 on this charge, only one of them was black, Nancy James, charged before the city's Court of Quarter Sessions in 1831.[103] Another sign of their economic marginality was the fate of thirty-seven-year-old Margaret Clark from Kentucky who was charged in December 1824 and discharged to the Guardians of the Poor three months later. Women who might eke out a living running a tippling house had their lives and businesses destroyed by the assessment of a $50 fine.

The punishment of women for public drinking was both sexist and classist in a city that long celebrated the ceremonial drinking of gentlemen's culture in taverns, private homes, and exclusive gatherings. While regular poor people who drank too much were simply deemed "intemperate," signaling loss of control of one's behavior, rich men who also drank too much and suffered the effects were granted a medical diagnosis, "Mania a Potu."[104] In defense of working-class drinking culture, one writer noted that only class and custom separated the habits of servants from their masters, stating, "With what consistency can the master ask the servant to restrain from whiskey, the poor man's drink, while he indulges in the unnecessary use of wine? How can he expect from him sobriety, industry, and economy, when he sets him an example in none of these things?"[105] Awareness of this hypocrisy did nothing to curtail celebration of alcohol's pleasures among wealthy men in refined settings while criminalizing the excesses displayed by commoners. Judge Jacob Rush was concerned with the latter when he stated, "For very good reasons, all civilized countries have agreed to punish drunkenness as a crime against social order and the public good. I believe it may be asserted with truth, that from this source originate almost *all* the enormities, that produce distress in private families, and the most destructive outrages on the public peace." Working-class men were particularly subject to the Judge's scrutiny. He wrote, "It is this vice, that makes so many helpless widows and distressed orphans—that fills our streets with wandering beggars—that crowds the sheriffs' dockets with executions, and is productive of innumerable quarrels, assaults, batteries, riots and manslaughters."[106] Women who drank in public places were under strict scrutiny, while men experienced a great deal of freedom and social sanction unless they became violent or abandoned their families.

This expansive policing of public drunkenness caused conflict between the constable's office and the prison authorities. Reformers and Inspectors argued that too many vagrants were held in prison for too little reason and that their presence undermined the penitentiary's effectiveness in reforming convicts.[107] The Board of Inspectors went so far as to argue that the "indiscriminate" admission of vagrants by the night watch was actually "very dangerous to the safety of the prison."[108] Overcrowding the prison with harmless people who drank too much undermined the ability of jailers, turnkeys, and reformers to do the real work of reforming convicts. The Board argued that thirty-day prison terms for public drunkenness were untenable. Walnut Street Prison was bursting at its seams. Watchmen relented and stopped packing the prison with people who simply drank too much, but the reintroduction of mild punishment for public drunkenness was not universally well received. Lawyer Job Tyson complained that the fine of sixty-seven cents and twenty-four hours in prison was not nearly enough for a crime responsible for so much destruction, one that "endangers so much the peace of families and society, debases the nature of man, destroys his intellectual vigour and disqualifies him for all kinds of useful exertion."[109] But others prevailed.

Violence

Women charged with physically assaulting the men, women, and children in their lives were barely punished at all. The typical punishment for an assault and battery conviction was a fine, while many charges were not prosecuted for lack of witnesses to appear in court. Only those too poor to pay the fines would be sent to prison, reinforcing the fact that punishment was for poor people. Women's violence threatened to expose the fallacy of several important myths of American national identity. Composure and control were key elements of middle-class identity for both men and women.[110] Self-mastery of one's emotional landscape was deemed vital to one's ability to serve in a position of public authority, as emotion played a key role in the struggle for social power and standing in the post-Revolutionary era.[111] Anger, on the other hand, signaled a loss of control. As Nicole Eustace has shown, anger was considered "the most passionate and problematic of all the passions."[112] Women's anger in particular was largely absent from colonial and early American public discourses.[113] While social and political elites could contain such representations, and probably also the women in their own homes, they proved unable to control the words and actions of women throughout the city. The court and prison records stand as tangible evidence of women's uncontrolled emotions. Overwhelmed by too much feeling and insufficiently submissive, they lashed out in defense, rage, and revenge.

Many working poor, servant, and enslaved women would have been accustomed to persistent violence in their lives. For some, violence might have seemed the only way to defend themselves, a loved one, or their property. In her business running a disorderly house, Mary Hines would have plenty of occasions where order was needed. The women and men she reportedly assaulted may have been employees, customers, or competition. Mary Hines, accused of being disorderly, keeping a house "for admitting street walking women," and assaulting and threatening a man, was held for five days.[114] Hines was a repeat offender. Charged on January 8, 1799, she served two months for "violently assaulting and beating the person of Catharine Lindsey."[115] In August of that same year, she was charged with "violently assaulting and beating the person of Elizabeth Benett," this time serving three months. Then, three days after her November 11 release, she was charged "on the oath of Elenor Glass with violently assaulting and beating her."[116] This time, she had the money to pay a small fine imposed. But Hines sought revenge on her accuser immediately upon release and found herself back in prison the next day. Hines's bursts of violence may have been fueled by alcohol and the loss of inhibition, but she was also determined to maintain order over her home and business under challenging circumstances.

Mary did what so many of her contemporaries and foremothers did. Even during the colonial period, women in Pennsylvania developed a reputation for violence, as nearly a quarter of all charges against women were for attacks.[117] More women were charged with assault and battery than any offense other than larceny.[118] Incidents of assault, battery, and threatening by women toward other women, men, and children rose steadily in the early decades of the nineteenth century, especially in urban areas. Most complaints against women for violence were made by their social equals, with grievances against those in their immediate work, family, home, or neighborhood circles, though some certainly concerned middling or elite women who were challenged, attacked, or undermined by servants, slaves, or social inferiors.[119] Assaults were not only a feature of life on the streets but could take place anywhere—at home, in someone else's home, in the tavern, at the marketplace, or at work. Anyone could report an assault to authorities—a witness, family member, victim, or agent of the state. Unlike vagrancy, it was not part of sanctioned surveillance of poor people in public.

Women accused of assault were deemed a nuisance. Despite persistent efforts by both men and women to draw attention to female assailants and persuade authorities to prosecute them, repercussions were minimal. Women were far more likely to be charged with assault than convicted. In 1807, for example, crimes against persons made up 30 percent of all charges against women, yet only 5 percent of all convictions. Assault and battery cases rarely went to trial.[120] Instead, charges were dismissed, witnesses failed to show up, or the accused woman agreed to a fine. A woman convicted of simple assault and battery, the most common charge in this category, was likely to be ordered to pay a fine and put down a certain amount of money as security for future good behavior. Assault and battery charges were the second most common charge heard by the Mayor's Court, increasing steadily in number from 1799 to 1823 and resulting in fines from one dollar to five dollars.[121] Cases tried before the Court of Quarter Sessions were more likely to result in serious punishments than those tried in the Mayor's Court.[122] Elizabeth Proctor served only three months for "attempting to stab" Marian Bainbridge, yet this was considered a severe punishment.[123]

The breakdown of assault targets by gender remains remarkably constant over the years. In 1807, 56 percent of charges against women for assault or threatening were brought by or on behalf of female victims, compared to 58 percent in 1795. The number rose slightly in 1823, as women brought 66 percent of the charges. The percentage of male victims was remarkably constant as well. Men were victims in 26 percent of the cases in 1795, 30 percent in 1807, and 24 percent in 1823. Incidents of assaults against women and men together, children, or of unidentifiable persons constitute the remainder of the charges. Although significant numbers of women were charged with assault and battery and held as prisoners for trial on those charges, a tiny number was actually sent to prison upon conviction.

Reports of "threatening" reveal the intimacy between women and the intensity of these encounters. Although Susan Dickson was accused of assaulting Elizabeth Vesey "with a billet of wood and with an intention it is believed the said Elizabeth to kill," she was released after one week.[124] Women who were victims of "threatening" behavior might escalate the actual threat by reporting it to the authorities. Woman after woman reported that she "is in danger of receiving a bodily hurt" or "that she considers her person in danger."[125] Accusers describe themselves as living in "personal fear" and "personal danger" and "bodily fear."[126] The methods used by many of the attackers reveal the intimacy between those who incited rage in each other. Mary Dunning was charged with assaulting and beating Elizabeth Turner "in her own house with brick bats."[127] Margaret Everet was charged by Lavinier Wallace with "having abused and dragged her about the street."[128] Martha Weir was charged by Camelia Widener with "attempting to choak her."[129] Ann Philips allegedly "struck" Mary Fox and "tore her frock and put her life in danger."[130] Women who pushed, pulled, and struck each other were often marked by the sweat, fibers, hair, and even blood of their victims. In the fear and heat of the moment, it is no wonder victims turned to authorities for help.

When men stepped in as coplaintiffs or witnesses to attacks against women, authorities instantly took them more seriously, and the charges were more likely to result in convictions.[131] Of course, taking the charge seriously was the least the judge could do when faced with a man who failed to protect his wife from assault by another woman. Rachel Smith was charged and convicted for assaulting Belinda Todd as well as harboring her husband.[132] Several men testified on behalf of assaults against their wives. Thomas Cummings accused Mary Johnson "with having as he has heard and fully believes committed an assault and battery on his wife Sarah Cummings."[133] According to Joseph Malcomb, Catherine Cress not only "beat his wife Mary" but also was in the habit of "going to his house at a late hour of the night and abusing his family."[134] Elizabeth Williams was released after one week, having posted security in the aftermath of being charged by James Wilson and his wife "with violent assaults and threatenings against their persons."[135] Women acted boldly to get what they wanted, defend themselves, or make a statement. And men failed miserably in their mastery of intimate patriarchy, unable to keep their wives safe from other women. Even working poor men could get the attention of authorities in ways women generally could not. African American Catherine Evenson was sentenced to one year of imprisonment on December 16, 1823.[136] Three members of the Combs family, George, Catherine, and Phebe, accused Evenson of assaulting and threatening to kill them while wielding a "naked knife."[137] The court stood by men who were victims or failed to protect the women in their lives from the violence of another woman.

Women also resorted to violence against their own husbands in an attempt to protect themselves, gain a semblance of control over their lives, or simply get revenge. Of the women charged with assault and threatening others in 1795, the only person imprisoned for longer than one week was Ann Young, who beat and threatened her husband. She was released after three weeks. Elizabeth Jones was imprisoned for one year for a seriously violent attack on her husband, Alexander Jones, and another man, Jacob Hall, both of whom claimed she intended to kill them. Jones was a thirty-year-old "yellow woman" from Boston who wanted to stay in Philadelphia. We can only imagine what compelled her attack: Repeated abuse at the hands of her husband? Mental illness? But why did she try to kill both men? Jones was said to have approached Hall "by striking him twice with a hatchet and then stabbing him in the back with a fork declaring at the same time she intended to kill."[138] Like men, women resorted to terrible violence, too. When assault was combined with more serious threats such as attempted murder or larceny, the state issued more severe punishments. Mary Reed was charged with assaulting and beating Ann Allen in addition to stealing "two boxes of tea and one box of thread." Reed served six months in prison on this charge, from June to December 1799.[139] Kitty Anderson was twenty-one in 1815 when she was charged with stealing stockings from two women named Elizabeth and Ann, abusing a different woman named Sarah, disturbing the peace, stealing $4.12 in bank notes from Mary, and breaking the Sabbath again by fighting.[140] Anderson was sentenced to one year at hard labor in prison. Physical assault was still deemed secondary and minor compared to taking another's property.[141]

Women, like men, turned to violence as a way to achieve a goal. Several reasons emerge to explain the light treatment of these women before the court. Their behavior was consistent with the culture of violence at the heart of Pennsylvania's history as well as the foundation of American nation building. Pennsylvania courts were generally soft on violent crimes throughout the eighteenth century.[142] Even then, high percentages of cases were thrown out, and many others were settled with small fines. Surprisingly, night watchmen, judges, and reformers had little to say about women's violence. Another explanation is the role of alcohol in fueling disputes. In one study, a city alderman reported that in his estimate 80 percent of charges related to assault, battery, and disturbing the peace "arise or occur *directly* from the use of spirituous liquors."[143] Authorities believed that most plaintiffs and defendants were intoxicated, making trustworthy testimonies nearly impossible. Violence, then, was a consequence of other vices and disorderly publics that threatened the social order, such as drinking, disobeying masters and mistresses, loitering, homelessness, gambling, unemployment, prostitution, or remaining unmarried. While the right to property and the sanctity of public spaces were prized, the state was uninterested in regulating interpersonal relationships and disputes—especially when they involved only women. And so what does this say about the place of women in punishment? We are left with an image of women debased by nature and refined only by class and custom. No one was responsible for the lives and behaviors of those women who could not control their emotions, because there was no reason for anyone to bother. Such outbursts betrayed the virtue of self-control and evenhandedness that was highly prized among elites. While acting out was not aggressively prosecuted or even criminalized, such emotional outbursts came to be expected of working poor women.

Stealing

Philadelphia markets were sites of great crowds, a diversity of people, an abundance of meat and produce from the country and coffee, spices, and other refined goods from around the world. The crowds included "every rank and condition in life from the highest to the lowest, male and female, of every age and color."[144] Women played an active role in the market as dealers, shoppers, hucksters, and thieves. One visitor from Massachusetts could not get over the diversity of women who sold produce, stating, "Several of the market-women, who sold fruit, had their infants in their arms and their children about them, and there seemed to be some of every nation under heaven." He was also taken with the plain and modest dress of the elite women who went to the markets accompanied only by their servants.[145] Biweekly trips to the market for food and other supplies provided

ample opportunities for women to steal or become victims themselves.[146]
Experienced thieves like Irishwoman Jane Henry and her Philadelphia-born
daughter Jane Henry, Jr., could wait patiently for an unsuspecting victim
and then split the task: one distracted while the other stole. They could
easily steal from market booths or unsuspecting shoppers and disappear
into the crowds. In December 1794, forty-five-year-old Jane, Sr., and her
nineteen-year-old daughter were convicted of stealing money from Elizabeth Price and cuff links from Anthony Trepar.[147] As risky, harsh, and
unpredictable as it was, Jane, Sr., preferred the freedom of life on the street
to life in the almshouse, where so many other poor mothers lived.[148] It is
easy to judge Jane, Sr., for exposing her daughter to a life of crime, but
she wanted to keep her family together and protect her daughter from the
Overseers of the Poor who would likely have indentured a younger Jane, Jr.,
out to a strange family. For some, the streets provided just enough suste-
nance and safety for women on the edge.

Images of colonial good wives and female submissiveness obscure the
resiliency, daring, and strength exhibited by women of the early national
city, who acted in bold defiance of a system that oppressed them. It is no
wonder women took the chance of stealing small household objects in
hopes of having something nice for themselves, getting out of debt, surviving for another week, purchasing a meal, or helping out a loved one. Petty
theft was one sign of women's resistance to an economic system that provided few rewards for their labor. Larceny charges show that working
women were not afraid to challenge the terms of property rights.[149]

Women who were currently or formerly enslaved may have felt entitled
to steal from whites who claimed ownership of them and profited from
their labor. Abolitionists argued that slavery itself was the real crime, turning people into property and denying those enslaved possessions of their
own.[150] The definitions of "property" and "ownership" were thus challenged by those who knew it was not right for one person to own another.[151]
The threat of theft was both public and private, as women targeted private
homes, often of their employers, as well as public spaces, including markets,
shops, streets, and taverns. The majority of women convicted of stealing
worked at service in the homes of middling and elite Philadelphians. The
association between servants and theft exposed the vulnerability and anxiety of those who relied on their labor but never quite trusted them in
their homes. When household goods went missing, servants were primary
suspects and would be severely punished. But for servants, slaves, and

others living on the social margins with no prospect for economic advancement, petty theft served as a source of retribution, compensation, or even rebellion.

Pawnshops played an integral role in the financial planning of the urban poor throughout the nineteenth century. Most of them were legitimate businesses whose owners had a vested interest in not accepting stolen goods for pawn so as to stay on the right side of the law, avoid police harassment, and build their businesses over time. However, the vast exchange of goods, the dynamic buzz of city life, and the willingness of women to hock small items of little value made it impossible to regulate legitimate versus illegitimate commerce. Only a minority of pawnbrokers were known to fence stolen goods.[152] Taking stolen goods to a pawnshop could backfire if the broker did not want to risk his reputation and he suspected an item was stolen. When a woman showed up with the silver case of a watch to be pawned in 1734, for example, the pawnbroker took it to a silversmith to be valued. He discovered it was an item stolen from a house fire, and had the woman arrested.[153] Some merchants and businessmen felt the system of trade, bartering, pawning, and dealing in stolen goods undermined their own businesses.[154] The line between legal and illegal was not always clear, especially concerning the practices of the informal economy. And so many turned to the streets to fence stolen goods—increasing their chances of being caught.

Larceny was always a serious crime in the eyes of Pennsylvania's colonists. The Quaker criminal code from 1682 punished property crimes through a combination of imprisonment, restitution, and corporal punishment.[155] When the British criminal code was imposed in 1718, larceny was the only felony that was not a capital offense.[156] In 1720, a new law gave magistrates more flexibility in sentencing, including the discretion to levy a fine in lieu of the public whipping provided the sum did not exceed twenty shillings. Inability to pay the fines and fees resulted in imprisonment in the workhouse.[157] When Pennsylvania overhauled its criminal code in 1786, the public whipping and excessive fees were removed. Larceny under twenty shillings was punishable by restitution, forfeiture of the same value to the state, and one year or less in prison; larceny over twenty shillings required the same with up to three years in prison.[158] After 1790, the penitentiary was literally filled with men and women convicted of larceny. Larceny charges had the highest conviction rates, and women convicted of larceny constituted at least 75 percent of women prisoners.[159]

Anxious to reestablish a social and political hierarchy in the wake of the revolution's democratic appeal, elites sought to rein in the poor by enacting severe punishments even for minor offenses. Penal authorities targeted property crimes like never before. At the bottom, the city's population was more numerous and poor than ever. The poor from England, Ireland, and Germany were lured to Pennsylvania by dreams of a future that Europe could never offer. As a wage-based free labor economy replaced long-standing relationships of dependency, formerly enslaved or indentured servants were left to fend for themselves, often without employment prospects or networks of family support. Workers faced an unpredictable seasonal labor market that left even skilled workers vulnerable during periods of unemployment. A cycle of wars and embargos contributed to economic booms and busts during the early decades of the young nation, creating an element of uncertainty even for middling people and wreaking havoc on the working poor. After the War of 1812, the city was in a depression that left one-third of the labor force unemployed. The city barely recovered when the Panic of 1819 hit, making everything even worse. That some turned to theft of basic necessities to sustain themselves and support family members was unavoidable.[160]

In 1799, when twenty-eight-year-old Mary O'Brien stole a plated lamp and two tablecloths from Edward Shippen's home on Fourth Street, she inspired outrage among Philadelphia's elites.[161] Shippen was noted as a Judge of Common Pleas who lived on Fourth Street with his family and two slaves. He was a member of one of the richest families in Pennsylvania. His namesake and great-great grandfather Edward Shippen stood at the top of Pennsylvania society during the early years of settlement, served on the high court, and possessed the greatest fortune in the colony at the time.[162] As part of the wealthy and powerful Shippen clan, Edward could have done without the tablecloths. But O'Brien's bold act showed she did not respect Shippen's authority and did not fear the repercussions of the newly strengthened penal system that was extremely harsh toward thieves. As a lawyer and judge himself, Shippen embodied penal authority. O'Brien was an Irish immigrant who was probably working as his servant when Shippen charged her with stealing. The two-year sentence she received was extreme even for Pennsylvania during the period, though she did receive a pardon after serving one year and eight months of her sentence.[163] Not only had she targeted one of the city's leading men, but she was also a repeat offender. She had been charged in 1794 with stealing from Edward Carrot and two years later was found guilty of theft with two accomplices, serving nearly one year in prison.[164] By the time O'Brien was charged by Shippen, she was a familiar face both in court and in jail. This time, the judge threw the book at her.

The tense relationship between elite men and women and poor women was visible in private homes, on the streets, and in jails, courthouses, and the press. Many commented on the practice of servants leaving home in the early evening to spend the night with family and friends, drinking, socializing, and carousing into the morning hours.[165] In 1809, Eve Spangler used "force and arms" to steal one tablecloth and two pounds of butter belonging to Ann Steel. Spangler was ordered to spend one month in the Dauphin County Jail as well as to restore the goods and pay a ten-cent fine.[166] Mary Cling targeted Abraham Bomgaugh and stole from him three pounds of chocolate and twenty-seven knives.[167] Such basic kitchen staples could be prized assets to the poor and struggling, but that did little to assuage the rage of those targeted. In 1787, Isaac Bartram, a successful merchant in his own right and son of John Bartram, the "Father of American Botany," ran an ad for the retrieval of a thermometer stolen from his yard.[168] Bartram claimed it was taken "by a Woman who asked for charity, as it was missing soon after she was gone, and as it is likely she will offer it for sale." He offered twenty shillings for its return. While he failed to give a description of the woman, neglecting her height, race, deportment, or clothing, he did give a detailed account of the missing item, identifying its brand along with the degrees of measure on the scale.[169] Readers were reminded that poor people could not be trusted, and anyone could be the victim of deception.[170] The powerful and wealthy Bartram sounded resentful, tinged with a bit of hopeful resignation while the woman, characterized as a manipulative imposter, was entrepreneurially savvy and invisible at the same time.

Violation of the law by poor women stealing goods of even slight value was seen to jeopardize the entire social order. One writer argued that the rule of law must come before human needs or feelings that were subjective and unreliable. He used a poor woman as his subject, writing, "A poor wretch, without education, without friends, without the knowledge of social order, takes a shift off a line to hide her nakedness; the law's eyes are wide open to see, and the law's hands are stretched out to seize her; she is thrust into a jail."[171] The writer imagines the arguments she would have made in her defense, stating, "Here, sir, is the identical shift; not a thread is taken

out; it is speck and span just as I put it on; I only used it a little; I thought
no harm of that; I fully intended to put it back on the line." While a feeling
person might be swayed by her need and willingness to return the shift, the
social order demanded otherwise. Instead, the author points out how a
judge should and would rule in such instance: "You had no business to
take or use what did not belong to you; you would all escape if the law
countenanced such subterfuges—society would be broken up—honest men
could not live—roguery would thrive." The author's choice of an unedu-
cated, friendless, impoverished woman to make a larger point about justice
suggests several important facts: knowledge of women's poverty and their
treatment before the courts was widespread and there was a limit to the
role of "feeling" in punishment; it applied to suffering inside of prisons but
was not extended to judges presiding over trials or sentencing.

Those imprisoned for theft faced stiff sentences that were made even
harsher for multiple offenses. Before formal identification cards or papers
were routine, women would change their names and provide prison officials with aliases in order to remain anonymous or avoid being charged
with a second or third offense. Aliases are revealed in the records when the
prison clerk figured them out and listed multiple names on a woman's
record. Elizabeth Wilson was only nineteen when she came to Philadelphia
as a slave from Cape François. In January 1795, she was charged with committing larceny at Samuel Middleton's house. While four others were sentenced, Wilson herself was discharged.[172] She began going by aliases to
evade authorities ever since. Under the alias Elizabeth Miller she was
charged in June 1796 with stealing or receiving stolen goods while out on
pardon on condition of leaving the state.[173] On July 26 that year she was
convicted of larceny in Delaware County, Pennsylvania, and sentenced to
two years in prison and fined three pounds. The clerk noted that Wilson
spoke "plain english" and had a "full face" as well as the fact that she lived
in Dover.[174] She learned to avoid authorities by changing her alias again to
Elizabeth Johnson when she was charged with Isaac Johnson in February
1797 on John Lee's oath with stealing fifty-six dollars from him. For some
women, the use of aliases, if undetected, could help repeat offenders avoid
more severe punishments set aside for them, demonstrating savvy in evad-
ing the legal system. For others like Wilson, they reveal just how small a
town Philadelphia was, and how, once in the system, it was nearly impossible to remain anonymous or escape the reach of the state.

Women working in occupations that provided them some degree of independence—grocer, milliner, baker, boarding house operator, schoolmistress, tavern keeper and mantua maker were rarely charged or convicted of theft.[175] But the majority of women in the city worked as servants, washerwomen, or seamstresses. Many women simply were not paid enough to make ends meet and resorted to theft to supplement their subsistence through a variety of tasks in the informal economy, including stealing or storing or selling stolen property. Servants earned about a dollar per week if they were lucky.[176] When one young woman left home to get away from her abusive alcoholic father, she thought she was lucky to find a job as a servant with a shoemaker. Even though the shoemaker treated her fairly and paid her typical wages, they were still "trifling" and barely enough to live on.[177] Seamstresses earned slightly more but still struggled to feed themselves after paying for rent (about half of their earnings) and fuel.[178] The correlation between poverty and crime was considered a commonsense connection and was scarcely remarked on in the early national city.[179]

Of all occupational groups, women working as servants were the most likely to be charged and convicted.[180] Servants often stocked up on clothing and other valuables when planning to run away. Clothing was a valuable asset, in terms of both monetary worth and social significance.[181] A servant might gain a nice outfit for Saturday night on the town or Sunday morning services, pawn it for some much needed money, or use it to start a new life that did not reveal his or her former status. One black woman was found guilty of larceny when her mistress, Mrs. Williamson, found her own missing dress in the possession of another woman. The runaway servant was caught and admitted to taking the dress from the Williamsons' kitchen, for which she was imprisoned for two years.[182] The ubiquitous runaway ads often listed items the person allegedly stole before they escaped. When twelve-year-old Margaret Repsher left her term of bound servitude, her master John Gaspard Brenton accused her of taking with her "a gold single cased WATCH, made at Paris, the maker's name unknown, runs on a diamond, the hour and minute hands set with brilliants, the chrystal wanting, with a steel chain and a gold seal, having three fleurs de lis engraved thereon."[183] Regardless of whether Repsher actually took the watch, she would be forever marked as a criminal by Brenton's assertion.

It is worth exploring why servants were those most commonly charged and convicted of theft. Working at service was a demanding life, day in and day out—even more so for those who lived under the constant surveillance of masters.[184] A critique of the lopsided distribution of wealth could easily lead workers to take something that was of little value to the rich but of tremendous value to them. But those stolen from took such attacks personally. This was especially true when servants or slaves stole from the homes in which they worked. Irish servant Catherine Waterson ran away, taking with her some valuables that her master listed in detail. Mr. Gibbons was clearly outraged and saved most of his words in the advertisement for a rhyming description of Catherine.[185] Gibbons described her as "Thick and clumsey made you see, Pretends a tayloress to be, She about 5 feet 4 inches high, Very apt to swear and lie. Of a down look; complexion dark, In her face much pock mark. As also very long black hair, Which she clubb behind did wear." He recounted her clothing in detail: "Two striped petticoats she had, One bird eye ditto, very bad, One striped linsey jacket she, With two check aprons, bore away, Two handkerchiefs about her neck, One a flag, the other check; Her hose blue worsted; clocks of white, And stuff shoes, as black as night." The goods included a "very good large silver spoon" and "a chain of silver." But he also wrote about her penchant for deception and quick answers. Gibbons suggested that she would soon be looking for work, having little money to get by on: "Tho'shortly for work she must call, As her money, if any, was but small, And to pawn that spoon or pincushion, She would be backward to begin. Therefore I desire with whome she be, He may think of himself and me, And safe secure her in some Goal, That I may have her without fail." Written in rhyme, the author's advertisement introduced literary flare to a staid and long-standing genre, revealing not only his writing skills but perhaps more importantly the depth of his attachment to his servant and the things she took from him. If she indeed stole housewares made of precious metals as accused, Waterson was facing some serious prison time. Thirty-three-year-old African American Ealoner Higgins was sentenced to three years for stealing five silver forks and one silver spoon valued at ten pounds along with a roram hat, made of wool and fur.[186]

Women who worked as bound servants in prosperous families did not generally benefit from their proximity to wealth and were left to fend for themselves when their terms expired.[187] When Susannah Kirk first arrived from Ireland, she worked for Abner Lukens as an indentured servant and then "worked out at service" for different families. In 1799, she was arrested for stealing a watch and two months later pressed charges against Rose

Stokes for "assaulting and beating" her before she landed in the poorhouse, sick and "rendered incapable of helping herself."[188] German immigrant Margaret Fisher was sentenced to two years of hard labor in prison for stealing "a gold locket and chain" and some other items in June 1815, over fifteen years after she had served out her indenture to Philadelphia rope maker Frederick Stall and spent some time in the almshouse with a venereal disease.[189] Twenty-three-year-old African American Margaret Browne was "raised in the family of Mr. Reiley" and served three months in 1796 for larceny. Sarah Weaver was "a small woman" and only eighteen when charged with larceny and sentenced to one year of hard labor. Sarah was notably "brought up in the family of Doctor Anderson" of Philadelphia.[190] A current or former working relationship with a wealthy or powerful family did nothing to protect these women from the brutalities of life—or punishment.

Only occasionally could those imprisoned who left a favorable impression on former employers or landlords still count on them for character references. Mary Fisher was charged with passing counterfeit money and acquitted. Still, she could not afford to pay the court fees and languished in prison. In May 1788, Thomas Cuthbert wrote to PSAMPP on her behalf, affirming that she carried herself "in an orderly and discreet manner" and found a "spirit of industry" that led him and his wife to think so highly of her they felt compelled to speak up for her under the circumstances. Cuthbert addressed his letter to Rev. George Duffield. Duffield then wrote to John Olden, who was on the Acting Committee of PSAMPP, communicating Cuthbert's message along with an endorsement from Dr. Morris, who also confirmed her industry and indigence.[191] The Cuthberts, however, were rather exceptional. Most were threatened by the insubordination of their hired, bound, or enslaved help.

It did not take much for elites to resent their servants and accuse them of insubordination, poor work ethic, and even theft. Conflict with servants was key to solidifying a woman's identity as "a lady."[192] Having problems with working-class women, viewing them as troubled, disobedient, and willful, served too many important functions for elite women to approach them any differently. Elizabeth Drinker repeatedly complained about her servants, claiming that "good Servants are hard to be had," and they frequently tried to get out of working—or working efficiently—whenever they could.[193] The fact that some of the most vulnerable and disposable workers wielded such power over Mrs. Drinker and other elites was amazing. That her servants (allegedly treated better than most) still maintained some sense of their own identity by insisting on visits with friends and family members, even at inconvenient times for their employer, enraged Drinker. When a former servant came calling for her freedom dues as required by law, Drinker called her "Impertinent and Saucy."[194] Drinker was not alone. Many mistresses at the time felt their servants were out of line, insubordinate, and believed they could do as they pleased.[195] Deborah Norris Logan complained about how hard it was to find "good servants," noting one black woman she fired for being "too warm in her place and very impertinent in her remarks."[196] The fact that even the slightest gestures of agency or autonomy by servants brought elite women such anguish and frustration reveals how desperate elite women were for displays of deference and respect.[197] But such conflict could also be generative, even vital, for women whose class identity was affirmed through their relationships with their poor servants.[198]

Such resentments and frustrations with regard to domestic servants were formalized in the 1820s as organizations were formed to regulate this much-needed workforce. In New York, those in a position to hire help articulated their frustrations in a collective way and moved to introduce the system of registration, discipline, and surveillance that was increasingly applied to the lower sorts in cities throughout the period. The Society for the Encouragement of Faithful Domestics, formed in 1826, noted in the opening words of its first report how damaging servants could be to family life: "*Bad* servants are alone sufficient, if not to destroy, at least to mar, much of the calm happiness of domestic life."[199] Part of the problem these women allegedly posed was that they were restless and loved change and adventure. This common attitude in young women led them to be "impatient of control, or of advice" that employers expected them to follow. Such tensions seemed minor, petty even. But servant women—so needed and so despised—came to carry a much greater burden in the young nation's aspirant republican families. The Society for the Encouragement of Faithful Domestics cast servant women as "evil" beings occupying space at the center of the family, and by extension, the nation, claiming, "A hostile body has been found in the bosom of every family, mingling in all its concerns, but with a separate and opposite interest."[200] And so the blame for any social chaos, political weakness, or economic unease was expanded from criminals, vagrants, runaway slaves, and the indigent poor to servants.

Philadelphians had compelling reasons of their own for starting a similar organization. From 1820 to 1835, servants were the majority of women charged with larceny.[201] The Philadelphia Society for the Encouragement of Faithful Domestics was founded in 1829. The sentimental family and well-being of children were chief concerns of the organization. The report of the Philadelphia Society asserted, "It is next to impossible to prevent the contamination of the tender minds of children, from that intercourse with corrupt and depraved domestics, against which no care or caution can sufficiently guard, when a family is afflicted with them."[202] Like their New York counterparts, Philadelphia's organizers also referred to this influence as evil.[203] Just who were these evil women with the power to destroy the family—and by extension—the nation? Largely Irish immigrants with African Americans a distant second.[204] Domestic tranquility was both fragile and vitally important to American national identity. Society's poorest workers were easy scapegoats for anxiety about the future.

Other observers noted the absurdity of the idea that servants were responsible for domestic discord. Instead, they argued that employers were the problem and domestics should form "A Society for the Encouragement of Faithful Employers." This response placed the blame squarely on the shoulders of privileged people with impossible expectations. Writer W. L. Fisher noted, "The effect is, if a servant happens to get several captious, fretful employers, who require unreasonable work, and hence chooses to change his place, he loses character, a record is preserved, a mark in reality is placed upon him, when, perhaps, much more than half the fault lies—not upon him."[205] Future employment prospects of those at service could be damaged by negative references from employers, but there was always a market for good servants who would submit to the orders and whims of employers. Hundreds of women imprisoned for theft throughout the 1820s declared their intentions to return to service upon release from prison suggesting there was still greater demand for servants than those willing or able to work.[206]

* * *

Women who challenged the social order by begging, stealing, drinking, and being paid for sex were socially, politically, and economically marginalized but by no means a minority. Women's experience of larceny is best understood collectively rather than individually. An underground economy of stealing or storing or selling stolen goods involved networks of men and women and provided a crucial source of income for many poor women.[207]

Rarely do these women appear on tax lists or censuses or in birth or marriage records. Only a select few of them made the local papers for their crimes, and even those reports contain little to help us understand the lives, dreams, struggles, and fears of this neglected group. Even more surprising is that a similar claim can be made about the men who shared their fate. In their exhaustive study of colonial crime and punishment, Jack Marietta and G. S. Rowe identified the Pennsylvania accused as "missing persons, or civilly nonpersons."[208] For women, this harsh reality was amplified by an economic system that obscured their labor and a legal system that erased them when they married. So, what do the lives of these women really tell us? The working poor were creative, crafty, and ingenious (just as elites feared) because their survival depended on it. They turned to the streets for food, drink, fun, companionship, alms, and opportunities. And yes, they even trained their children in their ways, hoping to instill in young people the skills, spirit and even cunning needed to survive.

The obstruction of their access to social and economic opportunity was devastating for poor women and men and their children. The excessive enforcement of vagrancy laws reflected local rather than state or national values of punishment. Constables and watchmen filled the prison with people to get them off the streets, even though this overwhelmed the prison and outraged reformers and Inspectors who claimed it worked against the greater aims of penal reform. The policing of women in public spaces reveals numerous contradictions in early republican life and thought. First, it exposes the conflicts between the principle of enlightened punishment espoused by reformers and the everyday actions and decisions of watchmen charged with policing the streets. Second, it shows that women were creative economic actors in the marketplace well into the antebellum period. The expansive policing of women's public activities was done in the name of national identity and the rule of law but served to weaken already tenuous ties of economic survival. Women who claimed independence and survival were punished for selling alcohol, sex, and used or stolen goods. The idea that women and men occupied "separate spheres" was promoted in the nineteenth century as a way to challenge the presence of women in public life. Women were to be relegated to the domestic sphere while men occupied and dictated public life. Even white middle-class women challenged this dichotomy with their volunteer and reform work.[209] But working women posed a different kind of threat by taking to the streets at night seeking community, pleasure, and money. They exposed the failure of intimate patriarchy, as husbands, fathers, and masters were less able to control the comings and goings of the women in their lives. They challenged the idea that women were primarily domestic and maternal beings, more concerned with caretaking and home life than sociality. They were punished severely for living their lives openly in the streets and yet barely at all when resorting to violence against others. Although physical violence was very much embedded in the framework of American national identity, women's embrace of drinking, swearing, and strolling was seen as a telltale sign of the failure of republicanism's vision for women.

CHAPTER 4

〜

Freedom's Limits

HISTORY HAS LOOKED kindly on Pennsylvania because of its antislavery legacy. It was the first state to pass a law abolishing slavery, inspired similar legislation in numerous other Northern states, and forced the issue of abolishing the international slave trade onto the national agenda. The ideology of freedom was widely celebrated in Pennsylvania while abhorrence of the slave trade boldly declared.[1] Though the Gradual Abolition Act of 1780 failed to free a single slave, it turned the state into a refuge for free blacks and those fleeing enslavement in border states.[2] But neither passage of the Act nor its many consequences were clear victories for African American freedom. The expanded penal authorities were quickly dispatched to punish those who sought their own freedom and resisted the authority of people claiming to be their masters. Many questions remained as to what impact abolition would have on the social, political, and economic opportunities afforded to free blacks. Would abolitionists and other elites take responsibility for the legacy of generations of enslavement and its effects on African American communities? Would prevailing theories of racial difference that long served as justification for enslavement be transformed by or further curtail the possibilities for freedom? Would attitudes toward the poor change as African Americans replaced Irish and English immigrants as those most in need? Would the criminal justice system, openly discriminatory to African Americans in the colonial period, be any different under American jurisdiction than it was under British?

The possibilities that post-Revolutionary emancipation presented were quickly foreclosed by a number of forces. Delegates to the Constitutional Convention in Philadelphia sanctified slavery in law, custom, and national identity. Talk of freedom, equality, and abolition had a negative impact on social relations and legal rights of African Americans, as slaveholders feared the loss of their "property," and everyone else feared disunion.[3] Antislavery advocates disagreed over the best approach for ridding the nation of the blight of slavery (gradual or immediate abolition?) as well as deciding the status of the formerly enslaved in the aftermath of abolition—were they citizens or expatriates? Local and national debates would fuel racist ideas, both deliberately and inadvertently. Abolitionists presumed African Americans needed supervision, while colonizationists declared them unfit for free society. Those against slavery did nearly as much to limit the life chances of newly freed blacks as slaveholders did. Pennsylvania had long been a stronghold of Quaker abolitionist sentiment, priding itself on humanizing views of African Americans, along with a commitment to education and opportunity. But even the most ardent abolitionists were taken by the colonization fever that swept the nation by 1820. Colonizationists relied on racist incriminations of African Americans' character and alleged propensity for criminality to fortify their views that blacks and whites could not peaceably coexist.

The treatment of African Americans in the courts and in prison reveals that the black community did not stand a chance of achieving legal or social equality in the young republic.[4] Simple analysis of inmates by race and ethnicity reveals persistent discrimination against African Americans before the courts. Black women shared this negative status with Irish immigrants for twenty years or so, but as the Irish became more assimilated into Anglo-American culture, African American women alone were shut out of opportunities for economic advancement.[5] Varied terminology used to describe racial and ethnic backgrounds reveals the malleability and changing function of race over time. Racial difference functioned both informally and officially in the prison and was shaped by discourses about masculinity, youth, criminality, and reform. The consolidation of racial categories into a simple binary of "black" and "white" coincided with an increase in violence and discrimination against African Americans at every level of economic, social, and political life. Liberty for African Americans proved to be, as Kali Gross has claimed, "temporal, fraught with strife, and ultimately, fleeting."[6] Still, African American women and men did what they could in an increasingly hostile social and political environment to assert their claim to the revolutionary promises of liberty and justice.[7]

Abolition

The Constitutional Convention met just a few blocks away from Walnut Street Jail. Delegates who fought over the role of slavery in the new nation would have passed the prison regularly. Though the Constitution itself does not mention slavery by name, its silence spoke volumes, serving to evade, legalize, and calibrate the institution.[8] In the three-fifths compromise, the Constitution fused together the two key aspects of slavery that divided delegates: economics and governance.[9] Leading abolitionist delegates such as Benjamin Franklin and Alexander Hamilton helped to shape the terms of the national discourse by their unwillingness to speak openly about the problem of slavery, during the convention and in its aftermath. In short, they modeled the imperative of silence regarding anything that might jeopardize the ratification of the Constitution and undermine the formation of a strong central government. The threat was not only slavery itself, but also the very act of talking about slavery.[10] It became obvious to all present that abolition—not slavery—would threaten the formation of a national government. Instead of taking a bold stand in favor of abolition at the moment of the nation's founding, antislavery delegates turned their contempt toward England and argued that slavery was something forced on the colonies by the British. It was politically safer to blame England for slavery than to take a stand in favor of national abolition.[11] Pennsylvanians also blamed the British for imposing a violent and faulty penal code on the colony. Their open public critique of the British penal code and quick, decisive steps to change it were an attempt to compensate for their unwillingness to take more decisive action against slavery.

The immediate post-Revolutionary period in Pennsylvania was one of some advancement for African American freedom, community, and opportunity.[12] Black leaders worked tirelessly to abolish slavery, improve the lives of community members, and challenge racist ideas. By 1785 there were only 420 enslaved people living in Philadelphia. African Americans successfully established churches, schools, businesses, and community organizations, making Philadelphia the center of the nation's free black community. Freedom, however, was always constrained by the very law that made it possible. As Joanne Pope Melish has shown, gradual emancipation itself was not a rejection of slavery but rather served to reproduce key elements of "the ideology practices of slavery" in free society. One manifestation of this dynamic was the way abolitionist discourses reinforced the idea that free blacks "would constitute an element of inherent disorder in need of continuing supervision and control."[13] African Americans were portrayed as being incapable of handling freedom, which further undermined their entitlement to it. Those enslaved who sought freedom by running away or fighting back were treated as rebels who represented the kind of disorder that was possible.

African Americans were joined in the fight for freedom by longtime Quaker activists who spread abolitionist sentiment in Pennsylvania, challenged some long-held racist views, and condemned slavery. They worked tirelessly for passage of the historic Gradual Abolition Act of 1780, which famously did not actually free a single slave. As early as 1789, the Pennsylvania Society for Promoting the Abolition of Slavery expanded its agenda to address the educational and economic needs of newly freed blacks to mitigate proslavery critiques that charged they were not capable of handling freedom.[14] The Pennsylvania Abolition Society continued to attack the constitutionality of slavery on multiple fronts, including sending a petition to Congress in 1790 lobbying for abolition of the international slave trade.[15] As the Society's president at the time, Benjamin Franklin advocated for "the Restoration of liberty" to slaves who "amidst the general Joy of surrounding Freemen" suffer in "Servile Subjection."[16] The Society of Friends then petitioned the Senate in 1793 for the complete abolition of slavery.[17] Neither effort worked, but by 1804 every Northern state had passed some form of gradual abolition act. When New York passed its act in 1799, it promised freedom for all by 1827.[18] White hostility grew exponentially as slavery's expiration date grew near.

The overall black population of Philadelphia tripled from 2,078 to 6,436 from 1790 to 1800, and then nearly doubled to 12,110 by 1820.[19] Whites became increasingly antagonistic toward free blacks, turning to legislative and penal authorities to regulate and punish them. Blatant interpersonal hostility became increasingly common, and white abolitionists could not be counted on to support or defend African American rights in freedom.[20] Penal reformers as a group were no longer committed to abolition. While there was considerable overlap between abolitionists and prison reformers in the founding years, especially Tench Coxe and Benjamin Rush, the causes diverged by the 1820s. PSAMPP member Roberts Vaux was "almost alone among his friends" in questioning the state's ongoing complicity with slavery in the 1820s.[21] Coxe himself switched sides, becoming a virulent racist and colonizationist. A series of court decisions and debates in the press confirmed that whites would fight most attempts for African American advancement. The cards seemed stacked against any hope that ordinary, poor, or struggling African Americans could ever be given the benefit of the doubt—let alone full equality and citizenship.

Even elite blacks doing benevolent work—the kind of work so celebrated among their white counterparts in the era of humanitarian sensibility—were subject to intense scrutiny. Black leaders were conscious to show their commitment to the greater good of all people and assumed active roles in a number of citywide benevolent projects in the 1780s and 1790s. When yellow fever ravaged the city in 1793, leaders of the African church organized nurses to aid the sick and offered to help the mayor in dealing with the crisis. Most notably, Absalom Jones, Richard Allen, and William Gray coordinated a great many activities. This act of generosity and good will might have generated respect or praise for the black community, but instead left them vulnerable to public critique by Mathew Carey, who stated in print that blacks charged exorbitant and exploitive fees for their caregiving services.[22] Even worse, he asserted that African Americans were caught stealing from the houses of the sick.[23] Jones and Allen were quick to fight back, claiming that Carey totally mischaracterized the behavior of black nurses and was himself profiteering by the publication of such characterizations. They wrote, "We believe he has made more money by the sale of his 'scraps' than a dozen of the greatest extortioners among the black nurses." If black leaders hoped to improve their public image by taking on such dangerous humanitarian work, they failed. Despite caretaking for whites during a public health crisis, black nurses and leaders were criticized as con men and thieves.

Carey's critique criminalized black civic behavior. As Jeannine Marie DeLombard argues, Carey's critique typified the commonplace refusal of black citizenship during the period.[24] In 1793, there was already an incredible double standard in place. While whites were also known to have taken advantage of people during the outbreak, the entire white race was not condemned for the actions of a few.[25] Absalom Jones labeled Carey's attack on African Americans as an attempt to "make us blacker than we are." Jones went out on a limb and risked alienating sympathetic white readers by comparing the actions of poor whites and blacks. He listed the many humane efforts of poor blacks and asserted, "We do not recollect such acts of humanity from the poor white people."[26] It was risky for Jones to publicly criticize the white community and to challenge Carey on these points, but his response signaled how tense relations had already become and how high the stakes were for African Americans.

Shortly after the epidemic passed, another crisis consumed Pennsylvania. One cannot overstate the impact of the Haitian Revolution on the prospects for African American freedom in Philadelphia, from reigniting sympathy for slaveholders to instigating fear of free blacks.[27] Freedom became conflated with violence, poverty, and criminality. Abolitionists faced a new challenge when French refugees from Saint-Domingue who settled in Philadelphia refused to free over 500 enslaved people who accompanied them. When forced to abide by the Gradual Abolition law, many tried to circumvent it by freeing the enslaved only to immediately indenture them as servants.[28] Further weakening the fight against slavery and blurring the line between slave and free, the Pennsylvania Supreme Court upheld the right of former French planters to follow this procedure, leading to a spike in the number of black indentured servants in the city. This was a terrible situation that greatly expanded the class of black servants who occupied an intermediate social status, higher than the enslaved but lower than white servants.[29] It still was not freedom.

Whites feared that French-speaking blacks were spreading the spirit of revolution and disorder. Countering abolitionists who authored numerous petitions and appeals to persuade the government to adopt their view, blatantly racist groups launched a campaign to prohibit admittance of free blacks into the state. In 1798 Pennsylvania's governor, Thomas Mifflin, sought to block any French-speaking blacks from entering the state at all.[30] Concern about the growing size of the free black community was vocalized again in the 1800s.[31] A bill before the Pennsylvania Senate threatened not only to prohibit admittance of free blacks into the state but also to restrict the movement of those already there. Many people spoke out in favor of legislation to prevent black immigration to the state. The real energy for this racial antagonism came from the city's leaders and an increasingly resentful middle class—not poor Irish fighting with African Americans over jobs.[32] It was the mayor, aldermen, and many citizens who petitioned the state to tax free blacks in order to support the poor.[33] These legislative efforts stand as a powerful testament to the intense, growing resistance to black freedom and equality.

White abolitionists became unreliable allies in the fight against anti-black discrimination as time went on. The radical abolition movement of black leaders and their white allies from the revolutionary era was replaced by a more moderate movement led by white people.[34] Many white liberal abolitionists, for instance, believed blacks were prone to crime. In its 1800 address to free blacks, the Pennsylvania Society for Promoting the Abolition of Slavery suggested that more of them attend church, that "your virtuous resolutions will be strengthened, the temptations to evil become fewer and weaker."[35] The Abolition Society's prescription for behaviors that free blacks should encourage among slaves identified the same behaviors the prison system sought to cultivate in inmates: "submission, obedience, and an obliging disposition."[36] Such behaviors were thought to elicit "human and gentle treatment" from masters, reiterating rather than challenging the viewpoint of slaveholders. Furthermore, the abolitionists called for free blacks to embrace education, place their children in virtuous white families where they might learn useful trades, and avoid interaction with those fallen.

Pennsylvania's location as a border state between slavery and freedom made it a popular destination for both runaways and free blacks. Most prisoners who listed a Southern state as their birthplace were of African descent—either born into slavery or children of slaves.[37] Free blacks flocked to Philadelphia and New York in search of kin, community, and employment.[38] Limited opportunities awaited them in Philadelphia, and their presence was widely criticized in the press as merchants, artisans, businessmen, and government officials worried about the increasing financial burden of the poor on the city.[39] One writer complained, "Many of these emigrants from the south are now paupers in this city, and will, *no doubt*, in the winter either have to be supported at the public expense, or will support themselves by thieving."[40] Many black women from the South would find work as washerwomen and servants for meager wages.[41] Others labored in the streets as hucksters or prostitutes. All were vulnerable to arrest simply for being black and free. The fact that so many worked in domestic service increased their chances of being suspected of or caught stealing, given all of the possible witnesses in the household.[42]

Fighting Slavery with Fire

Violence throughout the state, across the nation, and even around the world was used as justification for many local anti-black laws and policies, from restricting movement of free blacks to extending slaveholder rights to severely punishing those resistant to authority. While violence was a widely known fact of life justified in nation building, violence committed by African Americans was never excused but rather served as the justification for restrictions on black civic life. While representing only a small percentage of overall crimes, black women convicted of arson received the harshest penalty before the courts and the brunt of whites' greatest fears and anxieties. In 1794, arson was the last crime against property to be removed from the list of capital crimes. Attorney General William Bradford, Jr., belittled those who resorted to arson, describing it as a crime of revenge, most commonly committed by "slaves and children." He was right in that arson was often an action taken by those who had no other recourse to demand their personal or legal rights. It is no surprise, then, that black girls were most reputed to commit arson; they were also more likely to be convicted than white girls.[43] But Bradford critiqued the effectiveness of arson, arguing, "Its motive is revenge, and, to a free mind, the pleasure of revenge is lost when its object is ignorant of the hand that inflicts the blow."[44] Bradford's condescension toward arsonists reveals the real threat such bold actors posed.

For Bradford, white abolitionists, and elite blacks, arsonists crossed a line that even slavery did not justify. While enslaved people who ran away, broke tools, or talked back to their masters would have frustrated some or enraged others, these were minor transgressions compared to the more dramatic act of destruction caused by arson. Arson was no ordinary form of resistance. It signaled all-out war to whites by threatening not only property but also social hierarchy. In the 1790s, a crucial era for race relations in Philadelphia as elsewhere, dominant perceptions of black servants and slaves began to shift from that of deferential and obedient laborers to stubborn and violent rebels. A series of developments informed this change, including increased instances of running away and fighting back, news of the rebellion on Saint-Domingue, the arrival of refugees, and the migration of native-born free blacks as well as fugitive slaves.[45] Black Philadelphians learned of and annually celebrated the revolution that ended slavery in Saint-Domingue, which inspired their own efforts to abolish slavery in the United States.[46] Whites' fears that armed blacks would rise against them and demand humanity, dignity, and freedom were being realized.[47]

Fear of the spirit of violent revolution quickly spread up and down the Atlantic seaboard. Each report of fire—no matter where it was or what the cause—inflamed these anxieties.[48] Suspected arsons lit up the night skies of Virginia, Washington, Baltimore, New York, and New Jersey, in 1796 alone.[49] This issue was near and dear to Pennsylvanians as well. A white woman named Margaret Grogan was charged before the Supreme Court of Pennsylvania in November 1796 for setting a fire in Philadelphia but was ultimately found not guilty. That same month, fears were reignited when a tavern outside Harrisburg went up in flames, killing or injuring many of the forty people sleeping in the property, owned by Oliver Pollock, Esq.[50] Although that fire, too, was reported to be an accident, it spurred anxiety. Of course many fires were accidental during this time, when open flames were used for both light and cooking, and many homes were built entirely of wood. Regardless, each fire inspired fear of malicious intent.[51]

A fire in December 1796 in the middle of Philadelphia, on Market Street between Sixth and Seventh Streets, set off further alarms with the report that it "was kindled by some incendiary with a design to spread a conflagration."[52] This report was followed by an update on a recent New York City fire and news that the city council recommended the people set up a night watch. Philadelphians followed New York closely, as newspapers established these links day after day. The Mayor of Philadelphia, Hilary Baker, issued a proclamation offering a reward for the capture and prosecution of people "who may be found attempting to set fire to any part of the city of Philadelphia," noting that fires in Savannah, New York, and Baltimore all targeted "populous and wealthy cities."[53] Governor Thomas Mifflin also offered a five-hundred-dollar reward and promise of a pardon for information on all of the details involved in the arson plot.

The reporting and constant reprinting of stories of arson gave readers everywhere a chance to learn about the fires and form ideas about the propensity of black people to commit arson. The key factor in determining widespread alarm about a fire was not which city it started in but whether or not an African American was a key suspect. In 1797 another fire broke out in Philadelphia at the house of printer Andrew Brown, killing his wife and three children.[54] But Brown's apprentices and domestics seemed beyond suspicion because they all ran through the flames to escape (several sustaining injury), and none were charged with arson. Philadelphia readers took note when the *Pennsylvania Gazette* reported "four strangers of suspicious characters" who were picked up in Annapolis plotting a fire and suspected of playing a role in a recent arson in New York City.[55] The same article reports "a negro woman" was the prime suspect in a fire set in the Baltimore home of Samuel Orwig, Esq., that she was "belonging to."[56] During this era, the race of the suspects was more important than the place of the fire in fueling racial fear and antagonism throughout the young republic.

When a string of fires broke out in York County, Pennsylvania, home to the second-largest free black community in the state, everyone took note. The fires that broke out over the course of three weeks in February and March 1803 seemed to occur in waves, confirming white fears that they were a key tactic of black organized resistance. The historical records, which only provide the perspective of the white judiciary and newspaper editors, give the following account. A young black girl was caught setting fire to a barn at high noon, having misunderstood her order to set the fire at midnight, the time the previous fires had been set. Whites suspected the fires were an organized response to the conviction of a local black girl named Margaret Bradley for poisoning two white women—Sophia and Matilda Bentz, Bradley's mistress and her daughter. Bradley eventually served three years of a four-year sentence for poisoning in Walnut Street Prison.[57]

In the meantime, twenty-one African Americans were arrested for the fires. After so many people were imprisoned for the arsons, the group nearly succeeded in breaking open the jail.[58] The York authorities were in a frenzy.[59] Justices of the Peace George Lewis Leffler and John Forsyth and Burgesses Peter Mundorf and Rudolph Spangler issued an announcement encouraging the white people of York and all within a ten-mile radius to keep all slaves and servants under strict scrutiny. The order stated, "You are hereby notified, that such of you as have negroes or people of colour, to keep them at home under strict discipline and watch; so as they may be under your eyes at all times."[60] Free blacks were ordered to get work passes from the justice of the peace to ensure they would be able to get to work every day. York authorities felt justified issuing harsh restrictions for Pennsylvania's free black population.[61]

Organized resistance on the part of African Americans to violence and injustice at the hands of white Americans took on a new meaning after passage of gradual abolition in 1780. It threatened whites fearful of black autonomy and associated black freedom with lawlessness and chaos. In York County, the rate of slavery dropped dramatically. In 1783, there were 471 slaves in the entire county. In 1800 only 77 slaves were registered, and by 1810 just 22. Anxiety over the role of free blacks in York County percolated among whites in this area long known as a destination for freed slaves from Virginia.[62] It could be said that the punishment of Margaret Bradley for attempted poisoning was rather mild at only four years. Some women served nearly that much time for theft. The courts may have taken Marga-ret's age into account when issuing the sentence for the nineteen-year-old. Whites would have thought black rebellion over this sentence was ill-directed rage, when not long ago such a crime would have led to a far more severe punishment.

White elites' anxiety over abolition—and rage toward free blacks—became dramatically evident in the courtroom verdict issued against the alleged arsonists. In fact, abolition became the basis and justification for their punishment. The president of the court spoke to the black defendants, reminding them of the great obligation they owed to "the inhabitants of Pennsylvania, for their benevolent exertions to remove the blacks from a state of slavery," since so many were already free. The president then tried to demean the defendants, neutralizing the power, rage, and political mean-ing of their actions by disciplining them like children and "telling them of their ingratitude towards the citizens of PA, who had done so much for them."[63] Such infantilization was a new strategy in which a thinly veiled racist paternalism aimed to soften the damning restrictions and severe pun-ishments authorized by the state.

It turned out that far fewer people were actively involved in the plot than the original arrest indicated. A smaller group of six were charged and convicted together on one count of arson: Ruth Grimes, William Grimes, Hetty Dorson, Isaac Scipior, Isaac Spangler, and Abner Short were sen-tenced to twelve years in prison, half that time to be spent in the solitary dungeon cells.[64] This was an outrageously severe punishment for the time, three times greater than Bradley's original sentence for attempted murder. But this was not an ordinary time. The group found guilty included two slaves and four free blacks.[65] A powerful message was sent by both groups. The African American defendants, together free and enslaved, would work together and challenge slavery. The state, represented by the middling and elite white men who ran the court, would not tolerate expressions of auton-omy and resistance—or any claim to citizenship.

If many whites were fearful and uncertain as to what the place of free blacks would be in the polity, incidents like this gave them an excuse to pass restrictions to ensure their own security and authority. The report from the hearing warned both abolitionists and free blacks. To the aboli-tionist society, the president stated, "We do not call in question the purity of the motives that gave rise to this society; but we think it is, like other good institutions, liable to be abused, and has been abused by some of its members in this town."[66] To the black community, the message was even louder: though they had been denied access to a formal political voice, extralegal efforts to protest would be met with the harshest punishment. Freedom was tenuous and conditional at best—and resistance would not be tolerated.

Of all women sent to prison on arson convictions, only two of the thirteen were not designated racially as African American. Eve Dresh was found guilty of "burning the dwelling house of Jacob Ryes" in 1801. She received a sentence of two years and was pardoned by the governor after serving only two months.[67] No black women convicted of arson were treated so gently, suggesting she was white and/or someone helped to get her out of prison. Neither did Maria Cummins have a racial designation, and she died in 1821, one year into her five-year sentence for burning Samuel Williamson's barn in Chester County in 1820.[68] Women convicted of arson died at a higher rate in prison than those charged with any other crime, obviously because of the extreme length of the sentences. But this also raises the possibility that the severity of their crime exposed them to harsher treatment in the prison itself, including physical abuse, lack of medical care, and inadequate nutrition. Still, arson by white girls was perceived as an individual action, a sign of poor morals, a servant's refusal to listen to her master, or even her intrinsically evil spirit. The rebellion of white girls, whether American or foreign born, was never seen to represent their race.

Arson by black girls, however, was a different matter. Harsh punishments offered one way for the legal system to crush their resistance. As the most socially, economically, and politically oppressed and vulnerable people, young black women were treated with impunity when they resisted their abuse, took action, and rejected the authority of their masters—and by extension, the state. Nineteen-year-old African American Hannah Carson was sentenced to twelve years for setting fire to William Ross's house.[69] Ross worked as a river pilot and shared his home on Almond Street with Carson and his family before she burned it down.[70] Carson spent six years and six months in jail, making her one of the penitentiary's longest-serving inmates. Jane Wedge suffered the same fate after being convicted in Montgomery County and sentenced to five years in November 1802. She died in jail "of a lingering illness."[71] The legacy of the York trial lived on for years. Seven of the eight women sentenced to serious terms for arson after 1803 were of African descent.[72] An enslaved woman named Sabe was convicted of arson in Adams County in November 1804 and sentenced to five years and six months in prison.[73] Even twenty years later, York County courts issued severe sentences for arson. In 1822, a servant woman named Sal described as "a woman of colour" was sentenced to seven years. An eighteen-year-old black woman named Matilda Scott in 1823, convicted of arson and sentenced to two five-year terms in prison.[74] Scott died in prison after serving three years of her sentence. When these women and girls set fires, they were seen to be representative of the summary rebellion of the entire race.

Racial Classification

Pennsylvania's prison Inspectors and reformers refused to explicitly acknowledge the role of race in punishment. Like most efforts to order and classify prisoners in Walnut Street, racial segregation existed sporadically and unevenly among different groups of prisoners at different times. Individual jailers or inmates determined the extent to which people interacted across racial lines in the early years of the prison. This is apparent in the way the clerk documented the physical descriptions of prisoners on their admission, the categories Inspectors used in their periodic counting of prisoners, and the way reformers identified individuals. All these records show little attention to race in the 1780s and 1790s, and even 1800s.[75] For example, even in the prison sentence docket, the most reliable source of information about race, race is recorded less than 50 percent of the time before 1815.

The penal system did not explicitly acknowledge racial differences among inmates at its founding in 1790, nor was race an official part of penal organization. Scholars speculate about whether or not prisons were racially segregated during these early years. No policy officially called for segregation.[76] Cross-racial friendships and alliances thrived in the crowded prisons. Three women who were sentenced together in March 1796 escaped on May 26 of that year by "Getting into the dungeon through the arch and undermining the wall into Sixth street," including Phoebe Mines, a "negress," Margaret McGill from Ireland, and Catherine Lynch.[77] Some reports suggest that Irish and English inmates interacted casually with African Americans. One chronicler of Walnut Street noted the absence of racial segregation, stating, "At supper, I observed, they were all seated at the same table, a prospect that afforded, as you might well conceive, no small gratifi-cation."[78] This is consistent with a larger pattern of toleration of racial mingling among the lower classes in Philadelphia throughout this period.[79] In this sense, life in prison reflected life outside prison.

But other early reports portrayed both individual and institutional rac-ism. La Rochefoucault Liancourt pointed out that blacks were treated worse than whites, even when committed for the same crime. He critiqued this arrangement and called the Inspectors hypocrites for allowing such dis-crimination in light of the fact that "almost all the Inspectors belong to a society which pleads for the freedom of the blacks."[80] Another visitor pointed out the separation of black and white women in the dining area, asserting hypocrisy on the part of the reformers who advocated "liberty and equality for Negroes."[81] It seems racial segregation was enforced spo-radically by individual keepers or guards. While some inmates found friend-ship and alliances across racial lines, others preferred separation.

Records of reformers and Inspectors concerning individual prisoners under consideration for pardons or release reveal specific attention to the race of the inmate. For the first twenty years of record keeping, from 1787 to 1807, the PSAMPP Acting Committee only addressed race on an individ-ual basis and when concerning those of African or Native American descent. For example, Wanton Mingo was "a Black Man deranged and sick" held in the vagrants' ward, whom the committee requested be moved to the Bettering House.[82] The committee noted the plight of "Ruth Moore an Indian woman with her child committed," who petitioned the mayor for release.[83] PSAMPP paid the fees of "a black man unjustly confined" and provided "a black boy" with a shirt.[84] The Board of Inspectors followed suit. When Inspectors reviewed the cases of prisoners seeking pardons or release, they often named the inmates in their meeting minutes. Often peo-ple of African descent were listed by their race and without last names, while other prisoners had surnames and no racial designation. For example, on January 1, 1795, the Inspectors "Resolved that Mary Davis, Robert Gale, William McFait and three Blacks namely Lyndia, Fabice and Pierra be rec-ommended to the Governor for a remission of their fines."[85] On March 11, 1795, they recorded, "It appears that the time of Sentence of Hugh McGar-gle, John Conly, Ann Winters and Thomas a Negro has expired."[86] It appears that "Negro" or "Negress" often stood in for a surname. "Ellen a Negress" was recommended for pardon and remission along with three men with surnames and no racial designation.[87] African Americans without surnames were more likely to be slaves, and fewer slave women than slave men had surnames.[88]

Special attention to the racial identity of those convicted as well as to the language used to designate racial difference in prison records is vital for several reasons. First, it reveals a shared experience between African American and Irish women for a time and highlights the emergence of both "white" and "black" as racial categories, along with their accompanying privileges and oppressions. Second, it reveals the disproportionate burden black women have assumed historically in the criminalization of African Americans. Third, it reflects the impact of broader public debates over abolition, colonization, and freedom on the criminalization of African Americans.

The majority of women sentenced to Walnut Street Prison were of Irish or African descent and convicted of stealing small household items or personal effects.[89] On November 20, 1794, Isabella Word accused Sarah Roach and Sylvia Gardner of stealing or receiving two yards each of stolen red and yellow flannel.[90] One month later, twenty-six-year-old Roach and twenty-five-year-old Gardner were found guilty of two counts of larceny in the Mayor's Court of Philadelphia and sentenced to one year in Walnut Street Prison. Gardner was an African American woman, born in Philadelphia and bound to Captain Henderson. Roach, also African American, was born in Maryland and gave birth to a baby girl while in prison. Both women were pardoned by the governor on recommendation of the visiting Inspectors "for their late good conduct and orderly behavior" and discharged eight months into their sentences on August 4, 1794, on condition of leaving the state.[91] Rose Thornton and Elenor White were two of the many Irish women sentenced to Walnut Street. Rose Thornton was convicted of larceny in the Court of Quarter Sessions of West Chester in 1796. She was a thirty-two-year-old woman born in Ireland who had previously served out an indenture with George Seeds of Bradford Township, Chester County. Thornton was sentenced to two years and received a pardon from the governor after six months.[92] Elenor White was charged in May 1797 with robbing John Mur of a gold watch worth fifteen pounds. She was tried and convicted in the Mayor's Court in July and sentenced to six months. White, a twenty-three-year-old woman born in Ireland, was also released on condition of leaving the state after serving four months. She was identified as "tall stout made, freckled about the nose, long darkish hair black eyes speaks much with the Irish accent."[93] Women like Sarah, Sylvia, Rose, and Elenor filled the prison and had much in common.

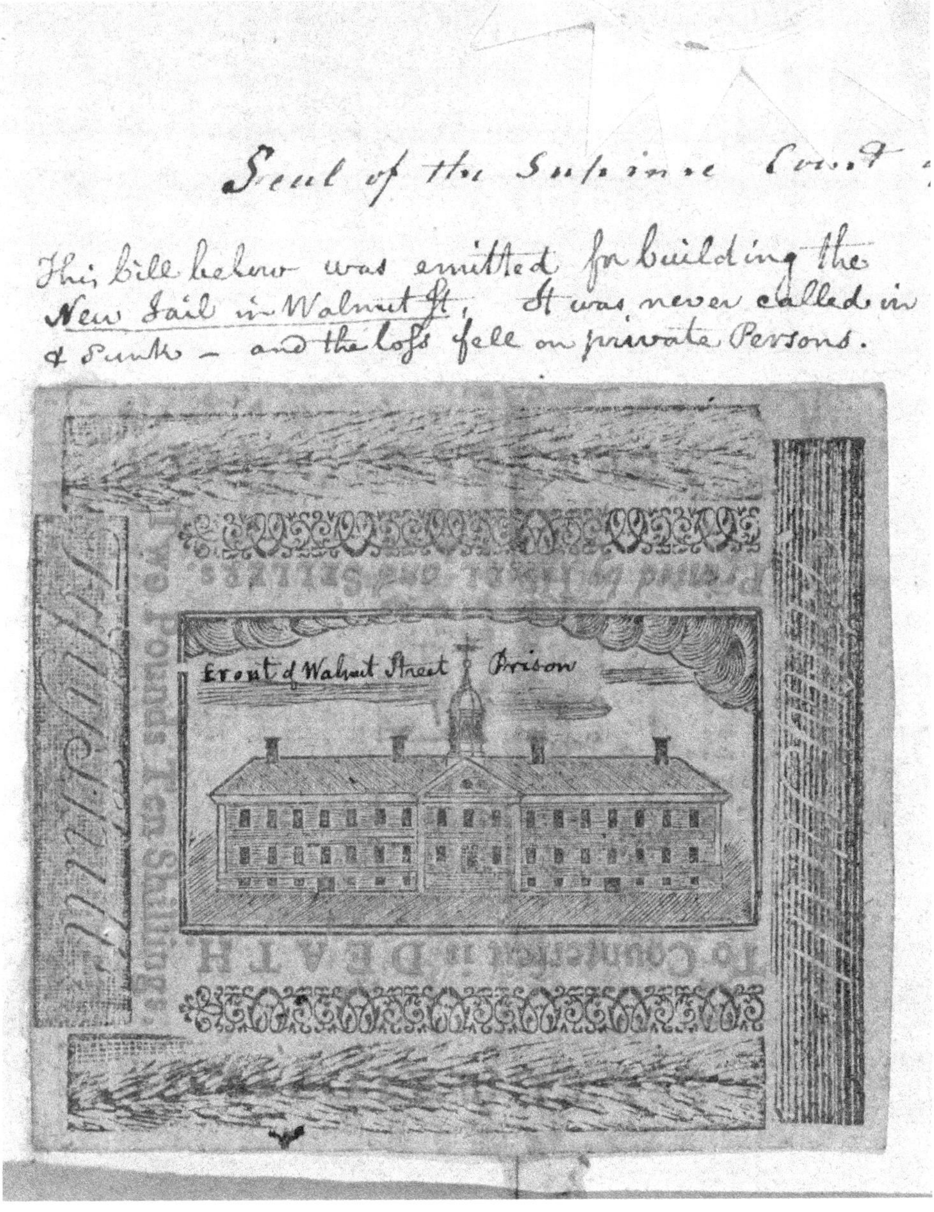

FIGURE 1. Two pounds ten shillings, currency with image of Walnut Street
Prison (1775). The Library Company of Philadelphia.

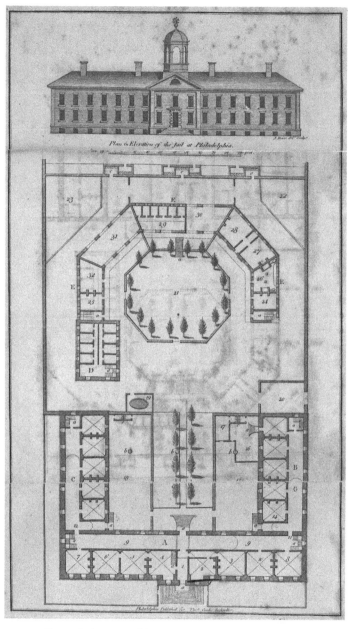

FIGURE 2. Plan and elevation of the jail at Philadelphia (1798) by Joseph Bowes for *Philadelphia Monthly Magazine*. The Library Company of Philadelphia.

(Opposite page) FIGURE 3. Apologies for tippling (1798) by G. M. Woodward. American Antiquarian Society.

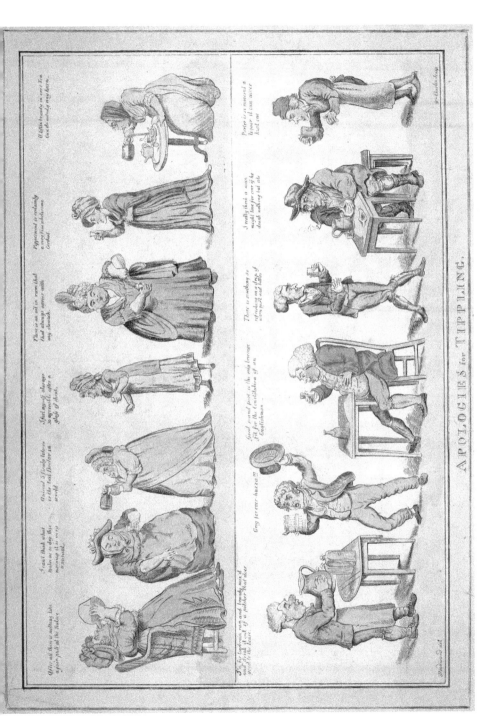

APOLOGIES for TIPPLING,

FIGURE 4. Goal, in Walnut Street Philadelphia (1799) by W[illiam] Birch & Son.
The Library Company of Philadelphia.

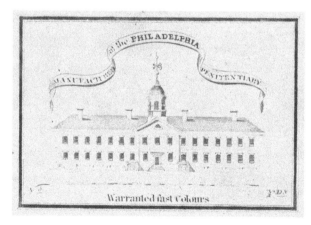

FIGURE 5. [Label for dyed cloth manufactured at the Walnut Street Prison, 500
block of Walnut Street, Philadelphia] [ca.1860] (restrike). The Library Company
of Philadelphia.

(*Opposite page*) FIGURE 6. Immediate emancipation illustrated (1833).
The Library Company of Philadelphia.

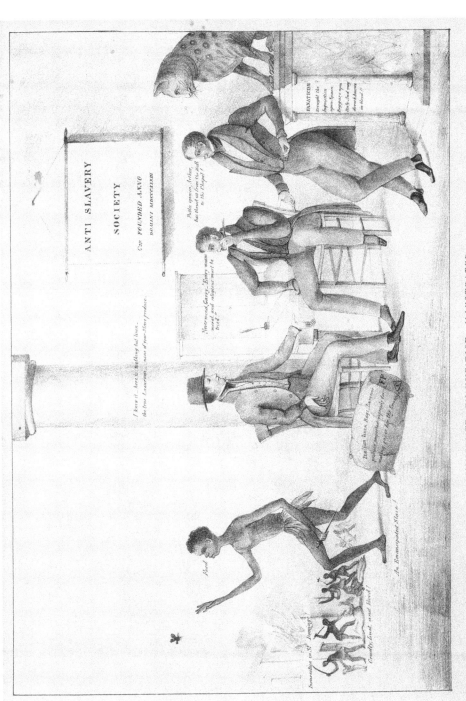

IMMEDIATE EMANCIPATION ILLUSTRATED.

A VIEW OF THE CITY OF BROTHERLY LOVE

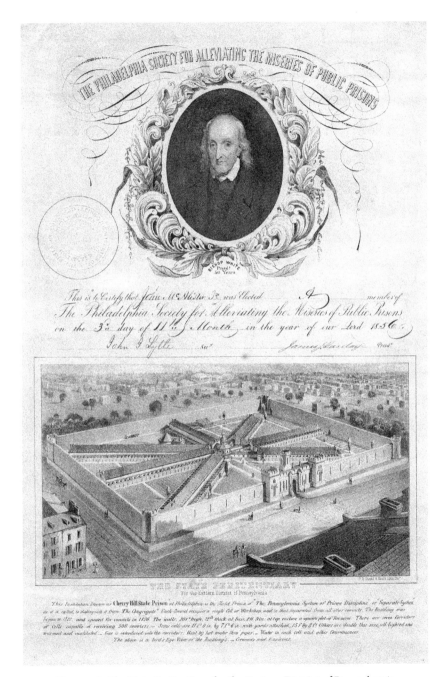

FIGURE 8. The State Penitentiary for the Eastern District of Pennsylvania
(ca. 1855) by James Fuller Queen. The Library Company of Philadelphia.

FIGURE 9. Joseph Ripka's Mills, Manayunk 21st Ward, Philadelphia (1856)
by W. H. Rease. American Antiquarian Society.

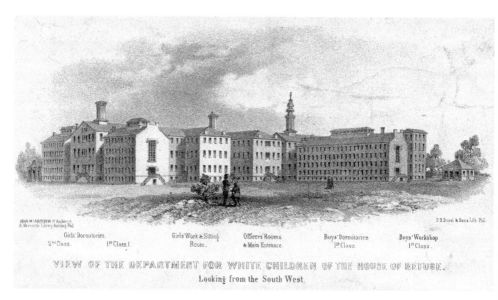

FIGURE 10. View of the department for white children of the House of Refuge:
looking from the south west (1858). The Library Company of Philadelphia.

African American and Irish women shared many experiences during this period. They experienced similar movement, dislocation, economic vulnerability, severed family ties, lack of safety net, and negative interactions with the English. African American and Irish women shared the status of forced servitude, long imposed on Irish laborers bound for passage to the colonies and increasingly imposed on African Americans in the transition from slavery to freedom. Gradual abolition required lengthy terms of servitude for former slaves and their offspring, further blurring the relationship not only between slave and free but also between servants of Irish and African descent.[94] Many women in their mid-twenties would have finished their terms of indentured servitude and then been left to fend for themselves. Working as a live-in servant, indentured or not, had many restrictions, but the near guarantee of shelter and food was no small security. Formerly bound or enslaved women were those most likely to be convicted of stealing. From 1795 to 1810, women under the age of thirty made up 59 percent of larceny convictions. In later years, that number skyrocketed. From 1820 to 1835, women under age thirty represented 93 percent of the convictions.[95] A young woman named Mariane, for instance, was only twenty-three when she was convicted in Mayor's Court in 1795 of larceny and sentenced to one year and a fine of two hundred dollars. She was pardoned on the condition that she leave the state and not return.[96] Similar factors also marked the life and struggle of Maria Dick, a thirty-year-old house servant charged with assault and battery in March and imprisoned because she could not afford the five-dollar fine.[97] Several months after her release, she was convicted of larceny and imprisoned for three years for stealing, ironically, a five-dollar bank note.[98] The hatred directed at the two groups was not identical, but their shared social location in Philadelphia lasted about thirty years, from the 1780s until the 1810s, at which point anti-black racism intensified and Irish Americans became more socially assimilated and privileged as "white" workers. Elites judged them against each other. Benjamin Rush relied on a shared assumption of black inferiority to criticize the poor from Europe. Rush claimed that former slaves were "more industrious and orderly than the lowest class of white people."[99] Former slaves were given the credit of industry only to further condemn poor whites.

Anti-Irish sentiment ran deep among the English, putting the Irish at the bottom of the social hierarchy among Pennsylvania's other European immigrants. Scots-Irish who emigrated to Pennsylvania hailed from the

borderlands between England and Scotland, an area of violence and lawlessness for hundreds of years.[100] Even leading Pennsylvania Quakers vehe-
mently condemned the humanity of the Scots-Irish, calling them "idle trash"
and "ye very Scum of mankind."[101] These sentiments were extended to the
Irish who immigrated during the post-Revolutionary period. Lower classes of
European immigrants also drew the attention of elite French émigré Moreau
de St. Méry, who described them as a people "upset and unruly, and without
property," who caused a great deal of trouble in American cities.[102] Irish
immigrants were stigmatized as lower class because of their ethnic differences
and poverty, which were inseparable for most. Few had safety nets for hard
times. Patrick Lyon was wrongly convicted of a crime in the 1790s and complained that hardworking immigrants struggling to make it in America were
unfairly suspected when crime occurred. Lyon asserted that he did not expect
hardworking and successful men such as himself to suffer from "prejudice,
malice, and injustice" in America.[103] Many Irish women found themselves
treated precisely that way. The majority of women in prison had far more in
common with Lyon, an Irishman struggling to get by amid great discrimination, than they did with Pennsylvania's elite and middling Anglo-American
women. Even prisoners of Anglo descent looked down on Irish immigrants
and African Americans. One of the best-known criminals of the 1820s, Ann
Carson, condemned the poor Irish and black women she shared time with in
prison. In her narrative, Carson presented herself in contrast to them, as a
truly refined woman who aspired to wealth, education, social respectability,
and republican motherhood.[104]

Reformers from Massachusetts to Virginia took pride in the small numbers of locals or natives who populated their prisons. This proved to be the
case in Walnut Street Prison, where only 6 percent of the women were born
in Philadelphia and 12 percent in Pennsylvania.[105] Only a small percentage
of African American women in Walnut Street were Philadelphia-born.
Officials used records of "birth" to determine residence, refusing to
acknowledge the reality of life in an era of tremendous disruption and
mobility. While few of these women were born locally, nearly all lived and
worked in Philadelphia or Pennsylvania homes for years, sometimes for
more than a decade. This suggests that African Americans with local ties
and support could avoid the harshest condemnations. It was true that U.S.-
born women of European descent were rarely convicted of crimes. Even
first generation Americans descended from Irish, German, or English-born
parents were likely to be spared the harshest condemnation offered up by

all-white judges and jurors. These statistics perpetuated the belief that crime and criminality lay beyond the purview of locals and were brought into communities by foreigners. Prisons were meant to protect locals from outsiders. For a period, then, Irish and African American women were united as "foreigners" and "outsiders" in the eyes of elites, moralists, constables, judges, and jailers, who treated them as belonging to the same class of useless and immoral people who disrupted their communities. The only decade when black women were not the majority of convicts was the 1790s, when European immigrants were the majority. The majority of the foreign born were from Ireland, with England a distant second. Only a handful of Germans, Dutch, Scottish, and Spanish were ever convicted, despite the high rates of German immigration and the sizable German neighborhood in the Northern Liberties area. Germans in Philadelphia were known for their strong work ethic and "peaceful character."[106] When only those convicts born in the United States are considered, black women made up even a higher overall percentage of those convicted.

Despite the many connections between African American and Irish women, African American women were treated worse when it came to sentencing and pardons. The most common sentence for larceny from 1795 until 1815 was one year. In the 1820s, this dropped to six months. Black women were more frequently convicted of minor charges than white women, resulting in a disproportionate number of black women receiving sentences of less than one year: in 1815, seventeen black women and five white women were sentenced to less than one year. Black women were also more likely than white women to receive the longest sentences. On average, nearly twice as many black women as white women were sentenced to two years or more. White women were rarely sentenced for two years or longer even for the most serious crimes. People of African descent were also more likely to be sentenced to solitary confinement than whites and slightly less likely to receive pardons.[107] All in all, they were rarely given the benefit of the doubt (as U.S.-born white women were) at any point in their interaction with the penal system. These subtle patterns of racial discrimination gave way to more explicit discrimination in the 1820s. In 1823, when the average length of sentences for larceny was reduced to six months, 45 percent of African American women benefited from this shift, compared to 65 percent of white women.[108]

Those sent to Walnut Street Prison were registered in a logbook by the clerk. The act incorporating the penitentiary called for prison keepers to maintain a record of "the names of their crimes, the term of their servitude, in what court condemned, the ages and the description of the persons of such as shall appear to be too old and infirm, or otherwise incapable to undergo hard labor."[109] The law did not officially require designation of the race or sex of the convicts. The prison sentence docket itself contained columns for the following categories: Name, Age, Court, Date, Crime, Sentence, Prosecutor, Description, Age, and the date and terms of their release. The Description column could include a range of information—or none at all. It might list a woman's race, place of birth, color of her hair or eyes, or any distinguishing feature. In rare cases it identified a woman's occupation and current or former employer. Sometimes it mentioned a woman's request or desire to stay in the city or go home to her parents. The most interesting feature is the way race and/or place of birth were sometimes mentioned—and how the language used to describe these things changed over time.[110]

During the 1790s and the first decade of the 1800s, race was listed as a description only for women of African descent. A number of different terms were used, including "negress," "negroe," "mulatto," "mulattress," and "black." "Negress" was by far the most common designation. It was always used for slaves—signaled by those listed with first names only—and sometimes for others as well. This racial designation was also gendered, as the masculine term "negroe" was rarely used describing women. Similarly, from 1794 to 1805, "mulatress" was used more commonly than "mulatto." Both "mulatress" and "negress" were categories rooted in slavery. In these early decades, the variations in terminology allowed for some degree of interpretation on the part of the clerk to classify the women. A number of factors, including place of birth, occupation, status as slave, servant, or free, and even skin tone would determine what language a clerk used. As the numbers of slaves in Pennsylvania waned, however, terminology in reference to African Americans became condensed. "Mulatress" was last used in 1804, and "negress" in 1807. As both "negress" and "mulatress" fell out of usage, they were replaced by the categories "coloured" and "yellow" and "black" and "mulatto." This signaled several important developments. First, gendered distinctions were falling out of usage as men and women were given similar descriptors. African American elites, organizers, and activists of the period used the term "African" when naming their organizations and churches, signifying shared ancestry and culture. This term never appears in the prison records, suggesting prisoners did not declare their racial identification; rather clerks assigned race to inmates based on their own assessment. Additionally, the term "African" held a certain amount of cultural authority in its use by elites that was probably not deemed appropriate in the description of prisoners. In the aftermath of slavery, color rather than status became the central signifier to mark African Americans. Free people increasingly described themselves as "colored" or even "black" after 1820. Penal records ignore the category of "colored" and instead embrace a stark dichotomy: black or white.[111] As time passed, fewer people were marked as yellow or mulatto, and more and more people of African descent were lumped under one category: black. The shifting language of race in the prison records reveals the development and solidification of a racial binary in the broader culture. The instability of racial categories between 1780 and 1810—an important period of change, contestation, and possibility—was foreclosed.

Only when the language used to describe African Americans was consolidated into the category "black" did the category "white" emerge.[112] Literally, no one was named "white" in the records before this turn, with one exception. Mary Wolfe was a twenty-one-year-old native Philadelphian convicted of receiving stolen goods in 1802. Her description, "A white girl born in this city, stout made, brown hair," marks whiteness a decade prior to its solidification as a class.[113] Whiteness came into being in response to and as a counter to blackness. Previously, women of European descent were listed by birthplace without any mention of race. In this era of sharper divides between those of African and European descent, even women native to Europe became identified as "white." In the first twenty years of the penitentiary, Irish and African American women shared a status as the poorest, most reviled, most highly incarcerated women in the young nation. The creation of whiteness signaled opportunity for Irish women and devastation for black women. With a linguistic turn, Irish women—those previously classified as foreigners—became white at a crucial moment. In the new racial order of the young nation, whiteness signified citizenship and inclusion. Racial classification—previously a category reserved for women of African descent—would apply to everyone now. While English and Irish women were previously designated distinctly by birthplace for decades, they now shared the racial designation of whiteness, as most were labeled "white woman" from 1815 on. Most Irish who arrived between 1815 and 1830 were from Ulster, and many did not even speak English.[114] While some of them stumbled, struggled, and lived on the margins of society, in and out of the almshouse, prison, and hospital, trying to survive, only rarely did their descendants follow in their footsteps. As more and more Irish put down roots and became assimilated to American culture, they were less likely to get caught in the crosshairs of the penal system. One reason for this was the improved economic prospects provided by manufactories being built throughout the Philadelphia region. The chief rising industries—shoes, textiles, and metals—largely excluded black women but served as a springboard for economic advancement of many immigrants.[115] As Irish and native-born white women were transformed into the wage labor force of early industrialization, black women were left behind and further criminalized.[116]

This new system of racial classification existed side by side with the old one, at least for a short time. Women could be both European and white—two categories that would later become conflated. Two women convicted in 1815 from North Wales in England were designated "white," while another woman from Liverpool was designated "English."[117] By 1823, however, the new system replaced the old. Women from all parts of England, even Liverpool, were white, as were Irish women and native-born people of European descent. While much has been written about racial hostility against the Irish in the antebellum period, these records suggest at least the small ways they were already being assimilated into white American culture and privileged above African Americans in meaningful ways. This bifurcation of race made things even worse for African Americans at a time when they were moving to Philadelphia in greater numbers. While those newly arrived in Philadelphia as free people or escaping slavery were more vulnerable than others, most blacks struggled to find work in anything but the most poorly compensated fields. Despite the fact that they worked as merchants selling rags, when two black women, Rachel Cooper and Ann Williams, were found with a bag of white rags, they were charged with theft. The reporter snidely remarked, "Not being satisfied with collecting merchandize through the day, they turned their minds to the much cheaper method of obtaining them by night."[118] Black women engaged in marginal economies were always suspect and rarely given the benefit of innocence by policing authorities. African American women were always under the watchful gaze of town authorities.

Perhaps most significantly, black women were represented in greater numbers in the prison population than black men. In 1800, blacks made up 30.6 percent of the overall prison population, while black women made up

45 percent of the women. Blacks were the majority of inmates overall by 1835, when Walnut Street Prison closed, but black women comprised the majority of women as early as 1803 and then consistently for years afterward.[119] On the other hand, white men continued to outnumber black men in prison, often by a two-to-one margin. For example, in 1818, there were 176 white men to 71 black men, and in 1821, 175 white men to 73 black men. While black men were still incarcerated disproportionately to their percentage in the population, black women carried the burden of the racial antagonism of the courts.[120] This harsh fact was obscured by public representation of prisoners as male.

Several larger forces contributed to the hardening of categories of racial difference inside the prison. Whites became increasingly vocal in their opposition to living peaceably with free blacks, even in Pennsylvania. This was manifest in formal lectures that challenged environmentalist theories of racial difference in favor of older, proposed legislation that would restrict the admission of free blacks into the state, and a growing colonization movement that promoted anecdotes of African American criminality to bolster its cause. In the decades preceding the War of Independence, environmentalist theories that situated the cause of African American inferiority in their limited access to education, culture, and free society prevailed. While the fundamental tenet of this theory was still racist—rooted in a belief that Africans were inferior to Europeans—it was progressive in that it held the social and economic forces of oppression responsible for this distinction. Riding the wave of Enlightenment thought, environmentalism largely supplanted older models of racial inferiority rooted in essentialist understandings of race, gender, and sexuality. But environmentalism lost traction as an explanatory model for racial difference in the 1810s.[121] Dr. Charles Caldwell was one of the people who attacked the environmentalist theory of racial difference, in a series of lectures, making space once again for an essentialist racist discourse.[122]

In 1813, Philadelphia officials including the mayor and aldermen introduced legislation that would restrict the passage and rights of free blacks in the state. Chiefly, they called for African Americans who broke the law to be sold by the state for a term of indenture to cover costs of restitution along with the registration of all free blacks.[123] Black leaders did what they could to challenge the legality and morality of these laws on numerous counts. Sailmaker James Forten spoke out passionately against the restriction of free blacks in Pennsylvania. The law would require all free blacks to register and carry proof of their registration at all times in addition to denying admittance to the state of any more free blacks. Worst of all, a person without papers would be imprisoned and sold into slavery. The threat of this proposal was so draconian and real that those arguing against it had to concede a fair number of points, including the idea that a strong penal system for the punishment of those disorderly among the community of free blacks was just and right. In his now famous essay, *Letters from a man of Colour*, the African American sailmaker, businessman, and lifelong freeman James Forten begged for the preservation of freedom for Pennsylvania's black community by calling for severe punishment of criminals. Forten's appeal makes four major points: impoverished former slaves deserve help, not punishment; there are esteemed men like him who are special and should be recognized as such; it is fine to punish black criminals to the maximum legal standard, I don't care; and the policing authorities cannot be trusted not to abuse their authority.

Forten's plea for help called for the support and protection of the citizens of Pennsylvania: "Where shall the poor African look for protection, should the people of Pennsylvania consent to oppress him?"[124] He appeals to their alleged sense of sensibility. Second, Forten pointed out that black men who own property, pay taxes, and are good citizens should not be subject to discriminatory treatment. Again, he positioned himself on the side of the authorities: "The villainous part of the community, of all colours, we wish to see punished and retrieved as much as any people can. Enact laws to punish them severely, but do not let them operate against the innocent as well as the guilty."[125] Forten argued that the criminal system already allowed for swift and forceful punishment of those who violated the law. Rather than police blacks, he argued, the state should police bad guys. He called for a strong system of laws and justice, stating, "We wish not to screen the guilty from punishment, but with the guilty do not permit the innocent to suffer."[126] Forten felt compelled to draw a line between good and bad blacks to get his point across to the punitive state legislature. Even black elites were resigned to the fact that a strong system of policing and punishment would be necessary conditions of freedom—and they hoped for at least a modicum of fairness. Even so, no abuse of penal authority could compare to slavery, or so Forten implied. Finally, Forten pointed out that police and jailors should not be trusted to carry out such a law, making a final appeal—"Men of feeling, read this!"—underscoring the point. Forten claimed the constable was already known to have great "antipathy" toward African Americans and would abuse this legislation to exact vengeance.

Forten was one of the earliest black elites who strategically distanced himself from the relationship between African Americans and criminal justice so as to further the cause of civil rights.[127] The fact that Forten had to concede so much in his plea signals how far anti-black sentiment had risen in just a short time. Leading abolitionists who had become uneasy with the prospect of free blacks in society joined in the growing racial antipathy, sometimes embracing colonization as the solution to slavery's end. Statesman and abolitionist Tench Coxe joined the chorus of men whose earlier sympathies for slaves did not translate into compassion and understanding for the plight of free blacks. Rather, over a period of twenty years, Coxe went from embracing environmental theories of racial difference to becoming a blatant racist—and he was not alone.[128]

Criminality thus became a place where race was constituted. Many cited incidents of black crime as a justification for their racism. Colonization advocate James Mease held free blacks responsible for the increase in property crimes in the 1820s. Mease proposed transportation for convicts, as was long practiced by the British. One "good effect" of this he claimed was "to relieve the country of the vicious part of the free black population, the increase of which, and the evils thereof, are obvious to all."[129] His perspective was increasingly common among those who saw slavery's evils but still held African Americans to be distinct and inferior.

This shift in attitudes about racial difference was reflected in institutional record keeping. Changing views of racial difference can be found in other areas of institutional life as well. While clerks consolidated the number of words used to identify African Americans in the official institutional record book, visiting reformers and Inspectors introduced a system of counting and classifying inmates by race. Reformers first took this step in 1808 when the PSAMPP Acting Committee reported, "In the east wing 96 untried prisoners, of whom 41 are negroes, many of these unfortunate creatures are in want of shirts and blankets—In the west wing are confined 46 females, some of whom stand in need of shifts and blankets."[130] This report highlights the gendered racial ideology that reformers embraced, noting the race of men, but not that of women. In 1809, Roberts Vaux and Thomas Wistar, on behalf of the Acting Committee, found "confined in the east wing 74 persons about 40 of whom are negroes and 37 female prisoners in the vagrant ward of the west wing—the men are many of them without shirts and otherwise poorly clad. Most of the women have no shifts."[131] Again, the race of the women was not worth mentioning, suggesting that even white women had little reform potential. The absence of concern regarding the race of women persisted for years, signaling general neglect of women and heightened attention to both the reformation potential of white men and the degradation of black men—and the need to keep them apart. In 1810, Inspectors began paying greater attention to race as a collective category. They tried to introduce racial segregation among the men in an attempt to institute order and break up alliances between Irish and African Americans.[132] But systemic segregation was still not an official policy, and attempts at segregation were easily undermined by circumstance. For example, when the Inspectors aimed to ease the overcrowding of "The Black Convicts Men's lodging rooms" they sacrificed racial segregation among the boys, noting, "This will be an encroachment on the well directed intention of the Board, in the separation of the black from the white boys."[133] Racial segregation was enforced formally, informally, and inconsistently throughout the prison.

As years passed, the process of classifying and counting inmates became ever more refined, including categories of race, sex, and sometimes age. This served the greater compulsion for mastery through precise quantification of people and objects. Furthermore, each encounter between inmates and the Inspectors, as they went about classifying and counting inmates, served as a scene of subjection that reinscribed the powerlessness of the counted.[134] In 1814, they described the subjects of their visits as follows: "73 men are confined in the east wing 47 of whom are negroes—in the West wing are 54 female prisoners, 30 of whom are black women."[135] In 1817, reformers identified prisoners by race, sex, crime, and age. In January 1820, this elaborate system provided the following description of the prison's 454 inmates: "Of these 251 were white men, 12 white Boys (under 18 yrs of age) 127 Coloured men, 10 Coloured boys, 22 white women, 2 white girls, 28 Coloured women, & 2 Coloured girls."[136] Reformers were interested in dividing groups of prisoners into ever more atomized subgroups. This came at a time when more general efforts to segregate prisoners by criminal classification were failing, leading most Inspectors and reformers to believe reform would never succeed at Walnut Street and that solitary confinement was the only way to prevent mixing among prisoners. Further itemization of inmates based on sex, race, and age only extended and intensified the process of objectification.

This reporting also reveals that black men were more likely than white men to have a period of solitary confinement as part of their sentence. While the report counted 251 white men and 127 black men in the prison overall in 1820, black men in the solitary cells outnumbered white men three to one. Visitors reported, "In one cell 6 Blackmen, in 2 Cells 3 blackmen each, and in one 4 white men." Interestingly, this number did not include the other 13 men who were deemed "refractory prisoners in Irons, who had attempted an escape" and were also held in the cells. This group—deemed the worst of all—was not racialized. Neither were the vagrants, whom visitors reported by age and sex, stating vagrant wards contained "158 males & 61 females; of these 12 were boys & 6 girls."[137] Racial classification was not made among the vagrants, described as a "motley crew" who lived and worked together with "very little distinction made as to colour or crime."[138] This heightened attention to naming race, counting people by race and gender, and segregating by race and age when possible developed quietly, slowly, and inconsistently—in stark contrast to how sexual difference was managed.

The slow movement toward racial segregation reveals the gendered nature of the racial ideology that shaped institutional practice. Race as the basis for segregation was most important in the ordering of male convicts. The organization of women by race began in 1814, coinciding with the consolidation of the language of race into "white" and "black." But that still did not mean women were segregated along racial lines. Just as women were encouraged to help each other, they also worked, ate, and roomed together regardless of race. As late as the 1820s, convict women still worked and dined together across racial lines in Walnut Street—even if they were counted and named separately.[139] This gendered racism was also mediated by age. Racial segregation among young boys was considered more important than among women but less important than among men. This pattern reveals the true aims and limits of reform. White men needed to be protected from everyone else, as they had both the greatest burden and the greatest potential for change. Children needed to be protected from adults as much as possible, even if it meant mixing children of different races together. An intersectional hierarchy of needs, expectations, and potential was woven through the prison, manipulating treatment of inmates based on age, race, and sex. Faced with undeniable evidence that the penal system was not reforming most of its inmates, reformers, judges, and Inspectors blamed the increasingly black inmate population. The belief that African

Americans were unreformable served to justify their segregation, isolation, and increasingly inhumane treatment in prison. Black men were separated from white men—and eventually black boys were singled out when space permitted. As black men were constituted outside liberal subjecthood by virtue of their perceived unreformability, imprisonment came to both signal and justify their exclusion from democratic personhood.

Essentialist views of racial difference were increasingly promoted as part of the colonization movement. When speaking before a meeting of the American Colonization Society in Newark in 1827, a Rev. Speaker condemned the incidents of black crime, advancing an essentialist viewpoint. Editors of *Freedom's Journal*, however, challenged his evidence. They asserted that three out of four crimes committed by black men were "grown out of the circumstances of his condition." Furthermore, the editor argued that white criminality was actually more pernicious and threatening. White male criminals were more "premeditated and vicious."[140] The editors made an important point that fewer and fewer people were willing to make: the imprisonment of African Americans did not show they were "more subject to crime, or their characters more debased" but rather reflected the misuse of punishment.[141]

In hindsight, it is easy to see how racism grew in the North through this period of political anxiety and economic stagnation. Visitors such as Alexis de Tocqueville observed that racial hostility was "stronger" in states that abolished slavery.[142] Fear of both European immigration and migration among free blacks was heightened in the 1820s. In New York City, someone complained that the influx of poor newcomers would overwhelm the system of public alms, stating, "The whites and blacks are pouring into our city from all quarters, and unless speedily removed will get such a footing by obtaining what is in law called a settlement, that it will be impossible for the commissioners of the Almshouse to get them away."[143] Perception was often different from reality, especially when it came to racial stereotypes and notions of dependency. Abolitionists collected data on African American people and communities, from literacy rates to employment categories, to neighborhood residence and more. Even though free blacks suffered in the worst jobs with the fewest opportunities for apprenticeships or training in skilled work, in 1832 they made up only 4 percent of those who received poor relief either in the almshouse or through outdoor relief.[144] Furthermore, they also made up a very small number of those convicted of serious crimes.[145]

Physical attacks on groups of African Americans became frequent, and the community was forced to constantly defend itself, navigate, and survive in face of this regular onslaught.[146] The church, a crucial part of the community's support and resilience, also became a target of attack.[147] Assaults on the black church struck at the heart of the community. Public complaints about noise and activity around black churches were sensationally criminalized. A group of whites attacked blacks in 1829 for being too loud during a church service.[148] Blacks who congregated outside the church were described as "noisy and riotous mobs" and subject to arrest in response to complaints from neighbors. One report assured readers that "ten or a dozen of the insurgents" were arrested, and this policing would continue nightly.[149] Associations between African Americans and criminality served to justify the extreme regulation of black public and social spaces, penalizing black civic culture. While groups of white or black women were charged with "rioting" in the 1790s, by the 1820s, this designation was reserved for black women alone.[150] All of the women found guilty of rioting in the 1820s and 1830s were African American.[151]

Worst of all was the ease with which people came to conflate black freedom with crime. Beaumont and Tocqueville famously observed, "The states which have many Negroes must therefore produce more crime."[152] They identified newfound freedom as the cause of black criminality, asserting that African Americans did not know how to use their minds and make good decisions for themselves. Freedom of thought, they claimed, was dangerous, asserting, "The day when liberty is granted to him, he receives an instrument, which he does not know how to use, and with which he wounds, if not kills himself."[153] Like many American abolitionists, they blamed slavery for creating the conditions that nurtured ignorance, but still viewed black crime through an individual psychological lens rather than a social and structural one.

In 1831, when Nat Turner inspired a group of his fellow enslaved Virginians to rise up against their captors, the dream of the enslaved and the fear of free whites were realized. With sixty whites dead at the hands of the enslaved, retaliation was swift, excessive, and widespread. The execution of Turner, his followers, and nearly 100 innocent slave bystanders was only the beginning. The rebellion fueled the colonization movement, providing justification for its agenda to remove all people of African descent from America. Shortly after the incident, a group met to formulate a petition to the Pennsylvania state legislature mandating colonization based on the idea

that free blacks in the North inspired the rebellion of enslaved.[154] William
Robinson served as chairman of the group that deemed colonization essential "for the maintenance of good order, a respectful observance of the laws,
the preservation of moral principle, religion, and our very union," thereby
giving up any claim that free blacks had to America.[155] The free black abolitionist movement quickly responded, claiming there was no evidence whatsoever that free blacks "have stirred up the slaves to insurrection."
Furthermore, they challenged the breadth and justification of the call to
colonization. "A colored man, born in the United States, has not more
affinity with Africa than he has with China; and if he has committed no
crime, he cannot be sent thither involuntarily."[156] But if he did commit a
crime, he would remain in America and lose any rights he once had
through incarceration.

The incarceration of African American women and men at higher rates
than whites sent a clear message about the limits of the freedom they would
experience in America.[157] But numerous groups of whites still viewed themselves as friends of justice and equal treatment for African Americans. To
better understand how the promise of freedom was eclipsed over and over
in various realms of society, we will consider one specific moment of hope
that proved short-lived. Long denied admittance to prison reform work,
female reformers found their cause in the 1820s when they discovered that
very young children were imprisoned alongside older and "hardened"
criminals. Female reformers projected purity and innocence onto those
children who were imprisoned, and argued this as the basis for their separation from others. They worried about "quite young girls, who were committed sometimes for trivial offences, and who were thus exposed, (for
there was no classification) to the company of women who were hardened
in crime."[158] They sought to prevent the situation in which "boys and girls,
inexperienced in vice, comparably innocent, and confined perhaps by hard
masters and mistresses for disobedience or neglect, associated with convicts,
hardened by age and abandoned to the basest crimes."[159] The group successfully lobbied for the establishment of a juvenile detention center as a
substitute for prison. Under the influence of the Association of Women
Friends, PSAMPP opened the House of Refuge in 1828 to help reform juvenile delinquents. Roberts Vaux promoted public education in part as a way
to prevent crime—and the House of Refuge as a way to steer children away
from a life of crime. As Vice President of the Board of Managers for the
House, he wrote the update on the new institution and solicited support

for its work. "So long as the House of Refuge remains an unfinished structure, the Penitentiary System of Pennsylvania, which is so justly her pride,
will be incomplete."[160] The House officially opened on November 29, 1828,
and quickly admitted a fourteen-year-old boy and "thus rescued it is con-
fidently hoped from the evils of a common prison."[161] The institution's
population quickly swelled—fifty-seven boys and twenty-three girls in 1829
and eleven boys and twenty-nine girls in 1830. They implemented a gendered division of labor in which boys were "employed in book-binding,
basket-making and wicker-works, shoemaking, tailoring, and carpenters'
work" while girls were employed "in sewing, washing, ironing, mending,
cooking, and housework generally."[162] Its Philadelphia location aimed to
serve where "the danger of idleness and crime is the most imminent."[163]
While Quaker women pushed for this organization, men still ran it. John
Sergeant served as president, while Vaux and Alexander Henry were vice
presidents. Women in leadership were designated part of the "Women's
Committee," headed by Margaret M. Collins, directress, Sarah Grimke,
treasurer, and Emily Smith, secretary. The Grand Inquest for the Court of
Oyer and Terminer in 1831 visited the House of Refuge and declared it "in
excellent condition" and, furthermore, asserted that it "be regarded as a
valuable auxiliary for the prevention of crime, and highly beneficial for
reforming the morals of the juvenile delinquents."[164]

Astonishingly, however, black children were refused admission. This is
not mentioned in the official report at all but can be inferred from two
sources. A survey of the plight of free blacks by abolitionists noted that the
high number of black men in prison in 1832 was a result of the exclusion of
black boys from the House of Refuge. While white boys under twenty-one
were removed from the prison to the house, black boys were "shut out."[165]
White girls were transferred from the prison to the house up to only age
eighteen. But even the abolitionist report neglected to mention the impact
of this practice on black girls who were also excluded. A later reflection on
the beginning of women's involvement in penal reform noted the role of
Quaker women in establishing the House: "They had the great satisfaction
of seeing the important object gained, at least so far as respects white children."[166] The refusal to admit black children into the House of Refuge also
served to inflate the percentage of prisoners who were black. Abolitionists
pointed this out in their 1838 report, claiming that to compare the number
of men of each race responsible for crime, one must also add in "all white
minor offenders" who were sent to the House of Refuge.[167]

By this time, two things were apparent: African Americans were disproportionately represented among inmates of both sexes, and education would be the key to the future hopes of black freedom. Abolitionists believed educational opportunities were vital: "The descendants of those who were brought into our country by force, and compelled to constant labour, with little attention to the cultivation of their minds, have a just claim upon us for instruction and assistance, to endeavor to render them more capable of encountering the difficulties of ignorance and poverty, and of becoming useful citizens."[168] By denying young African Americans convicted of their first offense the opportunity for special care, protection, and instruction reserved for white children who also crossed the line, officials authorized a cruel distinction. Black children born into freedom in America were treated more harshly than the many young European immigrant children who were taken in.[169]

Once the Abolition Society began studying institutional records and grand jury orders, the extent to which the penal system openly and flagrantly discriminated against African Americans became painfully clear. In 1837, of the 737 African Americans held on charges, only 123 were brought to trial, suggesting the remaining 614 were dismissed for lack of evidence or witnesses or even real charges in the first place. Even the Grand Jury of the Court of Quarter Sessions for Philadelphia acknowledged the rampant problem of magistrates widely imprisoning people on petty to nonexistent charges just to get them to pay a small fee. "The course pursued by many of the magistrates in Southwark and Moyamensing, is truly astonishing; it would seem that they are in the habit of committing individuals, who appear to be almost *pennyless* and *destitute* to prison, on the most frivolous grounds (merely for the sake of private employment)."[170] Poor African Americans were often unable to round up the necessary funds from family and friends for their release.

The hardening of racial categories was reflected in the organization of prison life as well. Some scholars believe greater racial collaboration and harmony existed within the prison than without, even during the tumultuous period from 1815 to 1830, because no riot or battle was organized along racial lines, and that may have been the case.[171] But institutional authorities were deeply invested in segregating prisoners by race. Black and white inmates were no longer even permitted to sit on the same benches in prison.[172] Together, race and sex segregation efforts in prison gradually formalized the groupings and hierarchies that increasingly ordered society.

Racial segregation inside the prison reinforced a dividing line between those former and future citizens targeted by reformative incarceration and those denied access to both citizenship and civic life.

Prison officials and reformers avoided discussing the role of race in punishment or the role of punishment in race relations because they could. No one dared declare penal authority was a tool to discipline and control free blacks, because calls for liberty and equality for all still lingered in the air. But they did not have to. Once blacks and whites were declared entitled to the same standing before the courts, the larger structural bias against African American economic prospects, social standing, and political rights all but ensured they would be incarcerated at higher rates than whites.

*　　*　　*

The broader culture became increasingly invested in theories that essentialized racial difference in the 1820s. While inmates in Walnut Street were classified chiefly by sex and then race, the practice was reversed in Eastern State. The 1845 Board of Inspectors report counting numbers of inmates listed them primarily by race—344 were "white" and 153 "coloured," for a total of 497 inmates that year.[173] The presence of men or women in each category was secondary, particularly as women numbered only 19 of the "white" people and 21 of the "coloured." The language of race remained flexible. Walnut Street records revealed use of the category "white" happened in direct relationship to the consolidation of multiple gendered racial categories into one—"black." While "white" persisted throughout the antebellum period as a seemingly stable category, references to people of African descent were open to personal bias and social manipulation—and a reemergence of the term "coloured." This meant little for actual incarceration rates. Black men were still imprisoned at rates significantly higher than white men, but black women became the face—and majority—of women in the penitentiary.

The penitentiary proved impervious to any amount of resistance, mismanagement, or abuse because political rhetoric could always distract the public from and give justification for the suffering and violation of real people. Political and social elites in Pennsylvania walked a fine line as champions of both punishment and abolition. Publicly fashioning themselves as friends of slaves in a period of heightened national controversy and tension about the future of slavery, those most involved with the penitentiary were unable to speak openly about popular theories of African American inferiority. Prison reformers from the 1820s and 1830s were known to have joined in the colonization movement. It should come as no surprise, then, that the threat of imprisonment loomed large over African Americans who resisted attempts to be removed to Africa. The failure of the colonization movement only inspired the expansion of penal authority, laying the foundation for a carceral state that has stigmatized, criminalized, and destroyed African American individuals, families, and communities ever since.

CHAPTER 5

~

Sexual Orderings

THE NEXUS BETWEEN sex and power throughout history is so ubiquitous that it can be difficult to see. It was manifested in a number of interesting ways in early American punishment.[1] The regulation of sexual activity within the prison heightened as punishments for many sexual crimes were relaxed. American reformers celebrated the fact that the new penal code was defined by logic, restraint, and fairness. To highlight this point, they emphasized that colonial British punishments for crimes such as sodomy, rape, and infanticide were characterized as excessive, punitive, and vengeful. By the early nineteenth century, American urban centers were defined by relatively relaxed sexual attitudes, in which sex outside marriage, frequenting of prostitutes, and single motherhood were accepted parts of life.[2] Frenchman Moreau de St. Méry stocked his bookshop with contraceptives intended for the many French colonials who sought refuge in Philadelphia, only to find Americans purchasing them in great numbers as well.[3] Protection from legal prosecution, however, did not signal widespread social approval. Sex between people of different races, people of the same sex, in exchange for money, or with someone other than one's spouse were still frowned on by religious leaders, reformers, and elites, even though everyone knew someone doing it. Sexual freedoms easily enjoyed by those beyond the reach of policing authorities by virtue of their class were denied to immigrants, African Americans, and the working poor who were closely monitored by the state.

The restriction of sexual intimacies in prison became a crucial site of discipline, functioning at the juncture of the body and the population at large.[4] Decisions about which expressions of sexuality to allow and which to punish were intimately tied to larger economic and social needs rooted in the heterosexual political economy. Initially, deviant forms of heterosexuality drew the most attention. Anxiety about corruption between different classes of prisoners became widespread, shifting the nexus of the threat from undesirable forms of heterosexual intimacies to more vaguely threatening relationships between people of the same sex. Particularly, reformers pointed to the threat of corruption across age differences: between older women and young girls or older men and young boys. This conversation was implicitly, though never explicitly, racialized, as "youth" and "innocence" were two categories defined by whiteness.[5] Later, this conversation became explicitly sexual and focused exclusively on men, in part because of the possibility for interracial sex. The fact that men engaged in "unnatural" intimacies with each other in prison came to represent everything that was wrong with the penitentiary, leaving solitary confinement as the only solution.[6] While different forms of intimacy were marked for regulation over time, each of these helped to establish new beliefs about sexuality. Heaping blame on women for embodying lustful desire and seducing men, this paradigm finally wore out its usefulness, in part because it left no room to reform men and their actions. Instead, this belief morphed over time, as people came to believe that men were the bearers of a natural innate sexual impulse, while women and children were innately innocent. One particular manifestation of this view emerged at the heart of international debates about prison design and the limits of reformative incarceration: the idea that men were now extensively and uncontrollably engaged in sexual intimacies with each other. The confines of punishment itself encouraged more widespread embrace of a previously taboo sexuality, creating the justification for an ever more punitive and expansive penal state.

British Barbarism

Pennsylvania Attorney General William Bradford played a key role in distinguishing the penal philosophy of the United States from that of Great Britain through extensive reflection on the purpose and effectiveness of punishment. At the request of the governor, Bradford wrote an essay summarizing the changes to the state penal code up to 1793.[7] In the essay, Bradford saved his harshest words not for those guilty of the most serious crimes but for the actions of Great Britain throughout the course of its colonial rule over Pennsylvania. He noted that founder William Penn's more humane laws were repealed by the queen, leaving Pennsylvania ruled by British laws from 1718 to 1786.[8] Bradford condemned Britain for threatening to destroy the young colony "with a mass of sanguinary punishments hardly endurable in an old, corrupted and populous country."[9] In emphasizing British barbarism, Bradford aimed to strengthen alliances among Pennsylvania's elite, legislators, reformers, and laborers and create a common enemy who could be easily blamed for many troubling legacies that might threaten the weak democracy, including excessive punishment and slavery.

The legacy of British barbarism lived on decades after independence because it served as a much-needed counterweight to democratic reforms.[10] British barbarism made American reform seem humane. Only by repeatedly looking to the past and producing an oversimplified characterization of colonial punishment could contemporary changes—fraught, contested, and of questionable success—become symbolic of something larger, better, and futuristic. Liberal reformers may not have been exaggerating Britain's penchant for excessive violence, but they also let their Quaker ancestors off the hook about what happened in Penn's colony.[11] A central subject of complaint among post-Revolutionary reformers was Britain's excessive reliance on the death penalty for as many as one hundred different crimes.[12] After the war, there were still thirteen capital crimes on the books, including "treason, murder, manslaughter by stabbing, serious maiming, highway robbery, burglary, arson, sodomy, buggery, rape, concealing the death of a bastard child, advising the killing of such a child and witchcraft."[13] Crimes with a sexual dimension, including rape, sodomy, and infanticide, became the basis for disavowing British barbarism.[14] Bradford set out to define America as different from and better than Britain because of its more lenient punishment of crimes stemming from sexual excess. This gesture signaled the complicated and central place of sex in carving out the new social and economic order.

The celebration of American sexual exceptionalism in debates over capital punishment highlights the importance of gender in punishment. One manifestation of this was Bradford's emphasis on the innateness of both female innocence and male lust, an idea that would have been soundly rejected not long before. Bradford explained this development and its larger significance for the penal system in his writings on infanticide, rape, and sodomy. Bradford played a significant role in the penal reforms and went on to become attorney general of the United States in 1794.[15] While his condemnation of Britain was overly simplified, his praise of William Penn strategic, and his characterization of his own generation's accomplishments overblown, Bradford, wittingly or not, set out a new sexual order. He laid the foundation for the protection of white men's sexual excess under law—and the denial of sexual desire for women of all races.[16]

Bradford argued that punishment for infanticide was a keen example of British barbarity. The long-standing Pennsylvania law of 1718 charging women who were found to have concealed the death of their child with murder, regardless of the evidence, had originated in England in 1624.[17] Infanticide was the only violent crime more often committed by women than by men.[18] Despite the "horrid severity" of this law, Bradford claimed that jurists had begun to introduce the "humane *practice* of requiring some proof that the child was born alive."[19] Even during the colonial period, however, very few women were convicted of infanticide. Between 1763 and 1790, just thirty-four women were charged with infanticide, and only five were executed.[20] The conflict between the letter of the law and judicial discretion was long a source of contention, as Pennsylvanians frequently levied accusations of corruption against judges for misuse of their power. In this instance, however, Bradford felt judicial intervention was necessary to protect women from a vicious law. He relied on logic to demonstrate the fallacy of convicting a woman without positive evidence of murder. He wrote, "May not the child perish from want of care, or of skill, in so critical a moment? A helpless woman, in a situation so novel and so alarming—alone, and perhaps, exhausted by her sufferings—May she not be the involuntary cause of her infants death?"[21] He positioned himself—and American independence—not only on the side of logic, restraint, and fairness, but also on the side of women. He sympathized with a young mother, overwhelmed by childbirth and without the skills necessary to take care of her infant. For Bradford, an enlightened penal code presumed the innocence of a weak woman instead of her guilt. Even if the child died because of her ignorance and fatigue, the American penal system would give the woman the benefit of the doubt. This new view of womanhood—that it was inherently weak and innocent rather than corrupt and debase—was just beginning to take hold, having been absent from similar conversations just ten years earlier.

The idea of female innocence developed out of larger social and scientific efforts to establish women as fundamentally different from—and weaker than—men. The long-standing one-sex model of humanity gave way to a two-sex model in the eighteenth century. What marked men and women as distinct shifted from culturally prescribed gender roles to biologically rooted sexual differences.[22] This concept created a new challenge in rape trials where women might previously have been considered responsible for seduction; now the fact of female innocence compelled another look. As Sharon Block has shown, however, a double standard endured that held women responsible even though belief in everywoman's inherent lustfulness was waning.[23] On the one hand, Bradford felt that it was natural that men would want to protect female innocence. He wrote, "Female innocence has strong claims upon our protection, and a desire to avenge its wrongs is natural to a generous and manly mind."[24] The idea of female innocence was so important to Bradford that it threatened long-standing social and legal bias in favor of white men accused of rape and other unwanted sexual intimacies. But it also had its limits.

Against convention, Bradford openly acknowledged the role of racial bias in the prosecution of rape charges, especially noting that his peers were unable to see innocence in black women. He criticized the laws that refused to grant enslaved women standing before the courts. Bradford wrote, "Why do the laws consider the violation of the female slave of so little moment as to secure the offender from punishment by excluding the only witness who can prove it?"[25] This contradiction exposed the problem of both bias and emotion in punishment, leading to an overzealous protection of white women and a total lack of protection of black women. Like so many of his contemporaries, Bradford was ambivalent about the experiences of actual black women. On the one hand, he claimed they should be deemed innocent and in need of protection, like white women. On the other hand, he scoffed at the idea of punishment for those who raped them, expressing uncertainty as to whether that would even be a violation. This vast contradiction between ideals and reality lays bare the deeply rooted cartographies of violence that justified exclusion of African Americans from legal protections.[26]

Dominant attitudes toward male sexual desire were also undergoing a transformation. For all his concern about female innocence, Bradford was far more interested in the protection of men's sexual freedom—even in cases of rape. Rape represented the culmination of what he perceived as most natural—male sexual desire for women. "This offence," he wrote, "arising from the sudden abuse of a natural passion, and perpetrated in the phrenzy of desire, does not announce any irreclaimable corruption."[27]

Because male sexual desire was natural, its excess or misdirection should not be punished.[28] This argument was a departure from expectations in Puritan New England, where the ability to control one's sexual urges was an important marker of masculinity.[29] Bradford argued that it would be unreasonable to expect the courts to punish men for acting on a natural impulse, stating, "The common sense of mankind revolts against the extremity of the punishment, and pardons or acquittals are the necessary consequence."[30] Ultimately, men's sexuality should scarcely if ever be subject to regulation, in part because white men have shown time and again their unwillingness to rule against each other in court. Black men would never face a jury of their peers and were punished with impunity on accusation of rape.

This legal justification for male sexual desire was merely an exclamation point to long-standing social realities. Everyone knew that most rape charges resulted in acquittals, with the exception of charges against black men for assaulting white women. Bradford's Virginia counterpart Edmund Randolph complained that juries "appeared to lay aside their natural abhorrence of the act, to seize the smallest symptoms of innocence," and he was right. The only innocence that seemed to matter in most rape cases was that of the man.[31] Much as American reformers disavowed British barbarity, so jurors disavowed the brutality of the violence of rape. The rare men found guilty were characterized as barbaric themselves. When the court ruled against William Lathrop in 1801 for the rape of a married woman, the conviction declared, "Such a creature as you are, is unfit for society. An enemy to chastity and virtue, you are more depraved than the savage that roams the wilderness; and in some respects are worse than a murderer."[32] The few white men convicted of rape were deemed inhuman.

By branding white male sexual desire natural or innate and seeking to protect its excess or misdirection from legal prosecution, Bradford defended not only rapists but also sodomites. Early Pennsylvania statutes established under William Penn against sodomy and buggery included both men and women, but women were never punished under these laws.[33] Sodomy and buggery became capital crimes in Pennsylvania in 1718 with the adoption of the British legal code.[34] Bestiality was met with greater disapprobation than sex between men because it evoked images of monstrous births from medieval times. Popular cultural references suggested that bestiality was a more serious crime than theft, but the will to execute offenders was lacking.[35] While sodomy was a mainstay on the lengthy list of capital crimes for most of the eighteenth century, people were rarely even charged with attempted sodomy, let alone found guilty of actual sodomy.[36] This reflects a degree of tolerance among the general public for those engaged in sodomy, but it also reflects the fact that a conviction required a high burden of proof, leaving many witnesses reluctant to formally bring evidence forward.[37] State officials were satisfied to remove sodomy and buggery from the list of capital crimes under revisions to the penal code, realizing the severity of the punishment only made it more difficult to successfully prosecute anyone. Sodomy and buggery became punishable by a ten-year prison sentence and surrender of all property, instead of by death.[38]

Sodomy and buggery were still deemed to be "crimes against nature," the worst kind of crime. In explaining why it was right to no longer punish sodomy with death, Bradford relied on proof, not ideology. He claimed that there was no evidence to support the idea that punishment by death effectively deterred people from committing sodomy—especially since men who were charged with sodomy or buggery claimed not even to know that it was a capital offense. Bradford could have rested his case here, but instead continued his reflection on the issue of male sexual desire. Pointing to marriage as a key social structure that helped prevent men from having sex with each other, Bradford wrote, "In a country where marriages take place so early, and the intercourse between the sexes is not difficult, there can be no reason for severe penalties to restrain this abuse."[39] Because men had easy and regular access to women for sex, he reasoned, they would not turn to each other to have their desires met.

The fact that men's natural sexual desire was aimed at women out of convenience and culture left the door open to a number of circumstances in which men might turn to other men for gratification.[40] Bradford claimed some men simply preferred sex with other men, citing the feelings of a man who knew sodomy was a capital crime, but did it anyway. Short of catching someone in the act, he noted, there was really no way to identify these people. Other men might turn to each other for sexual gratification when women were not around. As Regina Kunzel has shown, the concept of "situational homosexuality" was defined by social scientists in the 1940s and '50s as a way to contain the threat of homosexuality in prison by distinguishing prisoners from "true" homosexuals.[41] Bradford himself did not draw such a rigid line between the two groups. His theories left open the idea that anyone might turn to same-sex sex and anyone could enjoy or "prefer" it. He believed that certain social situations—such as the opportunity to marry at a young age—would deter men from trying it. His writings

were distributed through the country, challenging the long-standing practice of avoiding public discussion of sodomy.[42] With this gesture, Bradford
urged his peers to meet all kinds of crimes—even sodomy—with restraint
and logic rather than passion and revenge. Sodomy was not only something
that anyone might choose to engage in, but it was also simply a manifestation of men's natural sexual desire.

Of course Bradford was not writing about sodomy within a vacuum.
Other forces shaped which expressions of male sexual aggression were
appropriate as well. By the 1790s, the "pejorative effeminate sodomite" that
developed as a homoerotic type during the eighteenth century was growing
out of fashion.[43] Similarly, it was no longer socially acceptable for men to
have sex with boys.[44] Bradford used his platform to encourage this shift by
characterizing uncontrollable sexual desire for women as part of natural
masculinity. As a rule, however, same-sex sexuality, desire, and subcultures
were not really the target of legal reforms aimed at fixing the social order
in the 1790s. Bradford insisted once again that severe laws against sodomy
or buggery, like those previously used against adultery and witchcraft, were
"wholly unfit for an enlightened people of civilized and gentle manners."[45]
Instead, the state became far more invested in reining in the rampant
expressions of inappropriate heterosexual desire, such as extramarital and
interracial sex.[46]

Segregation and Corruption

The regulation of sexual intimacies was at the heart of the nationwide transformation of old jailhouses into penitentiaries. While visitors and observers
spoke passionately about the mistreatment of prisoners because of unsani-
tary conditions, limited amounts of food, and insufficient clothing and bedding, none of these issues were ever adequately addressed. Rather,
reformers targeted the behavior of prisoners and created rules that would
require inmates to demonstrate restraint and self-control. Restriction of
sexual intimacies and desires became a crucial part of reformative incarceration, as deviant forms of heterosexuality were used to bolster and stabilize
more desirable forms. Benjamin Rush characterized sexual intimacy in the
lower classes as contemptible, writing, "I wish I could add that the passion
of the sexes for each other, among those subjects of public charity, was
always gratified in a lawful way."[47] As elites cultivated a standard for sexual

desire that was controlled and channeled through marriage, they increasingly defined sexual practices of poor people as excessive and deviant.

The taming of passions became a key component of institutional discipline. In his widely cited essay "The Influence of Physical Causes upon the Moral Faculty," Benjamin Rush argued that physical experiences influenced moral reasoning in many different ways and must be curtailed. He wrote, "It is immaterial, whether the physical causes that are to be enumerated act upon the moral faculty through the medium of the senses—the passions— the memory—or the imagination. Their influence is equally certain, whether they act as remote, predisposing, or occasional causes."[48] Rush believed that the key to developing the moral faculty was to make the spirit of a man "tractable and submissive"—something much easier said than done.[49] But if the passions could be tamed through the regulation of sex, food, and alcohol, that seemed an obvious place to start.[50]

In the 1780s, the vestiges of the long-standing belief that women— particularly those of African descent and the lower classes—embodied sexual desire and danger remained. It was women's sexuality that first threatened the good order of the prison. The Grand Jury of the Court of Oyer and Terminer of Philadelphia visited Walnut Street Jail in 1787 and described a scene of debauchery, not the least due to the "general intercourse between the criminals of the different sexes" and the distribution of alcohol.[51] The report, published in the September 26, 1787, issue of the *Pennsylvania Gazette* continued, "There is not even the appearance of decency (from what they can learn) with respect to the scenes of debauchery that naturally result from such a situation." The grand jury blamed both men and women prisoners, complaining that the jail had become "such a desirable place for the more wicked and polluted of both sexes" that people signed "fictitious notes" in order to be committed. It was especially common among people who had recently been released to get recommitted as soon as possible. The jail was characterized by moral and sexual filth and chaos. This charge was one of several that moved a generation of politicians, jurists, and elites to overhaul the penal system and redefine the meaning and experience of imprisonment forever.

Appalled by the findings reported by the grand jury, the Acting Committee of PSAMPP made an official visit to inquire about the blight of the jail, which they felt "obviously originated in a too free open and unrestricted intercourse with the sexes."[52] In May 1787, the Committee reported more generally about the chaos at the jail, including the "dissipation and licentiousness diffused among all ranks in confinement, in consequence of an improper intercourse between the sexes."[53] Reformers implied both social and sexual interactions when referencing the problem of men and women intermingling, which was found among all groups of prisoners, including convicts, debtors, vagrants, and prisoners for trial.[54] Several arguments emerge from these and later attempts to regulate sex among prisoners. Illicit sexual activity represented lack of self-control, which reformation required. Women were in the way, blocking men's chances for reform. And deviant forms of heterosexuality threatened to undermine the sexual division of labor. Extramarital or interracial sex was seen as a threat to the social order that could be regulated within prison, if not outside it.

Efforts to restrict sex reflected multiple concerns about the threat to moral order. In a report to the Supreme Executive Council, PSAMPP echoed long-standing views that blamed women for sexually seducing men. The report suggests that unlike men who belonged in prison, most women were working as prostitutes and had deliberately sought arrest so they could "gain admission among the men."[55] The report also complained about the unrestricted interactions between men and women at all hours, stating, "Men and women had general intercourse with each other. And it was afterwards discovered that they were locked up together in the rooms at night." To fix this problem, PSAMPP suggested moving the women to a different section of the prison, away from the men. After a brief experiment with such separation, PSAMPP claimed that far fewer women were imprisoned—down to four or five from thirty or forty.[56] This statistic confirmed its theories. If some women did in fact have themselves sent to prison intentionally to engage in sexual activities with men for money, this was not terribly remarkable. Women had long ventured into areas dominated by men, such as seaports and military camps, to provide sex in exchange for money or goods, both within and outside the context of marriage.[57] Many poor working women supplemented their incomes by granting sexual favors.[58] The rhetoric that women had deliberately pursued imprisonment to better to engage in sex work, overshadowed the imprisonment of women for violating other gendered ideals by drinking too much, remaining unmarried, and socializing in the streets at night. This focus on women detracted from the role of class in defining access to sexual privilege among men. Elite men had long approved of each other's extramarital sexual dalliances—both actively and passively. But they thought that men in prison did not deserve such indulgences because they needed to learn to control their impulses.

While sexual restraint, virtue, and the stability of the nation became intertwined in the character of elite Anglo-American women in the post-Revolutionary period, poor and criminal women continued to represent the catalyst for men's lust.[59] Elite perceptions of the uncontrollable sexuality of poor women and black women combined with the large number of women held in prison on vagrancy charges for disorderly conduct resulted in a widely held belief that women in prison were sexually depraved.[60] This class-based bifurcation of sexual norms was advanced by Rush himself, who joked that extreme forms of government were analogous to two different types of women: "When we reject a republic, I wish we may adopt an absolute monarchy, for governments (like women, among whom it is said no one between a virtuous woman and a prostitute ought ever to please) should know no medium between absolute republicanism and absolute monarchy."[61] In the eyes of elites like Rush, women had very little room to navigate between the extremes of virtue and vice.

Women had for some time fought the assumptions that they were innately sexualized, an idea often used as justification for their sexual abuse or general mistreatment. Writing in 1779, one woman challenged the idea that women seduced men into sin, stating that this assertion seemed "calculated only to cast an odium on the fair sex." She turned the assumption upside down and challenged readers to see prostitutes for who they often were—women who were ruined by men promising them romance and marriage only to abandon them.[62] Only when it became apparent that the ideology of women's licentiousness would not serve the long-term purpose of reformative incarceration did its adherents relent. As long as women were the source of the corruption, there was little incentive to figure out how to change the men. But by marking men as those lacking self-control, a path to change and reform could be defined for male subjects/citizens.

Prostitution was not the only concern of reformers who appeared to separate women and men. A range of other sexual possibilities, including consensual sex, the chance of pregnancy, and sexual assault, may also have motivated the policy of sex segregation. The fact that any of these possibilities could have involved an interracial couple only exacerbated matters. While contemporary historians looking through the lens of heteroessential paternalism have suggested that reformers sought to separate men and women to keep women safe from the sexual advances of men, the historical record does not suggest this was the case unless we look specifically at white women and black men. The division may have incidentally protected women from some acts of coercion or violence by male inmates, but would also have left them more vulnerable to sexual abuse at the hands of prison guards, keepers, and visitors. The primary aim of the policy was to protect white men's *potential* virtue from being corrupted by any woman's *preexisting* licentiousness.[63]

Concepts of moral or sexual corruption did not emerge anew in the post-Revolutionary penal period but rather were deeply rooted in the theological writings and legal system of Puritan New England. Colonists imagined corruption in multiple ways, both literally and metaphorically. Most broadly, corruption constituted "polluted matter that compromised the wholeness of everything it touched."[64] Sin was one way of imagining corruption—and sexual wrongdoings topped the list of egregious sins, as they "combined immorality with bodily filth, resulting in an uncleanness that was physically embodied and morally reprehensible."[65] The plight of the prisoner, then, manifests a similarly embodied corruption that was both physically filthy and morally degraded. The parallels between prisoners and sexual deviants (both signified moral and bodily debasement) suggest that the very state of imprisonment was one of sexual degradation.

Teaching men and women in prison to distinguish between appropriate and inappropriate relations with each other was vital because companionship between the sexes was taking on a whole new meaning in society. Popular writers emphasized companionate marriages as key to a long and healthy life: "The fair sex should naturally expect to gain, from our conversation, knowledge, wisdom, and sedateness; and they should give us in exchange, humanity, politeness, cheerfulness, taste, and sentiment."[66] Furthermore, a highly prized social life should be defined by diversity: "the association of people of different dispositions and characters, judiciously blended together."[67] As companionate marriage, mixed-sex socializing, and diverse communities became more highly prized in society, prisoners were subject to increasing amounts of surveillance, separation, and isolation.

Though sexual difference served a vital function in enforcing the criminal law, authorities were at a loss when they were uncertain whether the suspect was a man or a woman. Such was the case when Samuel Johnson was caught burglarizing a home in Allegheny County and authorities discovered they were actually a woman passing as a man. Johnson's accomplice, John Clark, escaped. Johnson's sex was discussed at trial and reported in the local newspaper. Regardless, Johnson was convicted and sentenced to three years in the penitentiary—a long sentence that did not seem to grant her "consideration of her sex." Once Johnson was admitted to Walnut Street Prison, the clerk noted, "This woman had accustomed herself to wear mens cloaths for several years." Samuel was documented as Sarah, a white thirty-seven-year-old Virginian, with a "thin visage," who stood "four feet eleven inches high" who committed the crime "in mens apparel and was tried and convicted and brought to jail in the same."[68] It is interesting to note that after being discovered, Johnson was permitted to continue wearing men's clothing. Despite the three-year sentence, Johnson was discharged in less than a year, but not before challenging the belief that sex was easily discernible and labor best organized according to sex.[69]

Sex segregation served as the test for whether classification and segregation of inmates would help further larger institutional aims. In both Pennsylvania and New York, separating male and female convicts was the only form of segregation implemented to near perfection.[70] Further classification of convicts by degree of offense was frequently raised but proved too difficult for prison staff to implement.[71] Pennsylvania later introduced segregation by race, but this too was subject to available space and regularly disregarded. Further concerns arose about the mixing of convicts with those held in prison temporarily as vagrants or awaiting trial. New York reformer Thomas Eddy criticized Walnut Street Prison in Philadelphia for allowing convicts to interact with these other groups, especially untried prisoners, who were often found innocent. In both New York and Philadelphia, Thomas Eddy reported, "more than two thousand five hundred are annually committed; of whom not one fourth are found to be guilty; and that thus you have introduced every year more than 1800 persons, presumed to be innocent, into a school where every vice and every crime is taught by the ablest masters."[72] Eddy's careful critique blamed the architecture of the building, "circumstances not in their power to control," rather than his friends and peers—another sign that reformers valued their own needs and relationships over those of the suspect poor they allegedly helped.

Concerns about communication and corruption between prisoners were mapped onto new types of relationships including those between the old and the young. An observer noted the "dangerous intercourse" between older women and younger girls. Reformers were concerned about the influence convict women had on servants and slaves who were sent to prison by their masters to discipline them. This "dangerous intercourse" seduced women and girls "from their original innocence" while at the mercy of their owners.[73] Prison Inspectors worried about corruption between old and young inmates from the earliest years of the penitentiary, stating, "We have observed with pain the young apprentice and servant confined in the same apartment with the worthless vagrant and the novice in iniquity compelled to be the companion of the most hardy and abandoned villain."[74] One woman charged with theft (a charge she denied) and imprisoned at a young age credits her time in prison with transforming her from a state of innocence to one of total pollution. She wrote, "I entered it a child—I was innocent. I left it instructed in every vice. Those with whom I was compelled to associate took delight in polluting my mind."[75] Fear of hardened criminals corrupting innocent inmates could mean just that— those more experienced in vice teaching those less experienced. But innocence, as we have seen, could also be a synonym for whiteness, especially in the case of children. This is not to say that those corrupting them were necessarily African American, since immigrants and poor white Americans could be thought to be comparably evil and skilled in vice. But the lack of recognition of the innocence of black boys and girls suggests this public discourse was not aimed at helping them. Children, long imprisoned indiscriminately with adults, were increasingly identified as fundamentally innocent and in need of protection, but this characterization would not be extended to black children. The idea of "childhood" itself was developed in tandem with the carceral institutions of the early republic. Assessments of childhood innocence were ideologically driven by numerous forces, including race, class, gender, and alleged wrongdoing. Authorities would then determine whether or not a child deserved a second chance, the benefit of the doubt, and protection from corrupting adults.[76]

Women were characterized as the most despicable of negative influences—even more depraved than men. One report claimed, "the convict-women are, if possible, more depraved than the men; they have less reason, more passion and no shame."[77] In this characterization, women in prison were disregarded and dehumanized even more severely than the men. The writer, W. A. Coffey, described the women in prison as the worst sort: "Collected generally from the vitiated sewer of venality, they are schooled in its depravity, and practiced in its impudence. The utmost vulgarity, obscenity and wantonness, characterizes their language, their habits and their manners."[78] It's hard to imagine an evil these women were not capable of committing. Coffey further asserted that young, innocent, or novice women quickly become "proficient in wickedness" while in prison and ultimately many turned to prostitution after their release.[79] Other reports of young people point to the corrupting influence of older women on young girls before imprisonment. A fourteen-year-old Irish girl from New York became "a victim to the seductive arts of a villain" and was frequently charged with theft. A "little girl" from England was "induced by a wicked old woman" to steal for her. Both within and outside the prison, women served as corrupting influences on young girls—at least in prison, they could be stopped.[80] It is really difficult to discern the racial dimension of negative characterizations of corrupting older women, suggesting this designation could apply to anyone.

Any sexual dimension to this corruption was implied for the savvy reader but rarely named. This is hardly surprising, as same-sex intimacies were chiefly regulated through censorship and silence.[81] Only through the eyes of a Frenchman do we get a glimpse of the sexual pleasures—and corruptions—that women might have engaged in together in prison.[82] Moreau de St. Méry was routinely critical of the sexual proclivities of American women, including their lack of passion and their willingness to have sex with strangers. But he pointed out forms of sexual expression that might have easily occurred in prison, including masturbation and sex with other women. Of masturbation, St. Méry wrote that American girls "give themselves up at an early age to the enjoyment of themselves." He also explained the sexual pleasure they experienced with other women: "They are not at all strangers to being willing to seek unnatural pleasures with persons of their own sex."[83] It might be hard to believe that reformers, Inspectors, and guards would not explicitly report on such matters if they indeed witnessed women kissing, touching, embracing, or having sex with each other in prison, but the code of suppression regarding undesirable or illicit sexual expressions required they simply reduce all such possible intimacies to the vague category of "corruption," signaling the loss of innocence.

The regulation of same-sex intimacies between men also functioned through censorship, suppression, and silence. Newspaper references to the topic of sodomy, buggery, or bestiality were limited for a reason.[84] The public reporting in 1785 of the case of Joseph Ross, who had sex with an ewe, reveals the conflict between practices of reporting criminal convictions and the need to silence incidents of sodomy or buggery.[85] The story states, "Joseph Ross for a b***** crime with a ****, Angels and ministers of grace defend us!"[86] Another account of the same case reported, "The infamy of

Ross was very strongly proved; he was found guilty, and sentenced to be hanged."[87] Ross's situation was unusual, not only because he was executed but also because news of his misdirected sexual desire was reported in the press. Other cases were tried before the Supreme Court, but were not deemed newsworthy.[88] Lack of reporting was deliberate, serving an important function in rendering such desire both tantalizing and invisible. The silence speaks to a compelling wish to bury knowledge of such possibilities. In 1786, Benjamin Rush railed against the increasing tendency of printers to report on crimes with elaborate details by claiming the practice seduced young people to crimes. "It is of the utmost consequence," he wrote, "to keep young people as ignorant as possible of those crimes, that are generally thought most disgraceful to human nature."[89] This was especially true for sodomy and buggery. The mere reference to these practices could encourage people to try them, revealing the great fragility at the core of heterosexuality. The long-standing attempt to hide, erase, or minimize public awareness of illicit sex became the basic approach to all punishment.

The closest any Inspector's report came to acknowledging inappropriate sexuality among men in prison in the heyday years of the 1790s were the thinly veiled references of Inspector Caleb Lownes, who boasted that the introduction of beds with blankets and pillows was one way to separate men from each other. Lownes's comments suggested the possibility of touching, cuddling, masturbating, mutual masturbation, or sodomy. He recalled the situation in the men's cells: "The former practice of prisoners sleeping in their cloaths, and being crowded together without any regard to decency, was destructive to the health of the prisoners, and was attended with many other ill consequences, especially where men are collected in the manner they are in prison."[90] Lownes's intentionally vague statement suggested that violations of decency could be either physical or sexual or both. Other accounts avoid reference to physical intimacy but hint at intimate friendships between men in prison. One of the many visitors to the prison noted that a close relationship with another man made imprisonment bearable for one man. According to the observer, the brother of House Speaker General Muhlenberg fell on hard times and resorted to forgery. His conviction and subsequent stay in Walnut Street, however, had an upside: "He seemed very happy with a young sailor friend he had found and showed it, like all the other prisoners, in his smiling face."[91] This intimacy between two men, portrayed as friendship and devoid of explicit references to sexuality, was heralded as a relationship valued by the prisoner.

As Richard Godbeer has shown, this was a commonly held view of intimate friendship between middle-class and elite men during the period.[92] The story of Muhlenberg was captured by an esteemed European visitor. This positive characterization of a loving friendship between two inmates is a unique case in the prison records.

European views of same-sex intimacies had a great impact on Philadelphia at the end of the eighteenth century.[93] Historians agree about some of the obvious reasons why Philadelphia handled sodomy charges differently than both new and old England. In their colonial outpost, Philadelphians were far more invested in financial and political stability than they were in regulating morality. Clare Lyons has shown that expanding white male sexual privilege was an important part of the larger social and political project of creating a unified and inclusive model of white manhood. There was an active incentive to not punish white men for their sexual excesses—even sodomy. Still, Philadelphia never featured the Moll houses that were famous in eighteenth-century London.[94] Perhaps this lack of open socializing among men with sodomitical predilections was just enough to keep the larger social world of men from feeling threatened by them. Few could have predicted what came next. Reformers became obsessed with men having sex with each other—not in taverns or boardinghouses, places that often pushed the boundaries of both law and society—but right inside the prison, the belly of the beast of state authority.

Sex Panic

No one believed that imprisoning men with each other would lead to rampant sex among them. Both William Bradford and Benjamin Rush believed the denial of natural passion was a vital part of punishment. They expected men in prison to police each other. Though it was no longer a capital crime, sodomy was still viewed as a "monstrous vice" that would disgrace anyone who dared to try it. Such social disapprobation was vital in deterring men and boys from experimenting with sodomy because sodomy had not yet been defined as an act that would lead to or was equated with a homosexual identity.[95] This is most evident in the willingness of officials to house those convicted of sodomy or buggery within the general prison population. In 1790, John Pitts of York County was fined five shillings and sentenced to six months in prison.[96] In June 1795, thirty-seven-year-old African American ship carpenter Toby Morris was convicted of buggery in York County and sentenced to the maximum time allowed by law—ten years. He was pardoned by the governor in just under two years.[97] Seventy-six-year-old Samuel Boyer of Berks County was found guilty of buggery on August 10, 1804, and sentenced to six years in Walnut Street Prison. Boyer was pardoned by the governor less than a year later.[98] Official Walnut Street Prison records compiled by reformer Roberts Vaux also calculated six sodomy/buggery convictions, one each in the years 1795, 1804, 1805, 1821, 1823, and 1825, and one assault to commit sodomy in 1823.[99] A twenty-year-old white man from New York named David Van Guilder of Tioga County was convicted of sodomy on September 16, 1823, and sentenced to five years of hard labor.[100] Notably, these cases came from outside the city of Philadelphia—and none of these men were sentenced to solitary confinement during their imprisonment.[101]

Concern about sex between men was not timeless but rather emerged as a concern among Inspectors and reformers at a crucial point near the end of the first generation of penal reform.[102] Faced with overcrowded conditions and institutional failures in prisons throughout the Northeast, reformers began to publicly express their anxieties about men having sex in prison. By this time, penitentiaries were already under a great deal of scrutiny for failing at their major charge. In 1822, the question was not *whether* the penitentiary failed but rather *why*. One report asked, "Why has the Penitentiary System failed of producing its expected ends?" and "Can it be so modified and improved, so as to produce the results expected by its founders?"[103] There was a subtle shift from silence to reluctant speech about sex between men. A report commissioned by New York on the state of prisons throughout the United States demonstrated that sex between men was too much for even the most benevolent men, naming Virginia prison superintendent Samuel P. Parsons as a prime example. Parsons was said to manage the prison "with more wisdom, care, and uniformity" than most. But even Parsons could not manage to deter men from being together, stating himself, "There is too much intercourse among the prisoners, too many sleep together, and the contagion of vice is apparent."[104] Inmates engaged in masturbation, mutual masturbation, and oral or anal sex with each other, and no one could stop them.

New Englanders were the first to draw widespread public attention to the issue of sodomy. Inspectors from Connecticut complained about sodomy between men, reporting incidents of unnatural crime and mutual corruption as part of a detailed account of the successes and failures of punishment in their various institutions. The report was written and submitted to the state legislature by committee member Mr. Welles of Weathersfield. The *Connecticut Herald* covered the legislative session, reporting that, according to Welles, "Whenever the prisoners are confined in large numbers together at night, that unnatural crime is perpetrated, and that the convicts mutually corrupt each other." The committee recommended separation of prisoners during the night.[105] This excerpt from the report sounded the alarm, but the full text of the report offered even more detail about the problems at Connecticut's Newgate Prison. Sodomy was the first issue on the list of things going wrong. It was characterized as a new development caused by overcrowding: "From these various sources a mass of testimony has been obtained establishing in the minds of the committee, the existence in our penitentiaries of facts, of the most appalling and dangerous character. Of the existence of some of these facts, the committee had not at the time of their former report the least suspicion, and in their opinion they are to be attributed principally to the crowded state of the cells or night rooms."[106] This matter-of-fact statement is followed up by a passionate sense of defeat and vitriol. Sodomy, it turns out, seems to be everywhere. The report continues, "In our view the evidence is such as will warrant the belief, that in *some* of our penitentiaries, if not in *all* in which the convicts are placed in large numbers together in the cells, the crime of Sodomy has been perpetrated in numerous instances with entire shamelessness and notoriety." The widespread practice of sexual gratification among male inmates alarmed Inspectors because it was seemingly their fault, caused by the massive imprisonment of large numbers of men in very small spaces: "If that unnatural crime is ever perpetrated we should look for its commission among men shut up from all the enjoyments of society; among hoary headed convicts, condemned to long imprisonment, and whose passions and principles have been corrupted and degraded to the lowest point of debasement, and who are at night in numbers of from 4 to 32 persons locked together in cells which are not subjected to official inspection."[107] This statement marked the beginning of a new framework for understanding sodomy as a practice that arose from living in a crowded state of depravity.

Condemnation of sodomy in prison seemed to be emerging from every direction. The following year, 1827, Rev. Louis Dwight, secretary of the

Prison Discipline Society of Massachusetts, took to the road to spread his views. In New York, he outlined the principal evils of the penitentiaries, naming "unnatural crime" as one of six, including instruction in counterfeiting, pickpocketing, preparing instruments for pickpocketing, making false keys, and formulating new plots.[108] Dwight frequently took long horseback rides to clear and expand his lungs, which had been damaged by an accident in a chemical laboratory at Yale. He incorporated his ministerial vocation into these trips by distributing Bibles to prisoners along the way. These trips led him to his life's work.[109] His full report from Boston came out in August 1827, echoing the report from Connecticut. In Boston's prison, the directors, keepers, and convicts all confirmed the widespread practice of sodomy, the "unnatural crime." The chief magistrate of Massachusetts himself offered the results of his study: "A horrible offence is here committed between wretches, who are alike destitute of moral sentiment and without the reach of physical restraint. Nature and humanity cry aloud for redemption from this dreadful degradation."[110] In this dramatic account, the magistrate portrays sodomy as against both nature and humanity. Those who engage in this are "wretches" who lack both "moral sentiment" and "physical restraint." Now men would join women as an overly sexualized and degraded group within the prison.

But the worst part of the Massachusetts report—and the greatest source of shame, to the magistrate—was the fact that punishment produced sodomy: "Better even that the laws were written in blood, than they should be executed in sin."[111] He knew that the state was responsible for making sodomites out of criminals. The punitive regulation of sex was generative: not only did sex shape punishment, but punishment shaped sex.[112] A Boston publication picked up parts of the Massachusetts and Connecticut reports, highlighting the incidents of sodomy in prisons.[113] The unnamed group claimed they would start a circular letter to men in authority so that in the future, prisons would be constructed to prevent this from happening. The most revealing part of the campaign, however, was the solution: new prison design. Authorities seemed to quickly surrender the possibility that they could deter men from engaging in sexual acts with each other, making the prison a space of presumptive homosexuality.

Under Dwight's leadership, Boston's Society launched a witchhunt of sorts. Dwight brought his puritanical zeal to bear on New York and Philadelphia, much to the chagrin of the locals. Massachusetts's zealots criticized everything about punishment in Pennsylvania, from the lack of religious instruction to the "incomparably wretched" Walnut Street Prison to the sleeping arrangements of men (four hundred in sixteen rooms) to the fact that men "engaged in various sports" in the yard on the Sabbath.[114] Boston reformers pointed out that massive overcrowding of such a depraved group encouraged prisoners to "seek relief in the most vile and polluting abominations."[115] In 1827, Pennsylvania lawyer Job Tyson broke the official silence about conditions in his state's prisons. When he provided an overview of the penal code to date, he noted as an aside that sodomy in prison was a "sad and sickening" truth that was "frequent, daring, and open."[116] Tyson's statement was short and to the point. Little else had been said about it up to that point, and Pennsylvania's leading reformers were still using vague language in their communications. For example, in its memorial to the legislature in January 1828 asking for a law to authorize solitary confinement, PSAMPP avoided explicitly mentioning sodomy. It complained that population growth and the increased number of prisoners made it impossible to separate prisoners from each other, resulting in "a school of vice" instead of "a place of moral instruction and reform."[117]

The tone and volume concerning references to sodomy in prison were also muted throughout Roberts Vaux's many exchanges with English reformers debating the merits of solitary confinement. It was an important time for Pennsylvania, on the eve of the opening of Eastern State Penitentiary—finally, a prison designed properly for reformative incarceration. But solitary confinement was controversial, and many people argued against it. In a series of exchanges in 1827 and 1828, Vaux continued the practice of using vaguely suggestive language when describing inappropriate intimacies among prisoners. Vaux wrote a lengthy response to critic William Roscoe of Liverpool, England, in which he claimed that one of the main arguments in favor of solitary confinement was that it would prevent men from enjoying the company of each other. He wrote, "*By separate confinement*, therefore, it is intended to *punish* those who will not control their wicked passions and propensities, thereby violating divine and human laws . . . or making a mockery of justice by forming such into communities of hardened, and corrupting transgressors, who enjoy each other's society."[118] In his reference to sex, he avoided commonly used legal terms such as "sodomy" and "unnatural crime," instead alluding to desire and inclinations.

Roscoe replied by claiming solitary confinement itself was "inhuman and unnatural" and the far greater issue at hand.[119] Roscoe's countryman

Edward Livingston shared his opinion and tried to base his case against total solitary confinement on the idea that prisoners could benefit from interacting with each other during the day because it was only during the night that "promiscuous association" was common. It was only when the corrupt, hardened, and old offenders were able to isolate others beyond the watchful eye of guards and keepers that they had great influence, "initiating the young in the mysteries of vice and crime."[120] Livingston's point that men took advantage of boys was clear, echoing earlier concerns of "corruption," but his language was still vague.

After an elaborate assessment of the penal code, punishment generally, and the conditions of prisons, Pennsylvanian authorities came to a shared conclusion: they must get to the bottom of why their system was failing. Specifically, they wondered if the problems were rooted in the "system itself" or resulted from "imperfect or vicious" administration.[121] Reports of corruption and vice among inmates in prison were as old as the prison itself. PSAMPP already hinted at the troubles brewing in Walnut Street Prison in its 1816 publication. It admitted that the institution was failing, resembled European prisons, and was more a "seminary for every vice" than a place of reflection and reform. The situation was such that no one— even those novices in crime—could serve their time uncontaminated by depravity. Prison denied anyone the opportunity to "avoid the contamination, which leads to extreme depravity; and with which from the insufficiency of the room to form separate accommodations, he must be associated in his confinement."[122] Prison officials seemed to be taking some responsibility for creating and maintaining such degraded conditions.

Pennsylvania reformers begrudgingly acknowledged that sex among men in prison was a problem, but in a rather muted and nonsensationalized way. There are several reasons for this. Pennsylvania had developed a more moderate attitude toward sodomy in general. It was among the first states to remove it from the list of capital crimes, while Rhode Island and New Jersey still condemned people to death on the second charge of sodomy. After 1794, only murder was punishable by death in Pennsylvania.[123] The revised code passed in 1829 reduced punishment for sodomy as well to one to five years for the first offense and up to ten years for the second.[124] Another reason Pennsylvanians were less interested in discussion of sodomy in prison was the fact that their new prison based on total solitary confinement would soon open, making the entire point moot.

In 1828, the official report of the Pennsylvania Commission to Investigate Prisons was released. It identified three chief causes of the failure of the prison system in Pennsylvania: the increased number of convicts as a result of population growth, the frequent pardoning of too many prisoners without sufficient punishment, and the "flagrant evils" that spread among inmates in their time together during both day and night.[125] The report is sprinkled with examples of the dangers of prisons at night, such as the following: "It may be assumed as demonstrable, that the *night season* is that, in which the communication between convicts, who are in the same apartment, can take place with the greatest facility, and to the most dangerous extent."[126] In reflecting on what happens not only in Philadelphia but also in Boston, New York, and Baltimore, the report states, "All accounts agree in representing these night rooms as the means of the most corrupting communication, and the scenes of the most hideous depravity." But to highlight this, the commissioners looked to Boston.

Pennsylvania officials claimed no need to get into details, chiefly because the Massachusetts authorities had already dealt with the topic so eloquently in their own reporting. Maybe this was payback for feeling their hand was pushed by New England's Puritan zealots. Why air their own dirty laundry when they could just point to Boston and nod in agreement? The commissioners stated, "We allude to the nameless and unnatural crimes, which concurrent testimony proves to have been frequently perpetrated in those chambers of guilt and misery. We are spared the task of entering into any particular upon this subject by the nature of the offence." By explaining that their silence on the matter was conscious and deliberate, they remind us why references to same-sex intimacies can be so hard to find throughout history. Commissioners reminded the reader that just because they did not speak of unspeakable offenses did not mean they were not happening. Rather than get into the details of Pennsylvania's prison sex, Pennsylvania's commissioners spoke of their state as one among many—including Connecticut, New York, and Massachusetts—facing the problem. After thirty years of trying to set Pennsylvania's prison system apart from institutions in these other states, Pennsylvania officials admitted that their prisons, too, were places in which sodomy occurred. Sodomy thus became a uniting force, something that superseded long-standing state rivalries and divisions. Finally, the report reiterated that terrible quote from the Massachusetts governor condemning the fact that punishment itself was leading people to sin: "Better even that the laws were written in blood, than that they should be executed in sin."[127] This outcome was unacceptable.

But Pennsylvania authorities went further than their contemporaries in Massachusetts and New York. They used anxiety about intimacy among men in prison as further justification for solitary confinement—something widely under attack and not yet approved by the penal code despite the fact that construction of Eastern State Penitentiary had already begun. They believed fear of sodomy would win over skeptics of solitary confinement. The commissioners acknowledged that they would have avoided the topic entirely had it not helped make their case for solitary confinement. The report stated, "There is one feature in the miserable picture of evils produced by crowded night rooms, of a character so frightful and revolting that we would gladly pass it by without comment, did it not appear to us necessary to impress deeply on the minds of the legislature, the paramount importance of separate dormitories." General corruption, instruction in vice, illicit physical intimacies, and sodomy became the justification for the introduction of solitary confinement. The ensuing separations were widely acknowledged as necessities to prevent sexual as well as social intercourse.[128]

In light of all this debate, the public became curious about sodomy. Chiefly, they wanted to find out how men were being drawn into unnatural intimacies with each other, presuming that it was a mysterious skill that one needed to be taught rather than the unleashing of an innate desire. Inspectors tried to answer these questions, especially those that presumed condemned sodomites were moving throughout the prison and training others in its art. Inspectors provided no comfort with their answer. They had neither evidence nor recollection of "any prisoner having been convicted for any such offence committed in the prison."[129] This was a terrible answer that fueled collective anxiety because it suggested that men never before suspected or convicted of sexual intimacies with other men were able to figure out how to do it themselves. Neither the public nor the authorities could pin this development on individual, experienced, and visible sodomites. The only consolation was the fact that when men already in prison were caught engaging in "unnatural crimes" they were sent to the cells for punishment.[130]

Discussion of race is completely absent from the controversy over same-sex intimacies in prison. This is not altogether remarkable given that race was never openly discussed among reformers as a meaningful category in the establishment of the penitentiary in the first place. In fact, it served everyone's purposes to not openly acknowledge the ways the prison was quickly becoming a substitute for slavery in controlling African American lives. By the 1820s, when the controversy over sex between men erupted, the breakdown of inmates by race had white men outnumbering black men two to one. For example, in January 1820, 251 of the convicts were white men and 127 were black men.[131] While black men were greatly overrepresented in prison compared to their proportion of the population of Pennsylvania, they were still a minority of prisoners. Even though most men in prison were convicted of property crimes having nothing to do with sex, black men's sexuality was stigmatized as excessive through racial stereotyping under centuries of slavery. Therefore, race shaped the controversy over intimacies between men in a number of ways.

Given the lack of concern about regulating or punishing same-sex intimacies in society during this time, it is likely that the mixed race environment of the prison made this issue one of greater importance. While white men were free to sexually engage with nearly anyone without consequences, black men's sexuality was highly regulated by both law and custom.[132] If white men turned to each other for sexual pleasure, it would have been deemed immoral and unseemly but also a simple extension of their sexual prerogative. But black men had no such privilege, and similar expressions of same-sex intimacies would have quickly conjured stereotypes of hypersexuality and lack of control. While white men also enjoyed the freedom to exploit, dominate, and sexually humiliate black men under slavery, the tables could quickly be turned in prison, granting black men a chance to experience the other side of this power relationship.[133] The prospect of black men having sex together, corrupting others with their excessive sexuality, or even raping white men fueled the sex panic. As was the case with most instances of undesirable sexuality, however, none of this was spoken.

Vague references to corruption that were staples of reform rhetoric for decades were replaced by specific critiques of sodomy and unnatural vice. This public attack on inmates engaging in sodomy served several important functions in larger punishment discourses. With little evidence of successful reformation among inmates, sodomy gave reformers, keepers, and Inspectors a way out. As the ultimate example of penal failure, it came as a ready-made excuse for larger failures of reformative incarceration. Rather than figure out what was fundamentally wrong with punishment, they were able to focus on what was wrong with criminals. Rampant sodomy in prison became an excuse and rationale for the view that criminals were inclined to be sodomites, further evidence that sodomites themselves were fundamentally depraved and unreformable. This early conflation of criminality and sodomy helped establish correlations that later became more hardened into a distinct identity with this particular sexual desire at its core, resulting in the invention of homosexuality as a category of sexual deviance fifty years later.

Separate Spheres

The prison sex panics had different implications for separate spheres ideology and the potential role of women in prison reform work. The first wave against sex between men and women marked the prison as a debased place, off limits to elite women. Though elite and middling women were active in numerous charitable and reform activities in the post-Revolutionary period, they did not get involved in the prison reform movement that occupied so many of their fathers, husbands, and brothers from the mid-1780s on.[134] While men's organizations tackled wide-ranging issues and lobbied for legislation related to the slave trade, punishment, education, and colonization, the scope of women's activities was far narrower. Women's groups were generally religious, benevolent, charitable, and mutual aid projects that seldom called for a disruption of the social order.[135] Most of the women were compelled by Christian piety to provide food, clothing, and supplies for the poorest and neediest in the city. For about twenty years beginning in the mid-1790s, Protestants had pity on the poor and felt they were worthy of support. Numerous organizations popped up in major seaport cities. Philadelphia alone was home to half a dozen, including the Female Society for the Relief of the Distressed (1795), the Female Society of Philadelphia for the Relief and Employment of the Poor (1795), the Female Association of Philadelphia for the Relief of Women and Children in Reduced Circumstances (1800), and the Female Domestic Missionary Society of Philadelphia (1817).[136] Their generosity waned in the 1820s, as many came to view spiritual bankruptcy as the cause of poverty, and everyone blamed the poor for their plight.

In 1817, members of one of these organizations, the Female Domestic Missionary Society of Philadelphia, reported that they targeted women in prison for outreach along with those in the almshouse and hospital. Their schedule allowed for weekly visits to the hospital, twice weekly visits to the almshouse, and trips to the prison "as occasion might require." Without giving any details as to why, the managers reported that their efforts in both the prison and the hospital failed to achieve any "general effects," which left them to focus their energy on the almshouse. We should not think of their efforts as concerned with anything other than religious conversion. Prior to forming the society, founding members of the group met informally for "social prayer" and were so moved by the experience that they sought to share it with others, including those in "the abodes of sorrow" known as the almshouse, hospital, and prison. The women "administered the oil and wine of consolation 'to many a wounded soul'" in all three locations.[137] These efforts went entirely unremarked by the prison staff, Inspectors, and PSAMPP. But they do demonstrate interest on the part of religious women to address at least the spiritual needs of those in prison.

It is easy to see why the prison—a place deemed the most depraved of all—was off limits to virtuous and elite women. Fear of contagious immorality plagued reformers who were obsessed with classifying and segregating people based on their degree of moral corruption. They also feared the consequences of misdirected sympathy, an issue raised during the debate over public punishment.[138] Putting women deemed virtuous by their very embrace of sentiment and emotion would have undermined everything they believed in. Virtuous women might not be strong enough to resist the onslaught of emotions that visiting imprisoned women would surely instigate. Traits such as virtue, sensibility, and restraint were bedrocks of both family life and the nation, yet remained fragile. Physical filth, moral debasement, and the specter of violence all made the prison a threatening place for republican mothers, wives, and daughters. Besides, the prison was the domain of the state—a sphere that officially excluded women.[139] Women were shut out from working in or visiting the prison in any official capacity for decades.

All this changed in the 1820s. Several forces contributed to the emergence of women as prominent forces in penal management and reform. Reports of British reformer Elizabeth Fry's work with women in prisons all over England were circulating widely and inspiring women on this side of the Atlantic to follow in her footsteps, despite her critics. The earnestness of the sentimental project among men began to wane, and virtue became an increasingly feminized force. Both men and women began to embrace the idea that depraved or criminal women needed the effects of a virtuous woman to be reformed. As the ideology of "separate spheres" began to take root, female reformers were welcomed to visit women prisoners, and female matrons were sought out to oversee women's wards. As early experiments with incarceration came under attack from all angles, male keepers, Inspectors, and reformers were willing to try new things. Given that their efforts failed even for white men—those targeted by reformative incarceration—they were increasingly convinced they did not have all the answers and had barely given a second thought to the plight of women. Furthermore, women's criminality was increasingly visible in the 1820s as a result of a crackdown on public life, especially the informal economies so many women relied on: huckstering, prostitution, tippling houses, and fencing. During this time, Ann Carson emerged as the city's most famous criminal. It became impossible to ignore the fact that women were a regular presence in the streets, in the courts, and in the prisons.

The wealthy Quaker woman Elizabeth Fry began visiting London's Newgate Prison in 1814, having previously created a school for children whose parents were imprisoned. Fry established an organization of women to tend to the children of prisoners called the British Ladies' Society for Promoting the Reformation of Female Prisoners. Fry's work received wider recognition with the 1819 publication of reports from her prison visits with her brother Joseph John Gurney's *Notes on a Visit Made to Some of the Prisons in Scotland and The North of England*.[140] Fry achieved fame for her efforts across Europe and America, leading to both high regard for the efficacy of her work and criticism from fellow Quakers for the fame it brought her. Fry inspired multiple generations of Quaker women to action, even if their husbands and fathers were slow to support their efforts.[141] When Fry's organization—the British Ladies' Society—produced a manual with exact instructions on how to work with women in prison, there was no holding back the Quaker women of Philadelphia who wanted to follow her lead.[142]

Just as an early generation of men had approached prison work as an exercise in sentiment, so too did Fry and other female reformers focus on the cultivation of sympathy and feeling. This was crucial in order to draw prisoners into conversation and break through their "hardness." Accounts of Fry's work with women in prison emphasized that she approached the women with just the right countenance to avoid generating the laughter and ridicule prisoners were known to turn on visitors. Rather, Fry looked

at the women "with a kind and conciliating manner" and "with such sweet-
ness" as to win their confidence.[143] Fry was lauded in the British and American press as a pioneer philanthropist of vision, wisdom, and spirit. The keys
to her success were simple—a combination of her own outstanding character and example combined with humble instruction and creating opportunity for prisoners to work.[144] One public account of Fry's achievements was
juxtaposed to failures of American punishment, including the penitentiary
in Pennsylvania specifically. Even leading Pennsylvania reformers were willing to concede by now that women might have something to offer. Bishop
William White, president of PSAMPP for many years, wrote of prison
work, "From the ladies, therefore, whom heaven has blessed with affluence,
and the still greater gift of sympathy—from gentlemen, who acknowledge
the obligations to humanity."[145] While women were naturally sympathetic,
men were compelled to action only by obligation. Now, the penchant for
sympathy would make women ideally suited to effectively intervene in the
penal experiment. And so it began.

The female reformers were first officially permitted to visit women in prison
in 1823. Mary Wistar, wife of reformer and founding member of PSAMPP
Thomas Wistar, founded the Prison Association of Women Friends and
was joined by two other women in the Association's first prison visit. Her
husband accompanied the three women as they met with untried prisoners
and vagrants who had been moved to the new Arch Street Prison—away
from convicts.[146] The Board of Inspectors approved of this work, and Anna
Potts soon joined them as well.[147] Convicts stayed in Walnut Street and
remained off limits to female reformers. The women described those in
prison as mostly drunken vagrants who were "covered only by a few rags,"
along with those charged with a range of other minor offenses, chiefly
"petty thefts."[148] Elite Quaker women could see the harsh reality of poor
women's lives and tried to achieve things their husbands failed to do.

The female reformers who finally convinced PSAMPP and the Inspectors to let them begin a ministry of their own were the wives and sisters of
active male reformers. These men knew what prison conditions were really
like and aimed to protect white women of moral authority and refinement
from exposure to such a base, degraded version of black and white womanhood. When they learned that female reformers were to be admitted to visit
with the women, they sought to cover up their long-standing practice of
leaving vagrants and prisoners for trial nearly naked. In January 1823,

Inspectors visited Walnut Street, noting "the misery is very great among the untried and vagrants."[149] In anticipation of the admittance of elite benevolent women to the prison visitation circuit, the PSAMPP board passed a new resolution in May 1823 ordering new clothing. The Visiting Committee from then on was ordered "to afford clothing to such of the females in the vagrant [ward], as will render them fit objects to be seen by men and women visiting them together."[150] Male reformers tried to prevent their female counterparts from witnessing the spectacle of indecency that left so many women half-naked. What was tolerated—even essential—in the visitation dance between well-coiffed rich white men and partly naked poor black and white women was deemed inappropriate for the presence of elite white women. Conditions were improved, not necessarily for the benefit of inmates, but for the women who visited.

Changing ideas about sexual difference and the meaning of virtue were reflected in penal reform efforts. As women and emotions became increasingly associated with moral activity, men and reason became more exclusively associated with the utilitarian pursuit of self-interest.[151] This shift made space for female reformers who increasingly saw their admission to a ministry in prisons as only one small step in a larger reform project that would bring women into the prison as matrons, overseers, and role models. In 1824, after the deadly cholera epidemic moved through the city—and Arch Street Prison—the Association of Women Friends recommended the construction of a bathhouse for better hygiene and hiring a matron to supervise the women. The Board of Inspectors denied this recommendation but realized the equation had changed, as male reformers increasingly came to believe women were needed to help provide the moral road map out of a life of depravity toward one of virtue, submission, and salvation. The admission of white women as reformers—and eventually the appointment of a matron—signaled not only that women in prison were there to stay but also that elite women were pushing to have a voice in the management of a state-run institution. The lack of surviving organizational records, however, prevents analysis of the ambition of the organization beyond reference to their work by others.

The movement to employ matrons to oversee women in prison was rooted in both ideology and practice.[152] Practically speaking, women had been neglected in prisons for decades, perhaps even centuries. They scarcely figured in the reform agenda and were largely seen as a nuisance in the prison that needed to be tolerated rather than a vulnerable group worthy of protection or reform. Critics portrayed women in prison as boisterous, unruly, and overly sexual as justification for their neglect. One prison official recommended that steps be taken to protect guards and keepers from female inmates, writing, "Women should be kept in different prisons and be guarded by women. If women are in the presence of men, they will stir up natural feelings of desire."[153] Another widely circulated anecdote called for sympathy for the guards charged with female inmates, who were alleged to be more needy and demanding than men, claiming, "The Directors most ungallantly assert that these *four* make more trouble than the whole remaining ninety-three convicts of the other sex." This story went on to quote directors from another prison who complained, "I could cheerfully undertake the care of an *additional four hundred and fifty men* to be rid of the nine women."[154] And so the problem of women in prison became the problem of women—period. By framing guards as burdened and women as powerful, the accounts obscured the power of both guards and the state and the vulnerability of the women.

Inspired by both ideology and reality, white women reformers believed that black and white women prisoners would be protected from the mistreatment of white male prison keepers and guards if the women were under the supervision of a matron. Realistically speaking, women in prison were vulnerable to the whims and desires of the men who watched them. If visiting Inspectors or reformers witnessed inmate abuse at the hands of guards or keepers, they did not document it. The rare surviving accounts written by inmates include references to abuse, suggesting two important things: abuse was happening and women had no recourse for their physical or sexual mistreatment. One former inmate suggested that sexual abuse of the women was rampant and that the reform advocates were not invested in stopping it. Imprisoned as an accomplice to robbery, a charge that he was eventually cleared of, Patrick Lyon complained, "I suppose those advocates cannot deny that a keeper cannot at pleasure take the unfortunate women out of the west-wing, and keep them in the cells—for what purpose I suppose may be easily guessed at."[155] Lyon implies the keepers abused their authority and took women to the solitary cells—away from others—so they could rape them. He also suggests it was something reformers knew about and were unable or unwilling to stop. The fact that many women in prison on vagrancy charges were already stigmatized as sex workers only made it easier for male authority figures to justify sexualizing and abusing them. For example, Martha Patterson, who was picked up and held for one month on the charge of "being an idle desolate person and common street walker," and Ealoner Robison, charged for "being a common prostitute and keeping a bawdy house in Welch's Alley," would have been easy targets for guards.[156] Dozens of women like them would have been imprisoned at any given time with no recourse. Ann Carson, who was in and out of prison in the 1820s, described the abuse of an inmate who was dragged by a guard "but half dressed, down a flight of stairs and through a hall, just wet from scrubbing, to the cells, for a frivolous offence."[157] In the absence of weapons and without recourse to corporal punishment, guards could have freely engaged in rough handling of inmates as a way to exert their authority. If they knew of physical or sexual abuse of inmates, reformers did not make official note of this as they did of other forms of misconduct. Women inmates probably figured they would be even more vulnerable to abuse if they reported guards or keepers to Inspectors or reformers. Female reformers believed that hiring matrons to oversee women would put an end to this sort of violence.

Ideologically speaking, this principle was anchored in a belief that women were more fundamentally nurturing, passive, and less violent than men. Developments in the penitentiary of New York helped fuel this belief. The move to appoint a matron to oversee the women in New York's prison was accelerated by the publicity around the violent abuse of a white woman, Rachel Welch, in 1826. Welch was flogged by a turnkey and died after having become impregnated while in prison on a larceny charge.[158] A turnkey punished her by "beating or whipping" her during her sixth or seventh month of pregnancy, and she died shortly after giving birth. The turnkey was convicted of assault and battery and fined only twenty-five cents. The jury criticized the misapplication and overuse of punishment by flogging, calling it "barbarous and inhuman to the last degree," noting that the situation aroused public indignation. As if the public needed any more information to fuel its outrage, a newspaper ran the report from the trial describing the state of Rachel's body after the beating: "The female in question was bruised from her neck down to the middle of the back, so that the whole surface of the skin appeared purple, or black and blue, besides having several other marks on her sides and legs."[159] Only in this most egregious example of disregard for the life of a white woman did the chaos and lawlessness of prison violence and unchecked state authority become apparent; only then did women in prison become eligible for sympathy. Public outcry forced the issue of women's treatment in prison onto the legislature's agenda, calling for a detailed inquiry into Rachel's condition, punishment, and death.[160]

The revelations of prisoner abuse prompted debate about the role of corporal punishment in the prison, something Pennsylvania had already outlawed. Pennsylvanians boasted that their keepers were forbidden from even carrying "a stick, or any offensive weapon." Similarly, irons and fetters were prohibited in Pennsylvania but heavily used in New York.[161] In the wake of the New York scandal, Pennsylvania reformer Franklin Bache went to the press with an attack on corporal punishment in prisons and schools. Just because some people thought it was okay to punish schoolboys with flogging, he argued, did not make it right for schoolboys—or even inmates. Bache argued that flogging was entirely inappropriate under all circumstances except one—at sea among sailors.[162] The public debate over the use of corporal punishment and its devastating consequences for Rachel Welch is a little-known chapter in the great competition between New York and Pennsylvania to achieve greater virtue and success in punishment.

Events in New York helped Philadelphia's female reformers with their goal of getting matrons appointed to oversee women in prison. In his vast exchange with William Roscoe in defense of solitary confinement, Roberts Vaux wrote of the introduction of matrons as a done deal in 1827. Vaux stated, "Besides this abatement of expense in maintaining prisoners, very few keepers will be required on the new system, and as the females should be entrusted wholly to the custody of suitable individuals of their own sex, their services can of course be secured for less compensation than men."[163] The use of matrons to supervise women in institutional settings had long been common in the almshouse, the house of industry, schools, and hospitals. Finally, with the opening of Eastern State Penitentiary, the prison would employ a woman to supervise the women. But this formal approval did not result in the hiring and appointment of a matron, even with the knowledge they could pay such a woman "less" than a man. Rather, Eastern State Penitentiary became embroiled in a scandal of its own, rooted in its inability to properly manage female inmates, the exploitation of the keeper's wife, and the keeper's wife's abuse of her own authority.

Eastern State quickly became a site of the same kind of chaos and mismanagement that had plagued New York's penitentiary just a few years before and Walnut Street Prison for decades. Inmates communicated with each other, refused to work, and participated in a work slowdown. Guards formed alliances with inmates, to the frustration of reformers and Inspectors. Ministers undermined the authority of guards, and on and on.[164] Formal charges of impropriety and mismanagement included "practices and manners among the officers, both males and females, licentious and immoral in nature, generally known and participated in by the warden and his deputies." Cruel and unusual punishments were also discovered, including "iron gags, strait jackets, the practice of ducking, mad or tranquilizing chairs, severe deprivations of food."[165] Just five years after its doors were opened, America's model penitentiary appeared to be enabling the abuses it was alleged to stand against.

At the heart of the controversy was a woman—the gatekeeper's wife. Richard Blundin was hired as gatekeeper in part because he was married, and he offered his wife's labor to the institution as part of his own hiring. According to Inspector Thomas Bradford's testimony on the subject, Mrs. Blundin was "always having an oversight of the cooking, and when female prisoners were received, affording such assistance to them as became their sex and condition."[166] Bradford went to great lengths to distance the institution from any official responsibility for Mrs. Blundin's actions— emphasizing repeatedly that she was not compensated or deemed an ideal matron should the institution hire one. But, in the absence of anyone formally appointed to this role, people did refer to her as "female overseer."[167] Technically, Bradford would state, "The washing, making, and mending the clothes of the prisoners, as well as cooking and baking for them, was performed by Blundin's family; as the prisoners increased an assistant was allowed to him December 5, 1829, as appears by the report of the warden."[168] Bradford's evasion of responsibility for Mrs. Blundin served to distance himself and the penitentiary from her alleged indiscretions, including hosting parties in the prison, presenting herself drunk on multiple occasions, employing inmates in the kitchen, appropriating prisoner provisions for her own use, and carrying on too much influence (and possibly sexual intimacies) with warden Samuel Wood.

Failure to account for the domestic needs of the prison and to hire proper workers created the conditions for this scandal. The experience of Ann Hinton, the African American inmate who worked side by side with the white Mrs. Blundin in the kitchen, revealed this and other cracks in the system. Because so few women were sent to Eastern State and African American women made up the early majority, the warden decided not to hire a matron, despite having the Board's approval. Budget pressures in the early years led agents to make decisions based on practical conveniences over penal ideals. Mrs. Blundin herself was overworked and not compensated. She saw no reason why Ann Hinton, the first female prisoner at Eastern State, should not help her. Why leave a perfectly able black woman alone in her cell with her thoughts and prayers when she could help around the prison house? A number of people testified that Ann Hinton was treated differently from other prisoners, including William Mayall, a former officer, William Parker, a former inmate, and William Griffith, an overseer in the shoe department. Together, their testimony portrayed Hinton as a woman who was free to move about the grounds, actively participate in Mrs. Blundin's wild parties, and serve both Blundin and Wood in their own private domestic concerns.[169] For Hinton, punishment was not solitary reflection but coerced domestic labor.

While Mrs. Blundin had no formal institutional authority, she clearly dictated the daily routine of Ann Hinton—and possibly other women in the prison as well. Allowing a white woman to informally control the life and labor of a black woman in her domestic service was nothing new in early American household gender relations. But inside the modern penitentiary, it affirmed and confirmed white supremacy as an organizing and operating principle. The reproduction of the domestic relationship between black and white women that anchored the gendered hierarchies within racial slavery for centuries happened informally. It stands as one powerful example of how easily the abundant political manifestos about punishment's ideals were casually dismissed in the daily work lives of regular people.

Only in the wake of scandal were great changes made. In Pennsylvania, a matron was hired. The Board of Inspectors of Eastern State, recognizing the importance of the Association of Women Friends not only for its efforts to meet with women but also for the approval the Association might offer for the Board's latest efforts, invited the group to visit in November 1833. The women were impressed by the implementation of total isolation and the supervision of a matron. They divided their group of twenty-four into two branches and made regular visits at both Eastern State and the new county jail at Moyamensing. In 1835, it was widely accepted that women were best suited to superintend and counsel other women in prison.[170] In New York State, things moved even more rapidly to address the distinct needs of women in prison. The state legislature approved an act for the actual construction of *separate buildings* for female convicts in the two state prisons, Mount Pleasant and Auburn.[171] Pennsylvania's approach was less complete and banked on the idea that women were less likely to commit the most violent of crimes. With the opening of Moyamensing County Jail (and the closing of both Walnut Street and Arch Street prisons) officials planned to use the new jail to house vagrants, prisoners for trial, and all convicts sentenced to two years or less. While again undermining the long-standing value of segregating prisoners by class, this practice would allow Eastern State Penitentiary to be reserved for only the most violent criminals—who were seldom women.[172]

White women and men sought different experiences from their reform work. Women seemed to be less self-serving than their male counterparts. Men wrote openly about how benevolent work made them more "sensible" and better men than they might otherwise be. Records of women's comparable work received much less attention. Whereas constitutions, missions, and reports of various male benevolent associations seemed to always be reprinted in the press, women's were less so. Only in the 1830s did women's organizations begin to publicize their successes, and in these accounts we can see some of their original ambitions. One new narrative featured the positive influence virtuous elite white women could have on the most downtrodden and fallen girls by emphasizing the powerful connection between the two. Managers of the Philadelphia Orphan Society were thrilled to share in their fifteenth annual report that "an affectionate intercourse is preserved" between the young women who were raised in the asylum and their matrons. This was most evident in expressions of gratitude and requests for advice from the young girls.[173] Success was determined not by inspiring independence or a work ethic but rather by establishing strong bonds of trust and intimacy.

A publication by the Female Prison Association of Friends (formerly known as the Prison Association of Women Friends) celebrated the power of sentiment and redemption in the life of one woman.[174] Julia Moore had fallen far in her short life before landing in Eastern State Penitentiary with a seven-year sentence. After great resistance and terrible suffering, Moore came to accept the message of her regular visitors, the Female Friends. Interestingly, it was the harsh message of a male minister that first seemed to break this "lost, undone creature" and transform her countenance.[175] She then begged God for forgiveness and received her regular female visitors with a new attitude. Moore felt the kindness of both the physician and matron was far beyond anything her "hard-hearted" acquaintances had ever offered her. In prison, she wanted for nothing.[176] Transformed, Julia declared great gratitude for the women who met with her on a regular basis. It was said that Julia asked the Visiting Committee to send a message to one of her regular visitors who was unable to visit. Later she wrote the woman a letter herself in gratitude: "Experience plainly shows me he has made strangers my mother, father, sisters and friends. I have reason to bless the day I entered this Prison."[177] Women sought connection, friendship, and intimacy with those they visited. A relationship that just a generation earlier would have been suspect for its negative, corrupting, or sexual possibilities was now marked by the innocence of elite women and the penance of those condemned.

*　*　*

Reformers were unable to keep a handle on the range of sexual intimacies enjoyed by inmates. This was particularly threatening to the project of reformative incarceration, more so than other examples of rule breaking, resistance, and misbehavior. Some of their efforts to restrict communication between groups were widely publicized; others less so. Sex segregation was trumpeted in every report and story for years, suggesting that deviant forms of heterosexuality may have been less tolerated than historians have previously thought. But the principle of sex segregation was so important that it quickly became the bedrock of institutional order everywhere. It blended into the fabric of prison culture, normalizing heterosexual desire and setting the stage for more visible instances of same-sex intimacies. No one questioned the merit, utility, or fairness of restricting sex as a form of punishment. That too became folded into the logic of punishment. Penal authority leveraged sex as a tool of power and manipulation at will. When increased incidence of sexual intimacies between men coincided with public controversies over the soundness of solitary confinement, authorities took their great failure and turned it into the justification for their future. Each new change in policy with sex at its heart further obscured the dramatic expansion and the stunning failure of reformative incarceration.

～

Conclusion

THE MODERN PENITENTIARY was born of failure—not success. Samuel Wood, the first principal keeper for Eastern State Penitentiary, admitted as much when he condemned the impact of Walnut Street Prison on the cause of justice and reform. Wood declared, without shame or guilt despite having served on the Board of Inspectors for years, "I assert, without fear of contradiction, that it is not possible for the Legislature to devise a system where men will be more completely contaminated, hardened, and depraved, than in that college of vice, the Walnut Street Prison."[1] Though Wood and his fellow Inspectors, reformers, and keepers made Walnut Street what it was, he disavowed his relationship with the place, laying blame for its many failures on the structure itself, one that was soon to be abandoned forever.[2] This line of reasoning served several important functions. It continued the tradition of condemning the misuse of state authority while at the same time overseeing the expansion of the penal state. It left the door open for future success in punishment by linking the failure to one building—Walnut Street Prison—rather than to the group of people in charge, including judges, constables, Inspectors, and guards. Finally, this disavowal served to position Wood and his colleagues on the right side of history, as flexible and forward looking.

Punishment, however, was contradictory and hypocritical at its core. It is impossible to ignore how easily it morphed to advance the larger social aims of a given era. Its nascent years were compelled by uncertainty in the labor force sparked by the transition from bound to wage-based labor practices. Rhetoric about the need to put labor at the heart of punishment was explicitly about disciplining and controlling a workforce that embraced the spirit of freedom and revolution as its own. European immigrants along with African, Irish, and Anglo-Americans were in fact hardworking and resourceful in finding ways to stay afloat and support themselves and loved ones in the early American city. Rather than celebrate this group for their entrepreneurial spirit, governing elites made up new laws to regulate and criminalize them for huckstering, running tippling houses, and engaging in sex work. This group was less able to manage the paperwork and expenses required for proper licenses and rental agreements. They were punished for their industriousness or sent to prison, rather than coached through the process or provided with small loans. The effort to advance a heterosexual political economy by driving women from public spaces and paid work was not achieved by prison reform alone but certainly gained momentum as a larger social value by the mid-nineteenth century. The idea that women belonged "at home" rather than "at work" would serve to undermine women's opportunities for paid work and justify the ongoing restriction of their public lives. The celebration of the ideology of "separate spheres" along with the domestication of women inside of prison and other state institutions served to erase the legacy of women's public work from historical memory.

The movement to transform prisoners into a disciplined workforce failed entirely, but as textile mills popped up along the Schuylkill River to fill the growing demand for American-made goods, there was no shortage of opportunities for young white men and women to labor in prisonlike conditions for meager wages. As industry expanded in the 1830s and 40s, so to did racist views of African Americans, leaving them largely excluded from this growing workforce. Free blacks might be celebrated in some circles as a sign of larger social progress for human rights, but they were also quickly characterized in demeaning ways that suggested they were not prepared to participate in a democracy as citizens. The prospects for equal citizenship for African Americans were foreclosed in numerous ways large and small throughout the period. A key turning point with lasting significance occurred in 1828 when the House of Refuge, opened to save young children who committed minor infractions from prison, excluded African American children. At this moment, leading white reformers—both men and women—gave up on a generation of black children and solidified associations between African Americans and criminality in the process.

Analysis of the dynamic function of race and gender in these early years of punishment has provided many valuable insights. Elite white Protestant men used prison reform work as a source of self-improvement for the cultivation of a sensitive, expansive masculinity more appropriate to democratic society, replacing older, more aggressive expressions of patriarchal authority. While they visited both men and women in prison, women proved more amenable subjects for their efforts. White American manhood was made in the confines of a prison cell, and in encounters with the immeasurable suffering and vulnerability of poor Irish and African American women. White men's authority was uncontested. Their gestures, however minor, were deeply appreciated. They felt safe enough and important enough to express compassion rather than self-interest and mastery. Lost as these men were in their own experience, it mattered little that women's lives were scarcely improved by their efforts, and certainly none were truly transformed. The failure of reformers to measurably change the plight of those incarcerated did little to drive men away from the project. Rather, it confirmed the significance of the self-interested dimension of reform work.

Prison reform work was in fact a family affair for generations of Pennsylvania elites. It was a world comprised of fathers, sons, brothers, and nephews from the most influential families in politics, education, medicine, and business. Bartholomew Wistar served PSAMPP as his uncle Thomas Wistar did before him. Franklin Bache, great-grandson of Benjamin Franklin, was named prison physician. Charles Sidney Coxe was president of the Board of Inspectors and son of the influential merchant and politician Tench Coxe. Thomas Bradford, Jr., became an Inspector, following the path laid out by his uncle, former attorney general William Bradford.[3] If the underclasses caused chaos and disorder in the city streets, wharves, and public houses, they were more amenable to the social roles envisioned for them by this illustrious group once imprisoned. Their minor gestures of humanitarian relief for prisoners helped alleviate any misgivings or guilt they might feel about the larger political and economic forces that oppressed the masses while rewarding the few. Some might deem this characterization as harsh, discounting the fact that this group of men set themselves apart from many other equally rich and powerful people who would celebrate the brutal treatment of prisoners and advocate for the harshest punishments possible. But this study has set out to assess how a system so fundamentally flawed came to justify not only its very existence but also its rapid expansion during this formative moment in American history. And for this, I hold reformers responsible.

The only people missing from the penitentiary during its nascent years were middle- and upper-class white women. Though physically absent, the idea of them was everywhere. White married women had a new charge in the republican city: embrace education to become better wives to husbands and better mothers to sons! This role was defined not only by specific patterns of kinship but even more importantly by a class position that enabled a woman to pursue education and embrace domesticity. Though they too may have wished for the opportunity to live this kind of life, the stark reality for the working poor not only put domesticity and education out of reach, but also drastically strained family ties in every direction. Poor women of African, Irish, and even English descent were deemed failures and cast outside the boundaries of womanhood. This was no small matter but served to justify their abuse, disrespect, and general neglect whether in prison, the almshouse, the streets, a disorderly house, or the servants' quarters. The only group of poor women who benefited from this at all were Anglo-American women. Spared the marks of racial or ethnic difference or the wear and tear of immigration, American-born Anglo women received the benefit of their sex because of their race. No group was spared the full reach and weight of punishment like white women, making them the only group never really classified as criminal.[4]

Ideas about sexual difference and desire underwent tremendous changes in the late decades of the eighteenth and early decades of the nineteenth centuries. Women were long deemed to be full of desire and lust, capable of seducing any man. This influenced early policies against the imprisonment of men and women together for fear that women would lure men into sex and detract from their penitence. By the 1830s, this narrative was nearly turned upside down, especially for white women. Even poor white women were on their way to becoming "passionless," while white men were endowed with a renewed innate sexual desire that was socially celebrated and legally protected in nearly all but the most egregious circumstances of assault. Women were now victims of seduction rather than seductresses, but were still held responsible for the consequences of their seduction, as eighteenth-century white men seldom were. Those women seduced by the promise of marriage into sexual intimacies with men who later abandoned them were subjects of both pity and blame. Social norms that diminished the marital prospects for such women drove many of them to sex work at a time when it was increasingly criminalized. But the idea of passionlessness did not affect even all working women in the same ways. African American women were still thought to harbor unnatural and excessive sexual desire that marginalized them from other women and left them vulnerable to abuse with little recourse.

Men's sexuality became a subject of great importance in the 1820s. The rise of prison sex between men did a great deal to further belief in the idea that even white men were filled with uncontrollable sexual desire. Even though this idea was beginning to circulate before the creation of the penitentiary, it is fair to conclude that imprisonment made a vague theory into a convincing reality for men across race and class. The sexuality of African American men, long constrained under slavery, was still curtailed in freedom as white men and women together projected their discomfort with sexual desire onto black men, if for different reasons. Older people long held the dubious distinction of corrupting younger people in prison, a threat that was later mapped onto black men and boys, who might corrupt white men and boys with their sexual aggression. Even worse, black men might assert sexual dominance over whites if the groups were not consistently separated. The lack of open conversation about race in the controversy over same-sex intimacies reveals some important truths about the complicated, intertwined histories of racial minorities and same-sex sexualities. As Siobhan Somerville has shown, at the turn of the twentieth century, racist eugenics schemes were developed in tandem with categories of sexual deviance.[5] Many decades earlier, it can also be said that same-sex intimacies between inmates compelled the need for greater segregation by race. The mixing of male inmates of different races also shaped the desire for particular kinds of same-sex intimacies, whether consensual or forced. Sex between men—especially between men of different races—threatened to undermine both white supremacy and the heterosexual political economy. Neither could be tolerated.

The place of women in punishment was eclipsed by the opening of Eastern State Penitentiary because it was reserved only for those sentenced to one year or more—eliminating most women convicted of larceny, assault, and disorderly conduct. A new county prison was opened for these women and for men with similarly short sentences—Moyamensing Prison. But Moyamensing always stood in the shadow of Eastern State as it became the subject of extensive international media coverage and visits from writers, social critics, reformers, and political leaders. Punishment in Eastern State was referred to as the Pennsylvania System and came to represent American punishment more generally, though New York disputed this distinction and offered a slightly different model and philosophy of punishment. Regardless, women were scarcely represented in Eastern State when it began accepting prisoners in 1829. Even more notably, however, the first four women sentenced to serve their time in Eastern State were African American women convicted of violent crimes. One pundit mocked this pattern in the press, joking, "The statute books call the offence *manslaughter*, but *womanslaughter* would be more appropriate."[6] Women's crime was always taken less seriously then men's—even when it involved murder. Beyond the joke, however, this anecdote served a far more damaging function in conflating women's criminality with African American violence. Incidents of the everyday crimes of survival committed by poor women of all races were obscured, just as their place in county prisons across the country was ignored. Female criminality was embodied by African American women.

On the outskirts of the city, behind massive walls, Eastern State Penitentiary came to stand for everything that no county jail—even Walnut Street—ever could. With its airy design and Center City locale, the prison at Sixth and Walnut across from Independence Hall and next to Potters Field was open to the influence of the many people and ideas passing by. Once Eastern State was up and running, there would be no turning back. The strict discipline and painful isolation there were widely celebrated as a counter to the chaos of colonial punishment. The logic of punishment, with its precise ordering of time and space, enabled the penitentiary and those who ran it to stand as rational guardians of all who passed through its doors. The state positioned itself as a defender of freedom and arbiter of justice while obscuring its own violence.[7] As Chandan Reddy has argued, "State violence operating through and constrained by a drive for a monopoly on rationality, figured most often by attempts to concretize the meaning of rational freedom as a freedom from the threat of arbitrariness." *Liberty's Prisoners* has shown that state violence seemed muted during this era by the many laws passed that seemed to minimize violence, including the abolition of corporal punishment, the near abolition of capital punishment, and reduced sentences for a whole host of crimes. State violence, however, took on a different form, one that was more insidious, less visible, whose reach and impact was more difficult to discern. This violence—born of an enlightened justice crafted by the hands of the revolutionary generation's most esteemed men—was hidden, literally, behind the high walls of the great penitentiaries, emblems of democratic order and restraint.

Despite their investment in using penal authority to reassert social order in the young nation, state officials and reformers would never have foreseen the consequences of this strategy two hundred years later: the United States has the highest rate of incarceration in the world.[8] From their perspective, the legacy of excess in penal authority belonged to Europe, and they worked tirelessly to make punishment in America distinct and removed from British punishment, which they deemed barbaric. But in 2014, England had only the tenth highest incarceration rate in the world, imprisoning 148 people for every 100,000 people, compared to the United States, which imprisoned 737 of every 100,000 people.[9] The United States incarcerates women at a higher rate than any other country at 8.9 percent, while women make up only 5.5 percent of prisoners in England. In 2009, 1 in 300 black women was incarcerated in the United States compared to 1 in 1,099 white women and 1 in 704 Hispanic women. The effects of longstanding practices of criminalization of African Americans throughout American history have been exacerbated by mandatory minimum sentencing laws.[10]

While some nineteenth-century elites surely would have welcomed the opportunity to imprison poor people more liberally than they did, many remained sensitive to the exertion of unfettered state power amid a political culture that celebrated liberty, freedom, and democracy. The problem with the legacy of reformative incarceration as conceived and implemented between 1785 and 1835 is not that it was more violent, racist, punitive, or even rigid than earlier systems of criminal justice. In fact, none of those things is true. Punishment in the early national penitentiary was a generous gift of benevolent statesmen who could have resorted to more barbaric practices if they wished, but they did not. Rather, the founding generation are culpable for the expansion and misuse of the carceral state in the present because they designed and celebrated a system alleged to be more gentle, fair, and humane. This justified its expansive reach and alleviated whatever lingering concerns others might have about this great show of force. The penitentiary made the systemic manipulation of individuals, the classification and assessment of difference, and the restriction of one's life chances based on these differences seem both natural and neutral—a legacy with profoundly devastating consequences for American justice.

APPENDIX

Walnut Street Convicts by Sex, 1787–1810

Year	Women	Men	Total	% Women
1787	13	63	76	17.1
1788	13	112	125	10.4
1789	25	115	140	17.8
1790	20	71	91	21.9
1791	17	61	78	21.7
1792	19	46	65	29.2
1793	12	43	55	21.8
1794	11	43	54	20.3
1795	21	91	112	18.7
1796	20	114	134	14.9
1797	15	98	113	13.2
1798	19	119	138	13.7
1799	36	94	130	27.6
1800	19	87	106	17.9
1801	20	140	160	12.5
1802	19	70	89	21.3
1803	15	107	122	12.2
1804	29	88	117	24.7
1805	26	103	129	20.0
1806	26	132	158	16.4
1807	22	125	147	14.9
1808	30	150	180	16.6
1809	49	149	198	24.7
1810	52	177	229	22.7
Total	548	2398	2946	18.6

Pennsylvania General Assembly, *Report of Committee Relative to the Jail or Penitentiary in Phila-delphia* (Lancaster, Pa., 1811).

Women Convicts by Occupation, 1820–1824

	1820	1821	1822	1823	1824
Servant	17	23	25	29	28
Seamstress	4	2		2	2
Washerwoman	1	3	2	1	3
Milliner	2				
Laborer	1				
Cook		1			
Tobacconist		1			
Housekeeper			2		1
Spinster			2		
Huckster			1		
Whitewasher				1	
Tayloress				1	
Mantuamaker				1	1
Milk Girl					1
Shoebinder					1
Marketwoman					1
Woman of Pleasure					1

Prison Sentence Docket, Philadelphia Prisons System, PCA.

Women Imprisoned for Running Tippling Houses, 1820–1835
(They could not afford to pay the fine associated with conviction)

Date	Name	Race/ethnicity and age (when available)
1820	Margaret Mitchell	White, 24
1821	Elizabeth Hiram	German, 60
1821	Sarah Mills	White
1823	Mary McCarty	White
1823	Sarah Beard	n/a
1823	Ann James	White
1823	Jerusha Long	White
1823	Mary Fraley	White
1824	Margaret Clark	White, 37
1824	Hannah Parkinson	White
1825	Margaret Cassady	White
1825	Sarah Place	English, 24
1826	Bridget Matters	White
1826	Susan Place	White
1831	Nancy James	Black
1832	Margaret Morrison	White

Prison Sentence Docket, Philadelphia Prisons System, PCA

Women in Walnut Street Prison by Classification

	1795	1807	1823
Prisoners for trial	94	458	968
Convicts	21	23	92
Vagrants	134	213	482
Totals	249	694	1542

Prisoners for Trial Docket, Prison Sentence Docket, and Vagrancy Docket, Philadelphia Prisons System, PCA.

Women Prisoners for Trial by Categories of Charges (%)

	1795	1799	1807	1815	1823
Persons	18	20	30	19	23
Morals	37	43	37	57	36
Property	43	36	31	24	40
Total charges	103	210	458	928	968

Prisoners for Trial Docket, Philadelphia Prisons System, PCA.

Charges Against Women, Mayor's Court, Philadelphia

	1795	1799	1807	1815	1823
Adultery/Fornication	1	—	1	—	1
Assault/Battery	10	8	16	30	28
Counterfeit	3	—	—	—	6
Disorderly/Bawdy	3	3	8	17	5
Larceny	19	36	40	68	89
Misc	0	1	4	—	1
Riot	—	—	—	—	7
Tippling House	4	9	—	36	13

Mayor's Court Docket, Philadelphia Prisons System, PCA. Misc includes Conspiracy, Entering, Misdemeanor, and Nuisance.

Women's Larceny Convictions, 1795–1810

	Larceny	Other
1795	15	6
1796	30	2
1797	15	3
1798	14	3
1799	35	6
1800	16	4
1801	20	1
1802	20	3
1803	10	6
1804	20	12
1805	19	5
1806	26	2
1807	20	3
1808	23	7
1809	38	13
1810	36	19
Totals	357	95

Prison Sentence Docket, Philadelphia Prisons System, PCA.

Women's Larceny Convictions, 1820–1835

	Larceny	Other
1820	40	34
1821	56	26
1822	53	20
1823	65	27
1824	55	20
1825	57	40
1826	67	27
1827	47	29
1828	49	24
1829	48	15
1830	61	16
1831	59	14
1832	34	16
1833	28	19
1834	32	23
1835	23	12
Totals	774	362

Prison Sentence Docket, Philadelphia Prisons System, PCA. Beginning in 1831 women convicted to one year or more were sent to Eastern State Penitentiary: eleven in 1831 and 1832 respectively, eight in 1833, thirteen in 1834, six in 1835.

Women Convicted of Larceny by Age

	1795–1799	1820–1824
Under 19	15	54
20 to 29	40	159
30 to 39	19	73
40 to 49	8	28
Over 50	11	14
Not specified	26	69
Total	119	397

Prison Sentence Docket, Philadelphia Prisons System, PCA.

Women Convicted of Arson

Year	Name	Race	County	Sentence
1799	Hannah Carson	Black	Phila	12 years
1801	Eve Resch	—	Phila	2 years
1802	Jane Wedge	Black	Phila	5 years
1803	Hetty Dorson	Black	York	12 years
1803	Ruth Grimes	Black	York	12 years
1804	Sabe	Black	Adams	5 years
1804	Magdalin	Black	Phila	—
1804	Flora	Black	Phila	12 years
1820	Maria Cummins	—	Phila	5 years
1822	Sal	Yellow	York	7 years
1823	Matilda Scott	Black	York	10 years
1827	Rachael Robinson	Black	Phila	5 years
1828	Rebecca Brooks	Black	Franklin	5 years

Prison Sentence Docket, Philadelphia Prisons System, PCA.

Women Convicts by Race, 1795–1810

Year	African descent	European descent	Not listed	Total
1795	5	10	6	21
1796	13	14	5	32
1797	7	8	3	18
1798	5	6	6	17
1799	18	11	12	41
1800	9	4	7	20
1801	10	5	6	21
1802	10	4	9	23
1803	10	2	4	16
1804	8	10	14	32
1805	6	4	14	24
1806	13	2	13	28
1807	11	7	5	23
1808	13	6	11	30
1809	17	9	25	51
1810	21	1	33	55

Prison Sentence Docket, Philadelphia Prisons System, PCA.

Women Convicts by Race, 1820–1835

Year	African descent	European descent	Not listed	Total
1820	36	34	4	74
1821	46	35	1	82
1822	44	28	1	73
1823	51	32	9	92
1824	41	28	6	75
1825	57	40	0	97
1826	61	30	3	94
1827	49	21	6	76
1828	54	19	0	73
1829	45	16	2	63
1830	55	21	1	77
1831	51	22	0	73
1832	33	16	1	50
1833	29	14	4	47
1834	23	17	14	55
1835	11	9	15	35

Prison Sentence Docket, Philadelphia Prisons System, PCA.

Language of Race, Women, 1795–1810

Year	Black	White	Mulatto	Mulatress	Negro	Negress	Yellow	Coloured
1795			1			4		
1796	3		1		1	8		
1797	2		1	1		3		
1798	2		1	2				
1799	1		2	1		14		
1800				2		7		
1801				1		9		
1802	1	1		1		8		
1803	4			1	1	4		
1804	1			1		6		
1805	1	1	1			2	1	1
1806	9	1				3		1
1807	9					1		1
1808	6		3				2	2
1809	8	1	7		1			1
1810	12		1			1	5	2

Prison Sentence Docket, Philadelphia Prisons System, PCA. Most people designated by a European birthplace such as Ireland, England, Scotland, Germany, or Spain would be described as "white" by 1815.

Language of Race, Women, 1820–1835

Year	Black	White	Mulatto	Yellow
1820	23	34	11	2
1821	30	35	9	6
1822	31	28	9	4
1823	39	32	5	7
1824	30	28	6	5
1825	44	40	2	11
1826	38	30	3	20
1827	37	21	7	5
1828	37	19	10	7
1829	28	16	13	3
1830	42	21	11	2
1831	40	22	11	0
1832	24	16	81	
1833	23	14	5	1
1834	17	17	5	2
1835	7	9	2	2

Prison Sentence Docket, Philadelphia Prisons System, PCA. No entries under Mulatress, Negro, or Negress; one listed as Coloured in 1821. Race replaces birthplace as the most important and consistently reported characteristic by 1820.

NOTES

⚓

Introduction

1. The state constitution granted governing authority to a group of six men who made up the Supreme Executive Council, with one of them serving as president. Job R. Tyson, *Essay on the Penal Law of Pennsylvania* (Philadelphia, 1827), 52.

2. Eric Foner, *Tom Paine and Revolutionary America* (New York: Oxford University Press, 1976); Michael Meranze, *Laboratories of Virtue: Punishment, Revolution, and Authority in Philadelphia, 1760–1835* (Chapel Hill: University of North Carolina Press, 1996), 56; Clare A. Lyons, *Sex Among the Rabble: An Intimate History of Gender & Power in the Age of Revolution, Philadelphia, 1730–1830* (Chapel Hill: University of North Carolina Press, 2006), 209.

3. Gary Nash, *First City: Philadelphia and the Forging of Historical Memory* (Philadelphia: University of Pennsylvania Press, 2002); for analysis of Philadelphia's growth, see Susan E. Klepp, *Philadelphia in Transition: A Demographic History of the City and Its Occupational Groups, 1720–1830* (New York: Garland, 1989); and Klepp, *The Swift Progress of Population: A Documentary and Bibliographic Study of Philadelphia's Growth, 1642–1859* (Philadelphia: American Philosophical Society, 1991).

4. John Dickinson, Council Chamber, January 20, 1784, in Samuel Hazard et al., eds., *Pennsylvania Archives* 4th Ser., 3 (Harrisburg, 1874–1935), 953–54.

5. "Letter to Mr. Printer," *Freeman's Journal*, July 13, 1785. The juror's identity was known by the printer but not the public.

6. The question of women's place and the gendered dimensions of the social and political life of the early republic have been topics of sustained inquiry since 1980. See Mary Beth Norton, *Liberty's Daughters: The Revolutionary Experience of American Women, 1750–1800* (Ithaca, N.Y.: Cornell University Press, 1980); Linda Kerber, *Women of the Republic: Intellect and Ideology in Revolutionary America* (Chapel Hill: University of North Carolina Press, 1980); Jan Lewis, *The Pursuit of Happiness: Family and Values in Jefferson's Virginia* (New York: Cambridge University Press, 1983); Joan M. Jensen, *Loosening the Bonds: Mid-Atlantic Farm Women, 1750–1850* (New Haven, Conn.: Yale University Press, 1986); Christine Stansell, *City of Women: Sex and Class in New York, 1789–1860* (Urbana: University of Illinois Press, 1987); Jeanne Boydston, *Home and Work: Housework, Wages, and the Ideology of Labor in the Early Republic* (New York: Oxford University Press, 1990); Susan Juster, *Disorderly Women: Sexual Politics and Evangelicalism in Revolutionary New England* (Ithaca, N.Y.: Cornell University Press, 1994); Mary Beth Norton, *Founding Mothers & Fathers: Gendered Power and the Forming of American Society* (New York: Knopf, 1996); Catherine Allgor, *Parlor Politics: In Which the Ladies of Washington Help Build a City and a Government* (Charlottesville: University Press of Virginia, 2000); Susan Branson, *These Fiery Frenchified Dames: Women and Political Culture in Early National Philadelphia* (Philadelphia: University of Pennsylvania Press, 2001); Richard Godbeer, *Sexual Revolution in Early*

America (Baltimore: Johns Hopkins University Press, 2002); Mary Kelley, *Learning to Stand and Speak: Women, Education, and Public Life in America's Republic* (Chapel Hill: University of North Carolina Press, 2006); Lyons, *Sex Among the Rabble*; Rosemarie Zagarri, *Revolutionary Backlash: Women and Politics in the Early American Republic* (Philadelphia: University of Pennsylvania Press, 2007); Carolyn Eastman, *A Nation of Speechifiers: Making an American Public After the Revolution* (Chicago: University of Chicago Press, 2009); Susan E. Klepp, *Revolutionary Conceptions: Women, Fertility, and Family Limitation in America, 1760–1820* (Chapel Hill: University of North Carolina Press, 2009); Ellen Hartigan-O'Connor, *The Ties That Buy: Women and Commerce in Revolutionary America* (Philadelphia: University of Pennsylvania Press, 2009); Lucia McMahon, *Mere Equals: The Paradox of Educated Women in the Early American Republic* (Ithaca, N.Y.: Cornell University Press, 2012).

7. The idea of "republican motherhood" carved out an important historical and historiographical place for women where there previously seemed to be none. See Kerber, *Women of the Republic* and Norton, *Liberty's Daughters*. This concept was challenged by scholars who saw other opportunities and expectations for women in the period, including that of wife. See Jan Lewis, "The Republican Wife: Virtue and Seduction in the Early Republic," *William and Mary Quarterly* 3rd ser., 44, no. 4 (1987): 689–721. Though bodies of scholarship on the lives of enslaved, immigrant, poor, and working women have demonstrated the interpretive limits of a category defined principally for elite white women, the idea of "republican motherhood" has had tremendous staying power as the placeholder for women in the early republic.

8. "Letter to Mr. Printer," *Freeman's Journal*, July 13, 1785.

9. Alexis de Tocqueville, *Democracy in America* (London: Saunders and Otley, 1835).

10. G. J. Barker-Benfield, *The Culture of Sensibility: Sex and Society in Eighteenth-Century Britain* (Chicago: University of Chicago Press, 1992); Nicole Eustace, *Passion Is the Gale: Emotion, Power, and the Coming of the American Revolution* (Chapel Hill: University of North Carolina Press, 2008); Sarah Knott, *Sensibility and the American Revolution* (Chapel Hill: University of North Carolina Press, 2009); G. J. Barker-Benfield, *The Americanization of Sensibility* (Chicago: University of Chicago Press, 2010).

11. "Letter to Mr. Printer," *Freeman's Journal*, July 13, 1785.

12. "The Case of Eleanor Glass," *Freeman's Journal*, July 20, 1785.

13. On the malleability of patriarchy, see Judith M. Bennett, *History Matters: Patriarchy and the Challenge of Feminism* (Philadelphia: University of Pennsylvania Press, 2006).

14. Carroll Smith-Rosenberg, "Dis-Covering the Subject of the 'Great Constitutional Discussion,' 1786–1789," *Journal of American History* 79, no. 3 (1992): 841–73; Carroll Smith-Rosenberg, *This Violent Empire: The Birth of an American National Identity* (Chapel Hill, N.C.: University of North Carolina Press, 2010).

15. "Philadelphia, July 16, 1785," *Freeman's Journal*, July 20, 1785.

16. "Philadelphia, July 20," *Freeman's Journal*, July 20, 1785.

17. Negley King Teeters, *The Cradle of the Penitentiary: The Walnut Street Jail at Philadelphia, 1773–1835* (Philadelphia: Pennsylvania Prison Society, 1955); David Rothman, *Discovery of the Asylum: Social Order and Disorder in the New Republic* (Boston: Little, Brown, 1971); Michel Foucault, *Discipline and Punish: The Birth of the Prison*, trans. Alan Sheridan (New York: Vintage-Random House, 1995); Michael Ignatieff, *A Just Measure of Pain: The Penitentiary in the Industrial Revolution, 1750–1850* (New York: Pantheon, 1978); Michael S. Hindus, *Prison and Plantation: Crime, Justice, and Authority in Massachusetts and South Carolina, 1767–1878* (Chapel Hill: University of North Carolina Press, 1980); Thomas L. Dumm, *Democracy and Punishment: Disciplinary*

Origin of the United States (Madison: University of Wisconsin Press, 1987); Meranze, *Laboratories of Virtue*; Mark Kann, *Punishment, Prisons, and Patriarchy: Liberty and Power in the Early American Republic* (New York: New York University Press, 2005); Rebecca M. McLennan, *The Crisis of Imprisonment: Protest, Politics, and the Making of the American Penal State, 1776–1941* (New York: Cambridge University Press, 2008); Jennifer Graber, *The Furnace of Affliction: Prisons and Religion in Antebellum America* (Chapel Hill: University of North Carolina Press, 2011); Michele Lise Tarter and Richard Bell, eds., *Buried Lives: Incarcerated in Early America* (Athens: University of Georgia Press, 2012).

18. Negley King Teeters, *They Were in Prison: A History of the Pennsylvania Prison Society, 1787–1937* (Philadelphia: Winston, 1937).

19. Foucault's *Discipline and Punish* inspired important literary studies as well. See Peter Okun, *Crime and the Nation: Prison Reform and Popular Fiction in Philadelphia, 1786–1800* (New York: Routledge, 2002); Caleb Smith, *The Prison and the American Imagination* (New Haven, Conn.: Yale University Press, 2009); Jeannine Marie DeLombard, *In the Shadow of the Gallows: Race, Crime, and American Civic Identity* (Philadelphia: University of Pennsylvania Press, 2012); Jodi Schorb, *Reading Prisoners: Literature, Literacy, and the Transformation of American Punishment, 1700–1845* (New Brunswick, N.J.: Rutgers University Press, 2014).

20. Ignatieff, *A Just Measure of Pain*.

21. Dumm, *Democracy and Punishment*.

22. Meranze, *Laboratories of Virtue*.

23. Model studies of intersectionality in early America include Kathleen Brown, *Good Wives, Nasty Wenches, Anxious Patriarchs: Gender, Race, and Power in Colonial Virginia* (Chapel Hill: University of North Carolina Press, 1996); Bruce Dorsey, *Reforming Men and Women: Gender in the Antebellum City* (Ithaca, N.Y.: Cornell University Press, 2002); Kristen Fischer, *Suspect Relations: Sex, Race, and Resistance in Colonial North Carolina* (Ithaca, N.Y.: Cornell University Press, 2002); Jennifer Morgan, *Laboring Women: Reproduction and Gender in New World Slavery* (Philadelphia: University of Pennsylvania Press, 2004); Sharon Block, *Rape and Sexual Power in Early America* (Chapel Hill: University of North Carolina Press, 2006); Juliana Barr, *Peace Came in the Form of a Woman: Indians and Spaniards in the Texas Borderlands* (Chapel Hill: University of North Carolina Press, 2007); Ann M. Little, *Abraham in Arms: War and Gender in Colonial New England* (Philadelphia: University of Pennsylvania Press, 2007); Seth Rockman, *Scraping By: Wage Labor, Slavery, and Survival in Early Baltimore* (Baltimore: Johns Hopkins University Press, 2008); Jennifer Spear, *Race, Sex, and Social Order in Early New Orleans* (Baltimore: Johns Hopkins University Press, 2009).

24. I consulted 5,722 records from Walnut Street Prison, Philadelphia, including 1,802 records from the Prison Sentence Docket, 2,881 records from the Prisoners for Trial Docket, and 1,039 records from the Vagrancy Docket, PCA; 848 records from Dauphin County Jail, PSA; 741 Philadelphia city court records, including 262 from Quarter Sessions and 479 from Mayor's Court, PCA; 318 records from statewide courts, including 263 records from the Pennsylvania Supreme Court and 55 from the Pennsylvania State Oyer and Terminer, PSA; other county court records, including 194 from Chester County and 524 from Dauphin County, PSA.

25. This book builds on the early work of feminist scholars who used court records to write women into history: Toby L. Ditz, *Property and Kinship: Inheritance in Early Connecticut, 1750–1820* (Princeton, N.J.: Princeton University Press, 1986); Carol F. Karlsen, *The Devil in the Shape of a Woman: Witchcraft in Colonial New England* (New York: Vintage, 1989); Cornelia Hughes

Dayton, *Women Before the Bar: Gender, Law, and Society in Connecticut, 1639–1789* (Chapel Hill: University of North Carolina Press, 1995); Kathleen Brown, *Good Wives*; Terri L. Snyder, *Brabbling Women: Disorderly Speech and the Law in Early Virginia* (Ithaca, N.Y: Cornell University Press, 2003).

26. Barbara Johnson, quoted in Saul Cornell, "Early American History in a Postmodern Age," *William and Mary Quarterly* 3rd ser. 50, no. 2 (1993): 329–41.

27. Joan W. Scott, "Experience," in *Feminists Theorize the Political*, ed. Judith Butler and Joan W. Scott (New York: Routledge, 1993). This is also an important part of the turn to new historicism in literary studies; as Michael Warner argues, "meaning does not transcend context but is produced within it," in Saul Cornell, "Early American History," 334–35.

28. Studies of women that address this period include Nicole Rafter, *Partial Justice: Women, Prisons, and Social Control* (Boston: Northeastern University Press, 1985); and Susan Branson, *Dangerous to Know: Women, Crime, and Notoriety in the Early Republic* (Philadelphia: University of Pennsylvania Press, 2008). Studies of later periods include Estelle Freedman, *Their Sisters' Keepers: Women's Prison Reform in America, 1830–1930* (Ann Arbor: University of Michigan Press, 1984); Anne Butler, *Gendered Justice in the American West: Women Prisoners in Men's Penitentiaries* (Urbana: University of Illinois Press, 1997); Kali Gross, *Colored Amazons: Crime, Violence, and Black Women in the City of Brotherly Love, 1880–1910* (Durham, N.C.: Duke University Press, 2006); L. Mara Dodge, *"Whores and Thieves of the Worst Kind": A Study of Women, Crime, and Prisons, 1835–2000* (DeKalb: Northern Illinois University Press, 2006); Cheryl D. Hicks, *Talk with You like a Woman: African American Women, Justice, and Reform in New York, 1890–1935* (Chapel Hill: University of North Carolina Press, 2010).

29. Pennsylvania has been the subject of important histories of crime. See G. S. Rowe, "Women's Crime and Criminal Administration," *PMHB* 109, no. 3 (1985): 335–68; G. S. Rowe, "Black Offenders, Criminal Courts, and Philadelphia Society in the Late Eighteenth-Century," *Journal of Social History* 22, no. 4 (1989): 685–712; Thomas P. Slaughter, *Bloody Dawn: The Christiana Riot and Racial Violence in the Antebellum North* (New York: Oxford University Press, 1991); Jack D. Marietta and G. S. Rowe, "Violent Crime, Victims, and Society in Pennsylvania, 1682–1800," *Pennsylvania History* 66, Supplement (1999): 24–54; Jack D. Marietta and G. S. Rowe, *Troubled Experiment: Crime and Justice in Pennsylvania, 1682–1800* (Philadelphia: University of Pennsylvania Press, 2006).

30. Pioneering social histories of early Philadelphia put information about immigrants, working people, servants, slaves, and free blacks at our fingertips decades ago. See Jensen, *Loosening the Bonds*; Klepp, *Philadelphia in Transition*; Klepp, *The Swift Progress of Population*; Lisa Wilson, *Life After Death: Widows in Pennsylvania, 1750–1850* (Philadelphia: Temple University Press, 1992); Gary Nash and Jean Soderlund, *Freedom by Degrees: Emancipation in Pennsylvania and Its Aftermath* (New York: Oxford University Press, 1991); Gary Nash, *Forging Freedom: The Formation of Philadelphia's Black Community, 1720–1840* (Cambridge, Mass.: Harvard University Press, 1988); Sharon Salinger, *"To Serve Well and Faithfully": Labour and Indentured Servants in Pennsylvania, 1682–1800* (New York: Cambridge University Press, 1987); Billy G. Smith and Richard Wojtowicz, *Blacks Who Stole Themselves: Advertisements for Runaways in the Pennsylvania Gazette, 1728–1790* (Philadelphia: University of Pennsylvania Press, 1989); Billy G. Smith, *The "Lower Sort": Philadelphia's Laboring People, 1750–1800* (Ithaca, N.Y.: Cornell University Press, 1990).

31. For discussion of a politically engaged social history, see Stephanie M. H. Camp, *Closer to Freedom: Enslaved Women and Everyday Resistance in the Plantation South* (Chapel Hill: University of North Carolina Press, 2004), introduction; Walter Johnson, "On Agency," *Journal of*

Social History 37, no. 1 (Autumn 2003): 113–24. For more on the politics of history, see Michel-Rolph Trouillot, *Silencing the Past: Power and the Production of History* (Boston: Beacon, 1995). Contemporary critical prison studies commonly privilege a critique of punishment from the perspective of those imprisoned. Important recent work includes Patrick Timmons et al., "Punishment and Death; The Need for Radical Analysis," special issue, *Radical History Review* 96 (Fall 2006); Ruth Wilson Gilmore, *Golden Gulag: Prisons, Surplus, Crisis, and Opposition in Globalizing California* (Berkeley: University of California Press, 2007); Beth E. Richie, *Arrested Justice: Black Women, Violence, and America's Prison Nation* (New York: New York University Press, 2012); Dan Berger, *The Struggle Within: Prisons, Political Prisoners, and Mass Movements in the United States* (Oakland, Calif.: PM Press, 2014).

32. Michel Foucault, *The History of Sexuality*, trans. Robert Hurley (New York: Vintage, 1990); Sharon Marcus, "The State's Oversight: From Sexual Bodies to Erotic Selves," *Social Research: An International Quarterly* 78, no. 2 (Summer 2011): 509–32.

33. Foucault, *History of Sexuality*, 140–44.

34. On punishment and national identity, see DeLombard, *In the Shadow of the Gallows*; Smith, *Prison and American Imagination*; Karen Halttunen, *Murder Most Foul: The Killer and the American Gothic Imagination* (Cambridge, Mass.: Harvard University Press, 1998).

35. Pioneering work includes John D'Emilio, *Intimate Matters: A History of Sexuality in America* (New York: Harper & Row, 1988); Richard C. Trexler, *Sex and Conquest: Gendered Violence, Political Order, and the European Conquest of the Americas* (Ithaca, N.Y.: Cornell University Press, 1995); Martha Hodes, *White Women, Black Men: Illicit Sex in the Nineteenth-Century South* (New Haven, Conn.: Yale University Press, 1997); Catherine Clinton and Michele Gillespie, eds., *The Devil's Lane: Sex and Race in the Early South* (New York: Oxford University Press, 1997); Merril D. Smith, ed., *Sex and Sexuality in Early America* (New York: New York University Press, 1998); Martha Hodes, ed., *Sex, Love, Race: Crossing Boundaries in North American History* (New York: New York University Press, 1999); Janet Moore Lindman and Michele Lise Tarter, eds., *A Centre of Wonders: The Body in Early America* (Ithaca, N.Y.: Cornell University Press, 2001); Richard Godbeer, *Sexual Revolution in Early America* (Baltimore: Johns Hopkins University Press, 2002); Christopher Grasso, ed., "Sexuality in Early America," special issue, *William and Mary Quarterly* 3rd ser. 60, no. 1 (2003); Diane Miller Sommerville, *Rape and Race in the Nineteenth-Century South* (Chapel Hill: University of North Carolina Press, 2004); Sharon Block, *Rape and Sexual Power in Early America* (Chapel Hill: University of North Carolina Press, 2006); Thomas Foster, *Sex and the Eighteenth-Century Man: Massachusetts and the History of Sexuality in America* (Boston: Beacon Press, 2006); Lyons, *Sex Among the Rabble*; Thomas Foster, *Long Before Stonewall: Histories of Same-Sex Sexuality in Early America* (New York: New York University Press, 2007).

36. On the pivotal role of prisons in making modern sexuality, see Regina Kunzel, *Criminal Intimacy: Prison and the Uneven History of Modern American Sexuality* (Chicago: University of Chicago Press, 2008).

37. Feminist historians have long debated the value of privileging women as subjects of study and the best way to approach an intersectional analysis of race and gender. See Joan Kelly-Gadol, "The Social Relation of the Sexes: Methodological Implications of Women's History," *Signs: A Journal of Women in Culture and Society* 1, no. 4 (1976): 809–23; Nancy A. Hewitt, "Beyond the Search for Sisterhood: American Women's History in the 1980s," *Social History* 10, no. 3 (1985): 299–321; Joan W. Scott, "Gender: A Useful Category of Historical Analysis," *American Historical Review* 91, no. 5 (1986): 1053–1075; Denise Riley, *Am I That Name? Feminism and*

the Category of "Women" in History (Minneapolis: University of Minnesota Press, 1988); Evelyn Brooks Higginbotham, "African-American Women's History and the Metalanguage of Race," *Signs: A Journal of Women in Culture and Society* 17, no. 2 (1992): 251–74; Kathleen M. Brown, "Brave New Worlds: Women's and Gender History," *William and Mary Quarterly* 3rd ser. 50, no. 2 (1993): 311–328; Kathleen M. Brown, "Beyond the Great Debates: Gender and Race in Early America," *Reviews in American History* 26, no. 1 (1998): 96–123; Nancy A. Hewitt, "Taking the True Woman Hostage," *Journal of Women's History* 14, no. 1 (2002): 156–62; Stephanie Camp, "'Ar'n't I a Woman?' in the Vanguard of the History of Race and Sex in the United States," *Journal of Women's History* 19, no. 2 (2007): 146–50; Jennifer Manion, "Historic Heteroessentialism and Other Orderings in Early America," *Signs: Journal of Women in Culture & Society* 34, no. 4 (2009): 981–1003; Cornelia H. Dayton and Lisa Levenstein, "The Big Tent of U.S. Women's and Gender History: A State of the Field," *Journal of American History* 99, no. 3 (2012): 793- 817; Crystal N. Feimster, "The Impact of Racial and Sexual Politics on Women's History," *Journal of American History* 99, no. 3 (2012): 822–26; Michele Mitchell, "Turns of the Kaleidoscope," *Journal of Women's History* 25, no. 4 (2013): 46–73.

38. Important books that examine the relationship between slavery and punishment after emancipation include Roger Lane, *The Roots of Violence in Black Philadelphia, 1860–1900* (Cambridge, Mass.: Harvard University Press, 1986); David M Oshinsky, *Worse Than Slavery: Parchman Farm and the Ordeal of Jim Crow Justice* (New York: Free Press, 1996); A. Leon Higginbotham, *Shades of Freedom: Racial Politics and Presumptions of the American Legal Process* (New York: Oxford University Press, 1996); Gross, *Colored Amazons*; Hannah Rosen, *Terror in the Heart of Freedom: Citizenship, Sexual Violence, and the Meaning of Race in the Postemancipation South* (Chapel Hill: University of North Carolina Press, 2009); Bryan Wagner, *Disturbing the Peace: Black Culture and the Police Power After Slavery* (Cambridge, Mass.: Harvard University Press, 2009); Khalil Gibran Muhammad, *The Condemnation of Blackness: Race, Crime, and the Making of Modern Urban America* (Cambridge, Mass.: Harvard University Press, 2010); Hicks, *Talk with You like a Woman*.

39. In 1804 New Jersey joined Pennsylvania, New York, and all New England in passing abolition acts. Important studies of slavery in the North include Edward Raymond Turner, *The Negro in Pennsylvania: Slavery, Servitude, Freedom, 1639–1861* (Washington, D.C.: American Historical Association, 1911); Leon Litwack, *North of Slavery: The Negro in the Free States* (Chicago: University of Chicago Press, 1961); Mary Frances Berry, *Black Resistance, White Law: A History of Constitutional Racism in America* (New York: Penguin, 1971); Nash, *Forging Freedom*; Joanne Pope Melish, *Disowning Slavery: Gradual Emancipation and "Race" in New England, 1780–1860* (Ithaca, N.Y.: Cornell University Press, 1998); John Wood Sweet, *Bodies Politics: Negotiating Race in the American North, 1730–1830* (Baltimore: Johns Hopkins University Press, 2003); Leslie Harris, *In the Shadow of Slavery: African Americans in New York City, 1626–1863* (Chicago: University of Chicago Press, 2003).

40. See David Brion Davis, *The Problem of Slavery in the Age of Revolution* (Ithaca, N.Y.: Cornell University Press, 1975); Nash and Soderlund, *Freedom by Degrees*; Amy Dru Stanley, *From Bondage to Contract: Wage Labor, Marriage, and the Market in the Age of Slave Emancipation* (New York: Cambridge University Press, 1998); Richard S. Newman, *The Transformation of American Abolitionism: Fighting Slavery in the Early Republic* (Chapel Hill: University of North Carolina Press, 2002); Christopher Brown, *Moral Capital: Foundations of British Abolitionism* (Chapel Hill: University of North Carolina Press, 2006); Beverly C. Tomek, *Colonization and Its Discontents:*

Emancipation, Emigration, and Antislavery in Antebellum Pennsylvania (New York: New York University Press, 2011).

41. *The Trial of Alice Clifton for the Murder of Her Bastard Child* (Philadelphia, 1787).

42. William Bradford, *An Enquiry How Far the Punishment of Death Is Necessary in Pennsylvania with Notes and Illustrations, to Which is Added, an Account of the Goal and Penitentiary House of Philadelphia, and of the Interior Management Thereof By Caleb Lownes of Philadelphia* (Philadelphia, 1793): 26–29.

43. Peter C. Hoffer and N. E. H. Hull, *Murdering Mothers: Infanticide in England and New England, 1558–1803* (New York: New York University Press, 1981), 84. Also see Katie M. Hemphill, "'Driven to the Commission of This Crime': Women and Infanticide in Baltimore, 1835–1860," *Journal of the Early Republic* 32, no. 3 (2012): 437–61.

44. Gross, *Colored Amazons*, 26.

45. Leslie Patrick-Stamp, "Ideology and Punishment: The Crime of Being Black (Pennsylvania, 1639–1804)" (Ph.D. dissertation, University of California, Santa Cruz, 1989); David M. Oshinsky, *Worse Than Slavery*; Angela Yvonne Davis, *Are Prisons Obsolete?* (New York: Seven Stories Press, 2003); Michelle Alexander, *The New Jim Crow: Mass Incarceration in the Age of Colorblindness* (New York: New Press, 2010).

46. Edmund Morgan, "Slavery and Freedom: The American Paradox," *Journal of American History* 59, no. 1 (1972): 5–29.

47. Benjamin Rush, *An Enquiry into the Effects of Public Punishments Upon Criminals and Upon Society. Read in the Society for Promoting Political Enquiries, Convened at the House of His Excellency Benjamin Franklin, Esquire, in Philadelphia, March 9th, 1787* (Philadelphia, 1787); Peter Okun, *Crime and the Nation: Prison Reform and Popular Fiction in Philadelphia, 1786–1800* (New York: Routledge, 2002).

48. Vincent Brown, "Social Death and Political Life in the Study of Slavery," *American Historical Review* 114, no. 5 (2009): 1231–49.

49. Ibid., 1233.

50. On "life chances" as a concept in assessing structural oppressions, see Dean Spade, *Normal Life: Administrative Violence, Critical Trans Politics, and the Limits of Law* (Brooklyn, N.Y.: South End Press, 2011).

51. Eugene E. Doll, "Trial and Error at Allegheny: The Western State Penitentiary, 1818–1838," *PMHB* 81, no. 1 (1957): 3–27.

52. Walnut Street Jail was taken over by the British in 1777 when they occupied the city. After the British left, the colonial government used it as its own prison until the war's end. Teeters, *They Were in Prison*, 17–18.

53. Arch Street Prison was opened in 1817 and housed debtors and witnesses until 1823. Harry E. Barnes, *Evolution of Penology in Pennsylvania: A Study in American Social History* (Indianapolis: Bobbs-Merrill, 1927), 137.

54. Teeters, *They Were in Prison*, 332, 333.

55. Beccaria's work was first published in 1764 in Italian; early English editions include Cesare Marchese di Beccaria, *Essay on Crimes and Punishments* (London, 1767); *An Essay on Crimes and Punishments, Translated From the Italian; With a Commentary, Attributed to Mons. De Voltaire. Translated from the French* (Charlestown, 1777); *An Essay on Crimes and Punishments. Written by the Marquis Beccaria; of Milan. With a Commentary Attributed To Monsieur de Voltaire* (Philadelphia, 1778); *An Essay on Crimes and Punishments. By the Marquis Beccaria, of Milan. With a*

Commentary by M De Voltaire (Philadelphia, 1793). For elaboration on Montesquieu and his influence on Pennsylvania reformers, see Michael Meranze, "Penitential Ideal in Eighteenth-Century Philadelphia," *PMHB* 108, no. 4 (1984): 422–23.

56. Rush and Bradford both discussed these essays. See Rush, *An Enquiry into the Effects of Public Punishments* and Bradford, *An Enquiry How Far the Punishment of Death.*

57. Wilson helped draft both the state and federal constitutions; Homer T. Rosenberger, "James Wilson's Theories of Punishment," *PMHB* 73, no. 1 (1949): 45–63.

58. Western State Penitentiary was authorized in 1818 under a different design that allowed inmate communication and group labor during the day. It opened and functioned with remarkably little notice. After Eastern State Penitentiary opened in 1829, another act was passed to renovate the architecture of Western State so that it would be more conducive to solitary labor and confinement. PSAMPP, "Brief History of the Penal Legislation of Pennsylvania," *Journal of Prison Discipline and Philanthropy* 1 (1845): 12–13.

59. "State Prison Revolt, Philadelphia, March 29, 1820," *Weekly Recorder*, April 13, 1820.

60. Negley King Teeters, "The Early Days of the Eastern State Penitentiary at Philadelphia," *Pennsylvania History* 16, no. 4 (1949): 261–302, 261.

61. Studies that make this connection include Gary B. Nash, "Poverty and Poor Relief in Pre-Revolutionary Philadelphia," *William and Mary Quarterly* 33, no. 1 (1976): 3–30; John Alexander, *Render Them Submissive: Responses to Poverty in Philadelphia, 1760–1800* (Amherst: University of Massachusetts Press, 1980); Dorsey, *Reforming Men and Women*; Simon P. Newman, *Embodied History: The Lives of the Poor in Early Philadelphia* (Philadelphia: University of Pennsylvania Press, 2003); Tarter and Bell, *Buried Lives.*

62. Select feminist critiques of liberalism include Drucilla Cornell, *Transformations: Recollective Imagination and Sexual Difference* (New York: Routledge, 1993); Joan Scott, *Only Paradoxes to Offer: French Feminists and the Rights of Man* (Cambridge: Harvard University Press, 1997); Carole Patemen, *The Sexual Contract* (Stanford, Calif.: Stanford University Press, 1998); Denise Riley, *Am I That Name: Feminism and the Category of Women in History* (Minneapolis: University of Minnesota Press 2003).

Chapter 1. Rebellious Workers

1. Carole Shammas, "The Space Problem in Early United States Cities," *William and Mary Quarterly* 3rd ser. 57, no. 3 (July 2000): 505–42, 506.

2. Greater London Council and Office for National Statistics, 1801–2011, http://data.london .gov.uk/datastore/package/historic-census-population.

3. Shammas, "The Space Problem," 531–32.

4. Carole Shammas, "The Female Social Structure of Philadelphia in 1775," *PMHB* 107, no. 1 (1983): 69–83. See Shammas's discussion of Sarah Eve as an example of a woman who worried that her own integrity and status were compromised when she and some other women ended up without male chaperons in the middle of the city, where they were "surrounded by people of all ranks and denominations," 78–79.

5. The lower classes were less deferential to elites throughout the eighteenth century, even before the revolution, than previously imagined. See Michael Zuckerman, "Tocqueville, Turner, and Turds: Four Stories of Manners in Early America," *Journal of American History* 85, no. 1 (1998): 13–42.

6. Larceny was the most common crime for which women were convicted. See tables "Women's Larceny Convictions, 1795–1810" and "Women's Larceny Convictions, 1820–1835," in Appendix.

7. See A. Leon Higginbotham, *In the Matter of Color: Race and the American Legal System; The Colonial Period* (New York: Oxford University Press, 1980); G. S. Rowe, "Black Offenders, Criminal Courts, and Philadelphia Society in the Late Eighteenth-Century," *Journal of Social History* 22, no. 4 (1989): 685–712.

8. In the period 1790–1830, white female household heads increased from 13.3 to 18.7 percent; white male, age 16–25 from 4.4 to 11.3 percent; free blacks, from 2.4 to 7.4 percent. See Shammas, "The Space Problem," 534, "Table V: Estimated Proportion of Household Heads Drawn from Selected Greater Philadelphia Social Groups, 1790–1830." The source for Shammas's table is Tom W. Smith, "The Dawn of the Urban-Industrial Age: The Social Structure of Philadelphia, 1790–1830" (Ph.D. dissertation, University of Chicago, 1980), 168, 178.

9. PSAMPP, *Extracts and Remarks on the Subject of Punishment and Reformation of Criminals; Published by Order of the Society, Established in Philadelphia, for Alleviating the Miseries of Public Prisons* (Philadelphia, 1790); and Benjamin Rush, *An Enquiry Into the Effects of Public Punishments Upon Criminals and Upon Society. Read in the Society for Promoting Political Enquiries, Convened at the House of His Excellency Benjamin Franklin, Esquire, in Philadelphia, March 9th, 1787* (Philadelphia, 1787).

10. In the early years much was made of prisoners being eligible to keep the balance of their earnings once all fines, fees, transportation, and upkeep costs were paid. Occasionally women successfully petitioned to get the earnings of their husbands in prison. An account book reveals few prisoners received such funds. See Prison Stock Book, 1800–1805, Philadelphia Prisons System, PCA.

11. Religious counsel was promoted as a central part of reformative incarceration from the beginning, at least in theory. This is not surprising given the role of religious leaders and narratives of redemption throughout the colonial period. See Jennifer Graber, *The Furnace of Affliction: Prisons and Religion in Antebellum America* (Chapel Hill: University of North Carolina Press, 2011); and Daniel A. Cohen, *Pillars of Salt, Monuments of Grace: New England Crime Literature and the Origins of American Popular Culture, 1674–1860* (New York: Oxford University Press, 1993).

12. Sarah Cadbury, "Extracts from the Diary of Ann Warder, March 31, 1787," *PMHB* 18, no. 1 (1894): 51–63, 61.

13. French emigrant La Rochefoucault Liancourt also wrote of the scene, "Criminals, loaded with irons, and fettered through the streets, and along the roads, presented to the public the spectacle of vice rather than of shame and misery." François Alexandre Frédéric La Rochefoucault Liancourt, *On the Prisons of Philadelphia* (Philadelphia, 1796).

14. *PG*, March 29, 1786.

15. Bradley Chapin, "Felony Law Reform in the Early Republic," *PMHB* 113, no. 2 (1989): 163–83.

16. *Statutes*, XII: 280–81.

17. See J. Thomas Scharf and Thompson Westcott, *History of Philadelphia, 1609–1884* (Philadelphia, 1884) 1: 443–44. The revolutionary era sparked a rich tradition of organizing and resistance among working-class men. See Steven Rosswurm, *Arms, Country, and Class: The Philadelphia Militia and "Lower Sort" During the American Revolution, 1775–1783* (New Brunswick, N.J.: Rutgers University Press, 1987); Jesse Lemisch, *Jack Tar vs. John Bull: The Role of New York's Seamen in Precipitating the Revolution* (New York: Routledge, 1997).

18. Scharf and Westcott, *History of Philadelphia*, 1: 443–44; and *PG*, January 21, 1784.

19. A cook in Walnut Street Prison was paid three shillings three pence in 1795, while a whitewasher at Pennsylvania Hospital was paid five shillings five pence. See Minutes, March 11, 1795, BOI; Billy Smith, *The "Lower Sort": Philadelphia's Laboring People, 1750–1800* (Ithaca, N.Y.: Cornell University Press, 1990), 92.

20. Negley King Teeters, *The Cradle of the Penitentiary: The Walnut Street Jail at Philadelphia, 1773–1835* (Philadelphia, 1955), 28.

21. In North Carolina, outspoken women who were charged with being common "scolds" received a ride in a ducking stool. See Kristen Fischer, *Suspect Relations: Sex, Race, and Resistance in Colonial North Carolina* (Ithaca, N.Y.: Cornell University Press, 2002), 138–39. In Chester County, Pennsylvania, for example, public shaming such as the pillory or wearing a sign constituted only 2 percent of over two thousand convictions from 1682 to 1800. See Jack D. Marietta and G. S. Rowe, *Troubled Experiment: Crime and Justice in Pennsylvania, 1682 to 1800* (Philadelphia: University of Pennsylvania Press, 2006), 79.

22. Harry E. Barnes, *Evolution of Penology in Pennsylvania: A Study in American Social History* (Indianapolis: Bobbs-Merrill, 1927), 31–37.

23. On the prison as metaphor for a larger call for hierarchy and order, see Caleb Smith, *The Prison and the American Imagination* (New Haven, Conn.: Yale University Press, 2009).

24. *Statutes*, XII: 280–81.

25. Caleb Lownes, *An Account of the Goal and Penitentiary House of Philadelphia, and of the Interior Management Thereof By Caleb Lownes of Philadelphia* (Philadelphia, 1793), 77. This edition was published together with another essay: William Bradford, *An Enquiry How Far the Punishment of Death is Necessary in Pennsylvania with Notes and Illustrations, to Which is Added, an Account of the Goal and Penitentiary House of Philadelphia, and of the Interior Management Thereof. By Caleb Lownes of Philadelphia* (Philadelphia, 1793).

26. Scholarship revealing the power of collective organizing by prisoners since the 1960s includes Ruth Wilson Gilmore, *Golden Gulag: Prisons, Surplus, Crisis, and Opposition in Globalizing California* (Berkeley: University of California Press, 2007); Dan Berger, *Captive Nation: Black Prison Organizing in the Civil Rights Era* (Chapel Hill: University of North Carolina Press, 2014); Dan Berger, *The Struggle Within: Prisons, Political Prisoners, and Mass Movements in the United States* (Oakland, Calif.: PM Press, 2014).

27. *PG*, June 28, 1786.

28. Minutes, August 6, 1788, PSAMPP Acting Committee, Adams and Wistar Letterbook, PPS.

29. "On Tuesday, the 11th inst. several of the convicts endeavoured to make their escape by getting into the common sewer, but after a long and vigilant subterranean pursuit, we are informed they are all restored to their keepers." *PG*, September 19, 1787.

30. Scharf and Westcott, *History of Philadelphia*, 1: 453.

31. *PG*, August 20, 1788.

32. *Pennsylvania Mercury and Universal Advertiser*, January 13, 1789.

33. *PG*, December 31, 1788.

34. John M'Farland, *Some Account of John Burns, John Logan, John Ferguson, John Bennet, and Daniel Cronan, Who Were Executed Upon the Commons in the City of Philadelphia, on Monday the 12th of October, 1789, for the Murder and Robbery of John M'Farland* (Philadelphia, 1789).

35. *PG*, November 5, 1788.

36. J. P. M., *A description, with a perspective view, of the jail, in Philadelphia* (Philadelphia, 1789).

37. Rush, *An Enquiry Into the Effects of Public Punishments*, 6.

38. Rush, *An Enquiry Into the Effects of Public Punishments*, 7.

39. Negley King Teeters, *They Were in Prison: A History of the Pennsylvania Prison Society, 1787–1937* (Philadelphia: Winston, 1937), 95–6. Many of the people in attendance as Rush delivered his lecture in Franklin's house served as charter members of the Philadelphia Society for Alleviating the Miseries of Public Prisons the following year.

40. Meranze calls this phenomenon—that citizens "identified with the condemned or with the infliction of suffering on the condemned" without understanding the greater context of the punishment"mimetic corruption." Michael Meranze, *Laboratories of Virtue: Punishment, Revolution, and Authority in Philadelphia, 1760–1835* (Chapel Hill: University of North Carolina Press, 1996), 8 and chap. 3.

41. Caleb Lownes, *An Account of the Goal and Penitentiary House*, 91.

42. "Report of Visit to Jail Sept. 4. 1787," Correspondence, Box 1, Folder 9, PPS.

43. Work House Calendar of December 16, 1789 is revealing. It names four women convicts, three vagrant women, and one enslaved woman. The convicts were Mary Coningham (City Court, July 1788, larceny); Mary Williams (Quarter Sessions, June 1789, larceny); Isabel McKeever (Mayor's Court, June, 1789, receiving stolen goods); Elizabeth Mooney (Mayor's Court, September 27, 1789, larceny). The vagrants were Elen Armstrong and Jane Mooney, held on suspicion of larceny and Elizabeth Card for disorderly conduct. The enslaved woman was Ann Atkins, charged by the Mayor December 7, 1789 for running away. See Work House Calendar of December 16, 1789 in Samuel Hazard et al., eds., *Pennsylvania Archives* 1st Ser., 11 (Harrisburg, 1874–1935), 648.

44. *PG*, January 16, 1788.

45. These numbers remained roughly steady from 1787–1810, with women averaging 18.6 percent of inmates over the twenty-four year span; See Appendix "Walnut Street Convicts by Sex, 1787–1810."

46. See Jan Lewis, "'Of Every Age Sex & Condition': The Representation of Women in the Constitution," *Journal of the Early Republic* 15, no. 3 (1995): 359–87.

47. "Letter from Benjamin Rush to John Coakley Lettsom, Philadelphia, September 28th, 1787," in *Letters of Benjamin Rush*, vol. 1, *1761–1792*, ed. L. H. Butterfield (Philadelphia: American Philosophical Society, 1951), 443.

48. The period from the 1776 adoption of the Pennsylvania state constitution until the 1829 opening of Eastern State Penitentiary saw the most dramatic transformation of the penal code and modes of punishment deployed. See Meranze, *Laboratories of Virtue*; Teeters, *The Cradle of the Penitentiary* and *They Were in Prison*.

49. "An Acco.t was presented by Samuel Middleton amounting to L13.14.0 for sundry expenses incurred in apprehending in Baltimore and conveying to this prison, Pricilla Roberts, Cath.n Lynch, & Joan Holland, three convicts who made their escape on the 27th May last, which account the keeper is requested to pay out of the funds of the house and to place a proportion of the expense to the debit of each of the aforesaid prisoners." Minutes, September 20, 1796, BOI.

50. Phebe Mines, March 18, 1796, PSD; Margaret McGill, March 18, 1796, PSD.

51. Gary B. Nash and Jean R. Soderlund, *Freedom by Degrees: Emancipation in Pennsylvania and Its Aftermath* (New York: Oxford University Press, 1991), 140–41.

52. Servants and slaves standing up to or running away from their masters made up the single largest category of vagrancy charges in 1795: 40 of 134 total. This number was 17 in 1790/1 and 18 in 1807. 1790/1, 1795, and 1807, VAG.

53. Women were less likely to run away than men because of children. See Deborah Gray White, *Ar'n't I a Woman? Female Slaves in the Plantation South* (New York: Norton, 1985).

54. See Billy G. Smith and Richard Wojtowicz, *Blacks Who Stole Themselves: Advertisements for Runaways in the Pennsylvania Gazette, 1728–1790* (Philadelphia: University of Pennsylvania Press, 1989); David Waldstreicher, "Reading the Runaways: Self-Fashioning, Print Culture, and Confidence in Slavery in the Eighteenth-Century Mid-Atlantic," *William and Mary Quarterly* 3rd ser. 56, no. 2 (1999): 243–72.

55. *PG*, July 28, 1784.

56. Furthermore, servants and slaves would be treated similarly in the eyes of the law regarding the punishment for those aiding servants or slaves seeking freedom. The law states, "The reward for taking up runaway and absconding negro and mulatto slaves and servants and the penalties for enticing away, dealing with or harboring, concealing or employing negro and mulatto slaves and servants shall be the same, and shall be recovered in like manner as in case of servants bound for four years." "Gradual Abolition Act," in *Statutes*, X: 71.

57. Billy G. Smith, *Life in Early Philadelphia: Documents from the Revolutionary and Early National Periods* (University Park: Pennsylvania State University Press, 1995), 87–94.

58. The number was 1,897 to be exact; see Erica Armstrong Dunbar, *A Fragile Freedom: African American Women and Emancipation in the Antebellum City* (New Haven, Conn.: Yale University Press, 2008), 43.

59. This assertion is not to belittle the power of freedom but to give due recognition to the tremendous restrictions that characterized life for indentured servants and the lowest class of poor workers of all races.

60. "Better regulation of servants in this province and territories" (1700), *Statutes*, II: 54–56; "Supplement to the act entitled 'An act for the better regulation of servants in this province and territories'" (1771), *Statutes*, VIII: 29–31.

61. Leslie Patrick-Stamp, "Ideology and Punishment: The Crime of Being Black (Pennsylvania, 1639–1804)" (Ph.D. dissertation, University of California, Santa Cruz, 1989).

62. Patience, November 26, 1795, VAG.

63. Jantie "negress" October 10, 1795, VAG.

64. Sall "negress" August 12, 1790, VAG.

65. On the power of resistance, see Stephanie M. H. Camp, "The Pleasures of Resistance: Enslaved Women and Body Politics in the Plantation South, 1830–1861," *Journal of Southern History* 68, no. 3 (2002): 533–72. On slave conspiracies in prison, see the section titled "Brokering Power Behind Bars," in Richard Bell and Michele Tartar, eds., *Buried Lives: Incarceration* (Athens: University of Georgia Press, 2012). For important work on black resistance for a later period, see Robin D. G. Kelley, *Race Rebels: Culture, Politics, and the Black Working Class* (New York: Free Press, 1994).

66. On violence in slavery, see Nell Painter, "Soul Murder and Slavery: Toward a Fully Loaded Cost Accounting," in *U.S. History as Women's History: New Feminist Essays*, ed. Linda Kerber, Alice Kessler Harris, and Kathryn Kish Sklar (Chapel Hill: University of North Carolina Press, 1995); Saidiya V. Hartman, *Scenes of Subjection: Terror, Slavery, and Self-Making in Nineteenth Century America* (New York: Oxford University Press, 1997); Thavolia Glymph, *Out of the House of Bondage: The Transformation of the Plantation Household* (New York: Cambridge University Press, 2008).

67. Victorie "negress," July 29, 1795 and Victorie, August 3, 1795, VAG.

68. Louis Dwight, *Dear Sir, I see with great pleasure* (Boston, 1826).

69. *United States Gazette,* February 12, 1806.

70. For analysis of the ways slavers would manipulate the appearance and experiences of the enslaved to encourage a favorable sale, see Walter Johnson, *Soul by Soul: Life Inside the Antebellum Slave Market* (Cambridge, Mass.: Harvard University Press, 1999).

71. Clarissa Morris, February 11, 1807, VAG.

72. *PG,* November 6, 1795.

73. Susanna Ware, November 28, 1795, VAG.

74. Elizabeth Folmer, September 17, 1795, VAG; *PG,* June 9, 1784.

75. "On the oath of Charles Greguire with being his bound servants and have absconded from him and do refuse to return to his farm, to be kept until they be willing to return to their master or find some person who will pay their passage money." Anna Guster, December 11, 1795, VAG.

76. She ran away February 20, 1796; Anna Guster, December 11, 1795, VAG.

77. In 1790/1, of the 17 women charged with bad behavior or running away from a mistress, 14 were African American, 1790/1, VAG.

78. Phebe Bowers, "mulatto," September 11, 1790, VAG.

79. Mila "negress," March 28, 1791.

80. Elizabeth Nen, January 4, 1791, VAG.

81. Elizabeth McCoy, July 16, 1795, VAG.

82. Sarah Evans, September 17, 1795, VAG.

83. Elizabeth Folmer, September 17, 1795, VAG.

84. Jane "negress," September 2, 1795, VAG.

85. Margaret Mullen, September 18, 1795, VAG.

86. Elizabeth Nen ran away from Henry Clanse, 1791; Maria Tinmaten ran away from James Tremble twice, 1795; Betse Brown ran away from William Fiss, 1795; Ann Patterson ran away from Caleb Davis, 1795; Alice Cassady ran away from Captain James Foster in July, 1795 and then John Kean in September, 1795; Elizabeth Folmer, ran away from Thomas Palmer, 1795; Susanna Ware ran away from Samuel Clarkson, 1795; Anna Guster ran away from Charles Greguire, 1795; Sarah Uledbone ran away from the same James Tremble, 1795; Clarissa Morris ran away from George Springer, 1807; Flora Molder ran away from William Burns, 1807; Margaret Gibson ran away from John Austin, 1807; Hester Waters ran away from George Wood, 1807; Matilda Pringle ran away from Doctor James Tate, 1807, VAG.

87. Nance "negress," May 4, 1791, VAG.

88. Eliza Johnson, July 7, 1790, VAG; Hugh McCollough. had a pregnant servant earlier and petitioned to have her term extended by two years; Lyons, *Sex Among the Rabble: An Intimate History of Gender & Power in the Age of Revolution, Philadelphia, 1730–1830* (Chapel Hill: University of North Carolina Press, 2006), 90.

89. Matilda Pringle, November 2, 1807, VAG.

90. Eleanor Moor, August 21, 1790 and Rebecca "negress," August 11, 1790, VAG.

91. Marinet "blk girl", July 6,1807, VAG.

92. Catherine Frame, May 24, 1791, VAG. Frame appeared as a witness to the execution of a will in Chester County the following year, suggesting she found work with the Wayne family. *Chester County, Pennsylvania Wills, 1713–1825.*

93. *PG,* October 20, 1784; Phillis "negress," July 1, 1790, VAG.

94. *PG*, July 20, 1791; Mila "negress," March 28, 1791, VAG.

95. *PG*, October 27, 1790; Justinia "negress," August 15, 1795, VAG.

96. *PG*, October 25, 1780; Alice Cassady, July 13, 1795 and September 9, 1795, VAG.

97. *PG*, January 21, 1795; Catharine Louise Figg, July 10, 1795, PFT.

98. For an unusual account of a black mistress with a black female indentured servant, see Dunbar, *A Fragile Freedom*, 27.

99. Mary Meredith married Daniel January 13, 1768. Mary was administrator of debts and demands on his estate, which she conducted in the house of Widow Parry at Fourth and Arch, which was being kept by Elijah Weed, *PG*, May 14, 1777. Daughter Margaret died August 1777, age nine months; Record of the Inscriptions in the Tablets and Grav-stones in the Burial-Grounds of Christ Church, Philadelphia.

100. Dinah "negress," October 16, 1790, VAG.

101. Sarah Morton, August 1, 1795, VAG.

102. "Mr. Casper Souder's Tavern," *PG*, December 15, 1784.

103. Nancy "negress," July 26, 1790, VAG.

104. Calypso "negress," May 28, 1795, VAG.

105. G. S. Rowe, "Women's Crime and Criminal Administration," *PMHB* 109, no. 3 (1985): 335–68, 359.

106. Glymph, *Out of the House of Bondage*, 2.

107. Also see White, *Ar'nt I A Woman?*; Stephanie M. H. Camp, *Closer to Freedom: Enslaved Women and Everyday Resistance in the Plantation South* (Chapel Hill: University of North Carolina Press, 2004).

108. Glymph, *Out of the House of Bondage*, 24, 37.

109. PSAMPP, *Extracts and Remarks*. Negley Teeters described the pamphlet as "modest propaganda on penal reform in order to acquaint the general public with current methods of penal discipline, especially those in practice in England." Teeters, *They Were in Prison*, 31.

110. Robert Strettel Jones, "An Oration, Delivered in the College of Philadelphia, Before the United Company of Philadelphia for Promoting American Manufactures. March 17th, 1777," *American Museum, or, Universal Magazine*, March 1789.

111. Americanus, "On American Manufactures," *Columbian Magazine*, September 1786.

112. *Pennsylvania Journal and Weekly Advertiser*, April 12, 1788.

113. *Subscribers, Artisans, and Manufacturers of Philadelphia, To the Honorable the Senate and House of Representatives of the United States* (Washington, 1803).

114. Adrienne Hood, *The Weaver's Craft: Cloth, Commerce, and Industry in Early Pennsylvania* (Philadelphia: University of Pennsylvania Press, 2003).

115. Ronald Shultz, *The Republic of Labor: Philadelphia Artisans and the Politics of Class, 1720–1830* (New York: Oxford University Press, 1993), 166; the Society for the Encouragement of Manufactures and the Useful Arts survived for only one year, 1787–1788 but was followed several years later by the Pennsylvania Society for the Encouragement of Manufactures and the Useful Arts. Cathy Matson, "Mathew Carey's Learning Experience: Commerce, Manufacturing, and the Panic of 1819," *Early American Studies* 11, no. 3 (2013): 455–85, 458.

116. *Statutes*, XIII: 511–528.

117. George Meade, "Report of the Board of Inspectors of the Prison for the City and County of Philadelphia," *Universal Asylum and Columbian Magazine*, 1791, 398.

118. Bruce Dorsey, *Reforming Men and Women: Gender in the Antebellum City* (Ithaca, N.Y.: Cornell University Press, 2002), 11–49; Meranze, *Laboratories of Virtue*, 131–72.

119. Meade, "Report of the Board of Inspectors," 398.

120. Foucault claimed that the purpose of penal labor was the perpetuation of a power relationship rather than profit or training in a skill. Michel Foucault, *Discipline and Punish: The Birth of the Prison*, trans. Alan Sheridan (New York: Vintage-Random House, 1995), 243; also see Meranze, *Laboratories of Virtue*, 185–89.

121. Rush, *An Enquiry Into the Effects of Public Punishments*, 13. By privileging individual transformation, Rush was at odds with his own republicanism. This was one of many internal contradictions that doomed the reform movement. See Robert Sullivan, "The Birth of the Prison: The Case of Benjamin Rush," *Eighteenth-Century Studies* 31 (1998): 333–44.

122. *Statutes*, XIII: 511–528.

123. *First Annual Report of the Society for the Encouragement of Faithful Domestic Servants in New York* (New York, 1826), appendix.

124. Since work expectations were distinctly different for men and women for most of the eighteenth century, a gendered division of labor was not at all surprising. Mary Beth Norton, *Liberty's Daughters: The Revolutionary Experience of American Women, 1750–1800* (Ithaca, N.Y.: Cornell University Press, 1980), 13.

125. This was the case for enforcement of the 1786 Act to Amend the Penal Laws of the State, which failed to specify special treatment for women. See Jennifer Manion, "Women's Crime and Prison Reform in Early Pennsylvania, 1786–1829" (Ph.D. dissertation, Rutgers University, 2008), 13–17.

126. Minutes, August 18, 1795, BOI.

127. Minutes, June 5, 1798, BOI.

128. Minutes, November 7, 1796, BOI. It was uncommon for there to be any surplus from even men's labor.

129. For more on the intellectual framework for an intersectional approach to gender and disability studies, see Susan Burch and Lindsey Patterson, "Not Just Any Body: Disability, Gender, and History," *Journal of Women's History* 25, no. 4 (2013): 122–37.

130. Christine Stansell, *City of Women: Sex and Class in New York, 1789–1860* (Urbana: University of Illinois Press, 1987), 106.

131. Minutes, March 11, 1795, BOI.

132. Minutes, June 19, 1809, BOI.

133. Minutes, April 27, 1812, BOI.

134. "Letter to William Allen in London," October 18, 1816, PSAMPP Meeting Minutes, vol. 2, PPS.

135. Robert J. Turnbull, *A Visit to the Philadelphia Prison; Being an Accurate and Particular Account of the Wise and Humane Administration Adopted in Every Part of the Building; Containing also an Account of the Gradual Reformation and the Present Improved State, and the Penal Laws of Pennsylvania* (Philadelphia, 1796), 36.

136. "Considerations on the Late Laws of Pennsylvania, for Mitigating the Severity of the Penal Code of That State—With Satisfactory Reasons Why Its Success Has Not Equaled Public Expectation—and Proofs That As Yet It Has Not Had a Fair Trial," *American Museum*, June 1788, 510; There is no author listed for this essay, but it is consistent in voice and message with some of Carey's other writings. Thanks to Robb Keith Haberman for showing me this article.

137. "Observations On the Management of the Female Convicts, in the Work-house, Philadelphia," *American Museum*, June 1788, 512.

138. The publication was lauded by no less than George Washington, John Dickinson, and Tench Coxe in letters to the printer, *American Museum*, July 1788, 3. For an interesting take on the relationship between Mathew Carey and Benjamin Franklin, including Franklin's refusal to endorse the publication, see James N. Green, "'I was always dispos'd to be serviceable to you, tho' it seems I was once unlucky': Mathew Carey's Relationship with Benjamin Franklin," *Early American Studies: An Interdisciplinary Journal* 11, no. 3 (2013): 545–56.

139. "At a Meeting & c. 2 Mo. 6. 1789 and 20th and 26th," Correspondence, Box 1, Folder 13, PPS.

140. Caleb Lownes, *An Account of the Goal and Penitentiary House*, 84.

141. *Ordinances, Rules and Bye-Laws for the Alms-House and House of Employment* (Philadelphia, 1796), 7.

142. During the Revolutionary War, women were championed for their spinning, as a mundane domestic task became a shining sign of patriotism. The significance of spinning during the revolution lay as much in the attention and praise women received for the political symbolism of their work as in the actual increase in production. See Jeanne Boydston, *Home and Work: Housework, Wages, and the Ideology of Labor in the Early Republic* (New York: Oxford University Press, 1990), 31.

143. "Observations on the Management of the Female Convicts, in the Work-house, Philadelphia," *American Museum or Repository*, June 1788, 512.

144. Minutes, August 17, 1807, BOI.

145. Minutes, June 10, 1799, PSAMPP Acting Committee, vol. 6, PPS.

146. D. M'Kenzie, *"A just and true account" by a Person who has been an eye witness* (Philadelphia, 1820).

147. Minutes, March 8, 1804, PSAMPP Acting Committee, vol. 6, PPS.

148. Ann Carson, *The History of the Celebrated Mrs. Ann Carson, Widow of the Late Unfortunate Lieutenant Richard Smyth; With a circumstantial account of her conspiracy against the late Governor of Pennsylvania, Simon Snyder; and of her sufferings in the several prisons in that state* (Philadelphia, 1822), 300.

149. Turnbull, *A Visit to the Philadelphia Prison*, 25.

150. Ann Carson complained about losing her assets while in prison. See Ann Carson, *The Memoirs of the Celebrated and Beautiful Mrs. Ann Carson, Daughter of an Officer of the US Navy and Wife of Another, Whose Life Terminated in the Philadelphia Prison* (Philadelphia, 1838).

151. One woman was included, Elizabeth Clinton of York County; Prison Stock Book, 1800–1805, BOI, PCA.

152. The desired expansion would include weaving in addition to their spinning. PSAMPP, *Extracts and Remarks*, 11.

153. Mary Davis, January 7, 1796, PSD; Philadelphia City Directory, 1791.

154. "An Act to authorize the removal of the persons now confined in the Prune street apartment of the prison, of the city and county of Philadelphia, to the county prison in Arch street and for other purposes" (February 1823) in John Purdon, *A Digest of the Laws of Pennsylvania, From the Year One Thousand Seven Hundred, to the Thirtieth Day of March, One Thousand Eight Hundred and Twenty-four. With Some References to Reports of Judicial Decisions* (Philadelphia, 1824): 341; Also see Teeters, *They Were in Prison*, 86.

155. James Hardie, *The History of the Tread Mill, containing an account of its origin, construction, operation, effects as it respects the health and morals of the convicts, with their treatment and*

diet; also, a general view of the penitentiary system, with alterations necessary to be introduced into our criminal code, for its improvement (New York, 1824), 33.

156. Women in the almshouse—especially those on contracts, who were not inmates— enjoyed a wider range of work opportunities. Monique Bourque, "Women and Work in the Philadelphia Almshouse, 1790–1840," *Journal of the Early Republic* 32, no. 3 (2012): 383–413. Recent scholarship on the range of women's work in early America includes Seth Rockman, *Scraping By: Wage Labor, Slavery, and Survival in Early Baltimore* (Baltimore: Johns Hopkins University Press, 2008); Ellen Hartigan-O'Connor, *The Ties That Buy: Women and Commerce in Revolutionary America* (Philadelphia: University of Pennsylvania Press, 2009); Serena Zabin, *Dangerous Economies: Status and Commerce in Imperial New York* (Philadelphia: University of Pennsylvania Press, 2009). For a study of women's wage-earning labor that was pathbreaking in 1982, see Alice Kessler-Harris, *Out to Work: The History of Wage-Earning Women in the United States* (New York: Oxford University Press, 1982).

157. For analysis of the dynamic role women played in the marketplace from 1750–1820, see Hartigan-O'Connor, *The Ties That Buy.*

158. Claudia Goldin, "The Economic Status of Women in the Early Republic: Quantitative Evidence," *Journal of Interdisciplinary History* 16, no. 3 (1986): 375–404, 396.

159. Philadelphia Census, 1791. Thanks to Billy Smith for making his dataset available to me.

160. One woman, for example, was paid two shillings by the Philadelphia Common Council for "sweeping ye Court House & Stalls twice a week," Karin A. Wulf, *Not All Wives: Gender, Marriage, and Urban Culture in Colonial Philadelphia* (Ithaca, N.Y.: Cornell University Press, 1999), 141.

161. Karin Wulf, "Assessing Gender: Taxation and the Evaluation of Economic Viability in Late Colonial Philadelphia, " *PMHB* 121, no. 3 (1997): 201–35.

162. Almshouse Daily Occurrence Docket, October 2, 1792, Guardians of the Poor, PCA.

163. Almshouse Daily Occurrence Docket, January 2, 1791, Guardians of the Poor, PCA.

164. Almshouse Daily Occurrence Docket, June 8, 1792, Guardians of the Poor, PCA.

165. Almshouse Daily Occurrence Docket, September 30, 1792, Guardians of the Poor, PCA.

166. Almshouse Daily Occurrence Docket, November 23, 1790, Guardians of the Poor, PCA.

167. For elaboration on how sex-specific social, political, and economic roles shape and define categories of sexuality, see Adrienne Rich, "Compulsory Heterosexuality and Lesbian Existence," *Signs* 5, no. 4 (1980): 631–60.

168. See Boydston, *Home and Work*; Boydston, "The Woman Who Wasn't There: Women's Market Labor and the Transition to Capitalism in the United States," *Journal of the Early Republic* 16, no. 2 (1996): 183–206; Susan Branson, "Women and the Family Economy in the Early Republic: The Case of Elizabeth Meredith," ibid., 47–71.

169. Smith, *"The Lower Sort"*, 111–12, 118–19.

170. Smith, *"The Lower Sort"*, chap. 3; for a gendered analysis of the impact of this instability on merchants, see Toby L. Ditz, "Shipwrecked; or, Masculinity Imperiled: Mercantile Representations of Failure and the Gendered Self in Eighteenth-Century Philadelphia," *Journal of American History* 81, no. 1 (1994): 51–80.

171. Minutes, January 18, 1801, PSAMPP Acting Committee, vol. 6, PPS.

172. Minutes, March 8, 1804, PSAMPP Acting Committee, vol. 6, PPS.

173. Minutes, January 11, 1805, PSAMPP Acting Committee, vol. 6, PPS.

174. Minutes, August 17, 1807, BOI.

175. Minutes, February 20, 1809, PSAMPP Acting Committee, vol. 6, PPS.

176. This practice was not unique to Philadelphia. In the New York State Penitentiary, women prisoners were employed at "sewing, washing, ironing," and the prisoners made all of the clothes for inmates. See Inspectors of the State-Prison, *Report of the Inspectors of the State-Prison-Albany* (Albany, 1799), 3.

177. The long list of items she stole from Harriet Newton included Moroccan shoes, cottons stockings, a frock, a gown, and a shift; Kitty Spencer, June 12, 1807, PFT; she was sentenced to night months hard labor and fined $39.50; Kitty Spencer, September 27, 1807, PSD.

178. Rush noted this in his 1794 diary. Teeters, *They Were in Prison*, 52.

179. Minutes, January 7, 1795, BOI.

180. Minutes, January 12, 1796, BOI.

181. Minutes, October 9, 1820, PSAMPP Acting Committee, vol. 6, PPS; More ideal women can be found in the 1820 report; see Teeters, *They Were in Prison*, 88.

182. "A large quantity of nails and brads . . . for sale at very reduced prices" was advertised in local papers. Minutes, May 24, 1803, BOI. In 1807 the Board ordered the Visiting Inspectors "to send the linen cloths now on hand to the domestic manufactory warehouse to be disposed of to the best advantage." Minutes, July 20, 1807, BOI. A few years later they decided to sell "the surplus linen" at an auction, Minutes, May 7, 1810, BOI.

183. In 1820, the Committee on Manufactures "reported that they find the prices charged by the prison generally too high." Minutes, January 31, 1820, BOI.

184. Women's prison work in Philadelphia was never subject to this critique, but Foucault illustrated this debate in France in 1842: "The inconveniences of these prison workshops were even more evident for women, who were thus deprived of their labour, driven to prostitution and therefore to prison, where these same women, who could no longer work when they were free, then competed with those who were still at work." Foucault, *Discipline and Punish*, 241.

185. Minutes, June 5, 1798, BOI.

186. Minutes, March 2, 1818, BOI.

187. Minutes, January 25, 1815, BOI. This system would become the hallmark of punishment in other places on a more massive scale over the course of American history.

188. George Rugan, "Documents Accompanying the Commissioners' Report on Punishments and Prison Discipline," *Register of Pennsylvania*, April 19, 1828.

189. Jared Ingersoll, "Letter from Jacob Rush, Philadelphia, September 17, 1812 to Jared Ingersoll," in *Report Relative to the Penal Code 1813* (Harrisburg, 1813): 38–41, 40.

190. Roberts Vaux, *Notices of the Original, and Successive Efforts, to Improve the Discipline of the Prison at Philadelphia, and to Reform the Criminal Code of Pennsylvania: With a Few Observations on the Penitentiary System* (Philadelphia, 1826), 53.

191. In a letter to the chairman of the House of Representatives outlining their failures, the Inspectors agreed that the prison in fact did not reform inmates and would never be any different "without the means of classification or of adequate employment." Minutes, January 15, 1821, BOI. Another reason for the prison's doom was sheer numbers. By 1801, the average number committed had more than tripled since the early 1790s, making the desired reforms and personal attention of officers impossible; Orlando Faulkland Lewis, *The Development of American Prisons and Prison Customs, 1776–1845: With Special Reference to Early Institutions in the State of New York* (New York: Prison Association of New York, 1922), 39.

192. Minutes, January 12, 1799, PSAMPP Acting Committee, vol. 6, PPS.

193. Caleb Lownes, *An Account of the Goal and Penitentiary House*, 89.

194. This is evident in accounts of most visitors and Inspectors. See Turnbull, *A Visit to the Philadelphia Prison*; and Liancourt, *On Prisons of Philadelphia*.

195. In the political climate that led so many of Philadelphia's elites to avoid the topic of race or slavery as much as possible, Turnbull's discussion of the black women in Philadelphia's prison stands out. Turnbull's eulogist described this period: "After completing his preparatory professional course, and obtaining a highly honorable admission to the Bar, he went to Philadelphia, where he pursued his studies for a year; during which, in visiting the Penitentiary, he became so deeply impressed with the benignity and policy of that system of penal justice, that at twenty-three years of age, he wrote a Treatise on the Pennsylvania Penitentiary, which may now be referred to, not only as furnishing the unequivocal tokens of his future distinction, but which, at that time, attracted very decided notice and applause in Europe." James Hamilton, Esq., *An eulogium . . . Robert J. Turnbull* (Charleston: A.E. Miller, 1834), 11.

196. Turnbull, *A Visit to the Philadelphia Prison*, 48.

197. Even Foucault's example of an ideal prison room was based on women inmates: a workshop at Clairvaux in which he described a room full of women, working in silence under the watchful eye of a sister and a crucifix. Foucault, *Discipline and Punish*, 243.

198. "Extract," *Gazette of the United States*, December 17, 1798.

Chapter 2. Sentimental Families

1. On the replacement of older aristocrats with local elites, see the introduction to Carroll Smith-Rosenberg, *This Violent Empire: The Birth of an American National Identity* (Chapel Hill: University of North Carolina Press, 2010).

2. Manasseh Cutler, "New York and Philadelphia in 1787," *PMHB* 12, no. 1 (1888): 97–115, 109. Cutler served as senator from Massachusetts from 1801 to 1805.

3. Sarah Knott, *Sensibility and the American Revolution* (Durham, N.C.: University of North Carolina Press, 2009), 1.

4. Ibid., 190.

5. Karen Halttunen, "Humanitarianism and the Pornography of Pain in Anglo-American Culture," *American Historical Review* 100, no. 2 (1995): 303–34, 303.

6. On the power of desire in the sentimental family, Brian Connolly writes, "The feelings of love and affection between family members, in much literature regulating the relations between parents and children, were potentially erotic and, thus, incestuous. The only restraint on such desire was a clearly defined incest prohibition." Brian Connolly, " 'Every Family Become a School of Abominable Impurity': Incest and Theology in the Early Republic," *Journal of the Early Republic* 30, no. 3 (2010): 413–42, 442.

7. Negley King Teeters, *The Cradle of the Penitentiary: The Walnut Street Jail at Philadelphia, 1773–1835* (Philadelphia, 1955), 37–38; Negley King Teeters, *They Were in Prison: A History of the Pennsylvania Prison Society, 1787–1937* (Philadelphia: Winston, 1937), 89.

8. Samuel Rowland Fisher, "Journal of Samuel Rowland Fisher, of Philadelphia, 1779–1781," *PMHB* 41, no. 2 (1917): 145–197: 153.

9. Teeters, *Cradle of the Penitentiary*, 33.

10. She was hired to serve as principle keeper for three hundred pounds per year. The appointments states, "Her duty shall be to inspect the conduct of the keepers and prisoners, shall

receive the orders of the Board and issue them to the deputy who shall be amenable to her." The deputy keeper was Francis Higgins, paid half her salary and ordered to "take charge of the women, weavers, hacklers and generally to take charge of the house and superintend the conduct of the assistant keepers." Minutes, May 5, 1795, BOI.

11. E. F., "Prison Discipline: To the Editor of the Monthly Magazine," *Belles: Letters Repository, and Monthly Magazine*, July 1, 1819.

12. Rush named women as also in need of humanitarian sensibility reserved for those most detested in society: "The men, or perhaps the women, whose persons we detest, possess souls and bodies composed of the same materials as those of our friends and relations." Benjamin Rush, *An Enquiry Into the Effects of Public Punishments Upon Criminals and Upon Society. Read in the Society for Promoting Political Enquiries, Convened at the House of His Excellency Benjamin Franklin, Esquire, in Philadelphia, March 9th, 1787* (Philadelphia, 1787), 7; see also Thomas L. Haskell, "Capitalism and the Origins of the Humanitarian Sensibility, Part I," *American Historical Review* 90, no. 2 (1985): 339–61; Bruce Dorsey, *Reforming Men and Women: Gender in the Antebellum City* (Ithaca, N.Y.: Cornell University Press, 2002).

13. "Letter from Benjamin Rush to John Coakley Lettsom, Philadelphia, September 28th, 1787," in *Letters of Benjamin Rush*, vol. 1, *1761–1792*, ed. L. H. Butterfield (Philadelphia: American Philosophical Society, 1951), 443.

14. Jan Lewis, *The Pursuit of Happiness: Family and Values in Jefferson's Virginia* (New York: Cambridge University Press, 1983), 228.

15. Pennsylvanians did away with the position of governor, appointing a council in an attempt to keep any one person from wielding too much power. However, the new constitution of 1790 abolished the council and reinstated the position of governor. Pennsylvania State Constitution, 1776, 1790.

16. "At a Meeting & c. 2 Mo. 6. 1789 and 20th and 26th," Reports, Box 1, Folder 13, PPS.

17. Dorsey, *Reforming Men and Women*, 75.

18. Bruce Mann has characterized debtors' petitions as "narratives of failure," and many people would offer similarly negative assessments of those behind bars who begged reformers for relief. Bruce Mann, *Republic of Debtors: Bankruptcy in the Age of American Independence* (Cambridge, Mass.: Harvard University Press, 2002), 72–74.

19. "Petition signed Eliz.th Donovan her mark Workhouse 13 Feb 1788," Correspondence, Box 1, Folder 10, PPS.

20. "Petition of Susy Mines [or Susey]; Enquire of J. Harwell and Lewis Weiss, Esq," Correspondence, Box 1, Folder 9, PPS.

21. "The Petition of Sarah Collier a distressed prisoner in the goal of Philadelphia," Lists and Papers, Box 1, Folder 12, PPS.

22. "Petition of Elizabeth Elliot," Correspondence, Box 1, Folder 10, PPS.

23. "Catharine Usoons Address to John Morrison Nov. 1787," Correspondence, Box 1, Folder 9, PPS.

24. Dorsey, *Reforming Men and Women*, 18; also see Thomas Foster, ed., *New Men: Manliness in Early America* (New York: New York University Press, 2011).

25. "James Parkins letter to Wm Rogers January 9, 1788," Correspondence, Box 1, Folder 10, PPS.

26. "Copy of Representation to Council on Alex. Drians case del.d Septem. 1, 1787," Correspondence, Box 1, Folder 9, PPS.

27. "John McCrum's Address 14, May, 1788; to John Olden Esq," Correspondence, Box 1, Folder 11, PPS.

28. Minutes, March 8, 1804, PSAMPP Acting Committee, vol. 6, PPS.

29. Karin A. Wulf, *Not All Wives: Gender, Marriage, and Urban Culture in Colonial Philadelphia* (Ithaca, N.Y.: Cornell University Press, 1999), chap. 5.

30. "Sept 19, 1788 Jacob James Letter from the Goal to the Committee," Correspondence, Box 1, Folder 11, PPS.

31. Dorsey, *Reforming Men and Women*, 36.

32. "Patrick Kain," Correspondence, Box 1, Folder 12, PPS.

33. Ruth Bogin, "Petitioning and the New Moral Economy of Post-Revolutionary America," *William and Mary Quarterly* 3rd ser. 45, no. 3 (1988): 392–425, 420.

34. "Observations recommendatory of the Philadelphia Society for alleviating the Miseries of Public Prisons," *American Museum; or, Repository of Ancient and Modern Fugitive Pieces & c.,* May 1787.

35. Revolutionary antistatist zeal notwithstanding, PSAMPP more than any other reform organization inspired by the wave of humanitarian sensibility colluded intimately with the state. For profiles of important families and powerful men involved with the organization, see Teeters, *They Were in Prison*, 89–120.

36. Evidence of a commitment to sexual difference can be seen in institutional records regarding labor. See Minutes, 1794–1826, BOI; Jennifer Manion, "Women's Crime and Prison Reform in Early Pennsylvania, 1786–1829" (Ph.D. dissertation, Rutgers University, 2008).

37. Pennsylvania Supreme Court Docket, Philadelphia, April 16, 1787.

38. *Freeman's Journal*, May 2, 1787.

39. Minutes, May 31, 1787; Minutes, June 11, 1787, PSAMPP Meeting, vol. 1, PPS.

40. *Pennsylvania Journal of Prison Discipline and Philanthropy* (Philadelphia, 1845), 6.

41. Jacob Rush, "Upon Human and Divine Laws, and Their Consequences [Delivered at Reading, April 4, 1796]," in *Charges and Extracts of Charges on moral and religious subjects* (Philadelphia, 1803), 21.

42. "From the Harrisburg Republican. Pardon of Convicts," *Franklin Gazette*, July 14, 1820.

43. Ibid; and "From the Harrisburg Republican. Executive Pardons," *Franklin Gazette*, July 26, 1820.

44. Minutes, May 21, 1821, BOI.

45. In 1795, 62 percent, and 1799, 51 percent, of women convicted received pardons (11 percent in 1807, 6 percent in 1823).

46. Minutes, December 28, 1811, BOI.

47. Minutes, January 18, 1817, BOI.

48. "A Visit to the Penitentiary, From The Philadelphia Gazette," *New England Galaxy and United States Literary Advertiser*, June 29, 1827.

49. PSAMPP, "Constitution," *American Museum; or, Repository of Ancient and Modern Fugitive Pieces*, May 1787, 454.

50. See Jay Fliegelman, *Prodigals and Pilgrims: The American Revolution Against Patriarchal Authority* (Cambridge: Cambridge University Press, 1982); Dana Nelson, *National Manhood: Capitalist Citizenship and the Imagined Fraternity of White Men* (Durham, N.C.: Duke University Press, 1998); Mark E. Kann, *Punishment, Prisons, and Patriarchy: Liberty and Power in the Early American Republic* (New York: New York University Press, 2005).

51. Despite the persistence of what Judith Bennett refers to as a "patriarchal equilibrium,"" patriarchal authority was not static. Men continued to have major advantages over women in societies and periods marked by great advances for women; despite differences of race, class, and culture, the forms of authority and the degree of power change significantly. Judith M. Bennett, *History Matters: Patriarchy and the Challenge of Feminism* (Philadelphia: University of Pennsylvania Press, 2006), 57–58. For analysis of these issues on the frontier, see Honor Sachs, *Home Rule: Households, Manhood, and National Expansion on the Eighteenth-Century Kentucky Frontier* (New Haven, Conn.: Yale University Press, 2015).

52. For an analysis of the family metaphor for prisons, see Peter Okun, *Crime and the Nation: Prison and Popular Fiction in Philadelphia, 1786–1800* (New York: Routledge, 2002).

53. Brian Connolly, *Domestic Intimacies: Incest and the Liberal Subject in Nineteenth-Century America* (Philadelphia: University of Pennsylvania Press, 2014).

54. The expansion of relief and reformatory institutions occurred much earlier in the mid-Atlantic states than in New England. See David Rothman, *Discovery of the Asylum: Social Order and Disorder in the New Republic* (Boston: Little, Brown, 1971); Ruth Herndon, *Unwelcome Americans: Living on the Margin in Early New England* (Philadelphia: University of Pennsylvania Press, 2001).

55. Rush, *Enquiry Into the Effects of Public Punishments*, 10.

56. Philadelphia supported world-class botanical collections and gardens. Pioneering botanist John Bartram began planting his soon-to-be famous garden in 1728 a few miles from the city center. His son William Bartram followed in his footsteps, publishing a book called *Travels* in 1791 that chronicled the people and plants he encountered while traveling across America.

57. Dr. Darwin, "The American muse. Selected poetry. Idyllium. The Prison," *New York Magazine, or Literary Repository*, August 1796; also printed in *Philadelphia Minerva, Containing a Variety of Fugitive Pieces in Prose*, August 26, 1797; and *Universal Repository of Knowledge and Entertainment*, January 1798.

58. *Freeman's Journal or, The North-American Intelligencer*, April 10, 1787.

59. "Abigail McAlpines Letter 17 May 1788," Correspondence, Box 1, Folder 11, PPS.

60. Rush, *Enquiry Into the Effects of Public Punishments*, 16.

61. Ibid., 14.

62. Ibid., 10.

63. *PG*, August 7, 1782.

64. Orlando Patterson, *Slavery and Social Death: A Comparative Study* (Cambridge, Mass.: Harvard University Press, 1982).

65. On slave families, see Deborah Grey White, *Ar'n't I a Woman: Female Slaves in the Plantation South* (New York: Norton, 1985); Jacqueline Jones, *Labor of Love, Labor of Sorrow: Black Women, Work and the Family, from Slavery to the Present* (New York: Basic Books, 1985); Kathleen Brown, *Good Wives, Nasty Wenches, Anxious Patriarchs: Gender, Race, and Power in Colonial Virginia* (Chapel Hill: University of North Carolina Press, 1996); Jennifer L. Morgan, *Laboring Women: Reproduction and Gender in New World Slavery* (Philadelphia: University of Pennsylvania Press, 2004); Stephanie M. H. Camp, *Closer to Freedom: Enslaved Women and Everyday Resistance in the Plantation South* (Chapel Hill: University of North Carolina Press, 2004); Daina Ramey Berry, *Swing the Sickle for the Harvest Is Ripe: Gender and Slavery in Antebellum Georgia* (Urbana: University of Illinois Press, 2010).

66. This argument is elaborated by Leslie Patrick-Stamp, "Ideology and Punishment: The Crime of Being Black (Pennsylvania, 1639–1804)" (Ph.D. dissertation, University of California,

Santa Cruz, 1989). For a similar consideration of the connection between liberalism and the rise of the penitentiary, see Thomas Dumm, "Friendly Persuasion: Quakers, Liberal Toleration, and the Birth of the Prison," *Political Theory* 13 (1985): 387–407; and Dumm, *Democracy and Punishment: Disciplinary Origins of the United States* (Madison: University of Wisconsin Press, 1987).

67. Gary B. Nash, *Race and Revolution* (Madison: Madison House Publishers, 1990), 32–33.

68. Michel Foucault, *Discipline and Punish: The Birth of the Prison*, trans. Alan Sheridan (New York: Vintage-Random House, 1995), 232.

69. Patrick-Stamp, "Ideology and Punishment," chap. 3 and 153.

70. For more on servitude in early Pennsylvania, see Sharon Salinger, *"To Serve Well and Faithfully": Labour and Indentured Servants in Pennsylvania, 1682–1800* (New York: Cambridge University Press, 1987) and "'Send No More Women': Female Servants in Eighteenth Century Philadelphia," *PMHB* 107, no. 1 (1983): 29–48.

71. It was widely remarked that prisoners owed a social debt that they would pay through labor and suffering. Similarly, their punishment should pay for itself and not be a financial burden to the city or state. See PSAMPP, *Extracts and Remarks on the Subject of Punishment and Reformation of Criminals; Published by Order of the Society, Established in Philadelphia, for Alleviating the Miseries of Public Prisons* (Philadelphia, 1790), 11–12; Caleb Lownes, *An Account of the Alteration and Present State of the Penal Laws of Pennsylvania; Containing also An Account of the Gaol and Penitentiary House of Philadelphia and the Interior Management Thereof* (Philadelphia, 1793); Rush, *Enquiry Into the Effects of Public Punishments*.

72. M. Warville, "Of the Prison of Philadelphia, and Prisons in general," *New York Magazine, or Literary Repository*, December 1792.

73. Rush, *An Enquiry Into the Effects of Public Punishments*, 14.

74. Rush, "Upon Human and Divine Laws," 22.

75. Jennifer Graber unpacks the role of religious redemption and suffering in antebellum prisons in *The Furnace of Affliction: Prisons and Religion in Antebellum America* (Chapel Hill: University of North Carolina Press, 2011).

76. Sarah M. S. Pearsall, *Atlantic Families: Lives and Letters in the Later Eighteenth Century* (New York: Oxford University Press, 2008).

77. Ann Carson, *The History of the Celebrated Mrs. Ann Carson, Widow of the Late Unfortunate Lieutenant Richard Smith, with a Circumstantial Account of Her Conspiracy Against the Late Governor of Pennsylvania, Simon Snyder; and of Her Sufferings in the Several Prisons in that State, Interspersed with Anecdotes of Characters Now Living* (Philadelphia, 1822), 184–45; For extensive analysis of Carson's life, see Susan Branson, *Dangerous to Know: Women, Crime and Notoriety in the Early Republic* (Philadelphia: University of Pennsylvania Press, 2008).

78. See the tables "Women in Walnut Street Prison by Classification" and "Women Prisoners for Trial by Categories of Charges (%)" in Appendix.

79. Elizabeth Ferguson, April 4, 1791, VAG; Elizabeth Ferguson, Philadelphia City Directory, 1791; Mary Williams, August 29, 1795, VAG; Mary Williams, Philadelphia City Directory, 1795; Mary Brown, February 24, 1791, VAG; Mary Brown, Philadelphia City Directory, 1791. Brown's charge was a highly racialized one, as African Americans became increasingly burdened with accusations of disturbing the peace or "rioting" for gathering in large groups.

80. This practice continued throughout the antebellum period in the slaveholding South. See Brett Josef Derbes, "'Secret Horrors': Enslaved Women and Children in the Louisiana State Penitentiary, 1833–1862," *Journal of African American History* 98, no. 2 (2013): 277–90.

81. "Catharine Usoons Address to John Morrison Nov. 1787," Correspondence, Box 1, Folder 10, PPS.

82. Minutes, July 10, 1800, PSAMPP Acting Committee, vol. 6, PPS.

83. Minutes, April 28, 1817, BOI.

84. Minutes, July 10, 1800, PSAMPP Acting Committee, vol. 6, PPS.

85. Minutes, February 9, 1804, PSAMPP Acting Committee, vol. 6, PPS.

86. Minutes, January 12, 1789, PSAMPP Meeting, vol. 1, PPS.

87. Minutes, April 15, 1816, BOI.

88. This attitude was explicit at the House of Refuge, see Michael Meranze, *Laboratories of Virtue: Punishment, Revolution, and Authority in Philadelphia, 1760–1835* (Chapel Hill: University of North Carolina Press, 1996), 280.

89. Patrick-Stamp, "Ideology and Punishment," 185–86 from A. J. Dallas, *Reports of Cases Argued and Decided in The Supreme Court of the United States* (New York: The Lawyer's Co-Operative Publishing Company, 1882), 228.

90. John Alexander, *Render Them Submissive: Responses to Poverty in Philadelphia, 1760–1800* (Amherst: University of Massachusetts Press, 1980), 81–82.

91. "From the information derived by the managers it is apparent that fruitful sources of error and crime may be traced to the want of family discipline to the absence of that deep felt responsibility which teaches parents and masters and mistresses the necessity of knowing how each hour is passed by those under their care and with what companions they associate." Minutes, February 12, 1822, MAG Annual Meeting, box 1, vol. 1.

92. Jacob Rush, "Upon Drunkenness. Delivered before the Grand Jury of Luzern County, April 1801," in *Charges and Extracts of Charges on moral and religious subjects* (Philadelphia, 1803), 67.

93. Rush, "Upon Drunkenness," 67.

94. Mary Barry, June 19, 1792, PFT; Samuel, Myers, and Thomas were registered as merchants on the west side of Front Street in a household of nine people, Philadelphia Census, 1790.

95. Mary Barry, June 25, 1792, PFT; Manley was a shopkeeper on South Market Street; William Miller was a tobacconist on the north side of Front, Philadelphia Census, 1790.

96. The official almshouse docket noted, "The mother of the above three children is now confined in goal for stolen goods." Mary Barry, June 25, 1792, Almshouse Daily Occurrence Docket, Guardians of the Poor, PCA.

97. *Philadelphia Guardians of the Poor, Indenture Records, 1791–1822* (Southampton, Pa.: Bare Roots Publishing, 1998), PCA.

98. In the 1790s, about 50 children were indentured annually, and by 1810, the number doubled: for example, 1796–49, 1797–50, 1798–54, 1799–25, 1811–104. See *Philadelphia Guardians.*

99. While boys were indentured to a range of skilled craftsmen, the most that girls could expect to learn was the "art" of housewifery. Boys and girls were indentured in roughly even numbers. Few African Americans were indentured in the 1790s or 1800s, but this number rose in later years. See *Philadelphia Guardians.*

100. "Some Account of the Orphan Society in Philadelphia," *National Recorder*, September 16, 1820.

101. Almshouse Daily Occurrence Docket, August 16, 1800, in Billy G. Smith, *Life in Early Philadelphia: Documents from the Revolutionary and Early National Periods* (University Park: Pennsylvania State University Press, 1995), 45.

102. Age information deduced from records designate her as seventy in 1795, so age might be off by a year or two, PSD. Emigration information from Peter Wilson Coldham, *The Complete Books of Emigrants in Bondage, 1614–1775* (Baltimore: Genealogical Publishing, 1988), 46; and Peter Wilson Coldham, *Supplement to the Complete Book of Emigrants in Bondage, 1614–1775* (Baltimore: Genealogical Publishing, 1992).

103. Almshouse Daily Occurrence Docket, July 8, 1800, in Smith, *Life in Philadelphia*, 41.

104. Almshouse Daily Occurrence Docket, September 13, 1800, in Smith, *Life in Philadelphia*, 46.

105. Almshouse Daily Occurrence Docket, July 15, 1800, in Smith, *Life in Philadelphia*, 43.

106. This semipublic position was still quite restricted. For discussion of another sphere neither public nor private that women occupied during this period, see Mary Kelley's analysis of the role of civil society for educated and elite women. Mary Kelley, *Learning to Stand and Speak: Women, Education, and Public Life in America's Republic* (Chapel Hill: University of North Carolina Press, 2006).

107. See Minutes, PSAMPP Acting Committee, vol. 6, PPS.

108. Ruth Bloch, "Changing Conceptions of Sexuality and Romance in Eighteenth-Century America," *William and Mary Quarterly* 3rd ser. 60, no. 1 (2003): 13–42. As Bloch notes, "Women's taming of male aggression depended on the infusion of female qualities into men," 41. These men believed that by taking on those traits of women that were most admirable, they could effect the most positive change in society.

109. Dorsey, *Reforming Men and Women*, 20; on the precarious nature of masculinity, see Toby L. Ditz, "Shipwrecked; or, Masculinity Imperiled: Mercantile Representations of Failure and the Gendered Self in Eighteenth-Century Philadelphia," *Journal of American History* 81, no. 1 (1994): 51–80.

110. Minutes, April 5, 1798, June 10, 1799, December 26, 1799, April 10, 1800, January 18, 1801, February 11, 1802, April 7, 1803, April 28, 1803, March 8, 1804, January 4, 1809, December 15, 1810, PSAMPP Acting Committee, vol. 6, PPS. In later years, the committee appeared to visit less often and keep less detailed records.

111. Minutes, April 7, 1803, April 28, 1803, June 10, 1799, PSAMPP Acting Committee, vol. 6, PPS.

112. Minutes, December 26, 1799, PSAMPP Acting Committee, vol. 6, PPS.

113. Minutes, April 10, 1800, January 18, 1801, February 11, 1802, PSAMPP Acting Committee, vol. 6, PPS.

114. Philadelphia appointed three, while Northern Liberties and Southwark districts each appointed two. "An Act Giving Additional Powers To, and Changing the Mode of Appointment of the Inspectors of the Prison in Philadelphia, and for Other Purposes" (1809) *Statutes*, XVIII: 949–51.

115. Samuel Lorenzo Knapp, *Life of Thomas Eddy* (New York, 1834), 205.

116. Orlando Faulkland Lewis, *The Development of American Prisons and Prison Customs, 1776–1845: With Special Reference to Early Institutions in the State of New York* (New York: Prison Association of New York, 1922), 39–40.

117. Minutes, January 4, 1809, PSAMPP Acting Committee, vol. 6, PPS. Other reports echoed the same, including December 15, 1810; December 28, 1819; January 8, 1823; March 13, 1827; PSAMPP Acting Committee, vol. 6, PPS.

118. Minutes, December 15, 1810, PSAMPP Acting Committee, vol. 6, PPS.

119. Minutes, March 8, 1804, PSAMPP Acting Committee, vol. 6, PPS. The committee listed five women who they provided with shifts: Jane Joggle, Elizabeth Phillips, Chole Carpenter, Hannah Cole, and Margery McKinsey.

120. Minutes, March 8, 1804, PSAMPP Acting Committee, vol. 6, PPS.

121. Minutes, February 9, 1804, PSAMPP Acting Committee, vol. 6, PPS.

122. Teeters, *They Were in Prison*, 12.

123. Famous visitation accounts of traveling elites include Robert J. Turnbull, *A Visit to the Philadelphia Prison: Being an Accurate and Particular Account of the Wise and Humane Administration Adopted in Every Part of the Building; Containing also an Account of the Gradual Reformation and the Present Improved State, and the Penal Laws of Pennsylvania* (Philadelphia, 1796); François Alexandre Frédéric La Rochefoucault Liancourt, *On the Prisons of Philadelphia* (Philadelphia, 1796).

124. *Directions for the Inspectors, & c. of the Gaol of the City and County of Philadelphia* (Philadelphia, 1792).

125. Minutes, April 29, 1811, BOI.

126. Halttunen, "Humanitarianism and the Pornography of Pain," 324, 332.

127. Acting Committee members Thomas Harrison and Elisha Gordon pointed this out. *Federal Gazette*, February 10, 1792.

128. E. F. "Prison Discipline."

129. Jeremy Bentham, "Separation as between the Sexes," in *Panopticon: Postscript; Part II: Containing a Plan of Management for a Panopticon Penitentiary-House* 2, sec. 3 (London, 1791), 66–67.

130. Bentham, "Separation," 67–68.

131. Inspectors of the Eastern State Penitentiary (Pa.) et al., *First and Second Annual Reports of the Inspectors of the Eastern State Penitentiary of Pennsylvania: Made to the Legislature at the Sessions of 1829–30, and 1830–31* (Philadelphia, 1831), 10.

132. For more on solitude, see Eric Slauter, "Being Alone in the Age of the Social Contract," *William and Mary Quarterly* 3rd ser. 62, no. 1 (2005): 31–66.

133. "To Enos Hitchcock, Philadelphia, 24th April 1789," in Butterfield, *Letters of Benjamin Rush*, 1: 511–12.

134. "Representation of Prisoners in Jail Nov. 10, 1787," Correspondence, Box 1, Folder 10, PPS.

135. Ellis Paxson Oberholtzer, *Robert Morris Patriot and Financier* (London: MacMillan, 1903), 350, cited in Teeters, *They Were in Prison*, 57.

136. "An act for the Relief and Support of Poor confined Debtors, Approved April 4, 1792," in *Collection of the penal laws of the Commonwealth of Pennsylvania* (Philadelphia, 1794). They ordered three pounds, eight shillings, and seven pence worth of bread. Minutes, June 10, 1799, PSAMPP Acting Committee, vol. 6, PPS.

137. Minutes, January 9, 1804, BOI.

138. Minutes, April 3, 1815, BOI.

139. Minutes, March 14, 1808, BOI.

140. Ibid.

141. Ibid. The Board of Inspectors reported, "That children are prohibited from entering the prison, unless attended by an Inspector or by a parent who has permission from an Inspector." Minutes, April 15, 1816, BOI.

142. Minutes, April 15, 1816, BOI.

143. George Rugan, "Documents Accompanying the Commissioners' Report on Punishments and Prison Discipline," *Register of Pennsylvania*, April 19, 1828.

144. The first reference to spouses was in 1808; spouses were absent from records by 1828. Minutes, 1794–1828, BOI.

145. Assessment of the strength of intimate patriarchy is based on analysis of the judicial treatment of divorce, adultery, and fornication, as well as inheritance laws.

146. Ruth Bloch, "The American Revolution, Wife Beating, and the Emergent Value of Privacy," *Early American Studies: An Interdisciplinary Journal* 5, no. 2 (2007): 223–51, 244. The principle of familial privacy echoes the theory of James Wilson; see Jan Lewis, "'Of Every Age Sex & Condition': The Representation of Women in the Constitution," *Journal of the Early Republic* 15, no. 3 (1995): 359–87. Also see Nancy Cott, *Public Vows: A History of Marriage and the Nation* (Cambridge, Mass.: Harvard University Press, 2000).

147. Lewis, *Pursuit of Happiness*, 17.

148. Carole Shammas, "Anglo-American Household Government in Comparative Perspective," *William and Mary Quarterly* 3rd ser. 52, no. 1 (1995): 104–44, 104.

149. This push for greater freedoms had intensified further by the mid-nineteenth century, and patriarchal authority began disintegrating as people not only challenged the authority of the head of household but also forced the state to get involved in securing rights for women, slaves, freed blacks, and children. Shammas, "Anglo-American Household," 106.

150. Shammas, "Anglo-American Household," 144.

151. Jan Lewis, "The Republican Wife: Virtue and Seduction in the Early Republic," *William and Mary Quarterly* 3rd ser. 44, no. 4 (1987): 689–721.

152. On the role of marriage in refining a woman's "feminine virtues and graces of character," see "An Old Maid," *Ladies' Magazine and Literary Gazette*, July 1803, 289–95.

153. Lewis, "The Republican Wife," 699; also see Bloch, "Changing Conceptions," 39.

154. Susan Klepp, *Revolutionary Conceptions: Women, Fertility, and Family Limitation in America, 1760–1820* (Chapel Hill: University of North Carolina Press, 2009), 242–43; Klepp also argues that the post-Revolutionary morals laws targeted female sexual purity, as evidenced by increasing prosecution for fornication.

155. Clare A. Lyons, *Sex Among the Rabble: An Intimate History of Gender & Power in the Age of Revolution, Philadelphia, 1730–1830* (Chapel Hill: University of North Carolina Press, 2006), 187.

156. Those numbers in Philadelphia for sample years include one in 1795, two in 1799, and five each in the years 1807, 1815, and 1823. See 1795, 1799, 1807, 1815, and 1823, PFT.

157. By 1823, however, this changed, as most women held for trial were sent to the Mayor's Court or the Court of Quarter Sessions for a full hearing.

158. Jack D. Marietta and G. S. Rowe, *Troubled Experiment: Crime and Justice in Pennsylvania, 1682 to 1800* (Philadelphia: University of Pennsylvania Press, 2006), 88.

159. Also see Kann, *Punishment, Prisons, and Patriarchy*.

160. Meranze incorporated analysis of the family under penal reform by focusing on the almshouse, the Magdalen Society, and the House of Refuge. See Meranze, *Laboratories of Virtue*, chap. 7.

161. Carolyn Eastman, "'Marriage is no frolic'; or, the Rise and Fall of Nonmarital Sex in Early Philadelphia," *Reviews in American History* 35, 1 (2007): 25–31. Self-divorce was a long-standing tradition from seventeenth-century England; see Lyons, *Sex Among the Rabble*, 16.

162. Larceny was the most common crime for which women were convicted. See tables "Women's Larceny Convictions, 1795–1810" and "Women's Larceny Convictions, 1820–1835," in Appendix.

163. Margaret Miller, *Pennsylvania Packet*, July 8, 1784; Also see Kirsten Sword, "Wayward Wives, Runaway Slaves, and the Limits of Patriarchal Authority in Early America" (Ph.D. dissertation, Harvard University, 2002).

164. Margaret Miller, August 3, 1791, PFT.

165. Martha Jones, *Poulson's American Daily Advertiser*, June 13, 1803.

166. Martha Jones, February 24, 1807, VAG.

167. Mary Bray, *Aurora General Advertiser*, October 17, 1806.

168. Mary Bray, April 1, 1807, PFT.

169. Ann Morris, *Democratic Press*, November 29, 1813.

170. Ann Morris, January 20, 1815, PSD.

171. She was charged with assisting in robbing Joseph Michael of seven dollars, see Ann Morris, June 21, 1823; and then for assaulting Rachel Wimore, see Ann Morris, August 2, 1823, PFT.

172. Also see Christine Stansell, *City of Women: Sex and Class in New York, 1789–1860* (Urbana: University of Illinois Press, 1987), 4.

173. These crimes belonged in the category of riskier, higher-stakes criminal activity that usually fell beyond the purview of most women. For women, these charges were sometimes 0 but never more than 6 percent of all convictions. For men, they were variable: 11 percent in 1795 (nine charges); 22 percent in 1807 (twenty-six charges); 16 percent in 1823 (forty-two charges); PSD. Each was punishable by death under the 1718 law—and removed from the list of capital crimes by the penal reforms of 1786. Bradley Chapin, "Felony Law Reform in the Early Republic," *PMHB* 113, no. 2 (1989): 163–83, 178.

174. Under English common law, women who committed capital crimes were not held responsible. Instead, they were thought to be acting under the order of their husband. Murder and treason were exceptions.

175. Mary Barry, November 6, 1811, Pennsylvania Supreme Court, PSA.

176. Ann Price, November 10, 1823, PFT.

177. Ann Price, December 11, 1823, MCD; *New York Daily Advertiser*, December 11, 1823.

178. Ann Price, December 6, 1823, PSD.

179. Charles and Mary Boyles, September 12, 1811, Dauphin County Quarter Sessions, PSA.

180. Samuel and Christina Davis, September 1809, Dauphin County Quarter Sessions, PSA.

181. Reuben and Hannah Freshwater, July 29, 1816, Chester County Oyer and Terminer, PSA.

182. Margaret Price, February 28, 1795, PSD; *Aurora General Advertiser*, March 7, 1795.

183. "John McCrum's Address 14, May 1788 to John Oldan, Esq," Correspondence, Box 1, Folder 11, PPS.

184. December 26, 1786, Pennsylvania Supreme Court, PSA. "Wednesday January 31, 1787," *Freeman's Journal*, January 31, 1787.

185. "Elizabeth Emery's Narrative," May 27, 1788, Correspondence, Box 1, Folder 11, PPS.

186. "Elizabeth Emery's Narrative," May 27, 1788, Correspondence, Box 1, Folder 11, PPS.

187. Ibid..

188. "John McCrum's Address 14, May 1788 to John Oldan, Esq," Correspondence, Box 1, Folder 11, PPS.

189. Only when the prison was restructured and reimagined two years later was he uprooted from his position. This time, Reynolds tried to get reformers off his back by enlisting inmates to riot in response to the newly imposed rules that would govern the penitentiary. Also see Meranze, *Laboratories of Virtue*, 178, 189.

190. McCrum was probably telling the truth, as Emery herself was the one with a long list of criminal accusations; She was later held on vagrancy charges and convicted of a "violent assault and wounding of Thomas Dunn;" August 3, 1790, VAG; August 1792, PFT. In May 1797, Rebecca Nailor swore that Emery stole a "calico petty coat" that belonged to Memory Williams; May 1797, PFT.

191. "Philadelphia; Joseph Reed," *Evening Post*, July 11, 1823. Also "From the Phila.," *Salem Gazette*, July 15, 1823.

192. "Philadelphia; Joseph Reed"; "From the Phila."

193. Carson, *The History of the Celebrated Mrs. Ann Carson*.

194. "*Philadelphia, Jan. 25*," *Weekly Messenger*, January 30, 1823.

195. "The memoirs of Ann Carson," *New-Yorker*, March 30, 1839.

196. Ibid.

197. Linda Kerber, *No Constitutional Right to Be Ladies: Women and the Obligations of Citizenship* (New York: Hill and Wang, 1998), 11.

198. Foucault wrote about this as part of the system of individualization and documentation, the quest to know the offender. Foucault, *Discipline and Punish*, 251. I explore explicitly the racialized and gendered aspects of this dynamic between white male reformers and black and white female inmates.

199. For revolutionaries, society was a distinct sphere from the state—one with promise that was the main focus of "the sentimental project." Knott, *Sensibility*, 199.

Chapter 3. Dangerous Publics

1. Richard Godbeer, *Sexual Revolution in Early America* (Baltimore: Johns Hopkins University Press, 2002), 299.

2. Carroll Smith-Rosenberg, *This Violent Empire: The Birth of an American National Identity* (Chapel Hill: University of North Carolina Press, 2010).

3. Carroll Smith-Rosenberg, "The Female World of Love and Ritual: Relations Between Women in Nineteenth-Century America," *Signs* 1, no. 1 (1975): 1–29; Kathryn Kish Sklar, *Catharine Beecher: A Study in American Domesticity* (New Haven, Conn.: Yale University Press, 1973); Nancy F. Cott, *The Bonds of Womanhood: "Woman's Sphere" in New England, 1780–1835* (New Haven, Conn.: Yale University Press, 1977); Mary P. Ryan, *Cradle of the Middle Class: The Family in Oneida County, New York, 1790–1865* (New York: Cambridge University Press, 1981).

4. Rosemarie Zagarri, *Revolutionary Backlash: Women and Politics in the Early American Republic* (Philadelphia: University of Pennsylvania Press, 2007); Carolyn Eastman, *A Nation of Speechifiers: Making an American Public After the Revolution* (Chicago: University of Chicago Press, 2009).

5. On the history of English poor laws, see Lynn Hollen Lees, *The Solidarity of Strangers: The English Poor Laws and the People, 1700–1948* (New York: Cambridge University Press, 1998).

6. Legal scholars have critiqued the practice of adopting English vagrancy laws in America because the breakdown of social and economic organization that inspired the law of settlement

in England never really took place in North America. John Lise has asserted the fallacy in applying laws from "a medieval island country" to modern American life." John Lise, "Vagrancy Law: Its Fault & Their Remedy," *Journal of Criminal Law & Criminology* 5, no. 4 (1915): 498–513.

7. Gary Nash, "Poverty and Poor Relief in Pre-Revolutionary Philadelphia," *William and Mary Quarterly* 33, no. 1 (1976): 3–30, 5–6 and 10–12.

8. "An Act for the Better Employment, Relief and Support of the Poor Within the City of Philadelphia, the District of Southwark, the Townships of Moyamensing and Passyunk and the Northern Liberties" (1766) in *Statutes* I: 417- 424.

9. John Alexander, *Render Them Submissive: Responses to Poverty in Philadelphia, 1760–1800* (Amherst: University of Massachusetts Press, 1980), 118.

10. "An Act for Amending the Act, Entitled "An Act for the Better Employment, Relief and Support of the Poor Within the City of Philadelphia, The District of Southward, the Townships of Moyamensing and Passyunk and the Northern Liberties" (1767) in *Statutes*, I: 430–33.

11. Nash, "Poverty and Poor Relief," 17.

12. From May 1785 to May 1786, *PG*, June 28, 1786.

13. Karin A. Wulf, *Not All Wives: Gender, Marriage, and Urban Culture in Colonial Philadelphia* (Ithaca, N.Y.: Cornell University Press, 1999), 153–79.

14. James Mease, *The Picture of Philadelphia: Giving an Account of its Origin, Increase, and Improvements in Arts, Sciences, Manufactures, Commerce and Revenue* (Philadelphia, 1811), 124. The night watch was a loosely ordered police force: "There are thirty-two watchmen who cry the hour, and six who visit the boxes of the others, to insure a punctual performance of their duty; the whole are under the direction of the captain of the watch, who attends at the old court house in Second street, every night, to receive the vagrants, rioters or thieves, who may be taken up by the watchmen; and to take care of the oil, wick, & c." Also Mease, *The Picture*, 124.

15. Alexander, *Render Them Submissive*, 117–18.

16. "No. III Mr Fenno," *Gazette of the United States*, July 27, 1799.

17. For connections between the institutional regimes of the almshouse and the prison, see David Rothman, *Discovery of the Asylum: Social Order and Disorder in the New Republic* (Boston: Little, Brown, 1971). When examining the lives of women, this connection is even more pronounced.

18. See Lisa Wilson, *Life After Death: Widows in Pennsylvania, 1750–1850* (Philadelphia: Temple University Press, 1992), chap. 3.

19. *Committee to Digest a Plan for the More Effectual Relief of the Poor, A Plan for the Government of the Alms-House, and for Ordering the Affairs of the Poor in the City of Philadelphia, Township of Northern Liberties, and District of Southwark* (Philadelphia, 1805), 8.

20. *Committee to Digest a Plan*, 15.

21. In 1824, for example, of the 4,399 deaths in Philadelphia, only 590 occurred in the almshouse. Given the fact that the almshouse was a place of last resort for many of the city's poor, this percentage is low. But imagine the devastation for inmates when nearly two people a day died. *Evening Post*, March 30, 1825.

22. Alexander, *Render Them Submissive*; Billy G. Smith, *The "Lower Sort": Philadelphia's Laboring People, 1750–1800* (Ithaca, N.Y.: Cornell University Press, 1990).

23. Half of the women charged with vagrancy were described as "disorderly." VAG, 1790/1, 1795, 1807, 1823.

24. Margaret Hunsh, June 27, 1797; Mary Gordon, November 4, 1797; and Mary McCalla, July 17, 1797; Almshouse Daily Occurrence Docket, 1797; Guardians of the Poor, PCA.

25. Ann Craig, September 9, 1810, April 22, 1812, October 21, 1812, Almshouse Black Book, Guardians of the Poor, PCA.

26. Margaret Cooper, August 25, 1812; Abigail Burket, March 19, 1814; Elizabeth Brown, May 18, 1814; Almshouse Black Book, Guardians of the Poor, PCA.

27. "An Ordinance for the Appointment of a High Constable for the City of Philadelphia, and Prescribing His Duties (1798)," in John C. Lowber, *Ordinances of the Corporation of the City of Philadelphia; to Which are Prefixed the Original Charter, the Act of Incorporation and Other Acts of Assembly Relating to the City* (Philadelphia, 1812), 147.

28. *Philadelphia Gazette*, August 24, 1801; *Federal Gazette*, August 17, 1805.

29. Records for the year described as 1790 are actually from June 1790 to May 1791, capturing the first complete year of record keeping; years 1795, 1807, and 1823 are complete and contain records of all women charged; VAG. For a critique of Pennsylvania's adoption of English vagrancy laws, see Lise, "Vagrancy Law."

30. In 1790/91 (12 months) the total was 210; it dropped to 134 in 1795 and 213 in 1807; VAG. By 1820, nearly 110,000 people called Philadelphia home. Gary Nash, *First City: Philadelphia and the Forging of Historical Memory* (Philadelphia: University of Pennsylvania Press, 2002). In 1823 vagrancy charges against women totaled 482; VAG.

31. Bridget Cummings, August 14, 1790, VAG.

32. Elizabeth Boyd, Catherine Carr, Sarah McNullitz, and Dianna Smith, February 26, 1795, VAG; Mary Connor, February 20, 1795, VAG.

33. Vagrancy charges for idleness numbered only 14 percent in 1790 and 7 percent in 1795; by 1807, a whopping 52 percent were for idleness. In 1790 and 1795 respectively, only 20 of 210 (14 percent) and 9 of 134 (7 percent) vagrancy charges had to do with idleness. By 1807, a whopping 52 percent (110 of 213) were for idleness. In 1823, this number decreased slightly to 40 percent (193 of 482); VAG.

34. Wulf, *Not All Wives*, 142–46.

35. Lowber, *Ordinances of the Corporation*, 157.

36. "The clerk or clerks of the market . . . shall be entitled to detain, out of the rents of the stalls, by him and them collected as foresaid, after the rate of two and one half dollars in every hundred dollars," in Lowber, *Ordinances of the Corporation*, 159.

37. Candice L. Harrison, "'Free Trade and Hucksters' Rights!' Envisioning Economic Democracy in the Early Republic," *PMHB* 137, no. 2 (2013): 147–77, 156.

38. Ibid., 166.

39. Ibid., 167.

40. "No person or persons shall, at any time, except on market days and in market hours, sell or expose to sale, either on the shambles or stalls of the market, or on the pavements within or surrounding the same, any soup or soups, under the description of pepperpot or any other name whatsoever, or boiled Indian corn, pickled oysters or other dressed victuals," in Lowber, *Ordinances of the Corporation*, 157.

41. "Letter from William Hines, Dec 28, 1824, Philadelphia, to the mayor," Folder 3, Correspondence 146–96 (g–h), Joseph Watson Papers Collection, HSP.

42. "Letter from George Nagel and John Crox, June 23, 1825," Folder 5, Correspondence 273–96 (m–n), Joseph Watson Papers Collection, HSP.

43. "Letter from William Cammron, Thursday 28th, Sept 1825," Folder 1, Correspondence 3–94 (a–b), Joseph Watson Papers Collection, HSP.

44. Tench Coxe, "Address to an Assembly of the Friends of American Manufactures," *American Museum*, September 1787.

45. Alan M. Zachary, "Social Disorder and the Philadelphia Elite Before Jackson," *PMHB* 99, no. 3 (July 1975): 288–308, 294.

46. Americanus, "On American Manufactures," *Columbian Magazine*, September 1786.

47. Mary Carlisle, May 11, 1795, VAG. Mary was repeatedly a nuisance to the watchmen, who picked her up again in August, September, October, and December of that year. She was charged with being "idle lewd and disorderly," "a nuisance to the city," and "with being a most notorious and incorrigible disorderly woman." She was also charged with larceny "in picking the pocket of William Lealand of ten shillings" on December 17, 1791, PFT.

48. G. S. Rowe and Billy G. Smith, "Prisoners for Trial Docket and the Vagrancy Docket," in *Life in Early Philadelphia: Documents from the Revolutionary and Early National Periods*, ed. Billy G. Smith (University Park: Pennsylvania State University Press, 1995), 61–65.

49. Martha Patterson, July 31, 1790 and Margaret Miller, October 30, 1790, VAG.

50. Nancy Sumers, August 22, 1807, VAG.

51. Ann Galagher, October 6, 1795; and Rebecca Williams, August 29, 1795, VAG.

52. Sarah Gault (Snow), June 24, 1790, VAG.

53. Elizabeth Duffy, Hester Clark, Rachel Lane, Elizabeth Watson, and Mary Porter, June 17, 1823, VAG.

54. For more on this dynamic in the twentieth century, see Cheryl D. Hicks, "'Bright and Good Looking Colored Girl': Black Women's Sexuality and '"Harmful Intimacy' in Early-Twentieth-Century New York," *Journal of the History of Sexuality* 18, no. 3 (2009): 418–56.

55. Robert C. Smith, "A Portuguese Naturalist in Philadelphia, 1799: Excerpts from the Diary of Hipolito Jose da Costa," *PMHB* 78, no. 1 (January 1954): 71–106,100; and Kenneth Roberts and Anna M. Roberts, *Moreau de St. Méry's American Journey* (Garden City, N.Y., Doubleday, 1947), 313.

56. Claire Lyons, *Sex Among the Rabble: An Intimate History of Gender and Power in the Age of Revolution, Philadelphia, 1730–1830* (Chapel Hill, N.C.: University of North Carolina Press, 2006), 343–45; Marcia Roberta Carlisle, "Prostitutes and Their Reformers in Nineteenth-Century Philadelphia" (Ph.D. dissertation, Rutgers University, 1982); Marcia Carlisle, "Disorderly City, Disorderly Women: Prostitution in Ante-Bellum Philadelphia," *PMHB* 110, no. 4 (1986): 549–68.

57. Patricia Cline Cohen, *The Murder of Helen Jewett: The Life and Death of a Prostitute in Nineteenth-Century New York* (New York: Knopf, 1998).

58. Between 1790 and 1814; Lyons, *Sex Among the Rabble*, 339. Lyons counts not only those explicitly named as "prostitutes" or "street walkers" in her study, but also interprets records citing "no visible means of support" to include (or also mean) "anyone with no legal employment," which she suggests is what the city officials did at the time to justify or explain the imprisonment of those who actually did work, though illegally.

59. The widespread use of the term "disorderly" in reference to prostitutes, combined with the periodic street sweeps and imprisonment of such women, led to the misinterpretation of all vagrants and disorderly people as prostitutes. See Negley King Teeters, *They Were in Prison: A History of the Pennsylvania Prison Society, 1787–1937* (Philadelphia: Winston, 1937); Smith, "Portuguese Naturalist," 100.

60. Rodney Hessinger, *Seduced, Abandoned, and Reborn: Visions of Youth in Middle-Class America, 1780–1850* (Philadelphia: University of Pennsylvania Press, 2005).

61. Mission Statement, MAG Annual Meeting, box 1, vol. 1.

62. Minutes, December 17, 1806, MAG Board of Managers, box 3, vol. 4.

63. Minutes, April 4, 1807, MAG Board of Managers, box 3, vol. 4.

64. Minutes, April 4 and June 11, 1807, MAG Board of Managers, box 3, vol. 4.

65. In 1814 and 1815, for example, ten Magdalens named Philadelphia as their birthplace, while ten others came from Pennsylvania, Delaware, New Jersey, or New York. Four women had no place of birth listed. MAG Board of Managers, box 3, vol. 4.

66. Minutes, February 2, 1808, MAG Board of Managers, box 3, vol. 4.

67. Minutes, December 6, 1808, MAG Board of Managers, box 3, vol. 4.

68. Minutes, February 7, 1809, MAG Board of Managers, box 3, vol. 4.

69. Ibid.

70. Minutes, May 2, 1809, MAG Board of Managers, box 3, vol. 4.

71. Minutes, June 7, 1808, MAG Board of Managers, box 3, vol. 4.

72. Minutes, July 11, 1809, MAG Board of Managers, box 3, vol. 4.

73. Minutes, August 1, 1809, MAG Board of Managers, box 3, vol. 4.

74. "To the Magdalen Society of Philadelphia," *Register of Pennsylvania*, February 28, 1829. The report was signed by Alexander Henry, chairman, and Bartholomew Wistar, secretary.

75. Ibid.

76. Thomas R. Meehan, "Courts, Cases, and Counselors in Revolutionary and Post-Revolutionary Pennsylvania," *PMHB* 91, no. 1 (January 1967): 3–34, 13.

77. Louis Richards, "Hon. Jacob Rush of the Pennsylvania Judiciary," *PMHB* 39, no. 1 (1915): 53–68.

78. "An Act for the Prevention of Vice and Immorality and of Unlawful Gaming and to Restrain Disorderly Sports and Dissipation" (1794) *Statutes*, XV: 110–18, 110.

79. Ibid., 111.

80. Ibid., 113–14.

81. Ibid., 117–8.

82. Jacob Rush, "Upon the Institution of the Sabbath [Delivered before the Grand Jury of Luzerne County, August 1800]," in *Charges, and Extracts of Charges, on Moral and Religious Subjects delivered at sundry times, by Jacob Rush with a recommendation by the reverend clergy of the Presbiterian Church, in the city of Philadelphia to which is annexed the act of the legislature of the state of Pennsylvania, respecting vice and morality* (Philadelphia, 1803), 42.

83. Ibid., 38–39.

84. Jacob Rush, "Upon Prophane Swearing [Delivered before the Grand Jury of Luzerne County, November 1800]," in *Charges and Extracts*, 59.

85. Honest Woman, October 6, 1807, VAG.

86. Sarah Engles, June 3, 1823, VAG.

87. Hannah Johnson, December 7, 1823; Lydia Armstrong, June 28, 1823; Sarah Davis, February 27, 1823; Charlotte Palmer, January 19, 1823; and Sarah Williams, March 12, 1823; VAG.

88. Mary Hawse, July 29, 1795, VAG.

89. Mary Thompson, September 4, 1795, VAG.

90. Jacob Rush, "Extracts from a Charge on Patriotism [Delivered before the Grand Jury in Northampton County, April, 1799]," in *Charges and Extracts*, 35.

91. Even the Mayor's Court of Philadelphia, which typically heard cases for minor infractions, was no longer interested in prosecuting for fornication or adultery—at least against women. See the table, "Charges Against Women, Mayor's Court, Philadelphia" in the Appendix.

92. Susan Branson, *Those Fiery Frenchified Dames: Women and Political Culture in Early National Philadelphia* (Philadelphia: University of Pennsylvania Press, 2001); Simon Newman, *Embodied History: The Lives of the Poor in Early Philadelphia* (Philadelphia: University of Pennsylvania Press, 2003); Lyons, *Sex Among the Rabble*, 210–14.

93. Sarah Brown, June 30, 1807, PFT; July 12, 1809, PSD.

94. Peter Thompson, "'The Friendly Glass': Drink and Gentility in Colonial Philadelphia," *PMHB* 113, no. 4 (October 1989): 549–573; Sharon V. Salinger, *Taverns and Drinking in Early America* (Baltimore: Johns Hopkins University Press, 2004). On drinking and crime in England, see Dana Rabin, "Drunkenness and Responsibility for Crime in the Eighteenth Century," *Journal of British Studies* 44, no. 3 (July 2005): 457–77.

95. Dorsey notes that the reality of women's drinking for all but the poorest of women was hidden from view, happening largely in the private sphere. Bruce Dorsey, *Reforming Men and Women: Gender in the Antebellum City* (Ithaca, N.Y.: Cornell University Press, 2002), 99–102. References to drunkenness included 56 in 1790/1, 33 in 1795, 45 in 1807, 144 in 1835; VAG.

96. Margaret Fosset, September 6, 1790; and Mary Evans, June 22, 1790; VAG.

97. Mary Lane, November, 23, 1790, Almshouse Daily Occurrence Docket, Guardians of the Poor, PCA.

98. She was forty-two in 1803 when she was convicted of burglary and sentenced to three years in prison; Mary Lane, February 3, 1803, PSD; (Another woman named Mary Lane was also charged with larceny in Mayor's Court January 8, 1800, but this fifty-seven-year-old English woman was older and of different national origin, PSD). Mary made new friends in prison and became part of a more extensive network of people who lived on the margins of the law. In 1807 she was charged with Mary and Hannah for keeping a disorderly house, PFT. In June 1809 she was fined four dollars for assault and battery, probably a work hazard. Again in 1815 she was charged on two more counts of being disorderly, disturbing the peace and being riotous, and likely prostitution; in September, with two women named Sarah; in December with Mary Patten, Hannah Manuel, Jane McMullen, and Jacob Chandler, PFT.

99. Ann Floyd, March 5, 1813, Almshouse Black Book, Guardians of the Poor, PCA.

100. John Christy and Catherine Christy, March 15, 1812, Almshouse Black Book, Guardians of the Poor, PCA.

101. Matt Warner Osborn, "A Detestable Shrine: Alcohol Abuse in Antebellum Philadelphia," *Journal of the Early Republic* 29, no. 1 (Spring 2009): 101–32.

102. Mary Cobb, October 10, 1807, VAG; and Elizabeth Shaw, August 19, 1823, VAG.

103. Nancy James, March, 1831, PSD. Also see table "Women Imprisoned for Running Tippling Houses, 1820–1835" in the Appendix.

104. Matthew Warner Osborn, *Rum Maniacs: Alcoholic Insanity in the Early American Republic* (Chicago: University of Chicago Press, 2014), 86–87.

105. W. L. Fisher et al., *Pauperism and Crime* (Philadelphia: 1831), 47–48.

106. Rush, "Upon Drunkenness," in *Charges, and Extracts*, 64.

107. Minutes, May 19, 1795, August 24, 1798, and September 12, 1803, BOI.

108. Minutes, January 13, 1812, BOI.

109. Job R. Tyson, *Essay on the Penal Law of Pennsylvania* (Philadelphia, 1827), 61.

110. Jacquelyn C. Miller, "An 'Uncommon Tranquility of Mind': Emotional Self-Control and the Construction of a Middle-Class Identity in Eighteenth-Century Philadelphia," *Journal of Social History* 30, no. 1 (Autumn 1996): 129–148, 137.

111. Nicole Eustace, *Passion Is the Gale: Emotion, Power, and the Coming of the Revolution* (Chapel Hill: University of North Carolina Press, 2008), 161–62.

112. Ibid., 152–53.

113. Ibid., 191.

114. Mary Hines, May 21, 1795, PFT.

115. Mary Hines, January 8, 1799, PFT.

116. Mary Hines, August 14 and November 14, 1799, PFT.

117. Rowe cites 339 attacks, mostly of family members. Rowe, "Women's Crime and Criminal Administration," 342. For more on violence in Pennsylvania, see Thomas P. Slaughter, *Bloody Dawn: The Christiana Riot and Racial Violence in the Antebellum North* (New York: Oxford University Press, 1991); Jack D. Marietta and G. S. Rowe, *Troubled Experiment: Crime and Justice in Pennsylvania, 1682–1800* (Philadelphia: University of Pennsylvania Press, 2006).

118. Some research suggests that women in Pennsylvania were more violent than women in other states. See Marietta and Rowe, *Troubled Experiment*, 134.

119. This is Marietta and Row's explanation for male violence; I think it applies to women as well.

120. For this reason, none of the records from the Prisoners for Trial Docket appear in the records of the Mayor's Court or Quarter Sessions Court during the same years.

121. Women in prison charged with crimes against persons by year: 19 in 1795, 43 in 1799, 136 in 1807, 224 in 1823; number convicted: 1 in 1795, 0 in 1799, 1 in 1807, 7 in 1815, 15 in 1823, MCD.

122. Quarter Sessions Court cases had more ten- and twenty-dollar fines, while Mayor's Court averaged one and five dollars.

123. Elizabeth Proctor, December 11, 1799, PFT.

124. Susan Dickson, November 6, 1815, PFT.

125. PFT, 1807.

126. PFT, 1823.

127. Mary Dunning, December 16, 1815, PFT.

128. Margaret Everet, April 7, 1823, PFT.

129. Martha Weir, August 30, 1823, PFT.

130. Ann Philips, April 1, 1823, PFT.

131. See also Sharon Block, *Rape and Sexual Power in Early America* (Chapel Hill: University of North Carolina Press, 2006).

132. Rachel Smith, October 26, 1807, PFT.

133. Mary Johnson, September 23, 1823, PFT.

134. Catherine Cress, July 30, 1823, PFT.

135. Elizabeth Williams, March 27, 1795, PFT.

136. Catherine Evenson, December 16, 1823, PSD. Evenson was sentenced to one year in prison and transferred to Arch Street Prison after one month.

137. Catherine Evenson, October 25 and 27, 1823, PFT.

138. Elizabeth Jones, June 26, 1823, PFT and September 1823, PSD.

139. Mary Reed, June 22, 1799, PFT.

140. Kitty/Letty Anderson, March 27, April 17, July 12, September, 10, 1815, PFT; Letty Anderson, 1815, PSD.

141. Tyson, *Essay on the Penal Law*, 61.

142. Marietta and Rowe, *Troubled Experiment*, 152.

143. Alderman Badger, *Report on the Agency of Intemperance in the Production of Pauperism* (Philadelphia: J. Van Court, 1836), 8.

144. Manasseh Cutler, "New York and Philadelphia in 1787," *PMHB* 12, no. 1 (1888): 97–115, 112.

145. Ibid., 112.

146. On the frequency of shopping, see Mary Beth Norton, *Liberty's Daughters: The Revolutionary Experience of American Women, 1750–1800* (Ithaca, N.Y.: Cornell University Press, 1980), 22.

147. Jane Henry, Jun., December 18, 1794, PSD and December 16, PFT; Jane Henry, Sen., December 18, 1794, PSD and December 16, PFT; Minutes, August 4, 1795, BOI. Both were pardoned August 17, 1795, on condition of leaving the state.

148. Their lives of crime continued. In 1807 Jane Henry was again charged in Pennsylvania with receiving stolen goods, knowing them to be so, from Joseph Burrell and imprisoned for three months. She was, at the same time, convicted of the same for receiving goods from Samuel Moore. "Tuesday, June 16, 1807," *Poulson's American Daily Advertiser*, June 16, 1807. This was probably Jane, Sr.; Jane, Jr., turned her attention to other ventures in running a tippling house, for which she was fined fifty dollars in 1823; PFT, 1823.

149. See tables "Women's Larceny Convictions, 1795–1810 and Women's Larceny Convictions, 1820–1835" in Appendix.

150. "The right of slavery is a right to perpetrate all sorts of crimes; those crimes which invade property; for slaves are not suffered to have any, even in their own persons; those crimes which destroy personal safety, for the slave may be sacrificed to the caprice of his master; those crimes which make modesty shudder; my blood rises at those horrid images." *PG*, August 7, 1782.

151. As Leslie Patrick-Stamp has stated, "They knew about property since most had been subjected to slavery, and as slaves they had been forced to accept their fate as a possession of another" Leslie Patrick-Stamp, "Ideology and Punishment: The Crime of Being Black (Pennsylvania, 1639–1804)" (Ph.D. dissertation, University of California, Santa Cruz, 1989), 257.

152. Wendy A. Woloson, *In Hock: Pawning in America from Independence Through the Great Depression* (Chicago: University of Chicago Press, 2009), 128–29.

153. "Philadelphia, June 6," *PG*, June 13, 1734.

154. "Philadelphia, February 6," *PG*, February 6, 1772.

155. Burglary and theft were punishable by a three-month prison term and restitution of four times the amount stolen. If one was unable to provide such restitution, the prison term was seven years. Harry E. Barnes, *Evolution of Penology in Pennsylvania: A Study in American Social History* (Indianapolis: Bobbs-Merrill, 1927), 33. "An Act Directing the Punishment of Larceny Under Five Shillings" (1701) was passed, calling for a public whipping of up to fifteen lashes, simple restitution of goods or value, and costs of punishment. This lessened the burden of the excessive restitution that few could ever pay, *Statutes*, II: 159.

156. Simple larceny was charged with restitution of goods or value, payment of costs of prosecution, payment of fee to the government of the same value, commitment to the prison, and public whipping on the bare back of 21 lashes; a third offense raised the number of lashes from 39 to 50 and sent the person to the workhouse for one to four years. See "An Act for the Advancement of Justice and More Certain Administration Thereof" (1718), *Statutes*, III: 236; also, Barnes, *Evolution of Penology*, 39.

157. The punishment was public whipping of up to fifteen lashes on the bare back, and restitution; "An Act for the Trial and Punishment of Larceny Under Five Shillings," (1720) *Statutes*, III: 246–47. Early courts were known for punishing men and women similarly for theft. For

example, in 1750 a man who stole a linen shirt and pair of stockings, and a woman who stole a silk handkerchief were both punished with fifteen lashes to their bare backs. Quarter Sessions, January 30, 1750, York County, Pennsylvania; George Reeser Prowell, *History of York County, Pennsylvania* (Chicago: J.H. Beers, 1907), 480.

158. "An Act Amending the Penal Laws of This State" (1786), *Statutes*, XII: 280–289.

159. In 1799, for example, property crimes made up only 36 percent of the charges but a whopping 90 percent of convictions; of 210 women in prison awaiting trial, 36 percent were charged with property crimes, 20 percent with crimes against persons, and 43 percent against morals. Over 1,000 women were convicted of property crimes and sentenced to Walnut Street Prison between 1790 and 1835. For men, that number was slightly higher. For analysis of this based on a random sample of 1,068 charges against both men and women in prison during this period, see Batsheva Spiegel Epstein, "Patterns of Sentencing and Their Implementation in Philadelphia City and County, 1795–1829" (Ph.D. dissertation, University of Pennsylvania, 1981), 101–10.

160. On the economic upheaval of this period, see Ronald Shultz, *The Republic of Labor: Philadelphia Artisans and the Politics of Class, 1720–1830* (New York: Oxford University Press, 1993), 75, 165–166.

161. Mary O'Brien, January 2, 1799, PFT; Edward Shippen, Philadelphia Census of 1790.

162. Marietta and Rowe, *Troubled Experiment*, 51.

163. Mary O'Brien, January 10, 1799, PSD; Imprisoned again January 9, 1801 with Holland and McNiff, see Mary O'Brien, January 9, 1801, PSD.

164. Mary O'Brien, March 6, 1794 and July 9, 1796, PFT.

165. See Roberts and Roberts, *Moreau de St. Méry's American Journey*, 285.

166. Eve Spangler, May 1809, Dauphin County Quarter Sessions, PSA.

167. Mary Cling, January 1810, Dauphin County Quarter Sessions, PSA.

168. Bartram Family Papers, HSP.

169. *Pennsylvania Packet*, January 24, 1787.

170. On imposters and crafting of an identity, see Ann Fabian, *The Unvarnished Truth: Personal Narratives in Nineteenth-Century America* (Berkeley: University of California Press, 2000).

171. "To the People," *Weekly Aurora*, September 22, 1817. A shift was a garment commonly worn by women, made of cotton and sometimes longer than a shirt.

172. Elizabeth Wilson, January 14, 1795, PFT.

173. Elizabeth Wilson, June 6, 1796, PFT.

174. Elizabeth Wilson, July 26, 1796, PSD.

175. Occupations of female head of households, Philadelphia Census, 1790.

176. A man working as a cook or in maintenance might earn two to five times that amount. The only form of labor consistently mentioned in the records of women prisoners is that of domestic service; about 40 women of 400 records, PSD; Woloson, *In Hock*, 93. These women may not have been the poorest. In New York City from 1819 to 1847, servants were the only group of women workers who saved money. See Christine Stansell, *City of Women: Sex and Class in New York, 1789–1860*, (Urbana: University of Illinois Press, 1987), 157.

177. "Milledgeville Journal," *Weekly Visitor*, September 16, 1820.

178. Woloson, *In Hock*, 93.

179. This became more commonly discussed in the 1830s. For example, Joseph Tuckerman wrote at the time, "Unprepared, therefore, as I am to speak with confidence of the extent of the

influence of the low wages, for which females are often compelled to work, and of the difficulty which they often find of obtaining work, even at the small prices which are given for it, in leading them to dishonour and crime, I have yet no doubt that this is one of the causes, by which several are brought to debasement and ruin." Joseph Tuckerman, *Prize Essay: An Essay on the Wages Paid to Females for their Labour; in the form of a letter, from a gentleman in Boston to his friend in Philadelphia* (Philadelphia, 1830), 35.

180. See the table "Women Convicts by Occupation, 1820–1824," in Appendix.

181. Marietta and Rowe, *Troubled Experiment*, 95.

182. "The People vs. Emeline Williams," *American*, June 21, 1820.

183. "Five Pounds Reward," *PG*, September 21, 1785.

184. Stansell, *City of Women*, 158.

185. "Six Dollars Reward," *PG*, December 14, 1769.

186. Ealoner Higgins December 2, 1794, PSD; October 22, 1794, PFT.

187. There could be exceptions. The Drinkers were known to pay their servants better than average wages, for example.

188. Susannah Kirk, February 27, 1799 and July 25, 1799, PFT; July 16, 1800, Almshouse Record, in Smith, *Life in Early Philadelphia*; Sharon Salinger, *"To Serve Well and Faithfully": Labour and Indentured Servants in Pennsylvania, 1682–1800* (New York: Cambridge University Press, 1987), 131.

189. Margaret Fisher, June 19 and December 28, 1815, PSD; March 1815, MCD; May 19, 1815, PFT; Salinger, *"To Serve Well and Faithfully"*, 131.

190. Sarah Weaver, October 2, 1795, PSD.

191. "The Rev.d Geo. Duffield, May 3d, 1788" and "Dr. Duffield Letter, May 8, 1788, to Mr John Olden, Merch.t Secretary to the Acting Committee of the Relief Society," Correspondence, Box 1, Folder 11, PPS.

192. Stansell, *City of Women*, 161.

193. Elaine Forman Craine, ed., *The Diary of Elizabeth Drinker* Vol. 1 (Boston: Northeastern University Press, 1991), 326.

194. Ibid., 233.

195. Norton, *Liberty's Daughters*, 22–23.

196. Erica Armstrong Dunbar, *A Fragile Freedom: African American Women and Emancipation in the Antebellum City* (New Haven, Conn.: Yale University Press, 2008), 44.

197. Men were frustrated by their servants as well. Mary Fulton first made the papers in 1794 when she ran away from her boss, who offered a one-dollar reward for her return. Years later in freedom, she was charged by William Coyle for stealing "one sheet" from him worth only one dollar. Fulton worked for Coyle in his service or lived in the neighborhood with access to his clothesline. She was held from June until October 1807 on this charge. While no conviction was noted, she may have been held there by him as a form of punishment or because she was unable to pay the court or prison fees.

198. See Kathleen Brown, *Foul Bodies: Cleanliness in Early America* (New Haven, Conn.: Yale University Press, 2009), 253; and Stansell, *City of Women*, 161.

199. *First Annual Report of the Society for the Encouragement of Faithful Domestic Servants in New York* (New York, 1826), 1.

200. Ibid.

201. See the table "Women Convicts by Occupation, 1820–1824" in the Appendix.

202. Samuel Hazard, ed., *The Register of Pennsylvania, Devoted to the Preservation of Facts and Documents and Every Other Kind of Useful Information Respecting the State of Pennsylvania* (1829) III: 328–29.

203. Ibid.

204. New York reports that of 2,164 applications from domestics for registration with their society, only 259 were Americans. Most were Irish (1,279) and African American (460). *First Annual Report of the Society*, 9.

205. W. L. Fisher et al., *Pauperism and Crime* (Philadelphia: 1831), 47–48.

206. PSD, 1820–1835.

207. Serena Zabin, *Dangerous Economies: Status and Commerce in Imperial New York* (Philadelphia: University of Pennsylvania Press, 2009).

208. Marietta and Row, *Troubled Experiment*, 90.

209. Nancy Hewitt, *Women's Activism and Social Change: Rochester, NY, 1822–1872* (Ithaca, N.Y.: Cornell University Press, 1984); Lori D. Ginzberg, *Women and the Work of Benevolence: Morality, Politics, and Class in the Nineteenth-Century United States* (New Haven, Conn.: Yale University Press, 1992); Kathryn Kish Sklar, *Florence Kelley and the Nation's Work: The Rise of Women's Political Culture, 1830–1900* (New Haven, Conn.: Yale University Press, 1997); Anne Boylan, *The Origins of Women's Activism, New York and Boston, 1797–1840* (Chapel Hill: University of North Carolina Press, 2001); Dorsey, *Reforming Men and Women.*

Chapter 4. Freedom's Limits

1. For a discussion of those who condemned the slave trade but were not necessarily committed to abolition, see Christopher Leslie Brown, *Moral Capital: Foundations of British Abolitionism*, Omohundro Institution of Early American History and Culture Series (Chapel Hill: University of North Carolina Press, 2006).

2. Beverly C. Tomek, *Colonization and Its Discontents: Emancipation, Emigration, and Antislavery in Antebellum Pennsylvania* (New York: New York University Press, 2011).

3. John Wood Sweet, *Bodies Politics: Negotiating Race in the American North, 1730–1830* (Baltimore: Johns Hopkins University Press, 2003); Leon Litwack, *North of Slavery: The Negro in the Free States* (Chicago: University of Chicago Press, 1961); Richard Newman, "Prelude to the Gag Rule: Southern Reaction to Antislavery Petitions in the First Federal Congress," *Journal of the Early Republic* 16, no. 4 (Winter 1996): 571–99.

4. Edward Raymond Turner, *The Negro in Pennsylvania: Slavery, Servitude, Freedom, 1639–1861* (Washington, D.C.: American Historical Association, 1911); Mary Frances Berry, *Black Resistance, White Law: A History of Constitutional Racism in America* (New York: Penguin, 1971).

5. Pennsylvania was known for its significant population of Scots-Irish immigrants throughout the eighteenth century. In later years, particularly from the 1790s onward, immigrants were designated in the court and prison records as born in Ireland, which is why I use the term Irish rather than Scots-Irish for this group.

6. Kali Gross, *Colored Amazons: Crime, Violence, and Black Women in the City of Brotherly Love, 1880–1910* (Durham, N.C.: Duke University Press, 2006).

7. On motives for abolition during this period, see David Brion Davis, *The Problem of Slavery in the Age of Revolution, 1771–1823* (Ithaca, N.Y.: Cornell University Press, 1975); Christopher

Leslie Brown, *Moral Capital;* Early work connecting prisons to slavery includes Leslie Patrick-Stamp, "Ideology and Punishment: The Crime of Being Black (Pennsylvania, 1639–1804)" (Ph.D. dissertation, University of California, Santa Cruz, 1989); David M Oshinsky, *Worse than Slavery: Parchman Farm and the Ordeal of Jim Crow Justice* (New York: Free Press, 1996).

8. David Waldstreicher, *Slavery's Constitution: From Revolution to Ratification* (New York: Hill and Wang, 2002), 101.

9. Ibid., 102.

10. Ibid., 104.

11. Alan M. Zachary, "Social Disorder and the Philadelphia Elite Before Jackson," *PMHB* 99 (July 1975): 288–308.

12. Gary Nash, *Forging Freedom: The Formation of Philadelphia's Black Community, 1720–1840* (Cambridge, Mass.: Harvard University Press, 1988); Gary Nash and Jean Soderlund, *Freedom by Degrees: Emancipation in Pennsylvania and Its Aftermath* (New York: Oxford University Press, 1991); Julie Winch, *Philadelphia's Black Elite: Activism, Accommodation, and the Struggle for Autonomy, 1787–1848* (Philadelphia: Temple University Press, 1993); Turner, *Negro in Pennsylvania.*

13. There are many examples, from the way whites manipulated the laws to continue enslavement of children to outright kidnapping, and so on. Joanne Pope Melish, "The 'Condition' Debate and Racial Discourse in the Antebellum North," *Journal of the Early Republic* 19, no. 4, Special Issue on Racial Consciousness and Nation-Building in the Early Republic (Winter 1999): 651–72, 654; also Melish, *Disowning Slavery: Gradual Emancipation and "Race" in New England, 1780–1860* (Ithaca, N.Y.: Cornell University Press, 1998).

14. This argument came from proslavery people, colonizationists, and even gradualists. See Tomek, *Colonization and Its Discontents,* chap. 1.

15. Richard Newman, "Prelude to the Gag Rule: Southern Reaction to Antislavery Petitions in the First Federal Congress," *Journal of the Early Republic* 16, no. 4 (Winter 1996): 571–99, 577.

16. "Petition from Pennsylvania Abolition Society to Congress (1790)," cited in Gary B. Nash, *Race and Revolution* (Madison: Madison House Publishers, 1990), 145.

17. Turner, *Negro in Pennsylvania,* 82–83.

18. Leslie Harris, *In the Shadow of Slavery: African Americans in New York City, 1626–1863* (Chicago: University of Chicago Press, 2003), 96. For analysis of the history of research on this relationship by social scientists, see Khalil Muhammad, *The Condemnation of Blackness: Race, Crime, and the Making of Modern Urban America* (Cambridge, Mass.: Harvard University Press, 2011).

19. Nash, *Forging Freedom,* 137.

20. Gross, *Colored Amazons,* 37.

21. Zachary, "Social Disorder," 303.

22. Gary Nash, *First City: Philadelphia and the Forging of Historical Memory* (Philadelphia: University of Pennsylvania, 2002), 127.

23. M. Carey, *A Brief Account of the Malignant fever which prevailed in Philadelphia in the year 1793* (Philadelphia, 1830), 67–68.

24. Jeannine Marie DeLombard, *In the Shadow of the Gallows: Race, Crime, and American Civic Identity* (Philadelphia: University of Pennsylvania Press, 2012).

25. Absalom Jones and Richard Allen, *A Narrative of the Proceedings of the Black People, during the Late Awful Calamity in Philadelphia, in the Year 1793: And a Refutation of some Censures, Thrown upon Them in Some Late Publications* (Philadelphia: William W. Woodward, 1794), 9.

26. Ibid., 13.

27. Ashli White, *Encountering Revolution: Haiti and the Making of the Early Republic* (Baltimore: Johns Hopkins University Press, 2010).

28. Erica Armstrong Dunbar, *A Fragile Freedom: African American Women and Emancipation in the Antebellum City* (New Haven, Conn.: Yale University Press, 2008), 40–41.

29. Turner, *Negro in Pennsylvania*, 101.

30. Nash, *Forging Freedom*, 175.

31. Winch, *Philadelphia's Black Elite*, 18.

32. Nash, *Forging Freedom*, 223.

33. Turner, *Negro in Pennsylvania*, 152.

34. Bruce Dorsey, *Reforming Men and Women: Gender in the Antebellum City* (Ithaca, N.Y.: Cornell University Press, 2002), chap. 4.

35. Pennsylvania Society for Promoting the Abolition of Slavery, *An Address from the Pennsylvania Society for Promoting the Abolition of Slavery to the Free Black People* (Philadelphia, 1800), 4.

36. Ibid., 5.

37. Most of these women came from Virginia and Maryland, PSD.

38. See Harris, *In the Shadow of Slavery*; Nash, *Forging Freedom*.

39. See John Alexander, *Render Them Submissive: Responses to Poverty in Philadelphia, 1760–1800* (Amherst: University of Massachusetts Press, 1980).

40. "Pauperism," *New York Columbian*, August 10, 1820.

41. Harris, *In the Shadow of Slavery*, 81–82; Also see Tera Hunter, *To Joy My Freedom: Southern Black Women's Lives and Labors After the Civil War* (Cambridge, Mass.: Harvard University Press, 1997), chap. 4.

42. Gross, *Colored Amazons*, 34.

43. PSD; Patrick-Stamp, "Ideology and Punishment," 296. Very little has been written about arson by white girls. Of the eight arson cases recorded in one docket book of the Pennsylvania Supreme Court from 1779 to 1804 (by no means complete), four cases were against African Americans and four cases were against those of unknown race; only Negro Suckey from Cumberland County was convicted and sentenced to death. Of the twelve arson cases before the Court of Oyer and Terminer from 1799 to 1816, most were found "Ignoramous" or "Not Guilty." But all three women convicted were black and given lengthy sentences: Hannah Carson, twelve years; Flora, "a Negro," twelve years; and Magdalen, "a Negro," five years. Supreme Court Docket; Oyer and Terminer Docket; PSD. Of those women sent to Walnut Street Prison between 1795–1810 and 1820–1835, all whose race was designated were of African descent. See the tables "Women Convicts by Race, 1795–1810" and "Women Convicts by Race, 1820–1835" in the Appendix.

44. William Bradford, *An Enquiry How Far the Punishment of Death Is Necessary in Pennsylvania with Notes and Illustrations, to Which is Added, an Account of the Gaol and Penitentiary House of Philadelphia, and of the Interior Management Thereof By Caleb Lownes of Philadelphia* (Philadelphia, 1793), 31.

45. Nash, *Forging Freedom*, 173; Nash, *First City*, 125.

46. Nash, *First City*, 127.

47. This shift in perception takes off in the nineteenth century. See Thomas P. Slaughter, *Bloody Dawn: The Christiana Riot and Racial Violence in the Antebellum North* (New York: Oxford University Press, 1991), 33. Also see Nash, *Forging Freedom*; White, *Encountering Revolution*.

48. For analysis of this issue in an earlier period, see Jill Lepore, *New York Burning: Liberty, Slavery, and Conspiracy in Eighteenth-Century Manhattan* (New York: Knopf, 2005).

49. *PG*, May 4, October 5, December 14, December 21, 1796.

50. *PG*, November 16, 1796.

51. Sarah Morton was imprisoned for threatening to kill and set fire to the house of the widow Souder. Morton was held under vagrancy charges for a few days. Sarah Morton, January 5, 1795, VAG; Sarah Morton, January 5, 1796, PFT.

52. *PG*, December 21, 1796.

53. *PG*, December 28, 1796.

54. *PG*, February 1, 1797.

55. "Baltimore, Dec 28," *PG*, January 4, 1797.

56. "Baltimore, Dec 28," *PG*, January 4, 1797.

57. In 1820, a fourteen-year-old black girl set out to poison the daughter of Mr. and Mrs. Charles Wharton, Jr. The girl was alleged to have been with the family for only a few weeks before putting laudanum in the baby's bottle, which the mother fed to the infant and killed her. "Domestic Intelligence," *Weekly Messenger*, July 26, 1821.

58. Turner, *Negro in Pennsylvania*, 152–53.

59. Leslie Patrick-Stamp discovered a petition written by local residents to the governor suggesting that white people were also involved in setting the fires, but this aspect is not addressed in the hearing or coverage of the crisis. See Leslie Patrick-Stamp, "Numbers That Are Not New: African Americans in the Country's First Prison, 1790–1835," *PMHB* 119 (1995): 104 n. 20.

60. *To the Inhabitants of the borough of York* (York, 1803).

61. Jack D. Marietta and G. S. Rowe, *Troubled Experiment: Crime and Justice in Pennsylvania, 1682 to 1800* (Philadelphia: University of Pennsylvania Press, 2006), 250.

62. In 1821, a group of nearly 100 settled in the region and worked for lumber merchants along the Susquehanna River. George Reeser Prowell, *History of York County, Pennsylvania* (Chicago: J.H. Beers, 1907), 591–92.

63. *York Recorder*, May 25, 1803.

64. Ruth Grimes, William Grimes, Hetty Dorson, Isaac Scipior, Isaac Spangler, and Abner Short, May 19, 1803, PSD.

65. Isaac, "negro and slave of Peter Dinkle"; another Isaac, "negro and servant of Margaret Spangler"; Abner, negro; Hetty Dorson, mulatto; Ruth, mulatto; and William Grimes, negro. York County Court of Quarter Sessions, in Patrick-Stamp, "Ideology and Punishment," 105.

66. *York Recorder*, May 25, 1803.

67. Dauphin County Quarter Sessions, PSD.

68. Later that same year, another white woman, Judith Halliday, was found innocent of burning the barn of Arthur Andrews. Cummins was the only person found guilty of arson in Chester County between 1802 and 1830.

69. Hannah Carson, February 22, 1799, PSD; February 1799, Oyer and Terminer Docket, PSA.

70. Federal Census, 1790. Thanks to Billy Smith for sharing his database.

71. Jane Wedge, "negress," November 10, 1802, PSD.

72. See the table "Women Convicted of Arson" in the Appendix.

73. Sabe "negress," November 27, 1804, PSD.

74. Sal "a woman of colour" August, 1822, PSD; Matilda Scott, April 7, 1823, PSD; Matilda Scott died in prison in 1826, three years into her ten-year sentence; Sal was released after five and a half years.

75. Study of women convicts shows that race was recorded less than 50 percent of the time until 1815. This pattern was also reflected in the almshouse. Even in the early years of the nineteenth century, black men were less likely than black women to seek and receive help from the almshouse. Even more significantly, nearly twice as many Irishmen as black men entered the almshouse because they could not find work and of the majority of Irish people who received help, 68 percent were men. Nash, *Forging Freedom*, 180.

76. Noel Ignatiev, *How the Irish Became White* (New York: Routledge, 1995), 57.

77. Phebe Mines, March 18, 1796, PSD; Catherine Lynch, had no physical description recorded. A BOI report suggests it was actually five women who escaped, noting that the Board recaptured Pricilla Roberts, Catherine Lynch & Joan Holland in Baltimore and had to pay for their recovery. Minutes, September 20, 1796, BOI.

78. Robert J. Turnbull, *A Visit to the Philadelphia Prison: Being an Accurate and Particular Account of the Wise and Humane Administration Adopted in Every Part of the Building; Containing also an Account of the Gradual Reformation and the Present Improved State, and the Penal Laws of Pennsylvania* (Philadelphia, 1796), 39.

79. See Newman, *Embodied History*, 58; Clare A. Lyons, *Sex Among the Rabble: An Intimate History of Gender & Power in the Age of Revolution, Philadelphia, 1730–1830* (Chapel Hill: University of North Carolina Press, 2006); For information on the mid-eighteenth century, see David Waldstreicher, *Runaway America: Benjamin Franklin, Slavery, and the American Revolution* (New York: Hill and Wang, 2004), 94. Billy Smith notes that even by the end of the eighteenth century, most blacks lived in white households as servants, boarders, or domestics. See Billy G. Smith, *The "Lower Sort": Philadelphia's Laboring People, 1750–1800* (Ithaca, N.Y.: Cornell University Press, 1990), 195.

80. François Alexandre Frédéric La Rochefoucault Liancourt, *On the Prisons of Philadelphia* (Philadelphia, 1796), 44.

81. Robert C. Smith, "A Portuguese Naturalist in Philadelphia, 1799: Excerpts from the Diary of Hipolito Jose da Costa," *PMHB* 78, no. 1 (1954): 71–106, 101; Also pointed out in Kenneth Roberts and Anna M. Roberts, *Moreau de St. Méry's American Journey* (Garden City, N.Y., Doubleday, 1947), 302.

82. Minutes, July 10, 1800, PSAMPP Acting Committee, vol. 6, PPS.

83. Ibid.

84. Minutes, October 9, 1800, and April 9, 1805, PSAMPP Acting Committee, vol. 6, PPS.

85. Minutes, January 1, 1795, BOI.

86. Minutes, March 11, 1795, BOI.

87. Minutes, February 23, 1796, BOI.

88. Jean R. Soderlund, "Black Women in Colonial Pennsylvania," *PMHB* 107, no. 1 (1983): 49–68.

89. The first book of the Prison Sentence Dockets is missing. The second book begins in 1794.

90. PFT, November 20, 1794, Philadelphia Prisons System, PCA.

91. PSD, December 17, 1794; and Minutes, July 7, 1795, BOI.

92. Rose Thornton, August 17, 1796, PSD; She was previous charged with assaulting Mary McMullin and threatening her life, for which she served thirty days. Rose Thorton, June 28, 1792, PFT.

93. Elenor White, May 26, 1797, PFT; July 8, 1797, PSD.

94. Nearly all people bound as indentured servants before 1775 were free by 1783. Alexander, *Render Them Submissive*, 27–28.

95. That is, 55 of the 93 cases with data for age (of 119 cases total) for 1795–1810. From 1820 to 1835, there were a total of 397 larceny convictions; 228 had data for age and 213 of those were under the age of thirty. See the table "Women Convicted of Larceny by Age" in the Appendix.

96. Mariane, October 1, 1795, PSD.

97. Maria Dick, March 13, 1815, PSD.

98. Maria Dick, September 27, 1815, PSD.

99. "To Richard Price," Philadelphia, October 15, 1785, in *Letters of Benjamin Rush*, ed. L.H. Butterfield, vol. 1, *1761–1792* (Philadelphia: American Philosophical Society, 1951), 371.

100. Women in the post-Revolutionary penal records are described as born in Ireland, with no distinction made for Scots-Irish or ancestry in Northern Ireland, which is why I refer to them as Irish. For more on Scots-Irish, see Warren R. Hofstra, ed., *Ulster to America: The Scots-Irish Migration Experience, 1680–1830* (Knoxville: University of Tennessee Press, 2011); Patrick Griffin, *The People with No Name: Ireland's Ulster Scots, America's Scots Irish, and the Creation of a British Atlantic World, 1689–1764* (Princeton, N.J.: Princeton University Press, 2001); James G. Leyburn, *The Scotch-Irish: A Social History* (Chapel Hill: University of North Carolina Press, 1962).

101. The decision to import Scots-Irish to work as laborers was only regretted in hindsight by the Quakers, a decidedly nonviolent group, as culture clashes threatened the peace. Marietta and Rowe, *Troubled Experiment*, 69–70.

102. Roberts and Roberts, *Moreau de St. Méry's American Journey*, 265.

103. *Narrative of Patrick Lyon, who suffered three months severe imprisonment in Philadelphia Gaol; on merely a vague suspicion of being concerned in the robbery of the Bank of Pennsylvania: with his remarks thereon* (Philadelphia, 1799).

104. Susan Branson, *Dangerous to Know: Women, Crime and Notoriety in the Early Republic* (Philadelphia: University of Pennsylvania Press, 2008).

105. See official institutional penitentiary reports from Massachusetts, Maryland, New York, Virginia, and Philadelphia.

106. Roberts and Roberts, *Moreau de St. Méry's American Journey*, 264; Marietta and Rowe, *Troubled Experiment*, 68–69. While many German immigrants passed through the city, most settled in the country and managed to steer clear of penal authorities and the temptations and hardships of urban life. Roberts and Roberts, 280.

107. Batsheva Spiegel Epstein, "Patterns of Sentencing and Their Implementation in Philadelphia City and County, 1795–1829" (Ph.D. diss., University of Pennsylvania, Philadelphia, 1981), 123.

108. Jennifer Manion, "Women's Crime and Prison Reform in Early Pennsylvania, 1786–1829" (Ph.D. dissertation, Rutgers University, 2008), 151–154.

109. "An Act to Reform the Penal Laws of This State" (1790) *Statutes*, XIII: 511–528.

110. See the following tables in the Appendix: "Women Convicted of Larceny by Age"; "Women Convicts by Occupation, 1820–1824"; "Women Convicts by Race, 1795–1810"; "Women Convicts by Race, 1820–1835"; "Language of Race, Women, 1795–1810"; "Language of Race, Women, 1820–1835."

111. Melish, "The 'Condition' Debate," 667.

112. On the mutually constitutive relationship between black and white, see Barbara J. Fields, "Ideology and Race in American History," in *Region, Race, and Reconstruction: Essays in Honor*

of C. Vann Woodward, ed. J. Morgan Kousser and James M. McPherson (New York: Oxford University Press, 1982), 143–77; David Roediger, *The Wages of Whiteness: Race and the Making of the Working Class* (Cambridge, Mass.: Harvard University Press, 1991).

113. Mary Wolfe, June 10, 1802, PSD.

114. Ignatiev, *How the Irish Became White*, 44.

115. Nash, *Forging Freedom*, 217.

116. Ignatiev, *How the Irish Became White*, 134.

117. Elizabeth Thompson of North Wales, September 27, 1815, PSD, Mary Shuler (alias Nicholson) of North Whales, October 6, 1815, PSD; Ann Butcher of Liverpool, October 19, 1815, PSD.

118. "Moyamensing Police," *Public Ledger*, October 16, 1837.

119. Statistics for the general population come from Patrick-Stamp, "Numbers That Are Not New," 283; statistics for women come from my analysis of the PSD, 1794–1810, 1815, 1823; Patrick-Stamp (287) also has a table showing statistics for black women in prison 1794 to 1804.

120. Roberts Vaux, *Notices of the Original, and Successive Efforts, to Improve the Discipline of the Prison at Philadelphia, and to Reform the Criminal Code of Pennsylvania: With a Few Observations on the Penitentiary System* (Philadelphia, 1826).

121. Nash, *Race and Revolution*, 48.

122. Nash, *Forging Freedom*, 224.

123. Julie Winch, "The Making and Meaning of James Forten's Letters from a Man of Colour," *William and Mary Quarterly* 3rd ser. 64, no. 1 (2007): 129–38, 131; Winch, *Philadelphia's Black Elite*, 18.

124. James Forten, *Letters from a Man of Colour on a Late Bill Before the Senate of Pennsylvania* (Philadelphia, 1813), Letter I.

125. Ibid., Letter IV.

126. Ibid., Letter I.

127. Michelle Alexander shows a similar challenge among civil rights activists who felt they needed to distance themselves and their cause from issues of criminality and punishment. See Michelle Alexander, *The New Jim Crow: Mass Incarceration in the Age of Colorblindness* (New York: New Press, 2010), chap. 6.

128. Nash, *Forging Freedom*, 224–25.

129. James Mease, *Observations on the Penitentiary System, and Penal Code of Pennsylvania: With Suggestions for Their Improvement* (Philadelphia, 1828), 34.

130. Minutes, November 9, 1808, PSAMPP Acting Committee, vol. 6, PPS.

131. Minutes, January 4, 1809, PSAMPP Acting Committee, vol. 6, PPS.

132. Ignatiev, *How the Irish Became White*, 50–51.

133. Minutes, June 9, 1812, BOI.

134. See Saidiya V. Hartman, *Scenes of Subjection: Terror, Slavery, and Self-Making in Nineteenth Century America* (New York: Oxford University Press, 1997), chaps. 1, 2.

135. Minutes, January 10, 1814, PSAMPP Meeting, vol. 2, PPS.

136. Minutes, January 10, 1820, PSAMPP Acting Committee, vol. 6, PPS.

137. Ibid.

138. Person who has been an eyewitness, for a considerable length of time, *A Just and True Account, of the Prison of the City and County of Philadelphia; Accompanied with the Rules, Regulations, Manners, Customs, and Treatment of the Untried Prisoners, Who Have the Misfortune of Being Committed to This Place for Trial* (Philadelphia, 1820).

139. Ann Carson, *The History of the Celebrated Mrs. Ann Carson, Widow of the Late Unfortunate Lieutenant Richard Smyth; With a circumstantial account of her conspiracy against the late Governor of Pennsylvania, Simon Snyder; and of her sufferings in the several prisons in that state* (Philadelphia, 1822), 301.

140. *Freedom's Journal*, March 20, 1827.

141. Ibid.

142. Matthew Frye Jacobson, *Whiteness of a Different Color: European Immigrants and the Alchemy of Race* (Cambridge, Mass.: Harvard University Press, 1998), 29; Turner, *Negro in Pennsylvania*, 149.

143. "Pauperism," *New York Columbian*, August 10, 1820.

144. "Coloured Population of Philadelphia," *The Friend: A Religious and Literary Journal*, November 26, 1836.

145. Ibid.

146. In 1819 in Philadelphia, a group of three women stoned a black woman to death. *Philadelphia Gazette*, June 30, 1819, cited in Turner, *Negro in Pennsylvania*, 145.

147. While the success of the black church gave stability to the community, it threatened white ministers, who could no longer controlled what African Americans heard in church pulpits on Sunday morning. See Julie Winch, *Between Slavery and Freedom: Free People of Color in America From Settlement to Civil War* (Lanham, Md.: Rowman and Littlefield, 2014), 52–53. Also see Evelyn Brooks Higginbotham, *Righteous Discontent: The Women's Movement in the Black Baptist Church, 1880–1920* (Cambridge, Mass.: Harvard University Press, 1993); and Genna Rae McNeil, "African American Church Women, Social Activism, and the Criminal Justice System," *Journal of African American History* 96, no. 3 (2011): 370–83.

148. Nash, *First City*, 167.

149. *Daily Chronicle*, April 29, 1833.

150. Ann Green, Catherine Lynch, Jane Garland, Margaret White, and Sarah Alsted were charged with "being concerned in a riot and in general of infamous character" and sentenced to one month's imprisonment, September 14, 1790, VAG. Absence of racial designation suggests they were European immigrants or Anglo- and Irish Americans. A group of black women each described as a "negress" including Catharine Dewers, Mary Brown, Ann Duffield, and Rebecca Nailor were charged with "Riotius by assembling at the house of Pompey Carpenter and disturbing the peace of the neighborhood," February, 24, 1791, VAG. Ann Wall, Margaret Roberts, Mary Conner, and Ann Spencer were charged together, "being taken by the watch in a riot and drunk," to be kept one month, April 15, 1791. VAG. Again, no mention of race suggested European ancestry.

151. In 1821, Ann Stokely was convicted with two men (William Gray and James Brown, also dark mulatto men) and sentenced to three months in prison, Ann Stokely, December 1821, PSD; In 1825, a group of six black women (Maria Baker, Harriet Burley, Margaret Ever, Elizabeth Farthing, Harriet George, Amy Phillips) were also sentenced to three months, December, 1825, PSD; Maria Smith was a "yellow" woman charged with a black man, Hiriam Smith; both were sentenced to one month, January, 1825, PSD; From 1826 to 1834, six other black women spent between one and three months in prison on rioting charges: Hester Clymer, September, 1826; Matilda Smith, September, 1826; Margaret Fisher, September, 1828; Elizabeth Midcap, October 1834; and Elizabeth Stevens, October, 1834; Sarah Ann Smith, January, 1833; PSD.

152. Gustave de Beaumont and Alexis de Tocqueville, *On the Penitentiary System in the United States and Its Application in France* (Carbondale: Southern Illinois University Press, 1964), 93.

153. Ibid., 210 n. 18.

154. "Persecution in Philadelphia," *Liberator*, December 10, 1831.

155. Ibid.

156. Ibid.

157. For further consideration of these issues during reconstruction, see Michele Mitchell, *Righteous Propagation: African Americans and the Politics of Racial Destiny After Reconstruction* (Chapel Hill: University of North Carolina Press, 2004); Jim Downs, *Sick from Freedom: African-American Illness and Suffering During the Civil War and Reconstruction* (New York: Oxford University Press, 2012).

158. "Female Convicts and the Efforts of Females for Their Relief and Reformation," *Journal of Prison Discipline and Philanthropy* 1, no. 2 (1845): 113.

159. Job R. Tyson, *Essay on the Penal Law of Pennsylvania* (Philadelphia, 1827), 50.

160. *An Address from the Managers of the House of Refuge to Their Fellow Citizens* (Philadelphia, 1828), 5.

161. *The First Annual Report of the House of Refuge of Philadelphia with an Appendix* (Philadelphia, 1829), 5.

162. Ibid.,7.

163. Ibid., 9.

164. "Grand Inquest," *National Gazette*, April 23, 1831.

165. *The Friend: A Religious and Literary Journal*, November 26, 1836; on the age cutoffs, see "Fifth Annual Report of the House of Refuge of Philadelphia," *Episcopal Recorder*, June 29, 1833.

166. "Female Convicts and the Efforts of Females," 113.

167. *The Present State and Condition of the Free People of Color of the City of Philadelphia and Adjoining Districts, as exhibited by the report of a committee of the Pennsylvania Society for Promoting the Abolition of Slavery* (Philadelphia, 1838), 17.

168. William Rawle, "Miscellany: An Address from the Pennsylvania Society for promoting the Abolition of Slavery, for the relief of Negroes unlawfully held in bondage, and for improving the conditions of the African Race; on the origin, purposes and utility of their Institution," *Philadelphia Register and National Recorder*, May 15, 1819.

169. John Henderson, Joseph Watson, Job Brown, Thomas Bradford, Jr., R. L. Kennon, Joshua Boucher, H. V. Somerville, and Eric Ledell Smith, "Notes and Documents: Rescuing African American Kidnapping Victims in Philadelphia as Documented in the Joseph Watson Papers at the Historical Society of Pennsylvania," *PMHB* 129, no. 3 (2005): 317–45, 320.

170. *Present State and Condition of the Free People of Color*, 15. Prisoners were held in the newly established Moyamensing Prison, which replaced Arch Street and Walnut Street.

171. Ignatiev, *How the Irish Became White*, 59.

172. Turner, *Negro in Pennsylvania*, 146.

173. PSAMPP, "Art. VI. Sixteenth Annual Report of the Inspectors of the Eastern State Penitentiary of Pennsylvania, March, 1845," *Journal of Prison Discipline and Philanthropy* 2 (1845): 171.

Chapter 5. Sexual Orderings

1. Analysis of the regulation of sex in prison allows to distinguish more precisely distinguish between sexual difference, sexual intercourse, and other manifestations of sexuality. Gayle Rubin

argues that the dual meaning of the word "sex" constitutes a "semantic merging" that "reflects a cultural assumption that sexuality is reducible to sexual intercourse and that it is a function of the relations between women and men." Gayle Rubin, "Thinking Sex: Notes for a Radical Theory of the Politics of Sexuality," in *Pleasure and Danger*, ed. Carole Vance (New York: Routledge, 1984), 307; see also Heather Love, ed., "Rethinking Sex," special issue, *GLQ: Journal of Lesbian and Gay Studies* 17, no. 1 (2011).

2. See Richard Godbeer, *Sexual Revolution in Early America* (Baltimore: Johns Hopkins University Press, 2002); Clare A. Lyons, *Sex Among the Rabble: An Intimate History of Gender & Power in the Age of Revolution, Philadelphia, 1730–1830* (Chapel Hill: University of North Carolina Press, 2006); Thomas Foster, *Sex and the Eighteenth-Century Man: Massachusetts and the History of Sexuality in America* (Boston: Beacon Press, 2006).

3. "December 31, 1794," in Kenneth Roberts and Anna M. Roberts, *Moreau de St. Méry's American Journey* (Garden City, N.Y.: Doubleday, 1947), 177.

4. Michel Foucault, *The History of Sexuality*, trans. Robert Hurley (New York: Vintage, 1990), 147.

5. Sharon Block, *Rape and Sexual Power in Early America* (Chapel Hill: University of North Carolina Press, 2006), 205–9.

6. Mark E. Kann, "Sexual Desire, Crime, and Punishment in the Early Republic," in *Long Before Stonewall: Histories of Same-Sex Sexuality in Early America*, ed. Thomas Foster (New York: New York University Press, 2007), 280; also see Mark E. Kann, *Taming Passion for the Public Good: Policing Sex in the Early Republic* (New York: New York University Press, 2013).

7. The weight of Bradford's writing cannot be overestimated, as it was widely read and cited by both American and European elites, jurists, and reformers. Thirty years after its publication, Roberts Vaux wrote, "This excellent essay attracted superior attention, and produced more important effects, as coming from the pen of a profound lawyer." Roberts Vaux, *Notices of the Original, and Successive Efforts, to Improve the Discipline of the Prison at Philadelphia, and to Reform the Criminal Code of Pennsylvania: With a Few Observations on the Penitentiary System* (Philadelphia, 1826), 33.

8. William Bradford, *An Enquiry How Far the Punishment of Death Is Necessary in Pennsylvania with Notes and Illustrations, to Which is Added, an Account of the Goal and Penitentiary House of Philadelphia, and of the Interior Management Thereof By Caleb Lownes of Philadelphia* (Philadelphia, 1793), 16.

9. Ibid., 14.

10. French observers also accepted this characterization of the British penal code. See Gustave de Beaumont and Alexis de Tocqueville, *On the Penitentiary System in the United States and Its Application in France* (Carbondale: Southern Illinois University Press, 1964), 37.

11. On the brutality of punishment of crime in England, see E. P. Thompson et al., *Albion's Fatal Tree: Crime and Society in Eighteenth-Century England* (New York: Pantheon, 1976); V. A. C. Gatrell, *The Hanging Tree: Execution and the English People, 1770–1868* (Oxford: Oxford University Press, 1996); Peter Linebaugh, *The London Hanged: Crime and Civil Society in the Eighteenth Century* (New York: Verso, 2003).

12. Negley King Teeters, *They Were in Prison: A History of the Pennsylvania Prison Society, 1787–1937* (Philadelphia: Winston, 1937). Between 1718 and 1786, however, only 36 women were sentenced to death in Pennsylvania, and just more than half (19) pardoned; Pennsylvania actually executed a larger percentage of its condemned than a comparable region in England in the same

period. Jack D. Marietta and G. S. Rowe, *Troubled Experiment: Crime and Justice in Pennsylvania, 1682–1800* (Philadelphia: University of Pennsylvania Press, 2006), 75, 78.

13. Harry E. Barnes, *Evolution of Penology in Pennsylvania: A Study in American Social History* (Indianapolis: Bobbs-Merrill, 1927), 38–39.

14. Scholars critique the way colonizers justify military and political colonization under the rubric of women's rights. Spivak called this "white men saving brown women from brown men" as a critique of sexual exceptionalism rooted in colonialism. Gayatria Chakravorty Spivak, "Can the Subaltern Speak?" in Cary Nelson and Lawrence Grossberg, eds., *Marxism and the Interpretation of Culture* (Urbana: University of Illinois Press, 1988), 271–313. Also see Jasbir Puar, *Terrorist Assemblages: Homonationalism in Queer Times* (Durham, N.C.: Duke University Press, 2007); and miriam cooke, "Gender and September 11: A Roundtable: Saving Brown Women," *Signs: Journal of Women in Culture and Society* 28, no. 1 (2002), 468–70.

15. G. S. Rowe, *Embattled Bench: The Pennsylvania Supreme Court and the Forging of a Democratic Society, 1684–1809* (Newark: University of Delaware Press, 1994), 150, 202, 203; J. Thomas Scharf and Thompson Westcott, *History of Philadelphia, 1609–1884* (Philadelphia, 1884), 2: 1530–31.

16. For analysis of these issues in the post-Reconstruction South, see Mary Frances Berry, "Judging Morality: Sexual Behavior and Legal Consequences in the Late Nineteenth-Century South," *Journal of American History* 78, no. 3 (1991): 835–56.

17. "Advancement of Justice and More Certain Administration Thereof," (1718) *Statutes*, III: 202–203.This law was repealed by "An Act Amending the Penal Laws of This State" (1786), in *Statutes*, XII: 284.

18. Efforts to pin the crime on men—usually fathers—generally failed. For example, see *A Faithful Narrative of Elizabeth Wilson* (Philadelphia, 1786); Pennsylvania Supreme Court Records, PSA.

19. Bradford, *An Enquiry How Far the Punishment of Death*, 39.

20. G. S. Rowe, "Women's Crime and Criminal Administration." *PMHB* 109, no. 3 (1985): 359–60.

21. Bradford, *An Enquiry How Far the Punishment of Death*, 39.

22. Lacquer shows this developed simultaneously in multiple epistemologies and discourses. See Thomas Laqueur, *Making Sex: Body and Gender from the Greeks to Freud* (Cambridge, Mass.: Harvard University Press, 1990).

23. Block, *Rape and Sexual Power*, 37–52; Also see Sharon Block, "Rape Without Women: Print Culture and the Politicization of Rape, 1765–1815," *Journal of American History* 89, no. 3 (2002): 849–68; Wendy Anne Warren, " 'The Cause of Her Grief': The Rape of a Slave in Early New England," *Journal of American History* 93, no. 4 (2007): 1031–49.

24. Bradford, *An Enquiry How Far the Punishment of Death*, 29.

25. Ibid., 29–30.

26. Racialized, dehumanizing rhetoric about Africans, African Americans, and American Indians has long served as the ideological justification for violence with sexuality at its core. See Kathleen Brown, *Good Wives, Nasty Wenches, Anxious Patriarchs: Gender, Race, and Power in Colonial Virginia* (Chapel Hill: University of North Carolina Press, 1996); Martha Hodes, *White Women, Black Men: Illicit Sex in the Nineteenth-Century South* (New Haven, Conn.: Yale University Press, 1997); Catherine Clinton and Michele Gillespie, eds., *The Devil's Lane: Sex and Race in the Early South* (New York: Oxford University Press, 1997); Kristen Fischer, *Suspect Relations: Sex,*

Race, and Resistance in Colonial North Carolina (Ithaca, N.Y.: Cornell University Press, 2002); Jennifer Morgan, *Laboring Women: Reproduction and Gender in New World Slavery* (Philadelphia: University of Pennsylvania Press, 2004); Juliana Barr, *Peace Came in the Form of a Woman: Indians and Spaniards in the Texas Borderlands* (Chapel Hill: University of North Carolina Press, 2007); Ann M. Little, *Abraham in Arms: War and Gender in Colonial New England* (Philadelphia: University of Pennsylvania Press, 2007); Jennifer Spear, *Race, Sex, and Social Order in Early New Orleans* (Baltimore: Johns Hopkins University Press, 2009).

27. Bradford, *An Enquiry How Far the Punishment of Death*, 41.

28. On rape as natural passion out of control, see Block, *Rape and Sexual Power*, 226.

29. Foster, *Sex and the Eighteenth-Century Man*, chap. 3.

30. Bradford, *An Enquiry How Far the Punishment of Death*, 29–30. Under Penn, conviction for incest, sodomy, or rape led to forfeiture of one-third of one's estate and whipping, with prison terms of six months for sodomy and one year for incest or rape.

31. Bradford, *An Enquiry How Far the Punishment of Death*, 64.

32. "Wilksbarre, Penn," *Washington Federalist*, September 25, 1801.

33. The 1682 statute states, "That if any person shall be Legally Convicted of the Unnatural Sin of Sodomy or, joining with beasts, Such persons shall be whipt, & forfeit one third of his or her estate & work Six Months in the house of Correction at hard Labour, and for the Second Offense imprisonment as aforesaid during Life." "Law Against Sodomy and Bestiality" (1682) in *Statutes*, I: 32. See also Job R. Tyson, *Essay on the Penal Law of Pennsylvania* (Philadelphia, 1827), 13.

34. "An Act Amending the Penal Laws of this State" (1786) in *Statutes*, XII: 280–289, 286–87. During this seventy-year span, only twenty-three men were charged. Marietta and Rowe, *Troubled Experiment*, 88.

35. One broadside shows a man guilty of bestiality at the gallows with a woman guilty of theft. She claims, "You know your fault is far more base than mine, The most unnatural of any crime." See *A Dialogue between Elizabeth Smith and John Sennet* (Boston, 1773).

36. Thomas Foster, "Antimasonic Satire, Sodomy, and Eighteenth-Century Masculinity in the Boston Evening-Post," *William and Mary Quarterly* 3rd ser. 60, no. 1 (2003): 171–184.

37. Richard Godbeer, "The Cry of Sodom: Discourse, Intercourse, and Desire in Colonial New England," *William and Mary Quarterly* 3rd ser. 52, no. 2 (1995): 259–86. Historians dispute the rate or incidence of sodomy and the degree of tolerance among the general public. See John M. Murrin, " 'Things Fearful to Name': Bestiality in Colonial America," *Pennsylvania History, Explorations in Early American Culture* 65 (1998): 8–43; Doron S. Ben-Atar and Richard D. Brown, *Taming Lust: Crimes Against Nature in the Early Republic* (Philadelphia: University of Pennsylvania Press, 2014).

38. "An Act Amending the Penal Laws of this State," (1786) in *Statutes*, XII: 280–289, 281.

39. Bradford, *An Enquiry How Far the Punishment of Death*, 21.

40. See also Godbeer, "Cry of Sodom."

41. Regina Kunzel, "Situating Sex: Prison Sexual Culture in the Mid-Twentieth-Century United States," *GLQ* 8, no. 3 (2002): 253–70; and Regina Kunzel, *Criminal Intimacy: Prison and the Uneven History of Modern American Sexuality* (Chicago: University of Chicago Press, 2008), 101–103.

42. François Alexandre Frédéric La Rochefoucault Liancourt, *On the Prisons of Philadelphia* (Philadelphia, 1796), 32.

43. Clare A. Lyons, "Mapping an Atlantic Sexual Culture: Homoeroticism in Eighteenth Century Philadelphia," *William and Mary Quarterly* 3rd ser. 60, no. 1 (2003): 119–154, 127.

44. Randolph Trumbach, "Sex, Gender, and Sexual Identity in Modern Culture: Male Sodomy and Female Prostitution in Enlightenment London," *Journal of the History of Sexuality* 2, no. 2 (1991): 186–203.

45. Bradford, *An Enquiry How Far the Punishment of Death*, 21.

46. On this rampant sexual culture, see Godbeer, *Sexual Revolution*, chaps. 8 and 9; and Lyons, *Sex Among the Rabble*, chap. 4.

47. Benjamin Rush, *Medical Inquiries and Observations* (Philadelphia, 1805), 3: 124.

48. Benjamin Rush, *An Oration, Delivered before the American Philosophical Society . . . on the 27th of February, 1786, Containing an Enquiry into the Influence of Physical Causes upon the Moral Faculty* (Philadelphia, 1786), 11.

49. In this passage, Rush was recounting John Howard's belief that solitude was the best way to achieve this for "persons who are irreclaimable by rational or moral remedies." Rush, *An Oration, Delivered*, 23.

50. For a more extensive analysis of Rush's writings, see Sarah Knott, *Sensibility and the American Revolution* (Chapel Hill: University of North Carolina Press, 2009).

51. *PG*, September 26, 1787.

52. Minutes, April 11, 1788, PSAMPP, Adams and Wistar Letterbook, PPS.

53. Minutes, May 16, 1788, PSAMPP, Adams and Wistar Letterbook, PPS.

54. The term "intercourse" was commonly used to refer to social communication, or "frequent and habitual contact in conversation and action" with both social and sexual connotations. *Oxford English Dictionary*: "intercourse," n., meaning "sexual connexion"; examples include "An illicit intercourse between the sexes" (1798) and "Propagated by promiscuous intercourse" (1804).

55. "Report for Supreme Executive Council," Minutes, January 12, 1789, PSAMPP Meeting, vol. 1, PPS.

56. Ibid.

57. Timothy J. Gilfoyle, *City of Eros: New York City, Prostitution, and the Commercialization of Sex, 1790–1920* (New York: Norton, 1992); Elizabeth Alice Clement, *Love for Sale: Courting, Treating, and Prostitution in New York City, 1900–1945* (Chapel Hill: University of North Carolina Press, 2006); Kathy Peiss, *Cheap Amusements: Working Women and Leisure in Turn-of-the-Century New York* (Philadelphia: Temple University Press, 1986).

58. For more on prostitution and reform in Philadelphia, see Marcia Carlisle, "Prostitutes and Their Reformers in Nineteenth-Century Philadelphia" (Ph.D. dissertation, Rutgers University, 1982); Marcia Carlisle, "Disorderly City, Disorderly Women: Prostitution in Ante-Bellum Philadelphia," *PMHB* 110 (1986): 549–68; Rodney Hessinger, "Victim of Seduction or Vicious Woman? Conceptions of the Prostitute at the Philadelphia Magdalen Society, 1800–1850," *Pennsylvania History* 66, Supplement (1999): 201–22.

59. On changing representations of women, see Mary E. Fissell, "Hairy Women and Naked Truths: Gender and the Politics of Knowledge in 'Aristotle's Masterpiece,'" *William and Mary Quarterly* 3rd ser. 60, no. 1 (2003): 43–74. Fissel argues that the "naked or half-clad woman" who seemed to represent truth, nature, or beauty represented larger shifts in late eighteenth-century attitudes toward women's sexuality. She became more perfect, her sexuality more domesticated. See also Nancy Cott, "Passionlessness: An Interpretation of Victorian Sexual Ideology, 1790–

1850," *Signs: Journal of Women in Culture and Society* 4, no. 2 (1978); 219–236; Lyons, *Sex Among the Rabble*, 290.

60. Almshouse Admissions Book and Black Book, Guardians of the Poor, PCA; Lyons, *Sex Among the Rabble*, 305.

61. "To John Adams, Philadelphia, July 21st, 1789," in *Letters of Benjamin Rush*, vol. 1, *1761–1792*, ed. L. H. Butterfield (Philadelphia: American Philosophical Society, 1951), 522.

62. G. R-Ff-Y, "Occasional Letters to Bob Short," *Lady's Magazine; or Entertaining Companion for the Fair Sex, Appropriated Solely to Their Use & Amusement* 10 (September 1779): 462–63.

63. For more on sexual assault in early America, see Block, *Rape and Sexual Power*; Barbara S. Lindemann, "'To Ravish and Carnally Know': Rape in Eighteenth-Century Massachusetts," *Signs: Journal of Women in Culture and Society* 10, no. 1 (1984): 63–82; Cornelia Hughes Dayton, *Women Before the Bar: Gender, Law, and Society in Connecticut, 1639–1789* (Chapel Hill: University of North Carolina Press, 1995), 231–84; Kathleen Brown, *Good Wives*, 193–94, 207–11; Kirsten Fischer, *Suspect Relations*, 181–90.

64. Kathleen M. Brown, *Foul Bodies: Cleanliness in Early America* (New Haven, Conn.: Yale University Press, 2011), 58–93, 59.

65. Ibid., 59.

66. John Gregory, "Agreeable Effects of the Social Intercourse Between the Sexes, and Between the Aged and the Young of the Same Sex," *American Museum, or, Universal Magazine* (January 1792): 25–26.

67. Ibid.

68. Samuel/Sarah Johnson, December 4, 1799, PSD.

69. Tales of women cross-dressing to gain access to occupations and social freedom reserved for men abound. See Dianne Dugaw, *Warrior Women and Popular Balladry, 1650–1850* (Cambridge: Cambridge University Press, 1989); Peter Guillery, "The Further Adventures of Mary Lacy: 'Seaman', Shipwright, Builder," *History Workshop Journal* 49 (2000): 212–19; Alfred Young, *Masquerade: The Life and Times of Deborah Sampson, Continental Soldier* (New York: Knopf, 2004). For analysis of the cross-dressing, possibly transgender or intersex person known as Thomas/ine Hall, see Kathleen M. Brown, "'Changed . . . Into the Fashion of Man': The Politics of Sexual Difference in a Seventeenth-Century Anglo-American Settlement," *Journal of the History of Sexuality* 6, no. 2 (1995): 171–93.

70. Management of the debtors department was lacking. In 1790, PSAMPP called for the hiring of a salaried officer to supervise the debtors and ensure the separation of the sexes "in the day time as well as night." Minutes, October 18, 1790, PSAMPP Meeting, vol. 1, PPS; Also see Minutes, April 11, 1791, PSAMPP Meeting, vol. 1, PPS. Earlier concerns about women having "too much communication with the men" or having themselves admitted deliberately so they could have "communication" with the men persisted for nearly a decade. Minutes, April 5, 1798, PSAMPP Meeting, vol. 1, PPS; Minutes, January 12, 1799, PSAMPP Acting Committee, vol. 6, PPS; Minutes, June 10, 1799, PSAMPP Acting Committee, vol. 6, PPS.

71. *Board of Inspectors Report*, 1797. This was also an issue to New York authorities who reported, "The next error which we shall notice, as pertaining to our Penitentiaries, is the entire want of classification, if we except the division of convicts into sexes. Men and women are kept separately and here the rule of discrimination stops." *Report on the Penitentiary System in the United States, Prepared Under a Resolution of the Society for the Prevention of Pauperism, in the City of New York* (New York, 1822), 24.

72. Samuel Lorenzo Knapp, *Life of Thomas Eddy* (New York, 1834), 205.

73. Jennifer Manion, "Women's Crime and Prison Reform in Early Pennsylvania, 1786–1829" (Ph.D. dissertation, Rutgers University, 2008), 69–70.

74. Minutes, May 19, 1795, BOI.

75. "Milledgeville Journal," *Weekly Visitor*, September 16, 1820.

76. For scholarship on childhood in the nineteenth century and the idea of white children as naturally innocent, Anna Mae Duane, *Suffering Childhood in Early America: Violence, Race, and the Making of the Child Victim* (Athens: University of Georgia Press, 2011); Robin Bernstein, *Racial Innocence: Performing American Childhood from Slavery to Civil Rights* (New York: New York University Press, 2011); Anna Mae Duane, *The Children's Table: Childhood Studies and the Humanities* (Athens: University of Georgia Press, 2013); Brian Connolly, *Domestic Intimacies: Incest and the Liberal Subject in Nineteenth-Century America* (Philadelphia: University of Pennsylvania Press, 2014).

77. W. A. Coffey, *Inside Out; or, An Interior View of the New-York State Prison; Together with Biographical Sketches of the Lives of Several of the Convicts By One Who Knows* (New York, 1823), 61.

78. Ibid.

79. Ibid., 59.

80. John Sergeant, *An Address Delivered Before the Citizens of Philadelphia at the House of Refuge, on Saturday, the twenty-ninth of November, 1828 by John Sergeant, President of the Institution* (Philadelphia, 1828), 50, 53.

81. Same-sex intimacies in novels and plays reprinted during the period (sometimes French translations) were censored. Emma Donohue, *Passions Between Women: British Lesbian Culture, 1668–1801* (New York: HarperCollins, 1995).

82. One must turn to the broader Atlantic world discourses to learn more about same-sex intimacies between women, as the French, Dutch, and British considered the existence and meaning of sexual intimacies between women more openly than most Americans. In one famous 1792 case in Holland, twelve women were prosecuted. Then, between 1795 and 1798, eleven more women were tried for same-sex sex. See Theo Van Der Meer, "Tribades on Trial: Female Same-Sex Offenders in Late Eighteenth-Century Amsterdam," *Journal of the History of Sexuality* 1, no. 3 (1991): 424–45; Anna Clark, "Anne Lister's Construction of Lesbian Identity," *Journal of the History of Sexuality* 7, no. 1 (1996): 23–50; Martha Vicinus, *Intimate Friends: Women Who Loved Women, 1778–1928* (Chicago: University of Chicago Press, 2004); Sharon Marcus, *Between Women: Friendship, Desire, and Marriage in Victorian England* (Princeton, N.J.: Princeton University Press, 2007); Anna Clark, *Desire: A History of European Sexuality* (New York: Routledge, 2008).

83. Roberts and Roberts, *Moreau de St. Méry's American Journey*, 286.

84. Lyons, "Mapping an Atlantic Sexual Culture," 119–54.

85. Joseph Ross, August 31, 1784 and October 31, 1785, Oyer and Terminer Records, Pennsylvania Supreme Court, PSA.

86. "New York, Saturday Nov. 26," *Daily Advertiser*, November 26, 1785.

87. "November 28, a letter from Hannah's-town," *New Jersey Gazette*, November 28, 1785.

88. See Philip Bower of Philadelphia was charged with sodomy but dismissed, June 24, 1784; Solomon Brown of Fayeth was charged on three counts of buggery and dismissed, May 24, 1791; Jeremiah Sturgeon, Cumberland County, May 26, 1783, buggery, found guilty and ordered

hanged; John Mooney, Lancaster, buggery, May 12, 1788, guilty and ordered hanged; John Pitts, November 29, 1790, York County, buggery and attempt to commit buggery, guilty of latter, five shilling fine and three months in county jail; Amos Penrose, buggery, Philadelphia, November 26, 1809, guilty, ten years hard labor; Pennsylvania Supreme Court, PSA.

89. Rush, *An Oration, Delivered before the American Philosophical Society*, 35.

90. Caleb Lownes, *An Account of the Goal and Penitentiary House of Philadelphia, and of the Interior Management Thereof By Caleb Lownes of Philadelphia* (Philadelphia, 1793), 84–85.

91. Robert C. Smith, "A Portuguese Naturalist in Philadelphia, 1799: Excerpts from the Diary of Hipolito Jose da Costa," *PMHB* 78, no. 1 (1954): 71–106, 103.

92. Richard Godbeer, *The Overflowing of Friendship: Love Between Men and the Creation of the American Republic* (Baltimore: Johns Hopkins University Press, 2009); also see William E. Benemann, *Male-Male Intimacy in Early America: Beyond Romantic Friendships* (New York: Routledge, 2006); Nicholas L. Syrett, *The Company He Keeps: A History of White College Fraternities* (Chapel Hill: University of North Carolina Press, 2009).

93. Lyons, "Mapping an Atlantic Sexual Culture."

94. For more on molly house culture in England, see Rictor Norton, *Mother Clap's Molly House: The Gay Subculture in England, 1700–1830* (London: Gay Men's Press, 1992); Also see Randolph Trumbach, "Sex, Gender, and Sexual Identity in Modern Culture: Male Sodomy and Female Prostitution in Enlightenment London," *Journal of the History of Sexuality* 2, no. 2 (1991): 186–203; George E. Haggerty, "Keyhole Testimony: Witnessing Sodomy in the Eighteenth Century," 44, no. 2/3 (2003): 167–82; Charles Upchurch *Before Wilde: Sex Between Men in Britain's Age of Reform* (Berkeley: University of California Press, 2009).

95. Historians have long embraced the Foucaultian argument that prior to the late Victorian period, sodomy would not have been equated with homosexuality but was rather an act anyone might do, despite a persuasive critique of this understanding of Foucault. See David M. Halperin, *How to Do the History of Homosexuality* (Chicago: University of Chicago Press, 2002); This framework has also been challenged by research from the early period that suggests some people were known to prefer sex with those of the same sex and/or felt their desire for such reflected something innate. See Godbeer, "Cry of Sodom"; and Rachel Hope Cleves, *Charity and Sylvia: A Same-Sex Marriage in Early America* (New York: Oxford University Press, 2014).

96. John Pitts, November 29, 1790, Supreme Court of Pennsylvania, PSA.

97. Pardoned April 19, 1797; Toby Morris, June, 1795, PSD.

98. Pardoned May 31, 1805; Samuel Boyer, August 10, 1804, PSD.

99. Roberts Vaux, *Notices of the Original, and Successive Efforts, to Improve the Discipline of the Prison at Philadelphia, and to Reform the Criminal Code of Pennsylvania: With a Few Observations on the Penitentiary System* (Philadelphia, 1826).

100. David Van Guilder, September 16, 1823, PSD.

101. Boyer's indictment reads, "Forfeit all and singular his goods and chattels lands and tenements be imprisoned six years at hard labour fed and cloathed as the law directs pay the costs of prosecution and give security himself in $400 and one freeholder in like some for his good behavior and stand committed," Samuel Boyer, August 10, 1804, PSD.

102. Also see Stephen Robertson, "Shifting the Scene of the Crime: Sodomy and the American History of Sexual Violence," *Journal of the History of Sexuality* 19, no. 2 (2010): 223–42.

103. *Report on the Penitentiary System in the United States, Prepared Under a Resolution of the Society for the Prevention of Pauperism, in the City of New York* (New York, 1822).

104. Ibid.

105. "Connecticut Legislature," *Connecticut Herald*, May 16, 1826.

106. "Report of the Committee Appointed by the Legislature to Inspect the Condition of Newgate Prison," *American Mercury*, August 15, 1826.

107. Ibid.

108. "Thursday (Evening,) March 15," *New York Spectator*, March 20, 1827; "General Miscellany," *Christian Advocate and Journal*, March 24, 1827.

109. Orlando Faulkland Lewis, *The Development of American Prisons and Prison Customs, 1776–1845: With Special Reference to Early Institutions in the State of New York* (New York: Prison Association of New York, 1922), 289.

110. "From the Boston Statesman," *Essex Gazette*, August 4, 1827.

111. Ibid.

112. Carolyn Dean, "The Productive Hypothesis: Foucault, Gender, and the History of Sexuality," *History and Theory* 33, no. 3 (October 1994): 271–96; Kunzel, *Criminal Intimacy*, 7–9; and Foucault, *History of Sexuality*.

113. "General Miscellany," *Boston Recorder and Religious Telegraph*, August 31, 1827.

114. "Second Annual Report of the Board of Managers of the Prison Discipline Society," *Christian Spectator* 1, no. 10 (October 1, 1827): 554–57, 555.

115. Ibid., 554.

116. Job R. Tyson, *Essay on the Penal Law of Pennsylvania* (Philadelphia, 1827), 35. Tyson was later elected to the House of Representatives in 1855.

117. "Penitentiary System: Pittsburg Penitentiary," *Register of Pennsylvania* 1, no. 3 (January 19, 1828): 46.

118. Roberts Vaux, *Letter on the Penitentiary System of Pennsylvania Addressed to William Roscoe, Esquire, of Toxteth Park, Near Liverpool* (Philadelphia, 1827), 9.

119. "Report on Punishments and Prison Discipline," *Register of Pennsylvania*, 1, no. 14 (April 5, 1828): 209.

120. Edward Livingston, *Letter from Edward Livingston, Esq. to Roberts Vaux: On the Advantages of the Pennsylvania System of Prison Discipline, for the Application of Which the New Penitentiary Has Been Constructed Near Philadelphia, &c. &c* (Philadelphia, 1828), 6.

121. "Penal Code: Report on Punishments and Prison Discipline," *Register of Pennsylvania*, 1, no. 13 (March 29, 1828): 202.

122. Ibid.

123. Virginia punished sodomy by an enslaved person with death as well. Louisiana had no capital punishment. "Communications," *Free Enquirer*, November 14, 1829.

124. "New Penal Code," *Register of Pennsylvania*, 3, no. 18 (May 2, 1829): 280.

125. "Penal Code: Report on Punishments and Prison Discipline," *Register of Pennsylvania*, 1, no. 13 (March 29, 1828): 202.

126. "Report on Punishments and Prison Discipline," *Register of Pennsylvania*, 1, no. 14 (April 5, 1828): 209.

127. Ibid.

128. Beaumont and Tocqueville, *On the Penitentiary System*, 53–60.

129. A. Brackenridge, "Documents: Report of Punishments & Prison Discipline," *Register of Pennsylvania*, 1, no. 16 (April 19, 1828): 241.

130. Ibid.

131. Minutes, January 10, 1820, PSAMPP Acting Committee, vol. 6, PPS.

132. Thomas Foster, "Reconsidering Libertines and Early Modern Heterosexuality: Sex and American Founder Gouverneur Morris," *Journal of the History of Sexuality* 22, no. 1 (January 2013): 65–84.

133. Thomas Foster, "The Sexual Abuse of Black Men Under American Slavery," *Journal of the History of Sexuality* 20, no. 3 (2011): 445–64.

134. Nancy Hewitt, *Women's Activism and Social Change: Rochester, NY, 1822–1872* (Ithaca, N.Y.: Cornell University Press, 1984); Lori D. Ginzberg, *Women and the Work of Benevolence: Morality, Politics, and Class in the Nineteenth-Century United States* (New Haven, Conn.: Yale University Press, 1992); Margaret Morris Haviland, "Beyond Women's Sphere: Young Quaker Women and the Veil of Charity in Philadelphia, 1790–1810," *William and Mary Quarterly* 3rd ser. 51, no. 3 (1994): 419–46; Anne Boylan, *The Origins of Women's Activism, New York and Boston, 1797–1840* (Chapel Hill: University of North Carolina Press, 2001); Dorsey, *Reforming Men and Women: Gender in the Antebellum City* (Ithaca, N.Y.: Cornell University Press, 2002).

135. In fact, they often served the interests of the powerful. See Boylan, *Origins of Women's Activism*, 13.

136. Records for the following are at Haverford College Special Collections: the Female Society of Philadelphia for the Relief and Employment of the Poor was established (1795), the Female Association of Philadelphia for the Relief of Women and Children in Reduced Circumstances (1800).

137. "The First Annual Report of the Managers of the Female Domestic Missionary Society," *Religious Remembrancer*, November 22, 1817.

138. Rush, *An Enquiry into the Effects of Public Punishments upon Criminals and upon Society. Read in the Society for Promoting Political Enquiries, Convened at the House of His Excellency Benjamin Franklin, Esquire, in Philadelphia, March 9th, 1787* (Philadelphia, 1787).

139. On exclusion of women from the political body, see Carroll Smith-Rosenberg, *Violent Empire: The Birth of an American National Identity* (Chapel Hill: University of North Carolina Press, 2010), 150.

140. See Joseph John Gurney's *Notes on a Visit Made to Some of the Prisons in Scotland and The North of England in Company with Elizabeth Fry with some general observations on the subject of prison discipline* (Edinburgh, 1819).

141. Hannah More and John Griscom both praised her. "Female Convicts and the Efforts of Females for Their Relief and Reformation," *Pennsylvania Journal of Prison Discipline & Philanthropy* 1, no. 2 (1845): 98–117.

142. The manual was published by the British Ladies' Society for Promoting the Reformation of Female Prisoners in 1822.

143. "Prison Discipline," *Rhode Island American*, June 9, 1820.

144. "Miscellany," *Nantucket Inquirer*, March 15, 1824.

145. Vaux, *Notices of the Original and Successive Efforts*, 21.

146. The move to Arch Street was authorized by an act in February 1823; see Negley K. Teeters, *Cradle of the Penitentiary: The Walnut Street Jail at Philadelphia, 1773–1835* (Philadelphia, 1955), 105; and "Female Convicts and the Efforts of Females."

147. "Female Convicts and the Efforts of Females," 111; on the Society of Women Friends and the Female Prison Association (1852), see Teeters, *They Were in Prison*, 240.

148. "Female Convicts and the Efforts of Females," 112.

149. Minutes, January 8, 1823, BOI.

150. Minutes, May 14, 1823, PSAMPP Acting Committee, vol. 6, PPS.

151. Bloch argues that literary sentimentalism made virtue feminine. Ruth Bloch, "The Gendered Meanings of Virtue in Revolutionary America," *Signs: Journal of Women in Culture and Society* 13, no. 1 (1987): 37–58, 51.

152. Both Freedman and Rafter deal with this topic extensively. See Estelle Freedman, *Their Sisters' Keepers: Women's Prison Reform in America, 1830–1930* (Ann Arbor: University of Michigan Press, 1984); and Nicole Rafter, *Partial Justice: Women, Prisons, and Social Control* (Boston: Northeastern University Press, 1985).

153. *State Prisons and the Penitentiary System Vindicated, with observations on managing and conducting these institutions; drawn principally from experience. Also, some particular remarks and documents relating to the Massachusetts State Prison. By an officer of this establishment at Charlestown* (Charlestown: S. Etheridge, 1821).

154. "Anecdote for the Ladies," *Bachelors' Journal* 1, no. 11 (July 3, 1828); repeated here: "Anecdote for the Ladies," *Socialist* (North Adams, Mass., 1828–1829) 1, no. 8 (July 18, 1828).

155. Patrick Lyon, *Narrative of Patrick Lyon, Who Suffered Three Months Severe Imprisonment in Philadelphia Gaol; on Merely a Vague Suspicion of Being Concerned in the Robbery of the Bank of Pennsylvania: With His Remarks Thereon* (Philadelphia, 1799), 72.

156. Martha Patterson, July 31, 1790, VAG; Ealoner Robison, February 9, 1792, PFT.

157. Ann Carson, *The History of the Celebrated Mrs. Ann Carson, Widow of the Late Unfortunate Lieutenant Richard Smyth; With a circumstantial account of her conspiracy against the late Governor of Pennsylvania, Simon Snyder; and of her sufferings in the several prisons in that state* (Philadelphia, 1822), 305.

158. Rafter, *Partial Justice,* 6.

159. "From the Cayuga Republican Jan. 25," *Connecticut Herald,* February 7, 1826.

160. "Laws of New York," passed April 17, 1826, *Albany Argus,* May 11, 1826.

161. In Pennsylvania, prisoners could be "admonished" or denied meat or placed in the solitary cells. Thomas Foxwell Buxton, *An Enquiry, whether Crime and Misery are produced or prevented by our present system of prison discipline* (London, 1818), 96, compares Philadelphia and others.

162. Franklin Bache to Roberts Vaux, *National Gazette and Literary Register,* March 17, 1829; Bache was later joined by Lyman Cobb, who shared his views. See Lyman Cobb, *The Evil Tendencies of Corporal Punishment as a Means of Moral Discipline in Families and Schools, Examined and Discussed* (New York, 1847), 69, cited in Karen Halttunen, "Humanitarianism and the Pornography of Pain in Anglo-American Culture," *American Historical Review* 100, no. 2 (1995): 303–34, 323.

163. Vaux, *Letter on the Penitentiary System,* 10.

164. Jennifer Lawrence Janofsky, "Hopelessly Hardened: The Complexities of Penitentiary Discipline at Philadelphia's Eastern State Penitentiary," in *Buried Lives: Incarcerated in Early America,* ed. Michele Lise Tarter and Rick Bell (Athens: University of Georgia Press, 2012), 106–23.

165. Teeters, "The Early Days of the Eastern State Penitentiary at Philadelphia," *Pennsylvania History* 16, 4 (October 1949): 294–95.

166. Thomas B. McElwee, *A Concise History* (Philadelphia, 1835), 82.

167. Ibid.

168. Ibid., 81.

169. Leslie Patrick, "Ann Hinson: A Little Known Woman in the Country's Premier Prison, Eastern State Penitentiary, 1831," *Pennsylvania History* 67, no. 3 (2000): 361–375, 368–69.

170. "Female Convicts and the Efforts of Females," 114.

171. "State Prison for Female Convicts," *Niles Weekly Register*, May 23, 1835.

172. "New Prison in Moyamensing," *Hazard's Register of Pennsylvania*, 16, no. 15 (October 10, 1835): 229.

173. "Fifteenth Annual Report of the Philadelphia Orphan Society," *Register of Pennsylvania*, 5, no. 13 (March 27, 1830): 197.

174. Female Prison Association of Friends in Philadelphia, *An Account of Julia Moore: A Penitent Female, who Died in the Eastern State Penitentiary, in the Year 1843* (Philadelphia, 1844).

175. Ibid., 6.

176. Ibid., 10.

177. Ibid., 18.

Conclusion

1. Samuel R. Wood, "Sale of Walnut Street Prison," *Register of Pennsylvania* 7, no. 7 (February 12, 1831): 98.

2. On the opening of the new penitentiary, see "Eastern Penitentiary of Pennsylvania," *Rhode-Island American*, September 7, 1832.

3. *First and Second Annual Reports of the Inspectors of the Eastern State Penitentiary of Pennsylvania, Made to the Legislature at the Sessions of 1829–30, and 1830–31* (Philadelphia, 1831). Lesser families also carried on the tradition. The clerk of Eastern State, John S. Holloway, was the oldest son of Jacob Holloway, former keeper of Walnut Street. Thomas B. McElwee, *A Concise History of the Eastern Penitentiary of Pennsylvania, Together with a Detailed Statement of the Proceedings of the Committee, Appointed by the Legislature, December 6th, 1834* (Philadelphia, 1835), 8.1.

4. In the Louisiana State Penitentiary from 1835 to 1865, white women made up only 27 of 5,077 inmates held, and black women 179. See Brett Josef Derbes, "'Secret Horrors': Enslaved Women and Children in the Louisiana State Penitentiary, 1833–1862," *Journal of African American History* 98, no. 2 (2013): 277–90.

5. Siobhan B. Somerville, *Queering the Color Line: Race and the Invention of Homosexuality in American Culture* (Durham, N.C.: Duke University Press, 2000).

6. "Schuylkill Navigation," *Norfolk Advertiser*, November 30, 1832.

7. Chandan Reddy, *Freedom with Violence: Race, Sexuality, and the U.S. State* (Durham, N.C.: Duke University Press, 2011), 38.

8. The U.S. incarceration rate is about 750 for every 100,000 people. See Michelle Alexander, *The New Jim Crow: Mass Incarceration in the Age of Colorblindness* (New York: New Press, 2010), 6. On how this situation developed in the twentieth century, see Heather Ann Thompson, "Why Mass Incarceration Matters: Rethinking Crisis, Decline, and Transformation in Postwar American History," *Journal of American History* 97, no. 3 (December 2010): 703–34.

9. International Centre for Prison Studies, BBC News, "World Prison Populations" Special Report, August 2014, http://news.bbc.co.uk/2/shared/spl/hi/uk/06/prisons/html/nn2page1.

10. Gail L. Thompson, "African American Women and the U.S. Criminal Justice System: A Statistical Survey, 1870–2009," *Journal of African American History* 98, no. 2 (2013): 291–303.

INDEX

⤳

ACKNOWLEDGMENTS

〜

THIS BOOK OWES its greatest debt to my teachers, who inspired in me a love of history. They framed the past in ways that made it seem like the most important and exciting thing I could ever learn about. They taught me to write, pushed me to reflect, and made me excited to come to class every week. At Penn, I consider myself so lucky to have studied with Mary Frances Berry, Kathy Brown, Drew Faust, Lynn Hollen Lees, Matt Sommer, Tom Sugrue, and Mike Zuckerman. Drew lured me into the study of the past with her captivating lectures. Lynn taught me how to do research, kept me from falling through the cracks at Penn, and went out of her way to support me. Kathy inspired me to follow her footsteps and take on the somewhat staid field of early America.

At Rutgers, working with faculty who were committed to a politically engaged history proved crucial to my learning and sanity at a time when professionalization threatened to advance grade point averages over social justice commitments. Ann Fabian, Nancy Hewitt, Temma Kaplan, Jan Lewis, Phyllis Mack, Jennifer Morgan, and Deborah Gray White were the best guides through the comparative study of women's and gender history. And I met other students who shared my values, including Brian Connolly, Leigh-Anne Francis, Krystal Frazier, Abigail Lewis, Justin Lorts, Carla Mac-Dougall, Lucia McMahon, Michal Shapira, and Alex Warner. I was honored to be a fellow at the Rutgers Institute for Research on Women and Gender and participate in a weekly interdisciplinary seminar. Barbara Balliet gave me the opportunity to teach my first college courses and provided constant support. She also welcomed me into her community of feminist historians at the Baby Berks. Cheryl Clarke challenged me to not lose my passion and served as a model in juggling administrative and faculty duties.

The McNeil Center for Early American Studies provided a generous fellowship that allowed me to dive into the research and join an eclectic community of scholars including Kyle Farley, Chris Iannini, Julie Kim,

Sarah Rivett, and Aaron Wunsch. Amy Baxter-Bellamy made things happen smoothly and Dan Richter's dry wit made every gathering more fun. As the years go by, conferences and research trips add up. In this strange but beloved culture, I have made some great friends including Kate Adams, Tamar Carroll, Chris Castiglia, Paul Erickson, Erika Gasser, Dawn Peterson, Karen Krahulik, Amanda Moniz, Claire Potter, Seth Rockman, Honor Sachs, and Nick Syrett. The Committee on Lesbian, Gay, Bisexual, Transgender History has given me a home and a reason to actually look forward to the AHA.

In the summer of 2008, my beloved book club with Kathy Brown, Jim Downs, and Scott Wilds first met. As we gathered to eat, share stories, and argue over the readings, we became a fun, intellectual, non-traditional family of sorts. Many guests have come and gone, but thankfully Lori Ginzburg stayed after joining us a few years ago. Scott Wilds and Martin Bodtmann not only host book club but also have opened their home to me so that I could continue the research on this book. When I stay with them, I feel as if I have never left Philadelphia.

Jim Downs has been in my life since I first set foot in Philadelphia for college. We share inspiration, mentors, friends and a lifelong pursuit of critical engagement with the past. If the voices of prisoners emerge at all in this book, it is because of all the time we spent standing together at the corner of Sixth and Walnut streets, the former site of the prison, listening for them. My favorite radical writer-archivists Matthew Lyons and Claire McGuire moved in next door just as I was beginning the research and I am grateful for their encouragement. David Azzolina, Tina DiSanto, Lena Flower, Mary Lizzul, Tom Waldman, Julianna Walker, and Alex Welsh each entered my life at just the right time and I miss you all more than you know. My parents have always valued education and made sure that we had opportunities they did not. I will be forever grateful for their support. My older brother Jeff was my role model who charted the course for both our lives. He got As, so I wanted As. He went off to a fancy Ivy League school in the city instead of Penn State Schuylkill, so I did, too.

I received fellowships from several archives to enable research for this project including the Pennsylvania Historical and Museum Commission, the Library Company of Philadelphia, the Historical Society of Pennsylvania, and the American Antiquarian Society. The Philadelphia City Archives stores the records at the heart of this study and their reading room has become a second home. Special thanks to David Baugh, Connie King, Elizabeth Watts Pope, Linda Shopes, and Wendy Woloson. Connecticut College has been generous in funding my travel to conferences and archives to help complete this project. Students Elizabeth Boyland, Andrew Sowle, and Dvora Walker assisted with the research. Colleagues from across the college have supported my work and I am especially grateful to Armando Bengochea, Blanche Boyd, Joan Chrisler, Deb Eastman, Marty Grossel, Claudia Highbaugh, David Kim, Carolyn Patierno, Denise Pelletier, Tracee Reiser, Catherine Stock, and Marya Ursin for their wisdom and friendship.

Many people have given valuable feedback over the years, and I am forever grateful to Nancy Hewitt, Jan Lewis, Ann Fabian, and Jennifer Morgan. Nancy Hewitt is a model feminist scholar activist who approaches her work with great integrity and commitment. She puts students first and stands by us even when we choose unconventional paths or put activist values before our academic careers. Nancy is unbelievably thoughtful and engaged with my scholarship even to this day and I can never thank her enough for all that she has done to support my work and career. This project has benefitted from comments on conference papers by Wendy Woloson, Richard Godbeer, Nina Dayton, and Carroll Smith-Rosenberg. Special thanks to the organizers and participants at the Uncertain Knowledge American History Seminar at the German Historical Society and the *William and Mary Quarterly* Early Modern Studies Institute Workshop at the Huntington Library for their close engagement with my work. The readers for Penn Press, Bruce Dorsey and Brian Connolly, provided valuable engagement and thoughtful critiques that helped me make this into a better book than it would otherwise be.

I am so grateful to work with University of Pennsylvania Press and benefit from the critical eyes and astute guidance of Bob Lockhart and Kathy Brown. Bob promised early on that he understood how important it was to me to critique heteronormativity. His editorial acumen has steered this project in significant ways toward an engagement with several important concepts that have made the book stronger. Aside from being brilliant, kind, and witty, Kathy modeled an intersectional analysis of difference and power in the past that many of us have been trying to emulate ever since. She pushed me to develop and strengthen the arguments of the book while encouraging me to let more of my voice back into the writing. Alison Anderson has skillfully guided me through the final stages of manuscript preparation.

Many weekends and evenings have been given over to the completion of this book and I am forever grateful for the support of my love, Jessica Halem. She has taught me so much about the importance of community, the value of laughter, and the joy of unnatural vice. From the moment we met, my life has never been the same.